Aboriginal Peoples and Politics

Aboriginal claims remain a controversial but little understood issue in contemporary Canada. British Columbia has been the setting for the most intense and persistent demands by native people, and also for the strongest and most consistent opposition to native claims by governments and the non-aboriginal public. Land has been the essential question; the Indians have claimed continuing ownership while the province has steadfastly denied the possibility.

This book presents the first comprehensive treatment of the land question in British Columbia and is the first to examine the modern political history of British Columbia Indians. It covers the land question from its beginnings and gives detailed attention to the most recent court decisions, government policies, land claim developments, and Indian protest blockades.

Providing a new interpretation of Governor James Douglas, Paul Tennant views him as less generous to the Indians than have most historians and demonstrates how Douglas was largely responsible for the future course of the land question. In contrast to what many non-Indians assume today, the Indians of British Columbia began their land claims at the start of white settlement and persevered despite the massive efforts of missionaries and government officials to suppress Indian culture and despite Parliament's outlawing of claim-related activities. The Indians emerge in this book as political innovators who maintained their identity and ideals and who today have more strength and unity than ever before.

The author has conducted extensive interviews with many Indian leaders and has examined the inner workings of government agencies and Indian political organizations. Although sympathetic to native claims, he focuses as much on failures and deficiencies as on strengths and successes.

PAUL TENNANT is an associate professor in the Department of Political Science at the University of British Columbia.

Aboriginal Peoples *and* Politics

The Indian Land Question in
British Columbia, 1849-1989

PAUL TENNANT

University of British Columbia Press
Vancouver

Reprinted 1991

ISBN 0-7748-0347-9 (cloth)
ISBN 0-7748-0369-x (paper)

Canadian Cataloguing in Publication Data
Tennant, Paul, 1938–
Aboriginal peoples and politics

Includes bibliographical references.
ISBN 0-7748-0347-9
1. Indians of North America – British Columbia –
Land tenure. 2. Indians of North America –
British Columbia – Claims. 3. Indians of North
America – British Columbia – Government relations.
4. Indians of North America – British Columbia –
Political activity. I. Title.
E78.B9T45 1990   333.2   C90-091301-0

L787/

This book has been published with the help of
a grant from the Social Science Federation of
Canada, using funds provided by the Social
Sciences and Humanities Research Council of
Canada.

UBC Press
6344 Memorial Rd
Vancouver, BC v6T 1w5

For Laura Lee Antoine, Stefany Mathias, Harry Nyce, Jr.,
William Wilson, Jr., and Christopher, Douglas, Matthew, and Jonathan

Contents

Preface

The Indian land question is as old as British Columbia itself. The question remains as critical as it has ever been, and it is today more controversial than it has been for over a century. The Indian peoples of British Columbia have constantly sought to have the question resolved; their efforts to do so have been at the heart of their modern political history. White government officials have as constantly ignored, suppressed, and distorted the question. With very few exceptions, white scholars have avoided both the land question and modern Indian political history; implicitly, but effectively, they have sustained the official view and hindered informed public debate. My intent in this book is to remedy some of the deficiency. My purpose is not to test or demonstrate academic theories, nor is it to provide any detailed comparison with other jurisdictions. My purpose is to describe the history of the land question in British Columbia and to reveal something of the remarkable achievements of the Indian peoples in their steadfast pursuit of their land rights through peaceful political means.

Like most white British Columbians, I was raised and educated in ignorance of both Indians and the land question. In Kamloops, where I grew up, the Whites lived on one side of the river and the Indians lived on the other. The Indian reserve was the centrepiece of the local landscape, and the red-brick Indian residential school was for years the most prominent building in the valley. Yet, from the perspective I acquired, the Indians could have been on another planet. Only much later, as Indian students began to appear in my university classes and as they and other students turned to aboriginal issues, did I come to appreciate the creative political vitality of the Indian peoples of British Columbia and to see the need for a comprehensive examination of the Indian land question and Indian political activity.

My own research began in 1979. A visiting research scholarship, awarded by the University of Victoria and funded by the Canada Council, enabled me to spend much of 1980 travelling throughout the province interviewing Indian leaders, attending meetings, and examining documents in the offices of tribal councils and Indian organizations. During 1980 and subsequent years I attended meetings and assemblies of more tribal councils, forums, and Indian organizations in the province than did any other person, Indian or non-Indian.

I was the first political scientist to conduct such field research in British Columbia. I was welcomed almost everywhere; often I was the only non-Indian present. During this period I was also allowed access to the Department of Indian Affairs regional archives in Vancouver, and there I examined official records and correspondence dating from the mid-1950s to the late 1970s. My explanation of public policy and Indian politics during the contemporary period is thus based on my own contact with the major political leaders, upon my own examination of the relevant written material, and upon my own direct observation of all the important political developments during the last decade.

Since 1982 I have been an adviser to the Council for Yukon Indians as that organization and its member communities have gone about arranging their future through one of the great modern land claim agreements. My view that similar agreements are appropriate and feasible in British Columbia is thus based on direct knowledge of what has occurred in a neighbouring jurisdiction, where, aside from the absence of a provincial government, the historic circumstances are similar to those in British Columbia.

The literature on the subject in British Columbia begins with a remarkable volume, *Papers Connected with the Indian Land Question, 1850-1875*.[1] Put together more than a century ago as the product of white opposition to provincial government policies,[2] it contains a complete record of the beginnings and early history of the issue. Later, when white politicians thwarted the Indians by denying them access to it, the volume played its own part in the unfolding of events.[3] Happily, it has recently been reprinted under the auspices of the Provincial Archives and is now widely available.

Three scholars stand above others in having established the present-day foundations for study of the land question and of Indian history in British Columbia.[4] The late Wilson Duff, anthropologist, published *The Indian History of British Columbia* in 1964;[5] it is a brief introduction to the subject. Robin Fisher, historian, published *Contact and Conflict: Indian-European Relations in British Columbia, 1774-1890* in 1977;[6] it provides a substantial and authoritative treatment. Although I disagree with Duff and Fisher on some points, notably concerning the motives and policies of James Douglas, my intellectual debt to them is great.

Rolf Knight's *Indians At Work: An Informal History of Native Indian Labour in British Columbia, 1858-1930* was published in 1978.[7] Although focusing on labour from an economic perspective, Knight provides a broad, and indispensable, introduction to modern Indian history. Knight is sceptical of established academic interpretations. He regards Indians not as mere objects of history but as ordinary human beings who adapt, cope, and decide. Knight intends his book to do justice "to the lives and accomplishments of previous generations of Indian working people" and to acknowledge the potential of future generations.[8] Although my focus is on politics rather than economics, my approach and intent are similar to Knight's.

Among more recent studies, Brian Titley's biography of Duncan Campbell Scott presents much of relevance.[9] Insightful also, and as much for the present as for the future, is Frank Cassidy and Norman Dale's *After Native Claims? The Implications of Comprehensive Claims Settlements for Natural Resources in British Columbia.*[10]

Some words which I use in this book may need comment. "Aboriginal" is now permanently enshrined in Canadian usage through the Constitution, which recognizes the Indian, Métis, and Inuit peoples as the "aboriginal peoples" of Canada. "Aboriginal" does not mean first on the scene; it means, rather, present when modern history began or when colonizers arrived. Indians were and are the aboriginal peoples of British Columbia.[11] "Indian" and "aboriginal" and "native," as adjectives and nouns, are thus synonymous within British Columbia; each is commonly used by Indians and others; none has any pejorative connotation.

"Whites" is a trickier term. Until recent decades British Columbia Whites openly identified themselves as "Whites" or "white people." The fourteen early treaties, for example, state that the purchased Indian lands are to become the "property of the White people for ever." Until the late 1940s Whites in the province were eager to distinguish themselves from non-Whites and to protect white political interests, as they did in denying Indian claims, curbing Asian immigration, and prohibiting major non-white groups from voting.

Since that time there has been growth in the degree of white racial tolerance and in the size of the non-white, non-aboriginal population of the province. "Whites" has vanished entirely from official use and largely from public discussion. Whites, however, do continue to use the word privately among themselves, and they use it publicly in places where the land question is a controversial local issue.

Whites continue to occupy almost all positions of political power in the provincial and federal governments. In addition, as I show in Chapter 17, the pejorative image of the Indian long held by Whites still underlies provincial government policy. In fact, the Indian land question remains, as it has always been, a question between Indians and Whites.

Indians refer to "Whites" in both ordinary conversation and public statements. Often they use the word to mean all non-Indians, but this usage is hardly satisfactory. In New Zealand the Maori word "Pakeha" is widely used by everyone to refer to non-Maori.[12] Having an equivalent word in British Columbia would ease the discussion of aboriginal matters and obviate any need for the awkward and negative terms "non-Indian" and "non-aboriginal." Perhaps Indians could bestow a suitable name upon their fellow British Columbians (a name chosen after land claim settlements would perhaps prove more congenial than one chosen earlier). Those Whites who would hesitate to accept and use such a name would be showing their true colour.

"Politics" is the first and the final word pertaining to the land question. Politics is the fundamental human activity; politics is driven by the passions of peoples and the powers of governments; politics brings out the best and the worst in human beings. Defined drily by social scientists, politics is the identifying of, and dealing with, the fundamental issues and beliefs facing peoples or governments. Peoples can have politics whether or not they have formal governments. Governments cannot avoid politics; it is what they do. Issues cannot be dealt with until they are identified or, as is sometimes said, until they are put on the public agenda. Whether an issue is to be on that agenda is often a more controversial matter than is dealing with it once it is on. In British Columbia the land question has always been at the top of the agendas of the Indian peoples. Provincial government politicians have always denied that it belongs on theirs. The year 1989, however, did bring the first ever signs that the British Columbia government might be preparing to change its historic position.

My approach in this book is for the most part chronological. The first chapter describes the Indian peoples themselves, discusses aboriginal rights and land claims, and outlines the common Indian and non-Indian perceptions of those rights and claims. The next three chapters focus on the actions and omissions of governments from 1849, when the first colony was created, to 1887, by which time the Indian land question was firmly established in its present form. Chapter 5 examines the events of 1887, in which traditional Indian leaders presented a comprehensive set of demands and began the development of modern political forms and strategies.

Chapter 6 pauses in the chronology to consider the factors governing those forms and strategies; the chapter is thus an introduction and guide to Indian political activity during the present century. Chapters 7 and 8 examine the attainment of the first, and fragile, province-wide Indian unity and its curtailment by Parliament's outlawing of Indian claims activity in 1927. The following two chapters deal with the differing nature of political developments among coastal and interior Indians over the next four decades. Chapter 11 examines federal government policies of the 1960s that came to have quite unintended effects upon contemporary Indian political development.

Chapters 12 to 15 deal with the 1970s and 1980s, the tumultuous two decades in which communities and tribal groups wrested political control from the big province-wide Indian organizations, renewed the land claim struggles that had been interrupted in 1927, and turned to the courts. Chapter 16 analyses the major court cases and considers the province's legal arguments against aboriginal title. The final chapter examines the province's political arguments and assesses the likelihood of change in the province's denial of title and refusal to negotiate.

Acknowledgments

I am pleased to acknowledge the assistance of many persons and to mention first those who began as my students and remained willing to share their first-hand knowledge. They include Ardyth Cooper, Isabel Harrison, Darcy Mitchell, Bill Wilson, and Dave Zirnhelt, as well as Anne Atleo, Terry Brown, Phyllis Bonneau, Hugh Braker, Carole Dickie, Brian George, Ken Harris, Guy Lavallee, Milly MacKenzie, Robert Matthew, Henry Michel, Marion Mussell, Mike Nichol, Harry Nyce, Sr., Joe Williams, Edna Rose, Vern Salonas, Beverly Scow, Gordon Sebastian, Dolly Watts, and the late Greg Enright. Among other students whose research was of particular benefit are Wendy Aasen, Michael Bryant, Vincent Buckle, Pamela Bush, Jill Christensen, Grace Francescato, Stephen Fudge, Anthony Glavin, Stephanie Hudson, Radha Jhappan, Paul Kopas, Risë Massey, Wendy Morrison, and Andrew Webber. Invaluable assistance under provincial government student support programs was provided by Kenneth Anderlini, Kelly Clark, Charlotte Fincham, Mary Goldie, James McLennan, Lisa Spitale, Karen Trautman, and Lee Yow.

At the University of Victoria's BC Project, early support was given by Mercedes Ballem, Frances Bird, Terry Morley, Karen Ort, Jeremy Wilson, Norman Ruff, Neil Swainson, the late Walter Young, and, especially, Andrea Smith, my research associate.

Among those who went out of their way to provide assistance, information or interviews during my research were Dorothy Albert, Owen Anderson, Gordon Antoine, Max Beck, Bess Brown, the Honourable Thomas and Beverly Berger, the Honourable Frank and Tammy Calder, Stan Charles, Frank Collison, Ray Collins, Katie Cooke, Lori Davis, Jon Evans, Robert Excell, Dianne Fouladi, the Honourable Davie Fulton, Delbert Guerin, Guujaaw, John Hall, Ron Hamilton, Jan Hanna, Lillian Howard, Jennie Jack, Gene Joseph, Shirley Joseph, Clarence (Manny) Jules, Jeannie Kanakos, Manfred Klein, Nelson Leeson, Terry Leonard,

Francis Lewis, Bill and Lavina Lightbown, Carey Linde, Harold and
Betty-Lou Linville, Beverly Lopez, Brian Maracle, the Honourable
Leonard Marchand, Nathan Matthew, Bert McKay, Bill Mussell, Ed
Newman, Stephen Olson, Art Pape, Frank Parnall, Gary Patsey, Sophie
Pierre, Wilfred Price, Miles Richardson, Jean Rivard, Ron Rose, Rick
Salter, Robert Simon, Francis Smith, Don Sneddon, David Sparks, Vina
Starr, Neil and Barbara Sterritt, Peter Stone, Terry Stone, William
Tatoosh, Kathryn Teneese, Betty Tennant, Katie Thomas, Lulu Tizya,
Don Ursaki, Rueben Ware, Bob Warren, Hugh Watts, Fred Walchli, the
Honourable Guy Williams, Ed Wright, Vicky Wong, and the late George
Manuel.

A number of people helped in particular ways. Doreen Mullins provided pivotal prompting. Hubert Doolan, Gloria George, Leonard and
Kitty Maracle, and the late Butch Smitheram lent me their personal
papers; the Maracle Papers now form part of the University of British
Columbia Special Collections. Noel Bayliss gave me access to the
Department of Indian Affairs Archives in Vancouver. Susan Anderson
was a constant source of information. Bruce and Jan Cottingham eased
my way into the Nass Valley. Among the Nisga'a the late James Gosnell
made me welcome and opened many doors there and elsewhere. Ray
Jones was an insightful guide to the Upper Skeena and to Indian politics. Ethel Pearson and Shirley Scow were as generous with smoked
salmon as with information. Ardyth Cooper, Joe Mathias, George Watts,
and Bill Wilson were as warm in their hospitality as they were patient in
responding to my endless questions.

In the University of British Columbia Library George Brandak,
Robyn Fisher, Iza Laponce, Mary Luebbe, Tom Shorthouse, Alan Soro-
ka, and Frances Woodward were unfailingly helpful.

I am indebted as well to my fellow academics Robert Bish, Dale
Kinkade, Delloyd Guth, Michael Kew, Orest Kruhlak, Robert Mc-
Donald, Sam LaSelva, Michael M'Gonigle, Evelyn Pinkerton, Jay Powell,
Patricia Shaw, Robin Ridington, Sam Stevens, Wendy Wickwire, and,
especially, to Keith Ralston and Douglas Sanders. I am doubly grateful
to Alan Cairns, Frank Cassidy, Robin Fisher, and Arthur Ray for com-
menting on the entire manuscript and to the anonymous reviewers for
the University of British Columbia Press and the Social Science Federation of Canada for their very worthwhile suggestions.

None of these, however, should be held responsible for my interpretations or for errors in fact or conclusion.

Finally, several people were helpful in very special ways. Naida Hyde
gave good counsel. Jane Fredeman provided expert editorial guidance
from the beginning. Jean Wilson guided the manuscript through the
University of British Columbia Press. Mary La Liberté gave unfailing
support and encouragement.

Aboriginal Peoples and Politics

CHAPTER ONE

Aboriginal Peoples and Aboriginal Claims

The northwest coast of North America was a place of peoples. In the portion that would become coastal British Columbia, along the contorted shoreline, on the countless islands, and far inland along the many rivers, there was an extensive maritime population. Nowhere north of Mexico were there greater numbers or denser concentrations. To the east, across the great plateau of the interior, and north into the western reaches of the continental plain there were other peoples, but less numerous. Whites have consistently underestimated the original aboriginal population of British Columbia. Until recently the accepted estimate was less than 100,000.[1] The low number resulted in part from failure to recognize the extent of early post-contact epidemics and in part from the scarcity of archeological research, but it served as well the implicit purpose of demeaning aboriginal claims and buttressing white myths. In the 1970s and 1980s the estimates of the pre-contact population rose steadily. Today the estimate is between 300,000 and 400,000 for all of British Columbia.[2]

The aboriginal past is closer in British Columbia than almost anywhere else on the continent. Whites began to arrive in significant numbers only in the 1850s, and not until the 1890s did effective white control extend to the last of the major aboriginal groups. In almost every Indian community there are still elders who as children were taught by parents or grandparents who had grown to adulthood in self-governing communities free of control by Whites. Moreover, although the Whites brought devastating diseases and disruptive change, there was no armed conquest, no widespread displacing of villages, and relatively little forced admixing of differing communities. The aboriginal past was not cut off. Many aboriginal communities remained resident on ancestral sites. They could thus more easily keep alive their ways, their memories, and their ideals.

At the time the Whites arrived there were more than thirty separate aboriginal groups in what would become British Columbia. Each had a unique linguistic and cultural identity, as well as a name for itself and a territory which it made use of. The groups were as distinct from one another as were the various European nations of the time. While several of the smaller groups died out after contact, most survived. Today's groups are listed in Table 1.[3]

What to call these groups is an important consideration, for ambiguity or misunderstanding can easily occur. British Columbia Indians themselves refer to the groups as "tribes," "peoples," "nations," or "tribal groups," but none of these is completely satisfactory as a generic word. "Tribe" is the most ambiguous, for it is also applied by Indians to kin-groups and to local communities, while "people" (as in "my people") can mean anything from a kin-group to all British Columbia Indians. "Nation," which was commonly used in the last century by colonial officials, missionaries, and other white observers, does remain suitable, but ambiguity arises from the common use of "first nation," which normally refers only to the local community and not to the entire culture group. "Tribal group" is perhaps the best, since it is the only one of the four which is never applied to local communities, at least in British Columbia usage. It has also been the term most commonly used during recent years by those Indians seeking a greater political role for the language or culture groups. "Tribal group" will thus be used throughout this book. It must be emphasized that the purpose of using this term is to distinguish the groups listed in Table 1 from less inclusive entities such as kin-groups, bands, or local communities. "Tribal group" therefore has the same meaning as "nation" had in the last century; it refers to only one specific type of group; it is not a general term for collections of Indians.[4] The tribal groups are today the predominant political units among British Columbia Indians, and it is vitally important that they not be confused with other, less inclusive groups.[5]

From the beginning Whites have known most of the individual tribal groups by their correct Indian names. In some cases, however, Whites either got the name wrong or gave the group an English name. Among the best-known wrong names was "Nootka," which Captain James Cook applied to the people of the west coast.[6] One Indian explanation for the error is that Cook took the Indians to be calling out their name as his ship approached; in fact, the shouted phrase that could be taken as "Nootka" was a warning to watch out for underwater rocks.[7] The people's own name for themselves is "Nuu'chah'nulth." The English word "Carrier" was given to the Dakelh[8] and remains the common name in English. "Carrier" was also applied rather broadly; today the Wet'su-wet'en and the Babine are recognized as distinct groups. Another well-

TABLE 1: British Columbia tribal groups

Area	Tribal group	Population[a]	No. of bands
North coast	Nisga'a	3841	4
	Gitksan	3733	6
	Tsimshian	4330	7
	Haisla	1110	1
	Haida	2002	2
West/central coast	Nuu'chah'nulth	4971	15
	Kwagiulth	3815	14
	Heiltsuk	1670	2
	Nuxalk	889	1
South coast	Songish	1638	9
	Cowichan	2369	3
	Nanaimo/Chemainus	2224	7
	Comox	1064	5
	Sechelt	670	1
	Squamish	1899	2
	Sto:lo	4120	29
Southern interior	Nlaka'pamux	3568	16
	Lillooet	3353	10
	Shuswap	5088	17
	Okanagan	2137	6
	Kootenay	515	4
Central interior	Chilcotin	1946	5
	Wet'suwet'en	1212	2
	Babine	1597	5
	Carrier	4188	12
Northern interior	Sekani	685	3
	Beaver	767	5
	Slave	532	2
	Kaska-Dena	785	2
	Taku Tlingit	240	1
	Tahltan	976	2
TOTALS		67,934	199

[a]Populations are of registered Indian band members as of December 1987; figures are derived from Indian and Northern Affairs Canada, "Chiefs and Councillors, B.C. Region" (July 1988).

known name was "Kwakiutl." It was less a wrong name than a peculiar spelling; a preferred version is "Kwagiulth," which gives a more accurate pronunciation. Another, very recent, spelling change has seen "Nisga'a" replace "Nishga," which had much earlier replaced "Niska."

In the cases of the Haisla of Kitamaat, the Heiltsuk of Bella Bella, and the Nuxalk of Bella Coola, Whites originally applied the Indian place names to the local tribal groups. "Thompson," the name of the major river, was used until recently for the Nlaka'pamux people. "Tsimshian" can also be a source of confusion, since anthropologists use it to to refer collectively to the Nisga'a, Gitksan, and Tsimshian tribal groups, who have closely related languages. The three groups, however, do not regard themselves as one people.

Almost a dozen tribal groups in the southern part of the province fall within the broad Salishan linguistic category. All the south coast groups are "Coast Salish," while the Nlaka'pamux, Lillooet, Shuswap, and Okanagan are the "Interior Salish." In the central and northern interior the Athapaskan linguistic category is similarly broadly inclusive; indeed in that huge area only the Taku Tlingit are not Athapaskan-speaking.

Anthropologists identify two main types of traditional or indigenous society. One type is highly structured and has distinct politics based on rank, status, and hierarchy. This type emerges only among substantial populations, which in turn require bountiful natural environments. The other type is less structured and much more equalitarian; it is associated with small populations, often those having to gather food over extensive territories. Morton Fried distinguishes the two as "rank societies" and "band equalitarian societies."[9] The British Columbia tribal groups provide classic examples of each type.

The coastal groups were highly structured societies having clearly evident and permanent positions of political leadership. The interior groups were typically composed of small communities having little need for specialized politics. The general social and political differences between the coastal groups and the interior groups were thus fundamental, and many of the differences remain evident today. The coastal tribal groups are unique not only in British Columbia but also in Canada, and their presence does much to explain why the province's post-contact Indian political history has been distinct from that elsewhere in the country.

Among the gifts of the coastal environment is the giant red cedar tree (*Thuya plicata*). From the cedar the coastal peoples made the world's largest dug-out canoes and also large plank houses. Canoes allowed full use of the coastal environment; otherwise the sea and coastline could not have been harvested, and areas inaccessible by land could not have been settled. It was the canoes which allowed exploitation of areas extensive enough to provision sedentary winter villages with populations of several thousand. The canoes permitted ready communication among the villages composing a tribal group, and they enabled travel and trade up and down the entire coast. The cedar houses enabled a large number of people, usually family groups, to live under one roof, and many people could thus live compactly together in the winter villages. The "houses," or households, indeed, became the basic social unit in all the coastal groups. Had the cedar tree not existed, the coastal peoples could not have created their complex and sophisticated civilizations.

The households possessed property. There were pieces of land: house sites, launching places, places for hunting game, for berry-picking, and for root- and bark-gathering. There were buildings, canoes, and equipment, and less mundane items such as totem poles, wood and stone sculptures, paintings, and decorated screens. Houses could have rights to fish in certain waters, to harvest particular food species, to engage in certain activities, such as manufacturing stone tools, and even rights to use individual trees. Houses also owned "a host of ritual and intangible possessions,"[10] including crests, stories, songs, dances, and names. The coastal peoples, indeed, would seem to have had concepts of property at least as detailed and sophisticated as did Britain or other European nations.

Among the coastal peoples the households were grouped into lineages having common ancestry. The lineages reached their most detailed development on the north coast. Among the Nisga'a, for example, there were four clans, symbolized by the raven, eagle, wolf, and killer whale. Clan chiefs inherited their positions through their mothers. The certainty of inheritance allowed future leaders to be known and prepared from childhood, while matrilineal descent reduced the likelihood of conflict over succession. On the south coast succession was less certain, for chiefly rank could come through the mother or the father or even be decided on the basis of achievement; preparation of leaders could not be as definite, while dispute over succession was more likely. On the north coast the certainty of succession was a major contribution to the strength of the clans, while the clan network extending through the villages contributed to the strength and cohesion of the whole tribal group.

The large coastal houses enabled the holding of elaborate feasts and performances. These were the "potlatches" that were the hallmark of coastal societies. Potlatches served to legitimize political rank and authority, that is, to validate the rightful possession of prestige and the use of chiefly power and influence. At some time in his early life "the heir presumptive to a chieftainship would be presented formally to a group of guests at such an affair."[11] After the death of a chief the heir would assume his position in another potlatch. A chief would hold periodic potlatches to demonstrate his rank and wealth; he would do so by giving away large amounts of personal goods and items such as food, tools, and clothing. Economically, potlatches ensured a circulation of wealth; the prestige and rank of the chiefs was maintained by giving away wealth rather than by accumulating it. Conspicuous personal poverty was a requirement of chiefly office. The coastal peoples came as close as human societies ever have to resolving the perennial political problem of misuse of power for personal gain.

Potlatches were both the essential route to political influence and the vital means of maintaining authority and demonstrating prestige. Without potlatches no chief could have assumed or maintained his position, nor could any individual have been assured and reassured of his or her place within the house, extended family, or clan. Potlatches were the critically important institution within all coastal tribal groups.

Just as lineages and rank were the distinguishing features of coastal societies, so individual equality was the main principle among the interior peoples. Lacking the giant cedar, mostly unable to rely on water transport, and often having to travel extensively to harvest scattered resources, the interior groups lived generally as communities of immediate kinfolk. In the northern interior small and nomadic family groups were the basic social units. In the southern interior sedentary winter villages (often composed of sod-roofed pit houses) were more common, and rather large settlements, comparable to some on the coast, did exist in a few locations of abundant fish and game, notably along the Fraser and Thompson rivers.

Because they lived mostly in groups that were relatively small, the interior groups had less need for the complex organizational behaviour that evolved on the coast. In some of the Interior Salish groups where population densities were relatively high, however, permanent chieftaincies did exist. Among the Okanagan, for example, chiefly rank could be inherited, and one chief would even be regarded as the leader or spokesman of the whole tribal group.[12] Still, there was less need for politics as a specialized activity among the interior peoples, and so after contact there was less of a political tradition to build upon than was the case among the coastal peoples.

The higher population densities and smaller territories of the coastal peoples made specialized politics unavoidable. In practice, the responsibilities for protection and management of property could not have been separated from day-to-day decision-making. In the larger villages there would inevitably be disagreements, disputes, or violence between members of different houses and lineages; such matters would have to be settled by agreement of the chiefs. Co-ordinated public action would also be required, for example, in responding to the sudden appearance of fish and other food species, in reacting to storms and other threats of natural disaster, in taking defensive or offensive action against outsiders, and in planning for the future. Settling differences and co-ordinating common activities are the stuff of government and politics. As Roy

Azak, a Nisga'a clan chief, remarked in 1981, "There had to be the leaders of the village. There's four head-chiefs of every tribe [i.e, clan] that are leaders of the village. And it's still like that today."[13]

The form of politics at the tribal group level must have varied considerably up and down the coast and across the interior. Tribal groups having many communities over extensive territories would have had neither the means nor the motive for much overall co-ordination of activities. Those having fewer major villages and smaller territories would have been able to communicate and co-operate more readily, and in cases where neighbouring tribal groups were similarly cohesive there would have been an especial incentive for each group to maintain boundaries and to act collectively to protect tribal group interests. The Nisga'a and the Gitksan, among others, would have been such groups. In both groups elders of today affirm that clan chiefs from all the villages would meet periodically to adjudicate disputes between clans and villages and to make military decisions.

In the decades following the first white contact the drastic population decline and the changes in local economies had pronounced effects on local populations. Among every tribal group there were villages that simply faded away. Often the surviving populations of neighbouring communities came together, forming new ones. In almost every case these local consolidations occurred within tribal groups.[14] Continuity of the tribal groups themselves was thus not affected, although there were some changes in territorial usage. By the 1850s the situation had stabilized. Despite the ongoing population losses, the great majority of communities that were present at that time did survive and still exist today.

In controlling and administering the affairs of the Indians, the provincial and the Canadian governments in practice used local communities as the basic units. Tribal groups, in contrast, were officially and resolutely ignored. The Indian Act gave federal officials the authority to create "Indian bands." In most cases in British Columbia the members of one community were designated as a band, but not infrequently several communities were lumped together. Bands remain under the administrative supervision and control of the federal Department of Indian Affairs, or "DIA," as it is commonly called.[15]

The federal government recognizes as Indians only persons meeting provisions set out in the Indian Act. Such persons are referred to as "registered" or "status" Indians. Until the 1980s non-Indian women became registered upon marrying a registered Indian, while registered Indian women lost their status upon marrying anyone who was not registered.[16] Thus, the registered British Columbia Indian population includes several thousand women without Indian blood. Under the Indian Act only registered Indians can be band members. In 1987 the province's bands had a total membership of 67,934, while there were perhaps half again as many "non-status" Indians, that is, persons with Indian blood who were not registered.[17]

Today there are 199 bands in the province.[18] Table 1 gives the number of bands in each tribal group. Coastal bands tend to be larger than those in the interior. The former average 417 members; the latter, 300. Of the bands with more than 800 members, fifteen are coastal while eight are in the interior.

By the time of the first recorded European arrival on the west coast, Britain had considerable experience with Indians and Indian lands in North America. With the capture of Quebec in 1759 Britain had acquired complete control of the Atlantic coast and thus of the fur trade through the major river valleys westward into the continent. If that trade was to flourish in British hands, good relations had to be maintained with Indian tribes, for it was Indians who harvested the furs, and they could also be of military importance. While Britain seemed secure enough in the northern reaches through the Hudson's Bay Company, Spain was expanding northward from Mexico, and Russian traders were advancing southward from Alaska. The Pacific Coast between Mexico and Alaska had not yet been colonized, although Francis Drake had explored the California coast in 1579 and claimed it, ineffectually, for Britain.

The outcome of these various considerations was the Royal Proclamation of October 1763.[19] The proclamation recognizes Indians as "Nations or Tribes"; it extends British sovereignty and protection over Indians to the west of the existing colonies; it asserts that the Indians are not to be interfered with; and it acknowledges the Indians as continuing to own the lands which they have used and occupied. It begins by stating that

It is just and reasonable, and essential to our Interest, and the Security of our Colonies, that the several Nations or Tribes of Indians with whom We are connected, and who live under our Protection, should not be molested or disturbed in the Possession of such Parts of Our Dominions and Territories as, not having been ceded to or purchased by Us, are reserved to them, or any of them, as their Hunting Grounds. . .

And We do further declare it to be Our Royal Will and Pleasure, for the present . . . to reserve under our Sovereignty, Protection, and Dominion, for the use of the said Indians, all the Lands and Territories not included with limits of Our . . . new Governments, or within the Limits of the Territory granted to the Hudson's Bay Company, *as also all the Lands and Territories lying to the Westward of the Sources of the Rivers which fall into the Sea from the West and the North West.* [Emphasis added][20]

The proclamation does not take its assertion of British sovereignty as incompatible with continuing Indian land ownership. Precisely the opposite is the case. The nations or tribes are clearly recognized as "in possession of" the lands they have used and occupied. British sovereignty and continuity of pre-existing Indian land ownership go hand in hand. On this principle the proclamation is unequivocal.

That Indians are to have continuing title to their land is confirmed in the procedure that the proclamation sets out for the sale of Indian lands within colonies: "If at any Time any of the Said Indians should be inclined to dispose of the said Lands, the same shall be Purchased only for Us, in our Name, at some public Meeting or Assembly of the said Indians."[21]

The Indians were prohibited from selling lands prior to their being brought within a colony and from disposing of them to any private person or foreign official afterwards. While recognizing Indian nations or tribes as owning or holding title to their traditional territories, the proclamation sharply curtailed the freedom of the Indians to do as they wished with their lands. Indian title was thus to differ in three ways from the standard British fee simple title that would be granted to individual white settlers. Indian title would be held collectively, by each nation or tribe, and not by individuals. Indian title could be transferred only to the Crown. Indian title would be a continuation of pre-existing aboriginal arrangements; quite unlike the settlers' fee simple title, Indian title was being recognized rather than created by the Crown.

As Brian Slattery has observed, "The Royal Proclamation of 1763 has a profound significance for modern Canada. Under its terms aboriginal peoples hold continuing rights to their lands except where those rights have been extinguished by voluntary cession . . . In technical terms, the Indian interest constitutes a legal burden on the crown's ultimate title until surrendered."[22]

The principles of the Royal Proclamation were followed by governments in Canada east of the Rockies. Aside from a brief beginning, they were ignored in British Columbia, and ultimately the province came to assert that the proclamation did not apply to its territory and had not been intended to.[23] British Columbia Indians, however, came to regard the proclamation as guaranteeing their basic aboriginal rights. In their political thinking it gained the stature of a collective Magna Carta.

British Columbia Indians have had a remarkably consistent view of what their rights are and where those rights come from. This view can be summarized as follows:

1 Before Europeans arrived the various Indian peoples, as autonomous communities and tribal groups, managed their own societal affairs

and in so doing maintained jurisdiction over a particular territory (land and water) which they used and occupied and regarded as theirs. Self-government and land ownership thus existed as collective abilities, in whose exercise sub-groups (clans, houses, or smaller kin groups) participated.

2 Individual Indians also had abilities (such as hunting, fishing, and gathering food and materials in particular places) that they exercised, but the entitlement of individuals to exercise these abilities came to them only as members of tribal groups, communities, and sub-groups. Individual entitlements were thus derivative rather than primary.

3 Indian abilities and activities continued after white contact and under the new British sovereignty. That they did continue is a simple historical fact, but Indian communities and tribal groups were also morally entitled to carry on as they had before. In other words, because they were already living in organized societies, the Indian peoples had the right to continue governing themselves and owning their lands. Continuity of self-government and continuity of land ownership or title were thus collective aboriginal rights. The derived abilities and activities of individual members of communities or tribal groups were now individual aboriginal rights.

4 The British sovereign acknowledged aboriginal rights through the Royal Proclamation of 1763. Continuity of land title was explicitly recognized, while continuity of self-government was implicitly sanctioned. Treaties made in accord with the proclamation recognized the continuity of certain aboriginal rights, especially such individual rights as to hunt, fish and gather food.[24]

5 Particular aboriginal rights can be reduced or eliminated. A community or tribal group may voluntarily surrender a right—for example, by ceding title to some or all of its land to the Crown. The sovereign also has the legal authority, however unfair its exercise may be in practice, to limit or extinguish an aboriginal right by unilateral action—for example, by expropriating title or outlawing an aboriginal activity. Within an established system of government, however, legitimate curtailment of aboriginal rights can be accomplished only through explicit and lawful action; otherwise the "rights" would have so little substance as not to be rights in the first place.

The major collective aboriginal rights are thus seen as the right to self-government and the right to have aboriginal title recognized. Individual aboriginal rights devolve to members of the communities or tribal groups which possess the collective rights. In the Indian view the fundamental qualities of aboriginal rights are their "pre-existence" and their continuity.[25] Indians, of course, are not alone in their interpretations. Within Canadian and British legal philosophies, their views accord with principles of natural rights and with "the common-law doctrine of aboriginal rights."[26]

An aboriginal land claim is a demand by Indians upon governments. A claim has two parts, each equally essential and equally important: the demand that governments acknowledge that the claimant group held title to its land before contact and that the title has not yet been extinguished; the demand that governments negotiate with the group to reach a "settlement" or "agreement" similar to those which have been reached in most of the rest of Canada.[27] Since the federal government does acknowledge Indian land claims and is prepared to negotiate in British Columbia as it has done elsewhere, the actual target of the claims is the provincial government, which has always denied the existence of aboriginal title and has declined to negotiate.

The fact that there has been no specific action to extinguish aboriginal title over most of the province[28] is taken by Indians as the proof that it still exists and that Indians thus remain the owners of their original lands. As James Gosnell, chairman of the Nisga'a Tribal Council, put it in 1984: "We are the true owners of British Columbia. The Indians across the province own everything—the rivers, the trees, the bugs, the animals. You name it. Subsurface rights, the air, the rain, the whole shot. That's what we mean when we say we have aboriginal title to the land."[29]

Gosnell was also fond of saying that Indians own the province "lock, stock, and barrel." Such assertions always received much more attention in the news media and from white politicians than did Gosnell's repeated statements that Indians were willing to share and merely desired a fair settlement.

The historical fact is that aboriginal title does cover most of B.C. But whoever said we are seeking ownership of all of B.C.? Never has that been said. We are willing to share, and have said so hundreds of times. Aboriginal title is the starting point for negotiations. Exclusive ownership of B.C. will obviously not be the end point of the negotiations. We want an agreement that will finally recognize your laws and system of government, and in return you will recognize ours.[30]

As is evident in Gosnell's comment, the claim to land title has always been closely linked to the desire of Indians to control community and tribal affairs on their lands. Demands for self-government have always been implicit in land claims; in recent years these demands have become prominent and explicit. Terms such as "self-determination," "self-government," and "sovereignty" are often used. George Watts, chairman of the Nuu'chah'nulth Tribal Council, has said, for example:

We take the position that we are sovereign nations, that our existence stems from the fact that we were the first peoples here, that we have the aboriginal title to the land. But that sovereignty is one which could coexist along with the rest of Canada. We're not talking about being sovereign nations as far as having post offices, armed forces and monetary systems of our own. What we're talking about is having Indian governments within the Confederation of Canada.[31]

Underlying the land claims, but usually unspoken by Indians and unnoticed by non-Indians, is the passionate Indian desire that non-Indians, both ordinary people and government leaders, acknowledge and appreciate the simple historical fact that Indians were present in established societies of high attainment before Europeans arrived. For this reason, Indian demands for negotiation are almost always expressed with vigour and emotion, and they are usually phrased in terms of the claimant group's historic identity. For Indians, land claims negotiations are important not only because of the land, but also because they will signify that governments, and the non-Indian public, are acknowledging something of the historic and the present importance of Indian peoples. (It is partly for this reason that Indians have much preferred negotiating to going to court and have taken land claims to court only when despairing of government willingness to negotiate.) Government refusal to negotiate is thus taken as being much more than a refusal to talk about land; it is taken as belittling the worth and identity of Indian peoples.

In the Indian view, contemporary communities and tribal groups have the same essential connection with the land as did those same communities and tribal groups at contact. In most cases, indeed, present-day Indians do retain powerful emotional attachment to ancestral community, tribal group, and territory. This attachment, which is itself regarded by Indians as fundamental to their identity, is largely invisible to non-Indians, whose immigrant-derived society and culture are based upon exodus from established communities and upon individual rather than collective values. The fact that much social and lifestyle change has occurred among Indians is not seen by Indians themselves as having impaired historic continuity or Indian identity or as having removed the obligation of contemporary leaders to continue pursuit of land claim settlements.

Indians are acutely aware of the common non-Indian beliefs and assumptions that have served to denigrate the past and present identity of Indian peoples and thus to undermine the validity of contemporary land claims. One notion has been that Indians were too simple and unsophisticated before contact to be regarded as having individual or collective rights. This assumption is hostile to Indians, taking them to have been primitive creatures with no more rights than other wildlife, and it regards the land as having been essentially empty and unused until it was discovered and put to use by Whites. Accordingly, Indians had no rights in the first place and so could have none later. Although it has by no means disappeared, this notion is now less pronounced than it was in earlier decades.

Another notion, more subtle and seemingly less hostile, combines a concept of "Indianness" with certain assumptions about change and progress. Here, it is not disputed that aboriginal peoples and cultures may have existed in pristine, even sophisticated, form before contact, but it is assumed that they have since been subject to irresistible and irreversible decline and contamination as interbreeding occurred and cultures changed. This approach assesses continuity of identity, and thus of rights, by the criteria of racial purity and persistence of culture elements (such as language, religion, clothing, food, weapons, and means of transport). It does not deny that Indians may have once had rights, but it denies legitimacy to present-day descendants as claimants of those rights. It remains prevalent in British Columbia. In 1989, for example, in disputing Gitksan-Wet'suwet'en land claims in court, government lawyers were at pains to establish that the Indians eat pizza, watch television, and drive motor cars.[32]

There is an odd paradox in this second notion: the immigrant-derived dominant society regards innovation in meeting the challenges of the new land as an essential and creative aspect of its own culture (or national character or national identity) while tending to dismiss adaptive behaviour by Indians as "aping the white man" and as indicating loss of culture and rights. Presumably few non-Indians regard introduction of exotic foods, electronic communications, and modern transportation as having impaired the continuity of British Columbian or Canadian identity; nor would they assume that an Irishman becomes an Italian upon eating pizza.

The two common non-Indian notions are in fact complementary, serving to undermine both the historic and the contemporary bases of aboriginal rights. The first denies aboriginal rights on the grounds that Indians were in the beginning too different from Whites. The second view denies aboriginal rights on the grounds that Indians have now become too similar to Whites.

The two popular notions explain much of the refusal of the British Columbia government, and of most non-Indians in the province, to acknowledge any validity in the Indian claims. It is this refusal (rather

than any Indian demand) that is the most noteworthy feature of the
Indian land question. Most other governments in Canada, past or present, have felt obligated to acknowledge aboriginal title and to negotiate
settlements. But British Columbia governments have steadfastly acted as
though their portion of Canada were unique and so somehow exempt
from historical interpretations and legal principles commonly applied
elsewhere.[33]

CHAPTER TWO

The Douglas Treaties and Aboriginal Title

The British took their time in establishing British Columbia. For seventy years after the first white contact (of Juan Pérez Hernandez in 1774)[1] the fur trade between Indians and Europeans developed without any formal colonial control. It was only in 1849, after the Oregon Treaty of 1846 had set a southern limit to their influence, that the British established the Colony of Vancouver Island, giving charge of land and settlement to the Hudson's Bay Company. Then came the gold rushes. The Mainland was made a colony in 1858 and named British Columbia. James Douglas was governor of Vancouver Island from 1851 and of both colonies from 1858 until his retirement in 1864. The two colonies were united into the one colony of British Columbia in 1866. During the 1860s the present northern and eastern boundaries were established. British Columbia joined Canada in 1871, becoming a province within the Confederation.

Between 1774 and 1849 nothing occurred that can reasonably be regarded as having affected aboriginal title in British Columbia. The trading companies did build fortified posts, but the few Whites were everywhere vastly outnumbered, and the companies did not seek to intrude directly into the life or politics of the Indians. Control over Indian societies and Indian lands thus "remained in Indian hands."[2]

The new colony of Vancouver Island was formally administered by a governor appointed by the Colonial Office in London; however, the Hudson's Bay Company, having been granted control of land and settlement in the colony, was in a position to exert much more influence than the governor. The Company's chief official in the colony was James Douglas. He had been born in 1803 in British Guiana, his father a Scots trader and his mother "a free colored woman."[3] After 1826, when he was posted to New Caledonia, he had played an increasingly major part in the Company's operations from Oregon to Alaska and he had established Fort Victoria in 1843. His wife, whom he had married in 1828, also had a company background; her father was a trader, her mother, a Canadian Indian.

Douglas' first instructions relating to the new colony, sent from London by Archibald Barclay, the Company's secretary, dealt with Indians and land:

With respect to the rights of the natives, you will have to confer with the chiefs of the tribes on that subject, and in your negotiations with them you are to consider the natives as the rightful possessors of such lands only as they are occupied by cultivation, or had houses built on, at the time when the Island came under the undivided sovereignty of Great Britain in 1846. All other land is to be regarded as waste, and applicable to the purposes of colonization . . . The right of fishing and hunting will be continued to [the natives], and when their lands are registered, and they conform to the same conditions with which other settlers are required to comply, they will enjoy the same rights and privileges.[4]

Douglas acted almost immediately. In May 1850 he wrote to his superiors:

I summoned to a conference, the chiefs and influential men of the Songees Tribe, which inhabits and claims the District of Victoria, from Gordon Head on Arro Strait to Point Albert on the Strait of Juan de Fuca as their own particular heritage. After considerable discussion it was arranged that the whole of their lands . . . should be sold to the Company, with the exception of certain Village sites and enclosed fields, for a certain remuneration, to be paid at once to each member of the Tribe. I was in favour of a series of payments to be made annually but the proposal was so generally disliked that I yielded to their wishes and paid the sum at once.[5]

The complete text of the first of the sales agreements, the one arranged with the Teechamitsa, a Songhees community occupying what is now Esquimalt, is as follows:

Know all men, We the Chiefs and People of the "Teechamitsa" Tribe who have signed our names and made our marks to this Deed on the Twenty ninth day of April, one thousand eight hundred and Fifty do consent to surrender entirely and for ever to James Douglas the agent of the Hudsons Bay Company in Vancouvers Island that is to say, for the Governor Deputy Governor and Committee of the same the whole of the lands situate and lying between Esquimalt Harbour and Point Albert including the latter, on the straits of Juan de Fuca and extending backward from thence to the range of mountains on the Sanitch Arm about ten miles distant.

The Condition of, or understanding of this Sale, is this, that our Village Sites and Enclosed Fields are to be kept for our own use, for the use of our Children, and for those who may follow after us; and the land, shall be properly surveyed hereafter; it is understood however that the land itself, with these small exceptions becomes the Entire property of the White people for ever; it is also understood that we are at liberty to hunt over the unoccupied lands, and to carry on our fisheries as formerly.

We have received as payment Twenty seven pound Ten Shillings Sterling.

In token whereof we have signed our names and made our marks at Fort Victoria 29 April 1850.[6]

James Hendrickson provides the most detailed account of the unusual way in which the actual document was created.[7] Douglas had the chiefs indicate their approval at the foot of a blank sheet of paper;[8] he then wrote to Barclay asking for a suitable text to place on the upper portion of the sheet. Barclay responded with a text virtually identical to that already used by the New Zealand Company in purchasing land from the Maori. Douglas himself then copied the text, with the necessary additions of names, dates, and amount of payment, onto the original sheet of paper. The same text was used for subsequent purchases from other Indian groups.[9] Thus, as Hendrickson observes, it was New Zealand rather than Canada and the Royal Proclamation of 1763 that provided the immediate model for the Douglas transactions.

In all, nine purchases were made by Douglas in the spring of 1850 around Fort Victoria. In early 1851 similar purchases were made from two Kwagiulth communities at Fort Rupert at the north end of the Island. Later in the same year Douglas was appointed governor of the colony, but he retained his company position. In 1852 two purchases were made on the Saanich Peninsula, and in 1854 one was made at Nanaimo. For the most part the purchases were paid for not with the cash referred to in the documents, but with blankets and with the value of blankets inflated by several times their cost to the Company. Altogether the purchases involved some 358 square miles, which is about 3 per cent of Vancouver Island's area.

The fourteen purchase documents are variously referred to as the Fort Victoria treaties, the Vancouver Island treaties, or the Douglas treaties. Although the word "treaty" is not used in the documents and was not used by Douglas to describe them, Canadian courts ruled much later that the documents were and remain valid Indian treaties, with Douglas having arranged them as agent of the British Crown.[10]

It is sometimes assumed or implied that the treaties, or at least Douglas himself, recognized the Indians as properly possessing in the first place only those bits of land on which their houses stood or around which they had commenced the European practice of fencing garden plots.[11] According to this assumption, Douglas, following Barclay's instructions, did not regard the "waste" land as belonging to anyone and so purchased only the house sites and fields and then allowed the Indians to continue to occupy what was now company property.[12] This view can only derive from relying more on the wording of Barclay's instructions than on the wording of the treaties and thus failing to realize that Douglas in fact departed from those instructions.

The treaties plainly indicate that Douglas did not regard any land as unowned. The text recognizes each Indian community as initially own-ing "the whole of the lands" it traditionally occupied. A map of the treaty areas around Fort Victoria shows no gaps between the areas sold by the communities owning them.[13] The starting point for each treaty was that local communities of Indians were recognized as owning every square inch of their traditional lands. It was "their lands," excepting their "Village Sites and Enclosed Fields," as Douglas wrote to Barclay and as the treaties stated, that were being "sold to the Company."

Although differing in detail, the Douglas treaties are similar in princi-ple to the treaties concluded in 1850 between the colony of Canada and Indians in northern Ontario. The Ontario treaties were more generous in leaving land in Indian hands, using a formula of eighty acres for each family.[14] The British Columbia treaties followed no formula and left only a few acres to each Indian community, but they did leave these under aboriginal title, as was not the case in Ontario. The British Columbia treaties were more generous only in fisheries, acknowledging the unqualified and unlimited right "to carry on . . . as formerly."

The most important fact about the Douglas treaties is that they stand as unequivocal recognition of aboriginal title. It was with this initial acknowledgement that the British established their rule in British Columbia.

During the 1850s the white population remained small on both the Island and the Mainland. By 1852 fewer than five hundred Britons had emigrated to the Island colony, and about thirty had made some move to acquire land.[15] In Britain, Canada, and the eastern United States the reputation of the area among prospective settlers was much influenced by the wars and massacres occurring just across the boundary in Wash-ington and Oregon. The violence, which continued into the 1860s, kept the Whites in the colony fearful that Vancouver Island Indians would also fight to protect their lands.

By the 1850s the first Roman Catholic missionaries were reaching the colony and the mainland interior. The British government and Douglas encouraged Protestant missionaries with the aim of countering the potential Catholic influence and of pacifying the Indians as white settlement advanced. The Protestant missionary William Duncan arrived in 1857, having received free passage on a Royal Navy vessel. Further indication that settlement was expected to replace the fur trade as the major concern of the colony was provided by the creation of an elected assembly in 1856.

The slow course of events changed abruptly and forever in 1858 when the first gold rush occurred. Tens of thousands of Whites flooded uncontrolled northward by land and sea. To deal with the new situation the British Parliament made the Mainland a new colony and named it British Columbia. Douglas resigned his company position and was appointed governor of British Columbia as well as Vancouver Island. His Indian policies were somewhat different in the two colonies.

The remaining history of the island colony until it was merged into the much larger British Columbia in 1866 is relevant to the land question more for what did not happen than for what did. For several years the three centres of power for the colony—Douglas himself, the British government, and the elected Assembly—acted as though further treaties were imminent. They continued to acknowledge aboriginal title, focusing attention mainly on several southern areas that were of prime settlement potential but which were not yet covered by treaty.

Douglas soon opened the Cowichan, Chemainus, and Saltspring districts to white settlement without any purchase or extinguishing of Indian title having taken place. Although he did reserve from settlement the portions that would likely remain in Indian possession should treaties be arranged, most Whites feared violence and little settlement occurred. In March 1860 Douglas asked the House of Assembly "to provide means for extinguishing, by purchase, the native Title to the Lands" in the three areas. Otherwise, he said, the Indians might "regard the settlers as trespassers and become troublesome."[16] The assemblymen agreed that the land should be bought and paid for, but by the British government rather than from revenue raised in the colony, and so the assembly took no action.[17]

One year later the assembly prepared a petition formally requesting that the British government provide the necessary funds. In sending the petition to the Duke of Newcastle, now the colonial secretary, Douglas wrote that extinguishing the title was a "very necessary precaution," and he went on:

As the native Indian population of Vancouver Island have distinct ideas of property in land, and mutually recognize their several exclusive possessory rights in certain districts, they would not fail to regard the occupation of such portions of the Colony by white settlers, unless with the full consent of the proprietary tribes, as national wrongs . . .

Knowing their feelings on that subject, I made it a practice up to the year
1859, to purchase the native rights in land, in every case, prior to the settlement
of any district; but since that time in consequence of the termination of the
Hudson's Bay Company Charter, and the want of funds, it has not been in my
power to continue it. Your Grace must, indeed, be well aware that I have, since
then, had the utmost difficulty in raising money enough to defray the most
indispensable wants of Government.[18]

Douglas concluded by suggesting that a loan of three thousand
pounds sterling from the Imperial Treasury be used to buy the lands in
Cowichan, Chemainus, and Barclay Sound. The loan would be repaid
out of land registration fees paid by settlers. Douglas arrived at his price
by estimating that there were in the three districts one thousand Indian
"families" (that is, households or houses) from whom the purchases
would be made and assuming that each family would be satisfied with
three pounds in payment.[19]

Newcastle's reply reached Victoria in early 1862.

I am fully sensible of the great importance of purchasing without loss of time
the native title to the soil of Vancouver Island; but the acquisition of the title is a
purely colonial interest, and the Legislature must not entertain any expectation
that the British taxpayer will be burthened to supply the funds or British credit
pledged for the purpose. I would earnestly recommend therefore to the House
of Assembly, that they should enable you to procure the requisite means, but if
they should not think proper to do so, Her Majesty's Government cannot undertake to supply the money requisite for an object which, whilst it is essential to
the interests of the people of Vancouver Island, is at the same time purely
Colonial in its character, and trifling in the charge that it would entail.[20]

Thus, the British government would take no financial responsibility for
purchasing aboriginal title. There was, though, no suggestion whatever
that the British government was ceasing to acknowledge the title.
Indeed, Newcastle acknowledged in explicit terms "the native title to the
soil of Vancouver Island." Nor was the British government discouraging
further treaties; it would simply take no part itself in providing funds for
them. However, Newcastle gave no indication that the government
would compel treaties to be arranged. The decision was thrown back to
the colony.

The assembly continued to recognize aboriginal title and to urge
Douglas and, after 1864, his successor as governor, A.E. Kennedy, to
extinguish it. In 1862, for example, just after receipt of Newcastle's reply,
the assembly unanimously passed a resolution that stated "That this
House would view with approval the extinguishment by His Excellency

the Governor of Indian title at Cowichan, from the proceeds of land sales" and that went on to observe that the assembly itself could not raise the necessary revenue because it had no authority over either land sales or revenue from such sales (which remained in control of the Colonial Office in London).[21]

For its part, the assembly did authorize Douglas, and later Kennedy, to expend general revenues to extinguish Indian title. The estimates approved for 1864 still included more than nine thousand dollars for "Indian Claims—Payment for Lands."[22] Yet, neither Douglas nor Kennedy arranged any treaties. Shortage of revenue was the ostensible excuse, although both continued to acknowledge aboriginal title. In November 1864, for example, Kennedy stated to the assembly that "the growing difficulties with the Indian population must continue to increase while the extent of their lands is undefined and their just claims unliquidated."[23]

As the actions of the elected assembly and the content of newspaper editorials show, there was continual local white recognition of aboriginal title and continual support for its proper extinguishment. On 4 July 1859 the editor of the *British Colonist*, Amor De Cosmos, stated: "Why is Indian title to Cowitchen not extinguished at once? This [demand] is repeated over and over again, and yet no response is heard from the government. It may require judicious management, but it has to be done. The country expects it without delay. We want farmers,—and the best way to get them is to open the lands of Cowitchen to actual settlers by extinguishing the Indian title."

Two years later, at the time of the assembly's petition, De Cosmos's frustration at both Douglas and Downing Street was sharply evident. He believed that "nothing but negligence has prevented the extinction of the Indian title long ago"[24] and that unauthorized white occupation of Indian lands could not be prevented much longer:

The Indian title, we conclude, is the great bugbear to stop settlement. We won't extinguish it; the Home Government won't. We have not tried; the Home Government has not tried. We have after three years' agitation for a cheap land system embracing the whole colony, just sent off an address to Downing Street to extinguish the Indian Title. Our impression is, we might just as well ask the London police to quell a fight on the Indian reserve [i.e., the village site adjacent to the Victoria]. We are already told, "You must be self-supporting." If such is the case, we will have to extinguish the title ourselves. For months and years the Indians on the Reserve cut each other's throats every day, attacked pedestrians, fired into the town; and we are told: "Don't arrest them, or we will have an Indian war." We did arrest them; hung one of them; and now they are all as quiet as mice. We were . . . frightened by a bugbear. On the land question we are frightened by another: "Pay the Indians for the land or we'll have an Indian war." We don't believe it. We hold it to be our best policy to pay them, to avoid even the possibility of a war. But our government says it cannot provide the means. Granting such to be the case, shall we allow a few red vagrants to prevent forever industrious settlers from settling on the unoccupied lands?[25]

On receipt in Victoria of Newcastle's reply to the assembly's petition, De Cosmos felt vindicated and continued on the same theme:

The assembly is informed that they need not expect a farthing from Home to extinguish the Indian title; and they are rather sharply told that the extinction of title is a "trifling" matter, and to find the money themselves if they want to do it. Such a rebuke will rather cool the enthusiasm of address framers; if not give rise to the suspicion that the Duke of Newcastle has had an inkling from outside sources that the Indian question, which the admirers of Gov. Douglas have so long worked upon to prove his admirable fitness for his exalted position, is exploded in Downing Street—condemned as a "bugbear" to frighten old women.[26]

During 1862 the colony's attorney-general, a Douglas appointee responsible to Douglas, publicly encouraged settlers to homestead in the Cowichan area and promised government protection from the Indians.[27] De Cosmos, while still labelling the Indians a bugbear, continued to maintain that "the Indians have a right to be paid for their lands . . . it is high time that [the government] should come to a fair and definite arrangement and have it carried out to the letter. They will thus avoid the troubles that the question has given rise to in the Territories of the United States."[28] Several settlers were killed in the Cowichan area at this time. The *Colonist* gave much coverage to the murders and continued its sensational reporting of rumours of other killings further north. Yet De Cosmos continued to support the Indians' land rights:

Very little stress is placed upon the necessity of giving the Indians no cause for entertaining ill feelings against the Whites . . . There prevails among all members of the tribes whose lands have been taken by the Government, a great amount of ill feeling towards the dominant race. The cause of the animosity is simply the neglect of the Executive to make the natives compensation for the property we have appropriated belonging to them . . . In the present instance there is no excuse. Government have been authorized [by the assembly] to expend some $9000 in satisfaction of Indian claims at Cowichan—so they only are to blame for any trouble that may arise out of the non-payment to the natives of whatever is fair and just under the circumstances. It may now, however, be not available to take any steps for settlement of the claims in question until the perpetrators of the recent murders are brought to justice and have received their deserts. But after that it is only right that no delay should take place in removing from the Indians any just grounds of complaint against their White rulers.[29]

What, then, is to be concluded about the treatment of the Indian land question in the colony of Vancouver Island? It is indisputable that white public opinion, as expressed in newspaper editorials and, more significantly, by elected white representatives, did accept the principle of aboriginal title and was in favour of purchasing that title. To make this observation is not to ignore the very evident hostility, even outright racism, often expressed towards Indians by De Cosmos and others.[30] Among the Whites, notions of fair dealing in acquiring Indian lands could go hand in hand with contempt for Indians.

There was continuous and unanimous acknowledgment of aboriginal title in the colony by the three official actors: the Colonial Office, the governor, and the assembly. Yet no action on Indian title took place after 1859. Each of the three put the onus on the other two to act. None did.

One major view has the Indians "caught in the centre" between the authorities in London and the local assembly, neither of which was willing to provide the necessary funds.[31] In this interpretation, Douglas was also caught in the middle, politically willing but financially unable to arrange further treaties on the Island or the Mainland.[32] The corollary is the assumption that the first denial of Indian title occurred not under Douglas but after his retirement. An examination of the actual policies pursued by Douglas in both colonies, but especially on the Mainland, points the way to a different interpretation and provides an essential perspective upon future beliefs and actions of both Indians and governments in British Columbia.

CHAPTER THREE

The Douglas "System":
Reserves, Pre-Emptions, and Assimilation

There remains about James Douglas a major puzzle. Why did he fail to arrange further treaties to extinguish aboriginal title in British Columbia? On Vancouver Island he arranged no treaties after 1854; on the Mainland he arranged no treaties at all. For Vancouver Island the case can at least be made that he would have arranged more treaties had sufficient funds been available,[1] but the same is not true for the mainland colony. For the six years preceding the creation of the legislature in 1864, Douglas had complete control of the colony's administration. During that time he spent large sums, notably on roads to take miners into, and gold out of, the interior. He financed the roads, especially the Cariboo Wagon Road, with substantial loans "about which London was not fully informed."[2] Those same roads took the Whites into the areas of heaviest Indian population in the interior. Yet, despite the explicit assumption by the Colonial Office that he would arrange treaties and compensate the Indians for their lands, he made no move to do so. The cost of treaties, especially in the first few years, would have been a pittance compared to the amounts he was raising and spending for other purposes. Unlike the Colonial Office, Douglas himself does not appear ever to have explicitly acknowledged aboriginal title on the Mainland.

What Douglas did was proceed to create land reserves for the Indians and allow them the same rights as Whites to other lands. While the outline of Douglas's actual policies on both the Island and the Mainland is well known, their rationale and details have not been fully examined; nor has account been taken of the incompatibility between those policies and recognition of aboriginal title. It is these factors, however, that point to a solution to the Douglas puzzle.

In Britain during the 1850s there had been a decline of concern over the treatment of aboriginal and other non-white peoples in the colonies. Earl Grey, whose term ended in 1852, was the last of the great colonial secretaries to give high priority to protecting aboriginal interests.[3] The Aborigines Protection Society continued to exist, but its influence was now much reduced. In 1858 Douglas received instructions from Sir Edward Bulwer Lytton, the colonial secretary, concerning administration of the new colony.

I have to enjoin upon you to consider the best and most humane means of dealing with the Native Indians. The feelings of this country would be strongly opposed to the adoption of any arbitrary or oppressive measures towards them. At this distance, and with the imperfect means of knowledge which I possess, I am reluctant to offer, as yet, any suggestion as to the prevention of affrays between the Indians and the immigrants. This question is of so local a character that it must be solved by your knowledge and experience, and I commit it to you, in the full persuasion that you will pay every regard to the interests of the Natives which an enlightened humanity can suggest. Let me not omit to observe, that it should be an invariable condition, *in all bargains or treaties with the natives for the cession of lands possessed by them*, that subsistence should be supplied to them in some other shape, and above all, that it is the earnest desire of Her Majesty's Government that your early attention should be given to the best means of diffusing the blessings of the Christian Religion and civilization among the natives.[4] [Emphasis added]

These instructions demonstrate that the British government recognized aboriginal title on the Mainland. The British authorities expected it to be extinguished and the Indians compensated before settlement was allowed. Lytton's greatest emphasis, however, was placed upon the need to convert and civilize the Indians.

Lytton soon sent a further despatch to Douglas. Neither it nor Douglas's reply appear to have been used subsequently as more than sources of incidental scholarly quotations.[5] Their significance is thus easily overlooked. Lytton was concerned with "the present condition of British Columbia" and "the policy to be adopted towards the Indian tribes."[6] "The success that has attended your transactions with these tribes induces me to inquire if you think it might be feasible to settle them permanently in villages; with such settlement civilization at once begins. Law and Religion would become naturally introduced amongst the red men, and contribute to their own security against the aggressions of immigrants."[7] The village Lytton had in mind was that of the English countryside with its neatly fenced cottages, dominated by church and castle, surrounded by agricultural fields, and peopled by tenant farmers, craftsmen, and manual workers. Lytton now made no mention of aboriginal title or of treaties. Douglas's reply was lengthy, and its style, in marked contrast to that of his usual despatches, was enthusiastic. "With much pleasure," and "unhesitating confidence," he wrote:

I conceive the proposed plan to be at once feasible, and also the only plan which promises to result in the moral elevation of the native Indian races, in rescuing them from degradation, and protecting them from oppression and rapid decay. It will, at the same time, have the effect of saving the colony from the numberless evils which naturally follow in the train of every course of national injustice, and from having the native Indian tribes arrayed in vindictive warfare against the white settlements . . . Provided we succeed in devising means of rendering the Indian as comfortable and independent in regard to physical wants in his improved condition, as he was when a wandering denizen of the forest, there can be little doubt of the ultimate success of the experiment . . . Anticipatory reserves of land for the benefit and support of the Indian races will be made for that purpose in all the districts of British Columbia inhabited by native tribes. Those reserves should in all cases include their cultivated fields and village sites, for which from habit and association they invariably conceive a strong attachment, and prize more, for that reason, than for the extent or value of the land.[8]

Douglas intended to make the new villages self-supporting, relying on "voluntary contributions in labour or money of the natives themselves" and also on "the proceeds of the sale or lease of a part of the land reserved, which might be so disposed of, and applied towards the liqui-dation of the preliminary expenses of the settlement."[9] Douglas was especially concerned that individual Indians "be trained to habits of self-government and self-reliance." He rejected direct provision of gov-ernment money and services to the Indians, the policy then being followed on United States Indian reserves; for "notwithstanding the heavy outlay, the Indians in those settlements are rapidly degenera-ting." He was equally critical of the Spanish attempts to civilize the Indians in California.

The Indians . . . were well fed and clothed, and they were taught to labour; but being kept in a state of pupilage, and not allowed to acquire property of their own, nor taught to think and act for themselves, the feeling and pride of independence were effectually destroyed; and not having been trained to habits of self-government and self-reliance, they were found, when freed from control, altogether incapable of contributing to their own support, and really were more helpless and degraded than the untutored savages . . . To avoid the rock on which were wrecked the hopes of the Spanish missions, I think it would be advisable studiously to cultivate the pride of independence, so ennobling in its effects, and which the savage largely possesses from nature and early training.[10]

Douglas believed that the Indians should be taught to regard the reserve lands "as their inheritance" but that they should have "for the present, no power to sell or otherwise alienate the land." Nevertheless, the Indians were not to depend entirely on the reserves for their income and security: "the desire should be encouraged and fostered in their minds of adding to their possessions, and devoting their earnings to the purchase of property apart from the reserve, which property would be left entirely at their own disposal and control."

Douglas ended by expressing two principles which should guide the government in implementing "the system," as he now called it. The Indians "should in all respects be treated as rational beings, capable of thinking and acting for themselves" and "should be placed under proper moral and religious training, and left, under the protection of the laws, to provide for their own maintenance and support."[11]

While some of Douglas's terminology is now unfashionable, there can be no doubting his desire to ensure not merely the physical survival of the Indians, but also their attaining individual equality with the Whites. At a time when aboriginal peoples elsewhere were routinely being forced from their lands and often actively exterminated, Douglas displayed a spirit of tolerance, compassion, and humane understanding. To Douglas's enduring credit, he recognized that Indian social breakdown and personal demoralization were the product of white impact rather than of racial weakness. At the same time, he believed that traditional Indian ways could not survive in the new circumstances and that Indian salvation lay in Christianity and a European agrarian lifestyle. Moreover, Douglas was willing to develop long-term policy at a time when many Whites, and probably many Indians too, assumed that the rapid Indian population decline meant that short-term charity was the most that was needed of official policy-makers.

Upon receiving the description of Douglas's proposed system, Lytton replied, "I am glad to find that your sentiments respecting the treatment of the native races are so much in accordance with my own." But he had white welfare in mind as well. "Whilst making ample provision under the arrangements proposed for the future sustenance and improvement of the native tribes, you will, I am persuaded, bear in mind the importance of exercising due care in laying out and defining the several reserves, so as to avoid checking at a future date the progress of the white colonists."[12]

Lytton had proposed getting the Indians into English-style villages with the primary purpose of facilitating the accomplishment of his major goal, introducing Christianity and other elements of British culture. Douglas fully shared this goal, but his system included a further step. He saw the new villages, and the reserves on which they would be located, essentially as way stations and half-way houses. Once suitably prepared, by missionaries, educators, and other civilizing agents, the Indians would no longer require protection and tutelage. Confining Indians permanently to reserves would amount to continuing them in "a state of pupilage" and thwarting their "pride of independence" and new training in "self-government and self-reliance." The result would be to sap their morale and to drain the public treasury.

Essential to the system, then, was getting the Indians off the reserves and into the colonial society with the inducement being the equal right to pre-empt land. Lytton had not suggested this final step. For its time it was radical and unique. In no other new world colony was the equality of aboriginal and immigrant persons seriously accepted by senior officials and made the basis of actual policy at the start of colonial administration.

In presenting his system Douglas makes no mention of initial Indian ownership of the land, of compensation, or of negotiation with the Indians. Indians were now to be recognized as properly possessing at most only the pieces of land that they were cultivating or using for house sites. Douglas's principles had changed since his treaties. The lands outside villages and fields, the very category of lands that the treaties had acknowledged as being initially owned by the Indians and that had been purchased by means of the treaties, were now to be dealt with as though owned by no one and thus at the unilateral disposal of the Crown.

In his treaties Douglas had departed from his initial company instructions by acknowledging aboriginal title to all land regarded by Indians as theirs; now he was prepared to depart from Lytton's initial expectations by not acknowledging it. He now states explicitly that Indians see their security in their fields and village sites rather than in "the extent or value of the land." That his principles had changed was confirmed by his statement to the assembly in March 1862 that allocating and guaranteeing reserves was a means of satisfying Indian "claims on the land."[13] The statement can mean only that Indians were to be regarded as having legitimate claim only to their village sites and fields; it denies the principle of aboriginal title. Douglas's new principles would be adhered to by all future British Columbia governments.

Under the treaties there is at least the pretence that the Indian communities had decided how much land they wished to sell and how much to retain. Now the way is left open for government officials to determine the size and location of reserves. Under the treaties existing aboriginal title is left unaffected on the portions of land not sold by the Indians. Under Douglas's system Indians would have no ultimate control over the use or disposition of reserve lands—to allow it would be to acknowledge some continuing traditional authority and communal land ownership.

Officials would be able to lease or even sell reserve lands (but only to Whites) to benefit the Indians. Presumably Indians would have exclusive use of their villages and fields, but to the extent that reserves were made larger, the purpose would be to leave the way open for sale or lease to Whites. This element of Douglas's system anticipated the cutting-off of reserve lands which would occur in the 1920s.[14]

Indians, however, are to have access to new rights—the rights of individual British subjects to equal treatment under the Crown, including the right to pre-empt unsurveyed Crown lands. Indians are to be treated as though they were immigrants without prior land rights.

In his years as governor Douglas did implement his system. The actual setting up of the villages was entrusted to Christian missionaries. The missionary efforts, both Protestant and Roman Catholic, did involve to a major degree an attempt to create villages on the European model. In a number of cases, most notably under William Duncan among the Tsimshian and Bishop Durieu among the Coast Salish, model villages did indeed emerge. While the missionary enterprise did not reach its height until well after Douglas had retired, his ideals and those of the missionaries were in close agreement, and he provided substantial government support. He himself implemented the other two elements of his system: Indian reserves and Indian land pre-emption.

In allocating reserves Douglas's general approach was to lay them out before white settlers arrived in a locality and to allocate sufficient land to each local Indian community for village sites, for agricultural purposes, and for the protection of specific sites such as burial grounds. In early 1861 Douglas instructed R.C. Moody, the chief commissioner of lands and works in the mainland colony, to ensure that "the extent of the Indian Reserves . . . be defined as they may severally pointed out by the Natives themselves."[15] The next day Moody transmitted this instruction to W.G. Cox, one of the principal surveyors in the interior. Moody added, however:

I would, at the same time, beg of you to be particular in scrutinizing the claims of the Indians, as I have every reason to believe that others (white persons) [sic] have, in some instances, influenced the natives in asserting claims which they would not otherwise have made, the object of such persons being prospective personal advantages previously covertly arranged with the Indians. To instance this, I heard of men keeping Indian women inducing them or their relations to put forward claims in order that they (the white men) [sic] may so gain possession of the land.[16]

Two months later a member of the Royal Engineers, the elite military unit which did much of the surveying and road-building on the Mainland, was instructed by his superior to stake and mark in the Lower Fraser Valley "all Indian villages, burial places, reserves [i.e., those already laid out], etc., as they may be pointed out to you by the Indians themselves, subject, however, to the decisions of the District Magistrate as to the extent of the land so claimed by them . . . Be very careful to satisfy the Indians so long as their claims are reasonable, and do not mark out any disputed lands between Whites and Indians before the matter is settled by the Magistrate."[17]

As far as amount of reserve land was concerned, Douglas's approach was similar to that which he had used in arranging the fourteen treaties. The Indians were allowed to continue using the pieces of land they could be seen to be currently using in European terms, and in the case of arable land, they were allocated enough to grow their own food. In 1863, for example, Douglas wrote sharply to Moody:

An application has been made to me this morning by the Native inhabitants of Coquitlam River, for an additional grant of land contiguous to the Indian Reserve immediately opposite Mr. Atkinson's premises.

That reserve it appears is so small, not exceeding 50 acres of land, as to be altogether insufficient to raise vegetables enough for their own use.

I beg that you will, therefore, immediately cause the existing reserve to be extended in conformity with the wishes of the Natives, and to include therein an area so large as to remove from their minds all causes of dissatisfaction.[18]

The actual size of reserves allocated under Douglas is important in terms of his reputation and in light of later events. It is possible to conclude from portions of the quotations just given, as Fisher does, that "Douglas made it clear that the Indians were to have as much land as they wanted."[19] Robert Cail similarly concludes that "so long as Douglas was governor, the Indians had only to ask to receive additional land."[20] Wilson Duff asserts that Douglas's "policy was to give the Indians whatever plots of land they chose and as much acreage as they requested."[21]

In having Douglas so generous to the Indians, these conclusions downplay the role of the local white magistrates and discount the instructions that Douglas himself had from Lytton "to avoid checking at a future date the progress of the white colonists."[22] In addition, they do not give sufficient weight to Indian complaints such as the one from the chiefs of the Lower Fraser Valley: "Governor Douglas did send some years ago his men amongst us to measure our Reserve and although they gave us only a small patch of land in comparison to what they allowed to a white man our neighbour, we were resigned to our lot."[23] The interpretation that Indians obtained all the land they wanted must also assume that Indians, like Douglas himself, now regarded only their villages and adjacent areas as their rightful property. Coupled with the undeniable fact that most reserves were very small, this assumption implies that Indians no longer regarded themselves as owning the whole of the lands they had traditionally used. In attempting to reconcile the actual smallness of the reserves with Douglas's supposed generosity, Duff even suggests that "not being farmers," the Indians "did not ask for very much, in no case more than 10 acres per family."[24]

Douglas was not giving carte blanche to the Indians. In indicating where their reserve boundaries might be located, coastal communities, it would appear, were merely indicating the location of specific traditional sites and the extent to which they had adopted agriculture, and that had happened only recently, if at all.[25] In the southern interior, where Indians had begun raising horses and cattle during the fur trade and so could demonstrate extensive land use in European terms, reserves were often large. William Cox, for example, evidently having more trust in Indians than Moody did, allocated the Kamloops Indians many square miles,[26] including much prime agricultural land. Throughout both colonies, however, it was the government surveyors and magistrates, not the Indians, who were the final local arbiters on reserve acreage.

The question of Douglas's generosity in defining reserves comes down to numbers of acres and families. Duff accepts ten acres for each family as the maximum. Fisher, in contrast, concludes that it was the minimum and states that Douglas "included in his directions to those laying out reserves in British Columbia the provision that if the area demanded by the Indians did not equal ten acres per family then the reserves were to be enlarged to that extent."[27] The one letter of instruction that Fisher cites in support of this assertion was written on 6 April 1864, only days before Douglas retired, and so it could only have had minimal effect while he was governor. Moreover, the letter applies only to the marking out of reserves "between New Westminster and Harrison River, wherever reserves have not yet been declared and defined" and thus not to the whole colony.[28]

In one of his last speeches as governor, as he opened the first session of the mainland legislature, Douglas summarized his Indian policy and said about reserves:

The Native Indian Tribes are quiet and well disposed; the plan of forming Reserves of Land embracing the Village Sites, cultivated fields, and favorite places of resort of the several tribes, and thus securing them against the encroachment of Settlers, and for ever removing the fertile cause of agrarian disturbance, has been productive of the happiest effects on the minds of the Natives. *The areas thus partially defined and set apart, in no case exceed the proportion of ten acres for each family concerned*, and are to be held as the joint and common property of the several tribes, being intended for their exclusive use and benefit, and especially as a provision for the aged, the helpless, and the infirm.[29] [Emphasis added]

However, even Douglas's own very public and very official words cannot be the final ones on the acreage question, for at the time he spoke some reserves, including the one at Kamloops, contained much more than ten acres per family. So also, apparently, did at least one Fraser River reserve.[30] Moreover, in Douglas's previous instructions to field officials there had been no indication of any acreage formula.[31] During his last few months as governor, *after* his speech to the legislature, he did use ten acres a family as the *minimum* amount along the Fraser between New Westminster and Harrison River. Indeed, in this particular instance the surveyor, William McColl, stated soon afterwards: "In addition to the written instructions, I had further verbal orders given to me by Sir James Douglas, to the effect that all lands claimed by the Indians were to be included in the reserve; the Indians were to have as much land as they wished, and in no case to lay off a reserve under 100 acres. The reserves have been laid off accordingly."[32]

Thus, Douglas's statement to the legislature is at odds with his actions before and after. It presents another Douglas puzzle. His own final words, written from retirement a decade later, contradict what he said to the legislature: "It was never . . . intended that they should be limited to the possession of 10 acres of land, on the contrary, we were prepared, if such had been their wish, to have made for their use much more extensive grants."[33] Unfortunately for the Indians, it was Douglas's ten-acre statement to the legislature that would be seized upon by his successors.

In fact, Douglas did grant only limited reserve acreage to most communities. His system, however, left the way open for individual Indians to acquire vastly greater amounts of land than their reserves contained. To be too quick to perceive Douglas as generous in allocating reserve acreage is to overlook his system and its intention that Indians could freely pre-empt non-reserve land.

The ability to occupy and farm vacant unowned land as the first step in obtaining eventual ownership of it, that is, to pre-empt it, was a major aspect of white settlement on both the Island and the Mainland. Indeed, the ability of an enterprising individual to obtain free farm land and make it his own through his own labour was central to the white immigrant dream throughout North America. In the United States, where pre-emption was commonly referred to as "homesteading," the possibility that individual Indians might pre-empt land their community had surrendered was rarely, if ever, entertained, and in practice the possibility was removed by eliminating the Indians or confining them to reservations.

Douglas's intention that individual Indians be allowed to pre-empt land was thus unusual, if not unique. Certainly, in no other jurisdiction in North America was substantial Indian pre-emption envisioned. The implications of the pre-emption aspect of Douglas's system have not always been recognized. They are ignored or minimized by Shankel, Duff, and Cail.[34] The potential was quite simply that Indians, who in the 1860s greatly outnumbered Whites, would occupy and own most of the suitable agricultural land in the two colonies. Indians would thus assume a major economic role. Indians could also have major political influence, for Douglas presumably intended that Indians would have the normal political rights, including the franchise.

Widespread Indian pre-emption could occur only if many Indians were willing to give up traditional ways, to live in solitary families, to become farmers, and to forget aboriginal title. Pre-emption would be a process drawing out those Indians most amenable to assimilation and to co-operation with Whites. The two groups would be dependent upon one another and could, conceivably, even produce a biracial society, thus making British Columbia more similar, in this respect at least, to Mexico than to the United States or to Canada east of the Rockies.

The proclamations which Douglas issued allowed British subjects and aliens to pre-empt unoccupied, unsurveyed land. On the Island a married couple was allowed 200 acres and 10 more for each child; on the Mainland a person could pre-empt 160 acres and buy adjoining land at twenty-five pence an acre. Aside from prohibiting pre-emption of land in any "Indian Reserve or settlement," the proclamations made no mention of Indians or Indian lands.[35]

Indians did commence pre-empting, especially in the Lower Fraser Valley, the location of the most fertile arable land in the entire province. Officials feared that white hostility would result in conflict. In mid-1862 R.C. Moody wrote that "Indians are pre-empting in 'extended order' along the River and elsewhere to considerable extent" and that "such extent is likely to increase very considerably and very rapidly."[36] Moody appeared to suspect that Indians were colluding to protect their tribal lands from settlers and were not intending to live up to the requirement that they become individual homesteaders. In April 1863 he reported that "the Roman Catholic priests have moved the Indians to pre-empt as freely as any other persons . . . It is a growing question that will have to be met."[37] Douglas, however, appears to have been satisfied with the course of events, for he made no specific response to Moody's report.[38]

By this time there was much white sentiment that Indians should be confined to reserves and not allowed to pre-empt. In summarizing his Indian policy to the new British Columbia legislature, Douglas rejected the white concerns, stating that allocation of reserves was not "intended to interfere with the private rights of individuals of the Native Tribes, or to incapacitate them, as such, from holding land; on the contrary, they have precisely the same rights of acquiring and possessing land in their individual capacity, either by purchase or by occupation under the Pre-emption Law, as other classes of Her Majesty's subjects; provided that they in all respects comply with the legal conditions of tenure by which land is held in this colony."[39] What, then, is to be concluded about Douglas's treatment of the Indian land question? In particular, why did he arrange no further treaties?

In the colony of Vancouver Island both the British government and Douglas himself explicitly recognized aboriginal title; Douglas did so in the fourteen treaties and in many later statements. In the new mainland colony of British Columbia the British government began by acknowledging aboriginal title and assuming that Douglas would arrange "bargains or treaties with the natives for the cession of lands possessed by them."[40] But there Douglas himself does not appear to have recognized aboriginal title even rhetorically, and he certainly took no action to extinguish it.

Douglas seems not to have regarded his treaties as being of great consequence. Indeed, no reasonable person could have regarded them as having improved the lot of the Indians. The fourteen communities, most of them adjacent to white settlements, were the very ones suffering the greatest individual and communal ills by the time the mainland colony was created. The fact that a community's aboriginal title had been recognized and then extinguished by treaty seemed of little benefit to its surviving members once the treaty blankets had worn out.

Convinced that Indian ways could not survive and believing that the best hope for the Indians lay in assimilation, Douglas quite apparently regarded past title and further treaties as irrelevant to the task of ensuring a viable future for Indians. On the Mainland he faced no disagreement. On the Island, however, the assembly and portions of white opinion did regard title and treaties as important, although more because of white legalistic values and fear of Indian militancy than from any concern for Indian welfare. It was in face of this white pressure that Douglas continued rhetorically acknowledging title on the Island while doing nothing to extinguish it.

Douglas ignored treaty-making on the Mainland not because of lack of funds but because his system anticipated assimilated Indians who, having abandoned traditional communities for their homesteads, would maintain neither Indian identity nor Indian land claims. Despite the expectations of the British government, Douglas came in practice to deny Indian title and so to deny the relevance of the aboriginal past. His system opened the way, or so he believed, to a society, economy, and political system in which individual Indians could be prosperous, secure, and equal.

The legacy of Indian policy that Douglas left to his successors may be summarized as follows:

1 On a small fraction of Vancouver Island he had recognized aboriginal land title and extinguished it by treaty.
2 On the Island he had continued to acknowledge aboriginal title in word but not in deed; despite pressure from the public and the assembly and encouragement from the Colonial Office, he had taken no further action to extinguish Indian title.
3 On the Mainland he had not acknowledged aboriginal title in either word or action and had thus departed from the expectations of the British government.
4 He had implemented the beginnings of his "system" by encouraging missionary activities, laying out land reserves, and allowing Indians to become homesteaders off reserves.
5 He had established reserves of only a few acres per family and had explicitly enunciated in the mainland legislature, the most public forum possible, a policy of allowing no more than ten acres per family.
6 He had implemented legislation allowing Indians to pre-empt land and had resisted pressure from the white public by defending equal land rights for Indians.
7 Neither he nor the legislatures on the Island or the Mainland had taken any specific action that he or they regarded as, or that could be interpreted as, extinguishing Indian title outside the treaty areas.

The central elements in Douglas's land policy after 1854 were his de facto denial of aboriginal title, his granting of only small reserves, and his defence and encouragement of Indian land pre-emption.[41] Douglas envisioned a British Columbia in which Indians would have land rights equal to those of Whites. This vision did not materialize. Indeed, B.C Indians were not even to maintain equality with other Indians. As Clarence Karr observes, Douglas's policies led to their having "fewer rights, less land and less protection than most of their counterparts in the rest of Canada."[42]

Hidden within Douglas's legacy was a further feature which came to have effects he presumably did not anticipate. He had allowed Indian communities to choose the location, if not the size, of their reserves.

The surviving members of traditional communities could thus remain resident on preferred sites within their ancestral homelands and so could retain a sense of communal unity and an active connection with historic places and communal memories. Confined to their small reserves, they could nurture a deepening sense of injustice as they witnessed the takeover of their surrounding traditional lands without regard to aboriginal title. Douglas's approach thus facilitated the retention of the communal and tribal group identities that he assumed would vanish.

Douglas's greatest legacy, however, was *not* having extinguished aboriginal title. To the Indians he left title to their lands. To the Whites he left the unresolved Indian claims. To all British Columbians he left the Indian land question. Douglas is indeed the Father of British Columbia.

CHAPTER FOUR

Segregation and Suppression, 1864–87

Quite different Indian policies emerged following Douglas's retirement in the spring of 1864. His successors as governor left Indian policy to their subordinates. Joseph Trutch was the dominant policy-maker, serving until 1871 as chief commissioner of lands and works. Trutch had started his career as a surveyor, with little knowledge of Indians but considerable prejudice.[1] He personified settler interests and attitudes, considering Indians "as bestial rather than human," "as uncivilized savages," as ugly and lazy, and as "lawless and violent."[2] With governors no longer as active in policy as Douglas had been, Trutch's position gave him control over land matters. He used it to the full to reduce or eliminate the elements of Douglas's Indian policy legacy that were beneficial to Indians.

The Indian population continued to decline. In 1862 it was some 60,000. Then came a smallpox epidemic. One in every three Indians died.[3] Many Whites assumed that the "Indian problem" would ultimately vanish with the Indians themselves.[4] Although rarely made explicit, this comforting assumption was very likely in the minds of provincial officials as they casually ignored or dismissed Indian land claims.

Trutch was the first official to assert explicitly that British Columbia Indians had never owned the land. As this notion was so obviously contrary to the view that had been held by the British government, that had been initially followed by Douglas, and that had been accepted by the island assembly, Trutch was compelled to revise the history of the colony to suit his claim. In 1870 he informed the governor:

The title of the Indians in the fee of the public lands, or any portion thereof, has never been acknowledged by Government, but, on the contrary, is distinctly denied. In no case has any special agreement been made with any of the tribes of the Mainland for the extinction of their claims of possession; but these claims have been held to have been fully satisfied by securing to each tribe, as the progress of the settlement of the country seemed to require, the use of sufficient tracts of land for their wants for agricultural and pastoral purposes.[5]

Thus far he was seriously distorting the principles enunciated by British officials, notably Newcastle and Lytton, but accurately reflecting Douglas's de facto denial of title and view that reserves were adequate settlement of Indian claims. But there were still the Douglas treaties with their unequivocal recognition of Indian title. According to Trutch, Douglas had

made agreements with the various families of Indians . . . for the relinquishment of their possessory claims in the district of country around Fort Victoria, in consideration of certain blankets and other goods presented to them. But these presents were, as I understand, made for the purpose of securing friendly relations between those Indians and the settlement of Victoria, then in its infancy, and certainly not in acknowledgment of any general title of the Indians to the lands they occupy.[6]

In other words, the Indians had been bribed to give up their *claims* to the land not paid for the land itself. The none-too-subtle implication was that the Indians had not been serious in claiming to own the land or, at best, that they had been venal enough to give up principles for quick benefit. Trutch now needed only to discount the implications of the island assembly's having allocated funds to purchase title from the Cowichans. He provided a smokescreen of meaningless verbiage:

I can find no record of any promise having been made to these Indians that they should be paid for the lands in the Cowichan Valley which they may have laid claim to . . . But it is probable that the Cowichans . . . may have expected and considered themselves entitled to receive for their lands, which they held to be theirs, similar donations to those which had been presented to their neighbours, the Saanich Indians, years previously, as before mentioned, on their relinquishing their claims on the lands around their villages. It is further very likely that it was Governor Douglas' intention that such gratuities should be bestowed on this tribe.[7]

Underlying Trutch's revision of history was the view, already well established among white settlers, that Indians had been and remained primitive savages who were incapable of concepts of land title and who most certainly should not be perceived as land owners. Whether or not this view was expressed euphemistically, it fed the emerging white myth that British Columbia had been in essence an empty land, devoid of society, government, or laws. This myth legitimized the denial of aboriginal title and sanctified the new white doctrine that all land in the colony was not only under British sovereignty but also directly owned by the Crown.

The new myth and doctrine would prove remarkably enduring, in good part because they so perfectly served the interests of Whites and of provincial governments. There could be no better way to show that Indians did not own the land than by asserting that they had never owned it or even been able on their own to conceive of owning it. Contemporary Indian claims to title could now be dismissed as the self-seeking actions of Indians copying the more advanced concepts of property brought by the Whites. Treaties were now not merely unnecessary; they were impossible, for how could title which had never existed be acknowledged, let alone purchased? As for Indian reserves, they could now be seen as neither a right nor a recognition that the title to surrounding land had been surrendered. The use of reserves would be merely a gift from a generous monarch. Underlying the myth and doctrine would be the continuing white notion, first publicly advanced by Trutch, that Indian claims were motivated by conniving venality rather than honourable conviction.

So unquestioned became the white myth of an empty land and so entrenched became the doctrine of unencumbered crown ownership that the question of Indian title virtually disappeared from white public debate. Until after the turn of the century, such debate as there was, including that between the province and the federal government, centred not upon the fundamental question of title but on the lesser issue of reserve size. This issue involved no deep principle, but rather simply the degree of generosity the Crown should display in allowing Indians to use land they had no claim to. The shift from title to reserves as the major element in the Indian land question was a major, but unheralded, victory for Trutch and his allies, since it moved the public policy agenda onto safer ground for the Whites.

The full and equal right of Indians to pre-empt land had been a key element in Douglas's actual Indian policy. One of the first actions the legislature of the united colony was to amend the pre-emption ordinance: "The right conferred . . . on British Subjects, or aliens . . . of pre-empting and holding in fee simple unoccupied and unsurveyed and unreserved Crown Lands in British Columbia, shall not (without the special permission thereto of the Governor first had in writing) extend to or be deemed to have been conferred on . . . any of the Aborigines of this Colony or the Territories neighbouring thereto."[8] Indian pre-emption was thus abolished. Douglas's policy was shattered. The fate of the land already pre-empted by Indians is not now readily apparent; on this point the wording of the amendment is ambiguous. Possibly officials interpreted it as retroactively cancelling the Indian pre-emptions granted under Douglas. In any case, henceforth Indians could rely only on reserve lands, whose small extent under Douglas had been defensible principally because Indians were allowed and encouraged to pre-empt additional land. Indian families could now expect at most a ten-acre share of a reserve that had often been defined to exclude the prime land desired by Whites. A white settler family could acquire many times the acreage, and of prime land, right next door to a crowded reserve.

Douglas had treated Indians as immigrants in their own land but also as British subjects with equal rights, and he had favoured mixing of the two races and assimilation of the Indians. Under the Trutch regime, Indians became a residual category with fewer rights than aliens. Segregation and inequality would now be the hallmarks of British Columbia provincial Indian policy.

With Indians now confined to the reserves as far as use of land was concerned, Trutch proceeded systematically to reduce those reserves and to apply stringent pro-settler criteria in laying out new ones. No subject received greater attention in his correspondence with subordinates and with governors.[9] He displayed little of Douglas's sympathetic consideration of Indian concerns and complaints, although he does appear to have defended reserves from encroachment once they were laid out to his satisfaction.

Trutch was highly inventive in finding reasons to resurvey and redefine virtually every reserve already laid out. In his view "very few reserves had been staked off or in any way exactly defined," while details of boundaries had not been properly recorded and published.[10] The only record of most reserves, he implied, was furnished by the actual survey stakes, and these, of course, could be moved by the Indians. Where reserves seemed to exceed Douglas's stated policy of no more than ten acres a family, Trutch claimed that the surveyors must have misunderstood their instructions. He was industrious in counting Indians, or at least those who happened to be present and remain in sight when he or his officials came on the scene, and he was almost always successful in obtaining counts which justified cutting the acreage. In the interior, while allowing some exceptions, he generally applied the ten-acre maximum. The larger reserves were drastically reduced, including the one at Kamloops, which was cut on his instructions to less than half its former extent.[11]

Often Trutch justified reserve reduction simply because Indians had not yet adopted European farming methods, even though they had had only a few years to do so. In 1867 he wrote to the governor about the reserves laid out by McColl along the Lower Fraser in 1864.

The Indians regard these extensive tracts of land as their individual property; but of by far the greater portion thereof they make no use whatever and are not likely to do so; and thus the land, much of which is either rich pasture or available for cultivation and greatly desired for immediate settlement, remains in an unproductive condition—is of no real value to the Indians and utterly unprofitable to the public interests.

I am, therefore, of opinion that these reserves should, in almost every case, be very materially reduced.[12]

One year later the "public interest" had been served by the reduction of the Lower Fraser reserves by forty thousand acres, or more than sixty-two square miles. The surveyor assigned to make the reductions reported to Trutch that "in our reconnaissance in the Chilliwhack District we were accompanied by nearly all the settlers, some sixteen in number, who were very useful and obliging in pointing out . . . survey-or's posts."[13] Neither he nor Trutch evinced any suspicion that the settlers might already have shifted the posts they were so familiar with.

Later students of colonial Indian policy, white and Indian, have not been admirers of Trutch, excoriating him especially for denying title and reducing reserves and even perceiving his policies as unique in both respects.[14] However, in his de facto denial of title Trutch was simply following the well-established practice he inherited, and he was able to be credible in his doctrine of explicitly denying title in part because for more than a decade Douglas had been denying it implicitly. In reducing reserves and in allocating new ones, Trutch was adhering to the ten-acre formula enunciated by Douglas. In both cases Douglas thus bears much of the responsibility.

Trutch played the leading part on the British Columbia side in arranging the terms of union with Canada. The terms proposed by the province contained no mention of Indians, but term number 13 was added at Canada's insistence and written, it would appear, by Trutch himself.[15]

The charge of the Indians and the trusteeship and management of the lands reserved for their use and benefit, shall be assumed by the Dominion Government, *and a policy as liberal as that hitherto pursued by the British Columbia Government, shall be continued by the Dominion Government* after the Union. To carry out such policy, *tracts of land of such extent as it has hitherto been the practice of the British Columbia Government to appropriate for that purpose, shall from time to time be conveyed . . . to the Dominion Government* in trust for the use and benefit of the

Indians, on application of the Dominion Government, and in case of disagreement between the two Governments respecting the quantity of such tracts of land to be so granted, the matter shall be referred for the decision of the Secretary of State for the Colonies.[16] [Emphasis added]

Canadian officials, more than 2,000 miles from Victoria and having neither road nor rail connection to the west, were quite uninformed about the province's Indian policy. They assumed that it had, like their own, been in accord with the Royal Proclamation of 1763. Subsequently, one federal minister in charge of Indian affairs, David Mills, confirmed that Canada had believed that the Indians had surrendered their territories by treaty;[17] and another, David Laird, indicated that Canada had assumed that British Columbia reserves, like those in northern Ontario, contained at least eighty acres a family.[18]

Truch, who had travelled to Ottawa for the negotiations, obviously did not give full information, and he left the impression that British Columbia had indeed been liberal and generous in awarding reserves and other benefits. It was in this context that the Canadians accepted the promise of continued liberality and did not realize that Trutch's phrase "of such extent as it has hitherto been the practice . . . to appropriate" meant that the province would never in the future have to award more than ten acres a family for reserve purposes. The province's power to veto reserves exceeding ten acres a family would rest on the provincial Crown's now being recognized, in both the terms of union and under the British North America Act, as having direct title to public lands. The Canadian government would have no power to compel the provincial government to appropriate more than ten acres a family.

Sir John A. Macdonald and his Conservatives, like the provincial government, regarded the question of finances and of a transcontinental railway as the main issues in arranging union. It was in this connection that the province agreed to transfer large blocs of land to the federal government to promote railway development. Differences over Indians were not of major importance. Trutch emerged from the negotiations as the main provincial ally of Macdonald and his government.

Regardless of the terms of union, it might be supposed that union would have resulted in more favourable treatment of British Columbia Indians, for the British North America Act gave the federal authorities not only exclusive jurisdiction over "Indians and lands reserved for Indians" but also the power to disallow any provincial law. However, the federal authorities had no power to compel the province either to acknowledge Indian title or to exceed the ten-acre formula for reserves; and to use the disallowance power effectively on behalf of Indians would be to lose support among white voters. Thus, Canada's taking formal control of Indian administration did not result in any reversal of Trutch's policies. Trutch himself, appointed the province's first lieutenant-governor by Macdonald, was even successful in further entrenching those policies.

At Union the Indians still had one major provincial civil right, voting in provincial elections. This right was soon removed by the legislature.[19] Already denied land rights, Indians were now lumped together with non-white immigrants as ineligible for the most basic of political rights.

After Union the legislative vehicle for administering Indians and Indian lands was the federal Indian Act. By the mid 1870s its major features were in place, and "a Department of the Civil Service of Canada to be called the Department of Indian Affairs" had been established.[20] As it allowed only registered Indians to live (or be buried) on reserves,[21] the act served to divide families and to weaken communities. The act also provided for individuals to relinquish Indian status voluntarily.[22] It assumed that able and competent Indians would desire to leave their reserves, to live and work among non-Indians, to have the federal franchise (which was denied to registered Indians), and to become, in a phrase popular among federal officials, "full British subjects." The Indians, in sum, "were supposed to abandon their reserves and their special status and disappear into the general population."[23]

As Brian Titley observes, the Indian Act was "designed to protect Indians until they acquired the trappings of white civilization."[24] It protected reserves by defining them as federal crown lands held in trust for benefit of Indians, by prohibiting taxation of reserve land or property on it, and by providing that a reserve could be reduced only with the consent of a majority of the adult males in the band affected.

The act allowed the department to impose a "chief and council" structure, which, in spite its name, was copied from the typical Canadian mayor and council structure and was intended to induce bands to copy the municipal style of local government and to adopt the white view that local government should be subordinate to central authorities. Despite the implication of some local autonomy, the act gave sweeping powers of regulation over reserves and bands to the federal minister of Indian affairs and his officials.

Had tribal groups been recognized by the act, the political and administrative environment of Indians would have been very different. William Duncan, the north coast missionary, appears to have made the only recommendation along these lines, suggesting that the government ignore individual bands or local communities and instead "regard only the natural division of languages" and "grant a large district for the use and benefit of all the Indians of one language; that is, I would recommend one large Reserve for each tongue."[25] Seen in this light, the act's exclusive focus on bands served to inhibit the tribal strength and unity that Duncan's proposal would have facilitated.

In the same year that it accepted British Columbia into Confederation, Canada signed the first of the major treaties with Indians west of Ontario. By 1877 seven had been signed, covering most of the agricultural land in what would become the three prairie provinces. The treaties implemented the principles of the Proclamation of 1763. The Indians ceded their land title to the Crown in return for various payments, benefits, hunting rights, and reserves. The reserve allocation formula varied from 160 to 640 acres per Indian family, the intention being that an Indian family would have access to the same amount of land that a settler family would be allowed in the same region.[26] Over much of the prairies settlers were allowed access to the land only after government surveyors had laid out reserves. Acknowledgement, and extinguishment, of Indian title were thus accomplished east of the Rockies before most settlers had arrived. It was this same sequence of events that the Canadian officials assumed had already taken place west of the Rocky Mountains.

To administer the Indian Act in British Columbia Macdonald appointed Israel Wood Powell, a physician residing in Victoria, as Indian superintendent.[27] Powell set about dividing the province into Indian agencies and appointing agents to each of them. He also turned immediately to the problem of obtaining land for new reserves.[28] He soon became a trenchant critic of the provincial refusal to exceed the ten-acre amount and began to advocate the enlargement of reserves already laid out, especially as it became clear, in his words, that "many of the present reserves do not contain *five* acres of land to each head of a family."[29] His superiors in Ottawa endorsed his stand, in part because of active lobbying by Roman Catholic missionaries. In March 1873 the Macdonald cabinet officially requested the province to accept the eighty-acre standard and apply it both in laying out new reserves and enlarging established ones. The provincial government agreed to a twenty-acre standard, but only for new reserves and, in the end, reneged even on this agreement.[30]

To protest this response, Powell stopped laying out reserves. He was now convinced that further provincial intransigence would result in Indian violence, and he informed his minister that "if there has not been an Indian War, it is not because there has been no injustice to the Indians, but because the Indians have not been sufficiently united."[31] David Laird, the minister in the new Liberal federal government, supported Powell and wrote a lengthy report to his cabinet colleagues.

The present state of the Indian Land question in our Territory West of the

Rocky Mountains, is most unsatisfactory, and . . . is the occasion, not only of great discontent among the aboriginal tribes but also of serious alarm to the white settlers.

To the Indian, the land question far transcends in importance all others, and its satisfactory adjustment in British Columbia will be the first step towards allaying the wide-spread and growing discontent now existing among the native tribes of that province.

He observed that during union negotiations the federal officials "could hardly have been aware of the marked contrast between the Indian policies which had, up to that time, prevailed in Canada and British Columbia," and he noted that Article 13 in the terms of union "seems little short of a mockery" of Indian claims. He agreed with Powell that only lack of unity was preventing an Indian uprising. He recommended continued pressure on the provincial government to accept the eighty-acre standard for all reserves, and he suggested that the matter should be referred to the British colonial secretary for resolution should the province refuse.[32] The federal cabinet accepted his advice, at least to the extent of again requesting, in late 1874, that the province adopt the eighty-acre standard.

The extent to which the Indian land question was subject to public debate among white British Columbia politicians during the decades following union is now difficult to assess, in good part because there was no verbatim reporting of legislative debates. In this period the legislature did not have party politics or party government (and would not have until after 1900). There were premiers and governments, but they changed frequently. Government supporters and opponents could be identified, but neither side was a disciplined group. Independence was valued and practised. Measures put forward by opponents of a government could well be passed by the house.

However, the circumstances surrounding the province's response to the renewed federal request demonstrate not only that Lieutenant-governor Trutch and his allies sought to conceal information from the public and to prevent informed public debate but also that they faced white opposition to their Indian policies. There was even a possibility that the legislature might compel the government to adopt the eighty-acre policy.

In early 1875, during the legislature's debate on the federal request, William Tolmie moved that the government publish for examination by the house all papers relating to the Indian land question. Tolmie was an old Hudson's Bay Company hand with much experience among the Indians. His motion was adopted by the house despite being opposed by Premier G.A. Walkem. Immediately, William Smithe, then "leader of

the loosely organized opposition,"[33] moved that a committee be established to examine and report upon the papers and that it consist of
Smithe, Tolmie, John Robson, J.F. McCreight (who in 1871 had been the
province's first premier), and two members of the government, Walkem
and Robert Beaven. This motion was opposed by the government, but it
too was approved by the house.[34] Thus, contrary to what might be
assumed,[35] neither the motion to produce the papers nor that to set up
the committee was a government initiative.

Walkem and his government delayed as long as possible. The two
government members refused to attend meetings of the committee,
which went ahead and chose Smithe as chairman. Eventually, after a
concerted attack in the house charging a government cover-up, Walkem
presented a packet of papers to the Speaker of the assembly. Now
officially in the Speaker's custody, the packet was sent to the government
printer. After another month and nothing from the printer, it was discovered that the packet had disappeared. The papers were then discovered hidden in the office of one Mr. Good, the deputy provincial
secretary.[36] According to Smithe, Good informed him that the papers
had never been to the printer's and that Walkem's packet had been
simply "a bundle of nondescript odds and ends of papers."[37]

It was now close to the end of the session, at which time the committee would automatically cease to exist. The real papers were printed and
then reviewed by the committee, still without Walkem and Beaven; it
then prepared its report. According to the *Colonist*, the report observed
that "the Indians have complained, and have had good reason to com-
plain, of their treatment on the question of their land reserves,"[38] criticized the "utter unjustifiableness" of the government's policy,[39] and
recommended the adoption of the eighty-acre policy for existing and
future reserves.[40]

When Smithe attempted to submit the report in the house on Wednes-
day, 21 April, the day preceding the scheduled close of the session,
Beaven objected that it should not be received as the committee had
failed to consider evidence favourable to the government. Smithe
agreed to have the committee meet at 10 o'clock in the morning of the
next day to receive whatever the government would provide. Quite evidently, the government members were concerned not only that the
report would be damaging to them but also that the house might accept
its recommendations and direct the government to follow the eighty-
acre criterion. The government and its supporters now kept Wednes-
day's debates going until 5 o'clock Thursday morning, at which point,
obviously having taken careful note of which members were still present to vote, Walkem moved that the house adjourn until the precise
moment of prorogation at 2:30 that afternoon. The motion passed. Now,

even if committee members were awake to meet at 10 o'clock, there would be no time available in the afternoon for presentation of the report.

Smithe, Tolmie, McCreight, and Robson met at 10 o'clock and waited fruitlessly for Walkem and Beaven until just before 2:30, at which time the four went to the assembly chamber, hoping that Smithe would be allowed to present the report before Lieutenant-governor Trutch prorogued the session. Trutch, however, was ready and waiting, despite his well-established reputation for tardiness, and he prorogued the house out from under Smithe and his committee members. The *Colonist* reported that Smithe thereupon "handed a copy of the Report to a representative of this journal for publication. On hearing of this the Premier waxed very wroth and blustered about breach of privilege and such like; and the result was that the Chairman . . . was induced to withdraw the document."[41]

The committee report was never made public. The newly printed *Papers Connected with the Indian Land Question, 1850-1875*,[42] however, were henceforth a matter of public record and so could remain a permanent antidote to Trutch's revisions of history. Tolmie's motion thus led to a lasting result. (But not until 1985, when the Provincial Archives reprinted the *Papers*, was the document readily available. In the intervening decades white officials on at least one critically important occasion denied Indians access to it.)[43] Smithe, for his part, went on to become premier as well as commissioner of lands; in these positions he sought to advance none of the principles he had espoused in his committee report, but instead upheld the policies of Walkem and Trutch.

Deploring Walkem's success in suppressing the committee's report, the editor of the *Colonist*, now David Higgins, gave himself the last word, and posterity a lasting question. After urging the government to recognize Indian title and to grant larger reserves, he asked, "Shall it be written of British Columbia that she was the first province of the Dominion to oppress her natives and the last to do them justice?"[44]

David Laird and the federal Liberal cabinet had confined their request to the issue of reserve size and been unwilling to press the province on the questions of Indian title and treaties. Yet, there was one further and final federal plea on the subject.[45] Lord Dufferin, the governor-general, visited the province in 1876, making it a point to visit a number of Indian communities. In a speech in Victoria to leading citizens and government officials, Dufferin dealt directly with title:

We must all admit that the condition of the Indian question in British Columbia is not satisfactory. Most unfortunately, as I think, there has been an initial error ever since Sir James Douglas quitted office . . . of British Columbia neglecting to recognize what is known as Indian title. In Canada this has always been done: no government, whether provincial or central, has failed to acknowledge that the original title to the land existed in the Indian tribes and communities that hunted or wandered over them . . . The result has been that in Canada our Indians are contented, well affected to the white man, and amenable to the laws of Government.

Without mentioning the hostile role played by Trutch, Dufferin then explained how the lieutenant-governor of Manitoba was at that moment negotiating treaties with Indians in that province. He continued:

But in British Columbia, except [for the Douglas treaties] the Provincial Government has always assumed that the fee simple in, as well as the sovereignty over the land, resided in the Queen. Acting upon this principle, they have granted extensive grazing leases, and otherwise so dealt with various sections of the country as greatly to interfere with the prescriptive rights of the Queen's Indian subjects. As a consequence there has come to exist an unsatisfactory feeling amongst the Indian population . . . I consider that our Indian fellow subjects are entitled to exactly the same civil rights under the law as are possessed by the white population.[46]

Whether Dufferin's remarks were made of his own volition or at the instigation of federal officials is not clear. In any case, it is clear that the officials were no longer willing to press the issue. As Fisher observes, the federal government had by now "apparently given up any idea of extinguishing Indian title, partly because of the expense that would be involved and partly because Ottawa already had troubles enough with the 'spoilt child of Confederation'."[47]

On the reserve question, however, the federal pressure continued and the province did appear to bend by accepting a compromise that no specific acreage formula be used but that the needs and circumstances of each band be judged separately. Relative generosity occurred for a brief period in the late 1870s while G.M. Sproat was in charge of laying out reserves. Sproat, a self-taught ethnographer who had lived among the Nuu'chah'nulth,[48] enlarged some of the reserves reduced by Trutch, including the Kamloops reserve, which he expanded to fifty square miles.

John A. Macdonald returned to power in 1878 and subsequently asked Trutch (now a private citizen) for advice on a new reserve commissioner to replace Sproat. Trutch suggested his own brother-in-law, Peter O'Reilly, who had first worked with him before 1871 in reducing interior reserves.[49] O'Reilly took office in 1880. He began by reducing many of the reserves laid out by Sproat, and until his retirement eighteen years later, he allocated new reserves in the same spirit that he and Trutch had followed earlier. Almost everywhere his allocations left Indian dissatisfaction in their wake.[50] The Macdonald government, unlike its Liberal predecessor, was generally unsympathetic to Indian complaints. Nonetheless, wishing to take no chances, Trutch suggested, and Macdonald agreed, that all new reserves would require provincial approval.[51] The province, however, had no complaint with O'Reilly's reserves. Ultimately, then, despite the formal federal power over Indians and lands reserved for Indians, and thanks again to Trutch, the province retained control over the number, location, and acreage of Indian reserves.

The dominion government did use its authority to assume control over the Indians themselves and to do so entered into a partnership with the Christian churches. Christian missions, indeed, were now well established in most parts of the province. The earliest missionaries to reach the province had been Roman Catholics, brought by the fur-trading companies into the interior or to the south coast. Protestants— mainly Anglican and Methodist at first, later Presbyterian, Salvation Army, and, after 1925, United Church—concentrated on the central and north coasts, where the Catholics had made little effort or, in some cases, had been rebuffed by the Indians. Local missionary efforts could be especially focused and effective because there was almost no Catholic-Protestant competition at the community level.

On the coast the missionaries and the federal Indian agents quickly came to regard the resistance of clan and house chiefs as the most serious and specific impediment in their efforts to convert and civilize the Indians. Initially, the authority of the chiefs was tackled directly. By 1880 the Indian Act allowed the federal cabinet to depose "life chiefs" and provided that in cases where the department had imposed an elected band council "the life chiefs shall not exercise the powers of chiefs unless elected . . . to the exercise of such powers."[52] However, Powell and the agents did not at this time consider any band sufficiently advanced to be entrusted with an elected council, and so there was no effective way to limit the actual influence of the traditional chiefs.

It was in good part through the potlatch that the coastal leaders continued their own authority and were able to resist the control of church and government. Thus it was to the potlatch that missionaries and agents turned their attention. In their eyes it became the epitome of anti-government pagan depravity. As a result of their pressure and recommendations, the Macdonald government had Parliament amend the Indian Act in 1884. "Every Indian or other person who engages in or assists in celebrating the Indian festival known as the 'Potlach' [sic] . . . is guilty of a misdemeanor, and shall be liable to imprisonment for a term of not more than six nor less than two months in any gaol or other place of confinement."[53] The institution crucial to coastal societies, and in particular to their economies and political systems, was thus outlawed. In later years the prohibition would be further amended to the point that any gathering of Indians, other than a Christian church ceremony, could be labelled a potlatch and those present arrested and jailed. This circumstance had direct effects upon the political strategy eventually settled upon by British Columbia Indians in pursuit of their land claims. In any event, the close partnership of church and state in the suppression of Indian culture could have no better evidence than the use of prisons to curb the potlatch.

By the late 1880s there was unanimity among provincial politicians concerning the Indian question. Regardless of their faction or federal party loyalties, they believed the white myth that Indians had been primitive peoples without land ownership, and they accepted the white doctrine that extension of British sovereignty had transformed an empty land into unencumbered crown land. In the provincial view, the surviving Indians were mere remnants of an irrelevant past with neither the right nor the means to influence their own unhappy future.

CHAPTER FIVE

Demands for Title, Treaties, and Self-Government, 1887–99

The advance of white miners, farmers, fishermen, and loggers into each new area of British Columbia created much dissatisfaction among the Indians affected. Land was consistently the issue. "Indians everywhere were trying to convince the settlers that they had no business being there because the land belonged to them."[1] Letters and petitions to governments were commonplace both before and after union with Canada, and confrontations, demonstrations, and protest meetings occurred as settlement proceeded.[2] It was in the late 1880s that a new level of political awareness and organization began to emerge and with it a very specific set of Indian political demands for recognition of aboriginal title, for treaties, and for self-government. The demands would remain consistent, and unfulfilled, for the next century, and they would be the foundation of almost all future Indian political activity in the province. There was only one exception. At the turn of the century some Indians did gain a treaty, but this development occurred quite outside the main streams of both Indian and white politics and had no immediate effects upon either.

In the early decades the Coast Salish chiefs along the Lower Fraser were the most pressing in their demands. In 1872 they and hundreds of their people rallied outside the provincial land registry office in New Westminster. The crowd, composed exclusively of men and boys, posed rather cheerfully for a photograph.[3] Two years later, at the height of federal Liberal pressure on the provincial government concerning reserve size, the same chiefs organized a large protest assembly. It drew representatives from Coast Salish communities along the Fraser and the mainland coast and from the major Lillooet communities of the interior. Fifty-six chiefs approved a petition to Indian Commissioner Israel Powell asking for implementation of the federal proposal that reserves contain eighty acres for each family. "For many years we have been complaining of the land left us as being too small. We have laid our complaints before Government officials nearest to us; they sent us to some others; so we had no redress up to the present; and we have felt like men trampled on, and are commencing to believe that the aim of the white men is to exterminate us as soon as they can, although we have always been quiet, obedient, kind, and friendly to the whites."[4] Peter Ayessik and several other chiefs brought the petition as far as New Westminster, intending to present it directly to Commissioner Powell, but there they acquiesced to the suggestion, apparently from Powell, that they mail it instead. Their covering note stated that Powell could reach them "through Rev. Father Durieu, at New Westminster."[5] Powell does not seem to have responded.

Two rather different political developments occurred in the southern interior during the later 1870s, both causing considerable white anxiety.[6] In each case Whites blamed G.M. Sproat, the reserve commissioner, for allowing the events to proceed and even accused him of promoting Indian protests. The first development was the emergence of what was commonly referred to by Whites as an "Indian confederacy" in the southern Interior. In Sproat's words it was "the concerted action of the Okanagan and Shuswap Indians . . . to enforce what they considered to be their land rights." While believing that "confederacy" was "a large phrase that fills the ears of the ignorant and timid," Sproat did consider that "an outbreak of these Indians was . . . imminent." Under his guidance large reserves were allocated in the region and he claimed credit for averting any Indian action.[7] Among the leaders in the Indian activities had been Chillihitza, the pre-eminent Okanagan chief.[8]

The other development culminated in a large assembly at Lytton in 1879. Sproat described it as a meeting of "the Nekla-kap-a-muk Indians . . . summoned by themselves according to their rules."[9] The assembly took place "in a wooden building, erected expressly for the purpose, 240 feet long and proportionately wide."[10] Such buildings were unknown in that part of the province, but they would have been familiar to Sproat from his earlier life among the Nuu'chah'nulth of the west coast. Sproat's detailed account of the meeting strongly suggests that he sought to dominate the meeting and to introduce a governing body that would facilitate control of the Nlaka'pamux tribal group by the Department of Indian Affairs. According to Sproat, a new political structure, consisting of a head chief and thirteen councillors, was established by an assembly resolution which stated that "the Head Chief shall be elected . . . in such manner as the Queen may direct, and the Head Chief shall do what the Queen directs." Sproat intended, in fact, that the head chief would "be practically a sub agent."[11] In any case, the

Indians do not seem to have taken Sproat's efforts too seriously, for nothing seems to have come of them.

The arrival of white farmers, fishermen, and loggers in the Nass and Skeena valleys produced discontent among both Nisga'a and Tsimshian. Peter O'Reilly and the small reserves he allocated were a particular source of sustained complaint. In 1881 Chief Mountain led a Nisga'a protest delegation to Victoria. In 1885 three Tsimshian chiefs, John Tait, Edward Mathers, and Herbert Wallace, accompanied by the Anglican missionary William Duncan, became the first British Columbia Indian delegation to travel to Ottawa; their purpose was, in Wallace's words, "to tell them our troubles about our land."[12] The delegation met with Prime Minister Macdonald and received reassuring promises.

The north coast Indians were concerned about the fundamental issue of land title. Both the Nisga'a delegation to Victoria and the Tsimshian delegation to Ottawa raised the question. Subsequently the upriver Nisga'a sent a provincial survey crew back down the Nass, their instruments unopened. The Nisga'a had been refusing for several years to allow an Indian agent to be stationed in their territory. By 1886 Duncan and most of the people of Metlakatla, one of the two main coast Tsimshian communities, were making well-publicized plans to move across Chatham Sound to Alaska, where American authorities had promised a more generous land policy.[13]

During 1886 the Nisga'a chiefs were holding meetings in their communities to discuss the land question, some of which were attended by William S. Green, the Methodist missionary stationed in their area. The only Nisga'a village not to hold such meetings was Kincolith, the small breakaway village established at the mouth of the Nass by Anglican converts in 1864. Tsimshian chiefs at Port Simpson (the headquarters of the Methodist missionary Thomas Crosby) were holding similar meetings. By late 1886 the Nisga'a and Port Simpson chiefs had met and decided to seek a meeting with provincial and federal authorities.[14]

Provincial authorities and the white public, ill informed about the remote northwest coast, were becoming increasingly fearful of an Indian uprising. In these circumstances Premier William Smithe[15] and his government, presumably in response to a letter from Green or Crosby, agreed to an unprecedented joint meeting of senior federal and provincial officials with the north coast leaders.

The earlier actions of the Coast Salish, of the Shuswap and the Okanagan, and of the Nlaka'pamux had demonstrated that tribal groups were a natural unit for political discussion and that neighbouring groups with related language and culture could co-operate politically. They had also shown that Indian groups were willing to accept the aid and advice of missionaries—in part, presumably, because few Indian leaders as yet spoke English, fewer still could write it, and none knew the inner workings of government. These same features were evident on the north coast in 1886 and when Nisga'a and Tsimshian chiefs came down to Victoria in January 1887.

There is a world of difference between mailing off a petition, however many chiefs have signed it, and proceeding as a delegation of chiefs to meet directly with the highest government officials. It was evident before they even departed for Victoria that the north coast chiefs had no intention of merely having a perfunctory meeting. They had requested that verbatim transcripts be made of the meeting and that printed copies be sent to the Indians afterwards. Regarding themselves not as independent actors, but as delegates, the chiefs wanted their peoples to be able to see for themselves what had transpired in Victoria. The transcript request showed also that the chiefs were expecting a dialogue with government officials. They were not going to wait some distance away for a response to a petition; indeed, they were not bringing any petition. They wanted to explain their principles and demands directly to government policy-makers, and they hoped for a reasoned response. Moreover, their major express demand, that a public enquiry be held on the land issue, showed that the Indians assumed that the process of public discussion by Whites and Indians could contribute to a resolution of the land question.

As for the governments, the Victoria meeting also provided a new departure, at least of sorts. Premier Smithe, doubtless eager to be seen as protecting white interests by skilfully defusing a dangerous situation, acted as a courteous host, even going so far as to receive the delegation in the parlour of his own home. However, he and other provincial officials did draw the line at Methodist missionaries, whom the Indians wished to be present to act as interpreters. Firmly of the view that Methodists were causing much of the north coast unrest, the provincial officials insisted that the Indians come alone. (Possibly Smithe chose his home as the meeting place so he could exclude the missionaries; he could not as easily have done so had the meeting taken place in a government office.) Perhaps Smithe and his colleagues expected that the Indians would be incapable on their own of presenting a coherent defence of Indian land title and perhaps they thought as well that the chiefs could be more easily cowed without the missionaries.

The chiefs who took the greatest part in the meeting were the Tsimshian Richard Wilson and the Nisga'as Arthur Gurney, John Wesley, and Charles Barton.[16] Those present for the province included Smithe, Peter O'Reilly, and Attorney-General Alex Davie. Indian Commissioner Powell represented the Dominion. Barton acted as interpreter. The chiefs expressed bitterness at being depicted in white newspapers as violent and unpredictable; they emphasized their Christianity and their reliance on peaceful discussion. They responded clearly and cogently to questions and comments, although in several instances they refused to answer or to give details, explaining that the matters in question had not been discussed in the Indian meetings prior to their coming.[17]

In addition to making the immediate demand for an enquiry, the chiefs dwelt upon the principles of aboriginal title and Indian self-government, and they urged the governments to get on with treaties through which the Indians would retain sufficient land and resources for self-sufficiency. Title, treaties, and self-government were thus the paramount Indian concerns raised. Smithe and the other provincial officials refused to take the concerns seriously. They resolutely persisted in assuming that the chiefs' only real concern was reserve acreage. Powell, in contrast, seemed much more attuned to the Indians; at several points he elaborated upon Indian statements for the benefit of the provincial officials. Powell spoke to the chiefs as equals; Smithe, O'Reilly, and Davie were curt and condescending.

"Self-government" was not a phrase used in Barton's interpretation, nor did the chiefs delineate the concept as clearly as they did the concepts of title and treaty. They seemed to assume that they would continue to control their own affairs on lands they retained under the treaties. Nevertheless, retaining self-government was clearly a primary concern, as is shown by their insistence that Indian agents be kept out of their communities, but it was one that the Indians did not see as incompatible with British sovereignty. Wilson, the first chief to speak, immediately raised the issue of self-government. "What we want . . . is, to be free as well as the whites. You know if they catch a little bird and they put it in a cage . . . it will be in bondage; and that is the way it is with us, and it is what we have come to tell you. Can we be free under the law of Queen Victoria on the top of our land?"[18]

The provincial officials still assumed that reserve acreage was the Indians' main concern. As O'Reilly proceeded to defend the size of his reserves, Barton interrupted: "You see, Mr. O'Reilly, that is not what we came for, to argue about this land; but to tell you that we want to be free on top of this land . . . We don't refuse the law at all; we want it; and we want to be free under the British law—to be like the whites."[19]

As for land, the demand was clear:

Wesley: We want you to cut out a bigger reserve for us, and what we want after
        that is a treaty.
Smithe: What do you mean by a treaty?
Wesley: I have mentioned after a certain amount of land is cut out for the

Indians, outside of that we want such a law as the law of England and
the Dominion Government which made a treaty with the Indians.[20]

Smithe wanted to know how the Indians knew of treaties. Wesley
answered that "there are a good many Indians that can read and write,
and they are the ones who say this themselves."[21] Smithe replied by
asserting that no law required a treaty.

Powell: I think the grievance they have is this: that they want a treaty.
Davie: That is what they want.
Smithe: They are simply misguided.[22]

Davie now sought to rebut the claim to Indian title and the need for a
treaty. In doing so he ignored the province's own limited acreage policy
and proved his ignorance of the Douglas treaties: "Our duty is to protect
you, and give you all the land you can make use of. Surely you cannot
ask for more. The Indians around here might as well come and say that
the City of Victoria belongs to them . . . It would be perfect nonsense."[23]
Davie's statement was itself perfect nonsense. The land occupied by
Victoria had been acknowledged as belonging to Indians and bought
from them, through one of the Douglas treaties, before white settlement
had been permitted. The Victoria case thus confirmed the principles
advanced by the north coast chiefs. Apparently Davie was a willing
victim of Joseph Trutch's revision of colonial history.[24]

It was the premier's comments, however, which epitomized the white
founding myth and white title doctrine now so firmly entrenched in the
views of provincial officials. Smithe told the Indians: "When the whites
first came among you, you were little better than the wild beasts of the
field."[25]

He dismissed the Indians' views of land ownership.

The land all belongs to the Queen . . . A reserve is given to each tribe, and they
are not required to pay for it. It is the Queen's land just the same, but the Queen
gives it to her Indian children because they do not know so well how to make
their own living the same as a white man, and special indulgence is extended to
them, and special care shown. Thus, instead of being treated as a white man,
the Indian is treated better. But it is the hope of everybody that in a little while
the Indians will be so far advanced as to be the same as a white man in every
respect. Do you understand what I say?[26]

Undeterred by the lecture, Barton promptly responded, "I understand.
As I said before, we have come for nothing but to see about the land
which we know is ours."[27]

In the end, both governments did agree to the demand for a public enquiry, and a two-member, joint federal-provincial commission was established. Clement Cornwall, who had ranching interests near Ashcroft, was appointed by the Dominion, while Joseph Planta was appointed by the province. Both appointees were Anglicans.[28] Davie's instructions to Planta demonstrate, however, that the province still had no intention of taking Indian concerns seriously. The commission was to go north to hear the Indians' "views, wishes, and complaints, if any," but, Davie emphasized,

You will please be careful—while assuring the Indians that all they say will be reported to the proper authorities—not to give undertakings or make promises, and in particular you will be careful to discountenance, should it arise, any claim of Indian title to Provincial lands. I need not point out that the Provincial Government are bound to make, at the request of the Dominion, suitable reserves for the Indians, and it will be advisable, should the question of title to land arise, to constantly point this out.[29]

The provincial authorities thus had no intention of considering the question of title or the closely related question of treaties, even though these were the reasons for the Indians' request for the enquiry in the first place. Claims to title were to be deflected to the question of reserves, and the fiction was to be maintained that the province's reserve policy was fair and reasonable.

The commissioners proceeded to the north coast on a government steamer in mid-October 1887. The timing was good for the province since the approach of winter storms would allow only a brief period for travel in the region. In fact, autumn gales did interfere with Indian attendance at hearings and gave the commissioners an excuse for quick meetings and rapid departures. Hearings were held over five consecutive days: two at Kincolith, two at Nass Harbour, and one at Port Simpson. Witnesses spoke in their native languages. For the most part, in accord with provincial instructions, Indians rather than missionaries served as interpreters.

The Indian witnesses were well informed about the Victoria meeting. The transcripts had been received several months previously, and meetings had been held in which translations had been made and further discussions had occurred. It was as these meetings were taking place that the Tsimshian of Metlakatla had made their move to Alaska. This fact was much on the minds of witnesses in the October hearings; they regarded the Metlakatlans as refugees from persecution.[30] In the hearings the recurring themes were again title, treaties, and self-government. There were also complaints about O'Reilly's reserves and about

Indian agents. Yet, all major Indian spokesmen made clear their willingness to share land and resources with Whites and to accept white governmental authority. No threats were made. No hostility was expressed. Despair was evident, but should governments not be responsive to the Indian concerns, the only remedy mentioned was following the Metlakatlans to Alaska. One of the most comprehensive statements was given at Nass Harbour by the Nisga'a chief Charles Russ:

What we want is to speak about our property—our land. We want to have for ourselves . . . as much land as we need to use, and we want the words and hands of the chiefs on both sides, Indian and Government, to make a promise on paper—a strong promise—that will be not only for us, but for our children and forever. In the first place we did not like the name "reserve," but now it is all right—we want it. We don't want very much land for ourselves and the different villages; but if we have the reserves, there is one thing we want with them, and that is a treaty. We have no word in our language for "reserve." We have the word "land," "our land," "our property." Your name for our land is "reserve," but every mountain, every stream, and all we see, we call our forefathers' land and streams. It is just lately that the white people are changing the name. Now it is called the Indian reserve, instead of the Naas people's land. If you ask the Hydahs, Alaskas, Stickeens, Bella Bellas, and Fort Ruperts, they will tell you that all this country is the Naas people's land, and we don't know when any change was made, or when it was taken from us. But now it is called "reserve" we want the word "treaty" with it. The change that was made from "our land" to "reserve" was made by the white people, and "treaty" will have to come from them too . . . We don't ask much for ourselves . . . only a little bit compared with what is outside of it. All these mountains and lands outside of what we ask for are for you; we are not asking for it. Go up the mountains and you will see other mountains with nice valleys in between; all that is for you—the white people. But we want a solemn promise—a treaty. In the past we were a numerous people, and we used all the land; but we are not so many as we were, and we don't want it all now. We are different from the whites. We don't all live in one place, but have to scatter all over the country to make a living. We want sufficient land for our numbers. We want food, salmon, berries, animals for food and furs, timber for houses, canoes and boxes, bark for mats. Now these things are got in different places, and we want land where we can get them . . . We did not ask the Government to come and touch our land. They came; and when they commenced, then we began to see what we want and what we don't want. Our people used to be numerous, but they are killed out by bad things. Liquor and other things killed them out. Now the good has come we are increasing again, and we think our people will become very numerous, and if there is no [treaty] with them, the more numerous they become the greater the trouble will be. If we make a mistake now, we are making it not only for ourselves, but for our children, who will suffer.[31]

Commissioner Planta now reminded Russ of "the words of wisdom" spoken by Premier Smithe in Victoria to explain that the Queen owned all the land. These words, said Planta, should be translated into the Nisga'a language, "so that you might learn them by heart." The commissioner went on to emphasize the existence of the British North America Act, to quote from the terms of union, and to explain that both documents gave authority over Indians and reserves to the Canadian Parliament. Commissioner Cornwall added: "It is well for you to understand that there is no probability of your views as to the land being entertained."[32] Russ responded:

The words you have read to us we never heard before in our lives. When they made the laws that you speak about they had never been to see us; they did not know what we used or what we wanted. I would like to ask, sirs, if there was one chief of the Naas present when that law was made, and whether they asked him to speak for the Naas people? Or did they write a letter asking them about it? Why they never even sent a letter to tell us it was done. You see these chiefs present laugh. We cannot believe the words we have heard, that the land was not acknowledged to be ours. We took the Queen's flag and laws to honour them. We never thought when we did that she was taking the land away from us.[33]

Planta replied that the provincial government would always perform its duty by "setting apart" land "sufficient for all the purposes of the Indians." Russ's response was apparently heated. "Set it apart; how did the Queen get the land from our forefathers to set it apart for us? It is ours to give to the Queen, and we don't understand how she could have it to give to us." Immediately, in the words of the recording secretary, "an old blind Indian named Neis Puck jumps up and demands a hearing." Puck exclaimed: "I am the oldest man here and can't sit still any longer and hear that it is not our fathers' land. Who is the chief that gave this land to the Queen? Give us his name, we have never heard of it." The commissioners remained silent. Russ then suggested that the Nisga'a might, like the Metlakatlans, flee to Alaska: "We will do just the same; we will leave the country too. We love the land; we love the places where our fathers' graves are and where our children are buried; but we will leave them and go to a new country sooner than stay where it is said 'the lands do not belong to us.' We . . . don't want you to persecute us."[34]

Like Russ, most of the other Nisga'a chiefs sought to explain their feelings about the land and to point out their responsibility for it. Am-Clammon was one of these.

We are not common ignorant people, we know something. We know what good we get from the land. We have such strong hearts watching this river . . . The land belonged to our forefathers. It is like a long purse full of money, it never fails, and that is why we want to keep it. It belongs to us now, so we don't want any strangers to get our food away from us, our own land; it has never been done before, any strangers claiming our land . . . We take great care of the whole of the river and we don't want any one to come on it. It has often caused fighting years ago between the Tsimpseans and Naas people as to who should own the river. Now, since the word of God has been preached among us there has been peace.[35]

Troubled by the commissioners' refusal to take their concerns seriously, eleven upriver Nisga'a chiefs presented a written statement at the close of the Nass Harbour hearings.

What Mr. Commissioner Planta said . . . to the effect that we were not the owners of the land, but that the Queen owned it—did not satisfy us . . . we could not receive it into our hearts, and we wish to tell you that when we heard it again tonight we did not change our minds. The land was given to our fore-fathers by the great God above, who made both white man and the Indian, and our forefathers handed it down and we have not given it to anyone. It is still ours, and will be ours till we sign a strong paper to give part of it to the Queen.[36]

At Port Simpson the commissioners heard from the leaders of that community and from a few of the one hundred or so Metlakatlans who had not gone to Alaska. The Port Simpson leaders expressed the same major concerns as had the Nisga'a chiefs, but they gave greater attention to local government. They viewed municipal style government as desirable and had, under Thomas Crosby's guidance, already formed an unofficial local council; federal officials, however, had refused to deal with it. Richard Wilson was one of the principal witnesses.

They made no treaty with us about our land . . . We feel that we are not treated well by the Government taking our land, and selling it like that without consulting us; we feel very sad about it. We don't like [the condition of] our village. Look at the bridge and roads going to ruin; we are afraid that we shall always be oppressed like that; not only that, they have taken hold of the hands of the people and keep them down saying, "the Council have no authority." These Councillors were the strength of the village; they can't do anything now . . . We want for our foundation the law of British Columbia and the Dominion; let that law settle things for us properly, and not take away the law we had for ourselves . . . We don't want to keep this land and be strangers to the white people, so we wish . . . the same laws as the white people . . . We don't want the Indian

Act, or the Indian Agent ... We want the English law for our foundation, not that we wish to go against the Queen or her Governments; we are under that flag and we wish to have their laws.[37]

Just as doubtful as the Nisga'a had been that Planta and Cornwall were taking Indian concerns seriously, the Tsimshian chiefs too prepared a statement: "What we want is a municipal law, backed by legal authority, without the bondage of being under a bad Indian Agent, who would take us backwards rather than forwards. We have only one way left, after our patient waiting and protesting against the [land] surveys and the way our protests have been treated, and that is to follow our brethren into Alaska."[38]

During the five days of hearings several witnesses stated that their new Christian God was the source of their aboriginal title. One Tsimshian witness told the commissioners:

There is one thing the Tsimpseans and their chiefs wish—that it be acknowledged the land is ours, that God has put us on the land. You can see . . . you got your own land where God put you [i.e., in Europe] and this land is the same to us. We wish the Queen's laws so we may be free. In the presence of God it is a solemn thing, and the judgement of God is a solemn thing. The voice of God first came to you, and God will blame you if you don't settle things satisfactorily; you will be responsible to God. We want to have the Queen's law, so that we can live under her flag.[39]

In this view, Indians and Whites were equal before God and so should be equal under queens and governments. Whites were free under the Queen's laws, and those laws elsewhere in Canada had resulted in treaties for the Indians. The Indians wanted the same freedom and the same treaties. Indian agents and the Indian Act were seen for what they were: instruments for the suppression of Indians by Whites.

The enquiry report was harshly unsympathetic to the concerns raised by the Indian witnesses. While the commissioners did endorse the need for larger reserves, they dismissed the demands for recognition of title, for treaties, and for local self-government. For the first time a federal official, Cornwall, explicitly rejected the principle of Indian title. As their central theme the commissioners raised the ominous spectre of Indian disloyalty. They claimed that while the Indians of Kincolith and those remaining in Metlakatla "in all matters express themselves as loyal to the Federal and Provincial Governments," the other Indians had not concealed "their feelings of opposition to the views of the Government."[40] Opposition to policies was thus equated with opposi-

tion to government in general, while the numerous Indian assertions of
willingness to accept the Queen's law and flag were ignored.

The Anglican commissioners had two explanations for the unacceptable stance of the Indians. First, they noted "the curious coincidence"
of the disloyalty they perceived and the Methodist "missionary influence." They did not point out that the one Anglican Nisga'a village,
Kincolith, contained only a small fraction of the Nisga'a population;[41]
nor did they dwell on the fact that the Metlakatlans who had departed
because of the land issue had been Anglicans.[42] Second, the commissioners identified in the Indian character both a truculence and a primitive simplemindedness.

If an Indian conceives he has been illtreated, if he thinks he has a right which is
unrecognized, or which he is restrained from exercising, he becomes morose,
unyielding on the subject, as the Scotch say, a "dour" feeling with reference to
the matter takes possession of him, and no amount of reasoning with him will
enable to disabuse his mind of his possibly illconceived convictions.[43]

The Indians having acquired a little mental activity and a very partial knowledge of some of the things about which they are agitating, probably imagine
that they know a great deal and are thoroughly able to say what is good for
themselves. So in a way that would not call for particular attention were it not
seriously intended, they hold themselves as above and beyond the existing laws
which affect them as Indians.[44]

The commissioners made no attempt to deal with the substance of the
Indian claim to title or to provide any reasoned explanation why the
treaty policy followed in the rest of Canada should not apply in British
Columbia. The view that Indians were disloyal, stubborn, and mentally
inferior to Whites provided its own explanation and suggested its own
remedy. The remedy was to impose more control over Indians by government officials whose loyalty, unlike that of the Methodist missionaries, could be relied upon.

In past years the Indians of the North-West Coast have been left too much alone,
almost isolated from proper government regulation and control . . . [Their] ideas
ought to be firmly but kindly dealt with and changed. It can only be done by the
presence among the Indians of capable and experienced Government officials,
agents and magistrates. To leave them longer to pursue their course unaided,
uninstructed, as to the objects and purport of the law, and uncontrolled by the civil
power, would be fatal to any probability of future peace.[45]

The commissioners' recommendations thus confirmed the policies
and intentions that both governments had been pursuing. Indian land

claims should be ignored. Control over Indians should be exercised on the north coast, as elsewhere, by federal Indian agents operating under the Indian Act and by provincial police and magistrates. Within a few years the Northwest Coast Agency was established.

During the decade following the north coast enquiry the federal government evinced no concern over Indian title or the complete absence of treaties on the mainland of British Columbia. Then came the Yukon gold rush. Tens of thousands of Whites were on their way to the territory, the majority by sea through the Alaskan ports, but a good many by railway to Edmonton and then overland through northeastern British Columbia. Beaver, Slave, and Sekani Indians suddenly found themselves overrun. In 1898, just as the short summer travel season was well underway, several hundred Beaver Indians assembled at Fort St. John, blocked the flow of gold-seekers, and demanded a treaty that would delineate their lands and provide government protection against white encroachment.

At this time there was apparently no provincial presence in the area and certainly no provincial law enforcement officials. Federal Northwest Mounted Police were soon on the scene, however, and they feared violence, perhaps more from the anxious fortune seekers than from the Indians. The federal minister of the interior, Clifford Sifton, authorized the police to promise a treaty. Federal officials were already preparing for one, the eighth in the westward series of numbered treaties, with Indians in the neighbouring Athabasca district, which would in a few years become the northern half of the new province of Alberta. In December 1898 the federal cabinet approved an order-in-council authorizing the extension of Treaty 8 into British Columbia. The text of the order included discussion of Sifton's motives and concerns.

As the Indians to the west of the Mountains are quite distinct from those whose habitat is on the eastern side thereof, no difficulty ever arose in consequence of the different methods of dealing with the Indians on either side of the Mountains [i.e., treaties on the eastern side but not on the western]. But there can be no doubt that had the division line between the Indians been artificial instead of natural, such difference in treatment would have been fraught with danger and have been the fruitful source of much trouble to both the Dominion and the Provincial Governments.

The Minister submits that it will neither be politic nor practicable to exclude from the treaty Indians whose habitat is in the territory lying between the height of land and the eastern boundary of British Columbia, as they know nothing of the artificial boundary [i.e., the eastern border of BC], and, being allied to the Indians of Athabasca, will look for the same treatment as is given to the Indians whose habitat is in that district.[46]

The cabinet's motives were purely expedient. Had the Indians not threatened trouble, no treaty would have been initiated. Well aware that the province believed that it had already gained title to the land in question and was hostile to any notion of treaties, Sifton was not about to suggest asking it to share in providing treaty benefits. "Although the rule has been laid down by the Judicial Committee of the Privy Council that the Province benefitting by a surrender of Indian title should bear the burdens incident to that surrender . . . the Minister after careful consideration does not think it desirable that any demand should be made upon the Province . . . for any money payment in connection with the proposed treaty."[47] Sifton recommended that a copy of the order-in-council be sent to the province and that it be asked to confirm its willingness to relinquish land for reserves under the treaty. The double standard the federal government was forced to adopt in accommodating itself to the province's position thus became evident, for the cabinet was acting as though both the province and the Indians owned the land.

Whether the province replied is not clear, but it definitely expressed neither willingness to set aside reserves nor gratitude for the federal offer to pay all the treaty benefits. Federal officials now hit upon an ingenious way around the province's failure to provide land for the reserves. The federal government would allocate reserves out of the 5,500-square mile "Peace River Block," which the province had previously turned over to federal ownership for use in encouraging railway construction and agricultural development.[48] The province had not been thinking of Indian interests, but now it had no control over the land's disposition. In laying out the reserves, the federal officials followed the acreage formula used in the rest of Treaty 8—640 acres for each family of five.

The process of getting in touch with all the Indian communities was somewhat random. It was brought to an end in 1915. By that time the Slave and most, but not all, of the Sekani and Beaver communities had met with the federal negotiators and adhered to the treaty.[49] The Kaska-Dena communities were not contacted by the negotiators, nor were the Sekani in the McLeod Lake area.[50] Treaty maps should thus have shown a patchwork of surrendered lands. Instead, maps prepared by the federal government came to include the whole portion of British Columbia east of the Rockies, an area of some one hundred thousand square miles (about 27 per cent of the province's area).

British Columbia's failure to object to the treaty was quite inconsistent with its past (and future) assertion that aboriginal title had never existed. To be consistent, the province would have had to object to the acknowledgement of Indian title or, at the very least, to have made clear its view that the federal government was taking part in a fraudulent transaction by paying the Indians for something that did not exist. However, once they were assured that the province would not have to pay money or provide land for reserves, the provincial government leaders apparently felt no concern over any misguided desire of the federal government to act as though the Indians owned the land in a remote portion of the province having few white settlers. The provincial response, or lack of it, was, in fact, fully in accord with the view that claims to Indian title were so ill founded, irrelevant, and inconsequential that it made no difference whether they were ignored or denied.

Treaty 8 remains a fully valid treaty, now guaranteed along with all other Indian treaties by the Canadian Constitution. The treaty stands as irrefutable evidence that aboriginal title was recognized in a good portion of British Columbia and that the principles and procedures set out in the Proclamation of 1763 could be applied to Indians and Indian lands in the province.

CHAPTER SIX

The Politics of Survival

As the nineteenth century came to a close, "the Indians of British Columbia" had no common culture, no common language, and no common political tradition. At that time it must have seemed inconceivable to the Whites that the Indians, who appeared to be a dying race, would mount a prolonged political response to the denial of their land claims. Yet they did. This chapter pauses in the historical narrative to examine the general nature of the Indian response and the circumstances affecting it and thus provides an introduction to Indian political development in the present century.

When Indians from different tribal backgrounds come to have a common awareness and to seek to act in concert, the result is said to be "pan-Indianism."[1] The notion of a new, broader Indian identity is essential to the concept of pan-Indianism. The new identity goes beyond traditional attachments, sometimes replacing them completely, sometimes supplementing and building upon them. When traditional identities have been weakened, pan-Indianism appeals to uprooted or displaced individuals by giving them new identity and new hope. Often in these circumstances the goals of pan-Indianism are religious or spiritual, as in the numerous revitalization movements among Indians and other aboriginal peoples;[2] but the goals may also be political, seeking a better life for individuals.

When traditional loyalties and identities remain vigorous, pan-Indianism, if it arises at all, must appeal to those with authority and influence within traditional groupings. Such persons will likely be suspicious of notions of a broader identity, and unwilling to participate in joint action unless community or tribal group interests will likely benefit. In these cases pan-Indianism is in good part the outgrowth of tradition, and its goals will be to safeguard traditional interests; they will thus be largely political, if not entirely so. Successful pan-Indian activity of this sort will show itself not in mass movements but rather in the form of associations or bodies representative of traditional entities, and the new identity will be as much the result as the cause of the political co-operation.

The early United States and British Columbia experiences illustrate the two differing types of pan-Indianism. The United States experience is especially relevant because Canadian officials were aware of it and intended their own policies to lead to the same results in Canada. By the 1890s there were perhaps a few thousand United States Indians who had spent their formative years away from their home reservations as boarding pupils in government residential schools or as foster children in the homes of missionaries, government officials, or anthropologists. As a result of their off-reservation upbringing and the values inculcated in them, they had no strong attachment to their tribes of origin;[3] they identified with Indians in general throughout the United States. They were pan-Indians.[4]

The pan-Indians had a lifestyle and an outlook that made them very different from reservation Indians. A small but significant number of them had graduated from university; a notable few had become academic anthropologists themselves. Many were married to Whites or to members of other tribes; most were practising Christians; most were city dwellers; most had "occupations typical of white society." "Their feelings about the reservation mingled dislike of its constraints with nostalgia for the vanished childhood home." They "extolled the traditional values of Indian closeness to nature but envisioned the Indian future in terms of the professions, business, and modern farming"; they "frequently cited the immigrant experience as a desirable model for the Indian."[5]

The pan-Indians also had the skills, knowledge, and desire to become accepted, or at least to be perceived, as Indian spokesmen. It was they who formed and led the first modern regional and national Indian organizations in the United States. Working with active white supporters, among whom anthropologists and clergy were prominent, these organizations acted as pressure groups seeking reform both of government Indian policy and of Indian reservation life, in both cases with the aim of furthering Indian assimilation.[6] The leaders of the organizations thus acted as though they were immigrants, even to the point of forming ethnic associations to promote assimilation.[7]

The pattern of politics which emerged among British Columbia Indians was the opposite of the early assimilationist pan-Indianism of the United States.[8] British Columbia Indian leaders dedicated themselves to ensuring a distinct and continuing Indian existence. Theirs was the politics of survival. Three factors would seem to explain why they chose this path (and also why the individualistic pan-Indianism of the United States could not develop). First, relocating and intermixing tribal groups was the exception rather than the rule. The reserve policies pursued by James Douglas and his successors allowed members of tribal groups to remain resident in their traditional territories. Later the residential schooling system did serve to relocate and intermix Indian children, but even it was too little and too late to be able to erase community and tribal identities.

Second, there was a much greater continuity of Indian ideals and Indian leadership. Timing was one factor. The first pan-Indian leaders who did appear were in direct touch with tribal traditions as practised before white control over Indian communities was put in place. Even the new wave of Indian leaders emerging in the 1960s and 1970s was only a few generations removed. The special political tradition of the coastal peoples was a further factor in leadership continuity. More developed before contact than political traditions in the interior of the province (or in most parts of the United States), the coastal traditions had an easier time surviving contact. Indeed, they proved able to evolve and adapt within the new political regime even when that regime outlawed Indian claims activity.

Third, there was less exposure of Indian children to white families and white ideals in British Columbia.[9] Adoption of Indian children by Whites seems to have been almost completely absent in the early period.[10] White anthropologists, mostly from the United States, were active in the province from the 1880s onward, but they were not numerous and they seem usually to have made summer expeditions rather than living with the Indians for extensive periods. (The apparent exceptions are G.M. Sproat and James Teit,[11] but they were not academics and they became ethnographers after coming to live in the province.)

From the beginning, however, there were increasing numbers of mixed-blood persons in British Columbia. Those born to registered Indian women who had not married-out, and those whose fathers had, had Indian status and were usually raised on reserves. The majority of mixed marriages were between white men and Indian women. In these cases the Indian Act provision that the women must lose their status and leave the reserve ensured that few of the children were raised as members of an Indian community. The further provision that these children would not have Indian status, and thus could not attend Indian schools, made it unlikely that they would as adults identify strongly with Indians on reserves and, as a result, take political action to seek their betterment. (Such legislative provisions were absent in the United States, where children remained legally Indian providing they retained at least one-quarter Indian blood.) Furthermore, because they were stigmatized by most Whites, mixed marriages tended to involve Whites at the lower end of the social scale or those in the more isolated parts of the province. Raised in these settings, the children were less likely than otherwise to have the desire or the means to be politically active. In any event, and in contrast to what occurred in the United States, mixed-blood persons did not undertake any common political action or form any organizations in the early decades.

The first modern Indian political action in British Columbia was that of the north coast chiefs in 1887. Their goals of attaining recognition of title, achieving treaties, and ensuring self-government proved to be the goals of all British Columbia Indians. Subsequently, in Indian political thinking the Royal Proclamation of 1763 became the critically important statement of political justice pertaining to those goals. Britain, the source of the proclamation and in the early period still having colonial authority over Canada, came to be seen as the only possible source of remedy to the injustice being perpetrated in British Columbia. The Royal Proclamation and the British monarch became and remained important political symbols. As Whites erased the principles of early British land policy from their collective memory, those principles came alive to the Indians. Although "British Justice" was, quite literally, a rallying cry as they undertook their political response,[12] the adoption of British legal principles was no mere copying of white values. Not having encountered the principles in practice, the Indians became aware of them only after they had clearly affirmed their own ideals and enunciated their political goals. The principles were accepted so fully only because they accorded so completely with Indian views and demands.

The nature of Indian society itself had much effect upon the Indian political response. The tribal groups and their component communities, and the lineages and clans among the coastal peoples, remained of fundamental importance. Their existence provided much of the purpose of Indian politics, but it also imposed many restraints upon those who would be pan-Indian leaders. Such persons would at times be tempted by their own pan-Indian ideals to assume that "the Indians of British Columbia" were a real people who would act as one. Such beliefs would always founder on the hard facts of local or tribal group identities.

The pan-Indianism that did occur in British Columbia was rooted in aboriginal realities. Successful political activity beyond the level of tribal groups would have to build upon communities and tribal groups. Indeed, whether communities or tribal groups or some combination were the appropriate constituent units of political organization was to be a matter of much trial and error, and much bitter controversy. Tribal groups were the fundamental units of political action in the beginning, and in the end they would regain pride of political place.

Underlying all post-contact Indian political activity has been a dark and tragic reality. Although most Indian communities did survive and retain much ancestral memory, "anomy" was everywhere.[13] It showed itself in emotional depression, suicide, interpersonal violence, family breakdown, child abuse, misuse of alcohol and other drugs, and a whole range of other actions, from petty theft to arson, that reveal feelings of anger, helplessness, and loss of personal confidence and self-respect. Within stable societies, anomy remains an affliction of individuals, and its socially harmful effects can be treated or confined. Within societies whose traditional beliefs and customs and leaders are incapable of controlling rapid change, especially change for the worse, it becomes an affliction of whole communities. Among British Columbia Indians its manifestations increased directly with the degree of white contact and control. Few political leaders could remain untouched by the weight of suffering within their own families and communities, and for a number of them, past and present, alcohol came to provide both burden and refuge. The land question cannot be divorced from the underlying reality. Just as anomy results in good part from deprivation of land and resources, denial of rights and dignity, and withholding of self-government, so it could be expected to diminish were Indian political demands to be addressed.

The emergence of comprehensive Indian political activity was greatly dependent upon the ability of Indians to travel and communicate. Political co-operation beyond that of neighbouring tribal groups was inhibited during the early decades by the absence of a common language and by difficulties of travel. It is no accident that sustained political activity emerged at the turn of the century when English was becoming the new Indian lingua franca and when regular steamship services had linked towns and regional centres up and down the coast. Subsequently travel and communications became even more convenient on the coast as Indians came to own or operate commercial fishing boats.

In the interior the main line of the Canadian Pacific Railway was completed in 1886, but not until after the turn of the century was there the full network of feeder lines from north and south. The first interior political organizing took place at this time, with the major meetings taking place at Spences Bridge, the most convenient railway junction point for the greatest number of Indian communities. In later decades Kamloops, the other important railway junction, was the site of historic meetings. However, many Indian communities were far from railways. It was the automobile that opened the interior villages to political organization. Only in the 1950s did a sufficient number of Indians own automobiles to allow them to travel readily, either by driving or by hitching rides with other Indians,[14] and it was at this time that the first grass-roots political organizing occurred in the interior. Thus, both on the coast and in the interior the ability to travel freely was an important catalyst in the development of Indian political organizations.

For individual Indians survival was a matter of economics rather than politics. In part because reserves were often inadequate to provide a livelihood, in part for other reasons, many Indians participated in the white economy. Such participation did not amount to assimilation for, as Rolf Knight observes, "the pervasive and durable feature of native Indian workers was their identification, first and foremost, as members of particular 'tribal' Indian communities."[15] Nor, in most parts of the province, did Indian economic participation have any direct and positive political consequences. The coastal fishing industry provided the major exception, becoming the only economic sector in the province in which Indians were well paid and able to maintain a substantial presence. The west/central and north coast areas were the only areas in which prominent Indians were economically better off than most local Whites and in which the leading Indians were regarded by local Whites as their equals in ability and initiative. These factors contributed to the continuing political self-confidence of the Indians in that part of the province.[16]

Besides its economic benefits, there were particular features of the fishing industry that made it a most important factor in shaping and supporting coastal Indian political activity. Clan chiefs and house leaders became middlemen, "because, other things being equal, such persons could be more influential in recruiting labour among their people," and, because English was essential in their dealings with management, it was usually younger rather than older chiefs who obtained the positions.[17] Typically, these men would hire members of their own clans and villages, who would travel in whole families to the fishing grounds and canneries for the fishing season, which coincided with the period they would traditionally have spent harvesting food away from the home village.

Until 1923 Indians were not allowed to operate engine-powered boats in the north coast commercial fishery. With the restrictions removed, the leading Indians purchased their own boats, often using their control of the labour supply in the competitive market to extract loans for the purpose from cannery owners. As Drucker observes, "it is no accident that many of the best boats along the coast belong to chiefs."[18] The commercial fishing boats brought added wealth and prestige to the chiefs as well as a more extensive mobility and wider networks of contacts up and down the coast. The boats also further enhanced the ability of the owners to provide jobs and security for family and clan members. In addition, with their all-Indian crews working apart from Whites, the boats served as important nodes for continued use and transmission of native languages and beliefs, including political ideals. The coastal commercial fishermen were an important force in the evolution of Indian political activity, especially during the period of political prohibition from 1927 to 1951.

The nature and pace of the Indian political response was greatly affected by the white society's perceptions and opinions and, most directly, by the activities of Indian agents and missionaries. From the 1890s to the 1960s Indians were of little concern to the white public. Until after the Second World War the white fears and anxieties that had formerly focused on Indians were fixed on Chinese, Japanese, and Indo-Asian minority groups. To the white public Indians were now "merely a pitiful obstacle to progress and development, doomed to eclipse by the movement of history." The province's first white historians cemented this outlook by writing of the Indians in terms of "disgust, superiority, paternalistic condescension."[19]

While Whites apparently took it for granted that Indians would prefer not to be Indians, few Whites other than officials and missionaries had much contact with them. White opinion leaders—politicians, journalists, businessmen, teachers—were poorly informed about the Indians' own outlook and concerns. Until the 1920s, however, the question of Indian reserves did remain an item of white public discussion, especially in the southern portions of the province, where farmers, ranchers, developers, and municipal politicians pressed, in the end successfully, to have reserves reduced or eliminated to free the land for white use. Still later white British Columbia politicians were at the forefront in Ottawa as the land claims were successively investigated, denied, and outlawed. For a while in the early years there were white "friends of the Indians" offering their support, but ultimately the Whites and provincial politicians simply divorced themselves from Indian concerns.

By 1900 the province had been divided into fifteen Indian agencies, and the Indian agents were in position to exert continual administrative supervision over Indian communities. With the average number of Indians in each agency only some sixteen hundred, the agents could usually maintain close supervision. As Stephanie Hudson has shown in her study of their annual reports, the agents' goals for Indians can be summed up in two words that appeared frequently in their reports: "civilization" and "advancement." The words were synonyms for "assimilation."[20] It was the coastal Indians whom the agents regarded as providing the greatest challenge, for it became apparent that their traditional beliefs, practices, and institutions required active dismantling if assimilation was to succeed. In contrast, the agents apparently more often assumed that traditional ways were less of an impediment among interior Indians and would fade away of their own accord.

While there were some agents who came to sympathize with Indian political goals, who looked the other way when potlatches were held, and who gave supportive advice to Indian leaders, most were fully committed to the official goals of government. In partnership with missionaries, they suppressed, in addition to the potlatch, such major traditional cultural practices as matrilineal inheritance, customary marriage ceremonies, and the use of Indian personal names. They pressured adults to accept enfranchisement, that is, to give up their formal Indian status and right to live on a reserve. The targets of such pressure were especially those who knew English and who had accepted off-reserve employment; these were the very individuals with the knowledge and skills to be effective local political leaders.

The agents made all the day-to-day decisions regarding local matters on the reserves; even in later decades, when many bands had their own councils, the agents retained all important powers. The control by agents could extend even into the private lives of Indians, as, for example, in inspecting Indian households for signs of untidiness. The agents played the major part in removing children from their family and village in order to educate them free of traditional influence; no policy was more firmly believed in than this one. Controlled by agents and missionaries, many Indian communities found themselves under the very "pupilage" that James Douglas had warned against in devising his "system" for Indian advancement. The resulting degradation and incapacity were far from ennobling in their effects.[21] In general, the agents' presence and activities served to inhibit any community-level political activity based on tradition or intended to promote aboriginal claims. Open and consistent grass-roots support was thus not something that Indian political organizers could count upon.

For reasons of administrative convenience, agencies were often designed to contain only one tribal group. This practice, which presumably contributed to maintenance of tribal group unity and identity, was more evident on the coast because of the smaller tribal territories and denser populations. During the early years the only major exception on the coast was provided by the Northwest Coast Agency, the one imposed on the Indians after the enquiry of 1887. It was immense, extending from Bella Bella in the south to the Nass Valley in the north and covering both offshore islands and the mainland coast. No fewer than six tribal groups, including those with the most developed political traditions, were included within it: the Heiltsuk, Nuxalk, Haisla, Haida, Tsimshian, and Nisga'a. The Indian population was several times the

agency average in the province. The most remote villages, not easily
reached in even the best of conditions, were those of the upriver Nisga'a
in the Nass Valley. Given all these factors, the Indians in the agency
were subject in the early decades to much less government control than
they would have been had each of the six groups been under a separate
agent. The circumstance was a fateful one, for it was in this agency,
especially among the upriver Nisga'a, that modern Indian political
action received its critical early nurturing.

One of the more striking post-contact phenomena was the apparent
widespread conversion of Indians to the profession of Christianity. The
failure of traditional religion to account for and control epidemics and
social difficulties undoubtedly weakened traditional beliefs and practices. The epidemics, so obviously terrifying in their prevalence, were at
least in some cases,[22] and probably in many, explained by missionaries
as being punishment visited by God upon unbelievers. The missionaries' own immunity must have given credibility to such an explanation.
Another factor was the ceremonial appeal of church services; with their
music, oratory, and ritual, they were highly popular among Indians,
especially since many traditional social activities had been suppressed.

Many missionaries devoted great time and effort to learning the local
language, often encountering hostility until they had succeeded. Having acquired the language, and with it much knowledge of Indian ways,
they could gain the trust of potential converts more effectively and
convey the gospel directly. Many of the missionaries were men of strong
character whose obvious dedication and constant presence led to their
being accepted with gratitude and affection on the part of the Indians
whose welfare they sought to serve.

The manner and timing of missionary arrival served to divide the
province into two distinct missionary and religious watersheds as far as
Indians were concerned. The dividing line on Vancouver Island ran
from Tofino to north of Nanaimo, and on the Mainland from Desola-
tion Sound east to the summit of the Coast Mountains and then north to
the tip of the Alaska Panhandle. North and west of the line, the missionary enterprise was exclusively Protestant; east and south it was Catholic,
with the exceptions of the Anglican enclaves at Telegraph Creek and
along the Thompson and the Methodist stronghold around Chilliwack.

The Protestant zone thus coincided with territories of the tribal
groups having the most structured political systems. It was also the part
of the province least affected by white settlement. It had little arable
land, its topography discouraged overland access, and the coastal fishing and lumbering economy did not lead to the growth of large white
towns. For decades Indians composed local majorities in many parts of
the zone, including the upper Nass Valley, which remained for many

years the most isolated populous place in the entire province (it was penetrated by a road only in the late 1950s). In many cases the Protestant missionaries were the Whites in closest contact with Indian communities, and it was from them, or in local mission schools, that many Indians learned English. The Protestant missionaries were often assisted by their wives, who could deal directly with Indian women as male missionaries could not. As well, the Protestants allowed a much greater degree of indigenization of symbols and ceremonies, such as wearing Indian robes while preaching, than did the Catholics.

In contrast, the south coast and southern interior, the areas of heaviest Indian population in the Catholic zone, were from the 1880s onward subject to the full impact of white settlement, commerce, and transportation. Indians became local minorities almost everywhere. Since none of the early Catholic missionaries had English as their first language, many Indians learned English only later from the white settlers, most of whom were Protestants. In this process the Indians now encountered "the skepticism, agnosticism and anti-Catholic attitudes of white loggers, fishermen, and others," and as a result there occurred an "erosion of priestly authority."[23] The reputation of the Catholic missionary effort suffered a particular blow among Whites and Indians in 1892 "with the arrest, trial, and conviction of a highly regarded Oblate priest, Father Chirouse, for his acquiescent role in the double flogging of an adulteress in one of the interior villages of the Lillooet Indians . . . The trial was widely publicized and its effect was to seriously damage and weaken the entire social control system of the priests by removing its underlying sanction of force and coercion."[24]

Protestantism became part of Indian culture on the west/central and north coasts in a way that Catholicism did not in the rest of the province. One additional factor contributing to the acceptance of the Protestant sects was the political aid that a number of the missionaries gave to land claims efforts. The Protestant missionaries could be especially helpful because English was their first language and they were of the same ethnicity as were most government officials. Protestantism's major role in Indian political activity could have no better evidence than that provided by the three pre-eminent political leaders of the north coast. Peter Kelly was an ordained Methodist (later United Church) minister, Alfred Adams was a lay Anglican minister, and Frank Calder graduated from the Anglican Theological College at the University of British Columbia.

Of critical importance in establishing and maintaining the strong linkage between Indian political action and Protestantism on the coast was the continuation of the potlatch, in only slightly disguised form, within Protestant religious ceremonies. Having come to the north coast from Alaska in the early 1950s, Drucker was surprised, even perplexed, to discover that potlatches "were continued, quite openly" in Protestant church ceremonies despite having been outlawed. Studying the "mortuary and memorial potlatches," he observed that "marble tombstones substituted for totem poles" and that the missionary and the church choir participated in the exchange of gifts along with clan chiefs. Drucker noted that "clan and tribal secretaries keep minute [written] records of these transactions," that "no one seems to regard these affairs as other than perfectly normal and correct," and that the Indians "seem to assume" that the Christian elements "somehow change the character of the performance and legalize it."[25] Drucker did not make the rather important observation that missionaries and Indian agents were quite willing to make the same assumption. In effect, the Protestant churches gave sanctuary to the crucial traditional social and political institution of the coastal tribal groups.

On the north coast a full symbiosis occurred between Protestantism and the traditional clan system. In the 1950s the system was in full operation, "regulating marriages and establishing the framework within which the potlatch is carried on."[26] The vitally important potlatch feasts in which clan leaders received their inherited names and positions were now conducted, often in church halls, with blessings from the missionary and music from the church's brass band. The missionary himself would have been adopted into a house and clan, and a potlatch would have been held to sanctify his status. All these practices continue today.

Having found satisfactory ways of continuing their potlatches, the north coast Indians were not overly concerned when Parliament banned them. During the hearings of 1887, indeed, several Tsimshian spokesmen (whose descendants Drucker would study) went on at some length about their having become good Christians and having abandoned the potlatch. Among the Nuu'chah'nulth and, especially, the Kwagiulth, however, there was a pronounced effort not only to continue the potlatch but also to keep it separate from Christianity. It was this effort which the white authorities eventually sought to suppress. Even among these two groups, however, the Protestant church ceremonies incorporated important elements of the potlatch.

The belief that the Christian God had created the various peoples of the world and assigned them each their own lands quickly became an significant element in both Indian Protestantism and Protestant Indian political action. That the same God had allowed Whites to come to British Columbia did not cause any difficulty to the Indians, for plainly it was His intention that the white authorities should acknowledge Indian title and negotiate its proper transfer. This view may have been especially pronounced among Anglican Indians, since the British monarch was head of the church, the fountain of British justice, and the author of the Royal Proclamation of 1763. All in all, Protestantism and Protestant missionaries quickly became highly significant spiritual and political resources to coastal Indians.

Catholicism did not become nearly as ingrained in Indian culture. Catholic missionaries allowed little, if any, indigenization. Their garb and their churches were exact replicas of those in Quebec and Europe.[27] No British Columbia Indians became priests, despite Bishop Durieu's hopes that some would do so.[28] Few, if any, Catholic missionaries seem to have publicly supported claims to Indian title, although some did become active advocates on the reserve acreage question.[29]

A practice carried out by most early missionaries, but also by Indian agents, was the assigning of European family names to Indians. Doing so seems to have been regarded as an essential step in conversion to Christianity. Because missionaries commonly assigned names from their own ethnic groups, English family names became predominant in the Protestant areas, while French names became predominant in the Catholic areas. (In a number of north coast cases, Indians accepted the family names of the missionaries themselves.) Thus, on the central and north coasts names ordinarily provided no distinction between Whites and Indians, while they did in the rest of the province, where few Whites had French names.[30] Missionaries and agents insisted that family names pass in the European manner from man to wife and children, causing confusion with the north coast matrilineal custom. Contrary to white expectations, however, traditional names and naming practices did persist, most explicitly among the coastal lineages, but in the interior as well.[31] The traditional name thus remained an element contributing to the aboriginal identity of most individual Indians throughout the province.

It was quickly realized by agents and missionaries that suppression of traditional culture would not by itself promote assimilation. They regarded education of Indian children as the key. Effective schooling, in terms of regular attendance and inculcation of values, was impossible if parents retained influence over their children. The solution was to remove the children. Beginning in the 1880s, reaching its full development in the 1920s, and lasting into the 1960s, an effective partnership of church and state implemented this solution. Sixteen residential schools were established, each operated by one of the churches and funded by the federal government. The nine Catholic schools were all in the Catholic portion of the province. Five of the seven Protestant schools were in the Protestant coastal area; one was at Lytton; and another, the main Methodist school, was at Coqualeetza, near Chilliwack in the Lower Fraser Valley.

As Titley observes, schooling was intended "as an instrument of cultural annihilation" that would "transform the Indians into an unskilled or semi-skilled workforce while forcing them into the mould of Anglo-Canadian identity."[32] Agricultural pursuits were emphasized. The children provided much of the labour to maintain the schools; they worked as hard in the fields, barns, and kitchens as in the classrooms.[33]

Some parents willingly sent their children off to school; others did not. Stories abound among Indians of children forcibly removed from home and family by police and Indian agents or returned to school when they ran away. The children were often far from home. Children from the north coast were brought south to Port Alberni or Coqualeetza. Unless exempted by the agent, children from seven to seventeen years of age were required to be in school from September until May or June. Except when parents and children could read and write, there could be little if any family communication during these months. Stories are frequent of children not even sent home for the summer; some were kept at school continuously for years.

For children of broken, impoverished, or abusive families the schools could provide better physical and emotional surroundings than existed at home. In many cases, however, the schools were settings for much unhappiness. Separation from parents, relatives, friends, and familiar places could bring misery to a child, however healthful the school environment. But the schools were rarely healthful places. The Indian population had still not acquired the white immunities and the schools served as major transmission sites for all of the common infections and diseases, including, notably, tuberculosis. For the Indian children sickness and death were part of school life. Thomson observes, for example, that of the sixty-seven students discharged from the Kootenay school in a seven-year period "forty-seven were dead and three were sickly."[34] Sexual abuse by adults and by older students may also have been a common feature of school existence.[35]

Beatings, in the form of strappings, canings, or blows to the head, were the standard punishment in the schools; girls could also have their heads shaved. By far the most frequent stories told by those who attended the schools concern the beating of children for using their native languages. The goal was not simply to make English the everyday language; it was also, and explicitly, to have each Indian child incapable of using his or her mother tongue. In this way the fundamental cultural and personal link between tradition and posterity would be shattered, and assimilation would be promoted. In the early decades the majority of children coming to the schools knew little English. Added to the stress of separation from family, the regime of stigma and punishment suddenly attached to childhood language often had traumatic emotional effects. The children's conditioned response to their own language, and thus to much of their culture, often became shame, embarrassment, and avoidance. In many cases they lost the language during the years at school and so could not communicate fully with parents and older relatives. To lessen the anguish of their children, some parents hurried to learn English and ceased using their own language in front of their pre-school children.

The system of Indian schooling had profoundly important consequences for pan-Indianism and Indian political organization in British Columbia. By bringing together children from different tribal groups and widely separated communities and by keeping them together for long periods away from traditional influences, while at the same time isolating them from white society, the schools promoted a new and wider Indian awareness and identity. Schooling thus promoted pan-Indian awareness and provided future leaders with essential political resources. They could not have formed and maintained organizations had they not had the lingua franca that English provided, had they not been able to read and write, and had they not had networks of personal contacts composed of former schoolmates.

North coast children and graduates proved especially adept at making political use of their schooling. From its earliest days the Coqualeetza school produced more than its share of north coast leaders, including both Peter Kelly and Frank Calder. The Coqualeetza Friendship Society, composed of alumni, was the only non-political pan-Indian organization in the province prior to the 1960s. During the 1950s and 1960s, when residential school spaces were in short supply in the province, most north coast high school students were sent to a residential school in Edmonton, where they formed a fraternity which they called the "Edmonton Mafia." It had an explicit membership and a set of specialized roles for members. While the overt motives were nefarious (including providing post-curfew alibis and gaining night-time access to school food stores), the organization served to reduce homesickness and to emphasize north coast identity within the prairie school population. During the 1970s and 1980s the network of Mafia graduates contributed markedly to the pronounced political communication and co-operation among tribal groups on the north coast.

The division of the province into the Protestant and Catholic school catchment areas contributed to the emergence of two corresponding political zones, one consisting of the west/central and north coasts and the other of the south coast and the southern interior. It was within these two zones that separate pan-Indian outlooks emerged. The two political zones were not distinct before the 1920s, but they were pronounced from the 1920s until the late 1960s. They faded after the closing of the residential schools in the 1960s, but they did not disappear entirely. Contemporary Protestantism and Roman Catholicism were elements of the separate identities and also a cause of antipathy between the two, for each set of schools taught that the other faith was misguided and heretical.

Schooling and religion, however, were not the only factors contributing to the dual political pattern. The similarity and strength of political and other cultural traditions among the north coast peoples provided a core for pan-Indianism extending among tribal groups down the coast, while the same sort of similarity among the various Salish tribal groups was the basis of the common political outlook stretching across the southern reaches of the province.

A further consequence of the residential schooling was that it diminished individual incentive to protect aboriginal interests (since attachment to tradition was weakened) and decreased the likelihood that individuals would take political action (since self-confidence was eroded and a sense of dependency was inculcated). This effect was not uniform and seems to have been correlated with the strength of political and other cultural traditions. Where these were most developed, as on the north coast, the effect was less evident. It is also possible, but by no means demonstrated, that Protestant schooling implanted fewer political inhibitions than did Catholic schooling. Whatever the underlying causes, the Indian population became increasingly quiescent, even passive,[36] as the twentieth century progressed. The outlawing of claims activity in 1927 provoked no protest. After 1927 political activity disappeared entirely in the interior; it continued on the north coast, but in disguise. Political activity reappeared in the 1950s and 1960s among both coastal and interior Indians after the prohibition was lifted, but it did not attain widespread, active Indian support until the 1970s, when the Indian schools had been closed and the new generation of young Indian leaders had emerged.

Despite the enormous barriers placed in their way, British Columbia Indians did create and sustain a political response to the denial of aboriginal title. Despite their great differences and while seeking to retain their Indian identities,[37] the various tribal groups adopted uniform political goals and strategies pertaining to the land question. What is especially remarkable is that the political response emerged so quickly at such an early stage in the establishment of the new regime. Elsewhere many aboriginal minorities did come to the same response, but usually only much later (especially during the so-called ethnic revival in the 1960s) and not when the white regime was implementing its initial policies. Alone in the new world, with neither outside aid nor previous example to call upon, the Indians of British Columbia embarked upon sustained political action within the new political system, demanding that it live up to its own official ideals.

CHAPTER SEVEN

From Intertribal to Province-Wide Political Action, 1900–16

The early intertribal political initiatives, of the Salish in 1874 and of the Nisga'a and Tsimshian in 1887, were made by men who were traditional leaders in the full sense. They were the latest holders of positions that had continued from before contact, and they themselves had been raised in traditional ways. None had any formal schooling; few could speak English; none knew written English. The intertribal co-operation which they organized was limited to groups having closely related Indian languages. Since few traditional leaders, if any, could know much about the workings of the Canadian and provincial governments, their initiatives had to rely upon missionary advice and support.

By the turn of the century in every tribal group there were those, mostly younger people who had attended local mission schools, who were fluent in both spoken and written English. Included in this new generation were young men now inheriting, or otherwise acquiring, traditional leadership positions within clans and communities. In contrast to their predecessors, they were more knowledgeable about white society and government, and so they could communicate readily with government officials and other Whites. The new generation of community and tribal leaders retained much of tradition, but they had new skills and a wider outlook. They were both modern and traditional— "neo-traditional." Able to choose between tradition and assimilation, they chose tradition, but they sought to widen it, to adapt it, and to integrate it within the white political system. To do so they created organizations that were also neo-traditional.

A particularly important example of the generational change from traditional to neo-traditional leadership was provided by the Calders. Among the traditional Nisga'a chiefs attending the north coast hearings in 1887 was Job Calder, who had only recently taken an English name. He was husband of the "chiefess" Victoria, whose high rank was acknowledged both in her village of Greenville and among Nisga'a generally. Calder brought with him to the hearings his son Arthur,[1] then eighteen years old. Arthur Calder later inherited his mother's clan leadership and his father's English surname. By the turn of the century he was playing a leading role in Nisga'a politics.

Although a detailed understanding of developments within the various tribal groups must await the publication of their individual histories, it is clear that community and tribal spokesmen in all parts of the province continued after 1888 to assert their claim to land ownership and to object to the size and location of reserves. Spokesmen for the Coast and Interior Salish, the groups on whom white settlement was impinging most intensely, were especially vociferous. Among the Salish tribal groups, traditional leaders remained the principal spokesmen. They continued the pattern of complaint they had established in the 1860s and 1870s, but now with greater support and wider communication, as is shown by the assembly at Cowichan in early 1906 that brought together representatives from all the Coast and Interior Salish groups.[2] The assembly approved a delegation of three traditional chiefs—Joe Capilano, a Squamish, Basil David, a Shuswap, and Chillihitza, the Okanagan chief—to take their claims and complaints to London. The three met with King Edward, but they were rebuffed by the British government on the grounds that land questions were purely Canadian matters. While bringing together all of the Salish groups was a notable achievement and a step in the evolution of Salish pan-Indianism, the traditional Salish chiefs made no move to adapt Salish political structures or to form any alliance with non-Salish groups.

Nisga'a society and politics evolved rapidly after 1888. An intriguing element in this evolution was a Nisga'a newspaper. Founded in 1891 by the Anglican missionary J.B. McCullagh and called *Hagaga: The Indians' Own Newspaper*, it was initially published in the Nisga'a language by means of phonetic script. Later, a newspaper printing press was brought to Aiyansh by McCullagh and seven Nisga'a became competent typesetters. The paper began using English and seems to have been an important stimulus and means for the Nisga'a to learn to speak and write English.[3] By the late 1890s the Nisga'a had taken over the newspaper "and made it a vehicle for organizing the Land Movement in the region . . . to McCullagh's discomfort."[4] Renamed the *North British Columbia News*, the publication appears to have had "a fairly wide circulation" among both Indians and Whites in the Nass region.[5]

Among the Nisga'a festivals were "revival meetings" held in the immense wooden churches now appearing in each village. These meetings were simply potlatches in a new setting. Some of them were huge affairs, leaving vivid lifelong memories with the young children who attended.[6] At the potlatch/revival meetings the chiefs would give speeches on topics of public concern, with the land question always prominent. The meetings were a major means of keeping the Nisga'a public informed about the land issue.

In 1907 the Nisga'a chiefs formed the Nisga'a Land Committee. Their doing so was suggested by Charles Barton of Kincolith.[7] Fluent in English (it was he who had served as interpreter for the north coast chiefs in their Victoria meetings of 1887) and widely-traveled in North America, Barton was a good example of the neo-traditional leader. He brought the idea of the committee from Ontario, where he had encountered associations formed of neighbouring Indian communities.[8]

It was Arthur Calder, however, who appears to have organized the land committee.[9] It was based squarely on tradition, for it was structured to represent clans and local communities; in later years it had sixteen members with each of the four clans in each of the four villages having one representative. The position of committee chairman was rotated annually among the villages.[10] The formation of the committee was apparently the first instance among British Columbia Indians of a planned political restructuring for the purpose of achieving greater effectiveness in dealing with the white political system. The committee was clearly intended as something that white politicians and the white public could readily understand and would take more seriously than they had been taking traditional chiefs in traditional roles. Committee members proved adept in at least one further aspect of image making among Whites: they dressed the part, always wearing fashionable three-piece suits when travelling or meeting with government officials.[11]

By 1908 the north coast was the only major portion of the province in which the laying out of reserves was not substantially complete. Dominion and province were again in disagreement over the reserve question.[12] Dominion officials were urging the province to allow larger reserves, while the province was still refusing even to convey to the Dominion the lands already laid out. The provincial refusal, coupled with Premier Richard McBride's publicly stated views that reserve lands would be better used by Whites, caused much Indian unease. Then, in 1908, to pressure the federal government, McBride's government blocked the laying out of any further reserves. The effect was to leave the remainder of the major north coast valleys, including the Nass, completely open to white pre-emption without any attention to Indian concerns or any protection for Indian interests.

The Nisga'a Land Committee now initiated a meeting with the Port Simpson Tsimshian to discuss a broader political response.[13] The leaders of the two groups communicated with other coastal groups, precipitating discussion throughout 1909 about the formation of a political action group. As a result of the original Nisga'a initiative and the evident consensus among coastal tribal groups, an assembly was held in Victoria in December 1909.[14] North coast and Coast Salish leaders were the most prominent participants, and the assembly agreed to form an organization to be called the Indian Rights Association.[15] During the summer of 1909 a meeting of Interior Salish chiefs had taken place at Spences Bridge, with James Teit playing an active role. The chiefs had agreed to the formation of an association called the Interior Tribes of British Columbia.[16]

The year 1909 thus brought a burst of intertribal political organization. The Indian Rights Association was the most significant development, since it brought together for the first time north coast and south coast tribal groups and included groups, notably the Haida, who had not previously taken part in intertribal action. Peter Kelly, at about this time leaving school-teaching to become an ordained Methodist minister, was emerging as the major Haida spokesman.

As there had been in 1887, there was still in 1909 and later a belief among provincial politicians that Indians were getting their political ideas from Whites, especially from missionaries. The belief was undoubtedly prompted in good part by the common assumption that Indians were primitive and unsophisticated peoples. The assumption was held primarily by those who had little knowledge of Indians; contrary views were often held by those in close contact with them. In 1910, for example, the agent in charge of the Nass agency observed that the Nisga'a were "highly civilized, law-abiding and conscious of establishing the principles of international laws in regard to their ownership of land. They will defend their land even as the Boers have done."[17] Had missionaries been determining Indian political action, the organizations would likely have been formed much earlier. The fact that the first substantial intertribal political activity coincided with the emergence of the first generation of neo-traditional leaders provides further evidence that Indians were guiding the developments. Moreover, had missionaries been in charge, it is highly unlikely that the north coast Protestant and south coast Catholic Indians would have combined forces as they did so firmly from 1909 to 1927.

What the Indians vitally needed was legal advice. At this point, fortuitously, there arrived on scene Arthur O'Meara. He had become an Anglican missionary several years earlier, after having been a lawyer in Ontario for two decades. Until 1927 he was virtually the sole legal adviser to the Indian leaders. Upon his arrival he formed the Society of Friends of the Indians of British Columbia, composed mainly, it would appear, of Anglican churchgoers. The society raised money for Indian political activity and sponsored public talks, usually by O'Meara, on the

Indian question. Although he retained the confidence of the Indians, he was not popular among white politicians, most of whom regarded him as an irksome troublemaker. As Titley observes, O'Meara played "a major, and controversial, role."[18] With and without O'Meara, the Nisga'a Land Committee and the new organizations proceeded to lobby the provincial and dominion governments and again sent representatives to London.[19]

Prime Minister Wilfrid Laurier toured British Columbia in 1910, travelling the central and southern interior by rail and the coast by steamer. He received a number of Indian delegations, including the north coast leaders at Prince Rupert and a group of southern interior chiefs at Kamloops. Laurier seemed sympathetic to Indian complaints against the province, and some of the north coast leaders remembered him saying, "I think the only way to settle this question . . . is by a decision of the Judicial Committee [of the British Privy Council], and I will take steps to help you."[20]

Early in the next year a delegation of almost one hundred chiefs from up and down the coast and from the southern interior met with Premier McBride to urge provincial recognition of Indian title and a more generous approach to reserves. McBride was unmoved, and in reply he accused the Indians of taking bad advice from white advisers and "blandly stated that until a few months earlier he had not even known of any dissatisfaction existing amongst the Indian tribes."[21] Soon after, the chairman of the Nisga'a Land Committee, S.W. Pollard, wrote to the editor of the *Colonist* stating that the Nisga'a were "law-abiding and loyal subjects of the King," that they had thwarted the attempts of "unscrupulous whites" to provoke them, and that the main Nisga'a desire was to have "Nass River Valley lands . . . withdrawn from settlement and wholesale staking, until Indian claims are rightfully settled."[22]

After Laurier's visit the Dominion did increase its pressure on the province, but the impasse was resolved only after Robert Borden and the Conservatives had defeated Laurier and the Liberals in 1911, bringing with them an outlook on Indian matters welcomed by Richard McBride and his provincial Conservatives. Borden had J.A.J. McKenna appointed special commissioner of Indian affairs responsible for reaching agreement with the province. In September 1912 McKenna and McBride signed an agreement setting out a procedure to "settle all differences between the Governments of the Dominion and the Province respecting Indian lands and Indian Affairs" and to provide "a final adjustment of all matters relating to Indian Affairs in the Province." As Indians immediately noticed, the agreement dealt only with the reserve question. The agreement made no mention whatever of title, treaties, or self-government. The federal government had once again capitulated to the province's demands. The final adjustment was to be made without any attention to these three central Indian concerns.

The agreement provided for a royal commission of five members (two appointed by each government, with the fifth, the chairman, appointed by the other four) empowered to alter the size of any existing reserve. The commission would also have power to lay out new reserves. The province agreed to convey title to all reserve lands when the commission had finished its work and to stop refusing to allow reserve land to be disposed of for the benefit of Indians.[23] Section 2 of the agreement was key to the fate of reserves in British Columbia.

At such places as the Commissioners are satisfied that more land is included in any particular Reserve as now defined than is reasonably required for the use of the Indians of that tribe or locality, the Reserve shall, *with the consent of the Indians, as required by the Indian Act*, be reduced to such acreage as the Commissioners think reasonably sufficient for the purposes of such Indians. At any place at which the Commissioners shall determine that an insufficient quantity of land has been set aside for the use of the Indians of that locality, the Commissioners shall fix the quantity that ought to be added for the use of such Indians.[24] [Emphasis added.]

It did appear, then, that Indian interests would be fully protected against unwanted reserve reduction by the existing Indian veto set out in the Indian Act. Perhaps McKenna believed in the efficacy of the veto. Highly suspicious of anything the province would agree to, Indian spokesmen did not. The McKenna-McBride Commission, as it was commonly called,[25] was appointed in 1913 and spent the next three years holding hearings and examining reserves throughout the province. The hearings raised continual unease among the Indians. They also brought prominence to Andrew Paull, a Squamish who left his job as longshoreman to work as interpreter for the commission in the Salish-speaking areas of the province.[26]

The signing of the agreement and the setting up of the commission caused Indians to redouble their political efforts. In early 1913 the Nisga'a Land Committee, with O'Meara as its legal adviser and draftsman, prepared a lengthy petition to authorities in London. Among British Columbia Indians the petition became an important political text and political catalyst, as well as a symbol of the political struggle of all Indians for their land rights. In a covering letter (which was approved, along with the petition itself, at an assembly of the Nisga'a people called by the land committee), the Nisga'a stated:

Notwithstanding . . . the position . . . consistently taken by every representative of

Canada from the time of Lord Dufferin's speeches until the spring of the present year, and in defiance of our frequent protests, the Province has sold a large proportion of the best lands of our territory and has by means of such wrongful sales received a large amount of money.

While we claim the right to be compensated for those portions of our territory which we may agree to surrender, we claim as even more important the right to reserve other portions permanently for our own use and benefit, and beyond doubt the portions which we would desire so to reserve would include much of the land which has been sold by the Province.

We are not opposed to the coming of the white people into our territory, provided this be carried out justly and in accordance with the British principle embodied in the Royal Proclamation. If, therefore, as we expect, the aboriginal rights which we claim should be established by the decision of His Majesty's Privy Council, we would be prepared to take a moderate and reasonable position. In that event, while claiming the right to decide for ourselves the terms upon which we would deal with our territory, we would be willing that all matters outstanding between the Province and ourselves should be finally adjusted by some equitable method to be agreed upon which should include representation of the Indian Tribes upon any Commission which might be appointed.[27]

The three fundamental Indian concerns of title, treaty, and self-government ("the right to decide for ourselves the terms upon which we would deal with our territory") were thus put forward by the Nisga'a.

The petition itself contained a declaration of traditional Nisga'a land ownership and political sovereignty, an affirmation that the new British sovereignty had been accepted on the understanding that Nisga'a land ownership would be respected, and a disquisition on the relevance of the Royal Proclamation of 1763 to Nisga'a lands and to the Nisga'a "nation or tribe." Almost half of the petition's two thousand words were devoted to excerpts from the proclamation.[28] Until this troubled time the proclamation had been known to few, if any, British Columbia Indians, and its contents were an inspiration. For many Indians it was a moving revelation to discover that the British monarch, already seen as a symbol of justice, was the very one to have long since proclaimed the very principles that British Columbia Indians had been pursuing, seemingly alone.

Knowledge of the proclamation gave a powerful boost to pan-Indian sentiments. Each Indian could see his or her tribal group as one of the "nations or tribes" recognized and promised justice by the proclamation but denied it by the actions of provincial officials. Despite their diversity, all the tribal groups (except for the few affected by treaties) could feel as one in having been denied the promised justice. They could now be united in the conviction that the British Columbia government was the source of the injustice perpetrated against all the province's Indians. They could believe not only that the provincial officials had acted out of white self-interest and ignored commonplace notions of equity, but also that the officials had deviously ignored the instructions of their own sovereign. This interpretation became firmly fixed and added to the moral fervour of the Indian approach to the land question. Federal officials, having obeyed the proclamation east of the Rockies, were seen as less blameworthy.

To the Nisga'a the promises of the proclamation, combined with the existing Indian ideals of British justice, pointed to the obvious means of resolving the whole land question: once the injustice was brought to their attention, the highest British authorities would see to it that British Columbia Indians were treated as Indians had been elsewhere in Canada. This expectation explains the paradox of the Nisga'a petition: it makes no specific demands; it simply lists the promises and the failures to fulfil them. It assumes that the statement of the injustices will cause them to be corrected. Before 1913 the Nisga'a Land Committee had issued statements that "our case is now before the Privy Council in England and we are expecting a settlement of the difficulty at present existing between ourselves and the Government of this Province at an early date,"[29] and this statement was repeated in the petition.

There was much misunderstanding, at the time and later, about precisely which British authority the Nisga'a were addressing in their petition. The petition, however, was addressed to "the King's Most Excellent Majesty in Council,"[30] with the covering letter addressed to the secretary of state for the colonies, the cabinet member responsible for colonial affairs. The petition was thus intended for the cabinet or government of the day, but it was addressed to the Privy Council, the formal entity of which the cabinet is the only active part.[31] The petition was not addressed to the Judicial Committee of the Privy Council, the highest Imperial court, as Canadian officials at the time, and scholars later, assumed.[32]

There is much indication, however, in the petition and in later public statements in various parts of the province that the Nisga'a and other Indians did regard the Privy Council as a real and active body which could, if it chose, remedy the situation in Canada. Apparently the Nisga'a remained convinced that their claim had somehow been lodged with it, and in subsequent years Indians in other parts of the province would express the same article of faith concerning their own claims, often with some reference to the monarch as having a personal hand in the matter.

Government officials in Canada generally used the term "privy council" to refer to the Judicial Committee of the Privy Council,[33] which could normally act on a Canadian matter only on appeal from a Canadian court decision. As long as neither Indians nor a government had initiated a court action and been allowed to appeal the decision, the Canadian officials insisted that nothing could be before the "privy council." There was, though, the outside possibility that the British cabinet might refer the matter to the Judicial Committee; Canadian officials, devoutly hoping that it would not do so, did not admit this possibility in their dealings with British Columbia Indians.[34]

The adamant Indian belief that their claim was before the "privy council" was an important factor in Indian politics and government action until 1927. It seems to have given hope and confidence to the Indians that justice would eventually be done and in particular, to have led them to be less concerned than they otherwise might have been with the lack of government response within Canada to their demands. The belief exasperated officials, who thought that it kept the Indians intent on their political action and thus inhibited them from assimilating.[35]

In the year of the Nisga'a petition, Duncan Campbell Scott, well known as a Canadian poet, became deputy superintendent general of Indian affairs after three decades of rising through the ranks. His was the "narrow vision" that would dominate federal Indian policy until his retirement in 1932.[36] Scott was fully committed to assimilation. "I want to get rid of the Indian problem," he stated on one occasion, "Our objective is to continue until there is not a single Indian in Canada that has not been absorbed into the body politic and there is no Indian question, and no Indian Department."[37] While he accepted the principle of aboriginal title in British Columbia, he believed that the Indians had been adequately compensated in the form of reserves and money spent on their health, education, and welfare. In his view, the land claims were motivated by hopes of "receiving compensation of a very large value either in money or privileges."[38]

One of Scott's major early initiatives was intended to undercut the influence of the Nisga'a petition and to deflect Indian attention away from political action. Scott was seeking also to head off any thought the British government might have of pressuring Ottawa to deal seriously with the Nisga'a petition. Senior DIA officials were apprehensive that Britain might be entertaining precisely such thoughts.[39] On Scott's advice the federal cabinet passed an order-in-council in March 1914 stipulating that the federal government would refer "the Indian claim to the lands of the Province of British Columbia" to the Exchequer Court of Canada "with right of appeal to the Privy Council" (that is the Judicial Committee) providing that three main conditions were accepted by the Indians. First, that if the courts did decide "they have title to the lands," the Indians would do two things: they would surrender the title completely in return for the same sort of treaty benefits awarded else-where in Canada, and they would accept the recommendations of the McKenna-McBride Commission as final in relation to reserves. Second, that any obligations of the province for any of its past actions would be fulfilled by its granting the land for the reserves. Third, the province would take part in the court case, represented by legal counsel of its own choosing, while the Indians would be "represented by counsel nominated and paid by the Dominion."[40]

The Indians were outraged. They were especially angry about having to promise to accept reductions in their reserves and about having a government lawyer forced upon them and given charge of their inter-ests. The Indian Rights Association, the Interior Tribes, and the Nisga'a Land Committee rejected the conditions.[41] Scott's proposal, in fact, prompted moves towards wider political co-operation.

The years leading up to 1916 were active ones for the Nisga'a Land Committee and for the two political organizations. In contrast to the committee, the Indian Rights Association and the Interior Tribes of British Columbia were not highly structured. Their activities consisted of periodic assemblies in which policy statements would be approved and delegations authorized to meet with governments. The various delegations seem to have been the main structures within the organiza-tions, for no executive groups or individual leaders emerged to play any dominant role. Money was a continual problem, especially for travel. (As they crossed the prairies to Ottawa, the British Columbia leaders must have envied the prairie chiefs who were given railway passes as treaty-signing bonuses.) Presumably the Coast Salish leaders played a key role in the occasional co-ordination between the two organizations, as they did in the 1911 meeting with Premier McBride. Missionaries also played their part in spreading news of meetings and other activities.

The leaders of most tribal groups were willing to subsume their politi-cal action within one of the organizations. The Nisga'a were the only notable exception; they played a leading part in the Indian Rights Association, but they also devoted much energy to efforts of their own. At this stage, and until well after 1927, local Indian communities in the central interior and northern interior did little more than send the occasional delegate to assemblies or conferences.

By 1915 the Interior Tribes had expanded its support to include both the northern Shuswap and, for the first time, a non-Salishan group, the Kootenay. The organization remained in communication with Coast Salish chiefs, a number of whom attended an Interior Tribes assembly at Spences Bridge in February 1915. The assembly endorsed the Nisga'a petition; it also prepared its own petition and authorized a delegation to take it to Ottawa. While the meeting marked an important step in the evolution of coastal-interior co-operation, the participants do not seem to have regarded themselves as forming a new organization.[42] Had they done so, the Ottawa delegation would likely have included coastal chiefs rather than, as appears to have been the case, having consisted solely of interior chiefs (one Kootenay and seven Interior Salish) and James Teit.[43]

At about this time a Nisga'a delegation met with Scott and the minister of Indian affairs in Ottawa. The Nisga'a defended their petition, explained their reasons for rejecting the order-in-council, and sought assurance that appearing before the McKenna-McBride Commission, which they had so far declined to do, would not be regarded as an abandonment of their claim to aboriginal ownership. Scott and the minister assured them that dealing with the commission "would not prejudice their larger claim to aboriginal title."[44] Nisga'a chiefs subsequently took part in commission hearings, using the opportunity to re-emphasize their claim to title. In the spring of 1916, with the commission's report soon expected and with little Indian optimism evident anywhere about its contents, the Nisga'a spent six fruitless weeks lobbying in Ottawa, hoping to gain agreement that the report would not be implemented until their petition had been acted on in London. Scott would give no assurance and urged the Nisga'a to accept the terms of the 1914 order-in-council.[45]

Andrew Paull and Peter Kelly organized a conference in June 1916 on Paull's Squamish reserve in North Vancouver. No fewer than sixteen tribal groups were represented: the Kootenay and the four Interior Salish groups (Lillooet, Nlaka'pamux, Okanagan, and Shuswap) from the southern interior; the Chilcotin and at least one Carrier group from the central interior; the Kaska-Dena and the Tahltan from the northern interior; the mainland Coast Salish and the Cowichan from the south coast; the Nuxalk from the central coast; and all four north coast groups (Nisga'a, Tsimshian, Haida, and Gitksan). Thus, tribal groups from literally every corner of the province were represented, although undoubtedly a number of the representatives were self-chosen without much consultation within their respective tribal groups. The only large groups not represented were the Nuu'chah'nulth and the Kwagiulth.[46] The conference formed itself into the Allied Indian Tribes of British Columbia.[47] The Indian Rights Association evidently regarded itself as dissolved with the formation of the Allied Tribes; the Interior Tribes, however, remained in existence.

The first major speaker at the conference was the young Nisga'a Andrew Barton, who stated, "our main desire is the acknowledgement of our tribal rights to the land . . . We claim that our right should be declared in court before we choose what treaty to accept." Two main resolutions were approved by the conference: one of them rejected Scott's order-in-council; the other approved the formation of a steering or executive committee, which was, in the words of the resolution, "to work for the preservation of all rights and claims in co-operation with the Nishga tribe."[48] Kelly was made chairman of the committee, whose members included the old interior chiefs, Basil David and Chillihitza (by this time known as John Chillihitza). James Teit was appointed committee secretary. Immediately, the committee wrote to Borden in Ottawa and the secretary of state for the colonies in London: "While it is believed that all of the Indian Tribes of the province will press on to the Judicial Committee, refusing to consider any so-called settlement made up under the McKenna Agreement, the Committee also feels certain that tribes allied for that purpose will always be ready to consider any really equitable method of settlement out of court which might be proposed by the Governments."[49] The aim of the Allied Tribes was thus to take the land claims through the court system to the Judicial Committee, but the way was left open for direct negotiations with provincial and federal governments.

British Columbia Indians had now created a province-wide political organization to pursue the land question. Among coastal tribal groups the foundations for the organization had been established by the activities of neo-traditional leaders within tribal groups, especially among the Nisga'a. Among the interior groups neo-traditional leaders had yet to emerge, and traditional chiefs such as Basil David and Chillihitza continued as tribal group spokesmen. The strength and unity of the political marriage of coast and interior and of new and old within the Allied Tribes would soon be tested.

CHAPTER EIGHT

Cut-Offs, Claims Prohibition, and the Allied Tribes, 1916–27

The decade commencing in 1916 was a fateful one for the Indian land question and for Indian political activity. It began with the Allied Tribes united in representing the majority of tribal groups. It brought momentous judicial decisions in London, reduction of reserves and further suppression of Indian rights in British Columbia, and a full-blown parliamentary investigation of the land question and the claims of the Allied Tribes in Ottawa. It ended with the outlawing of claims-related activities and the disappearance of the Allied Tribes.

The McKenna-McBride Commission[1] spent 1913 and the next two years holding hearings and examining reserves throughout the province. Many Indians spoke at the hearings, frequently expressing fear that reserves would be reduced without Indian consent. McKenna and the other commissioners just as frequently reminded them that the Indian Act guaranteed that no reduction, or "surrender," of any reserve could occur without the consent of a majority of the adult males of the band affected. Nevertheless, the commissioners took the approach that they could recommend reductions without taking account of the views of Indians and that it would be up to the federal government to obtain Indian consent.

The verbatim transcripts of the hearings provide a wealth of information about Indian views and concerns. In the central and southern interior there was much complaint and worry about reserve size, the unsuitability of reserve land for agriculture, and the frequent lack of access to water for irrigating crops and raising stock. There were also frequent assertions of Indian title and demands for treaties. John Chillihitza, for example, still the leading Okanagan chief, explained that his father had allowed Peter O'Reilly and G.M. Sproat to lay out reserves on the understanding that compensation would be paid later for lands occupied by settlers. "My father said 'All right, we will take our small piece where we are going to live, and we will talk about our interests in the big outside lands,' and [O'Reilly and later Sproat] said 'All right'."[2] On the coast the primary concerns were aboriginal title and the need for treaties, and demands for these were expressed again and again. The Indian Rights Association wrote to a number of communities urging them to boycott the hearings because title was being ignored; some did so, while spokesmen for others appeared at the hearings but insisted on speaking about title.

McKenna and the other commissioners became adept at turning references to original ownership into questions relating to current reserves and current needs. When unsuccessful they would dismiss a witness or close the hearings, as they did, for example, at Hazelton, when the commission was hearing from Gitksan spokesmen. House chiefs from the community of Kuldoe sought to speak about title and self-government, but they were cut short by the chairman. William Jackson, a house chief in the Kisgegas community, then came to the witness table and insisted, apparently heatedly, on raising the same issues.[3]

Jackson: We are asking to get back the land of our grandfathers—we want our places, and we want our places to be free as they were before; as our fathers had a free living in their own land, we want to be the same way. God gave us this land where we were brought up, and it was free. There was no one bothering us and we want the land just as it was before the white man ever came into this country.

Commissioner: William Jackson and Indians of the Kisgegas Tribe: You need not speak to us about holding this land the same as your grandfathers did—the world moves along, and you in your lifetime must move with it.

Jackson: What is moving this world?

Commissioner: You will have to go to a wiser lot of men than the Kuldoes to find that out—but you will have to move with the world. If you don't you will be wiped out.

Jackson: Who gave us this land—it was God. We heard it and all we know is that you people are taking away our land. This is our land—our own. No one [from] one house [can] serve as boss in the other house.

Chairman: We are sorry you have not seen fit to answer our questions, and all that remains to be done is to wish you Good Bye.[4]

In June 1916, when the commission made its report (only days after the founding meeting of the Allied Tribes), Indian reserves in the province totalled 713,699 acres (or 1,115 square miles). The commission

recommended that 666,640 acres (1,042 square miles) be confirmed as
existing reserve lands and that 87,291 acres (136 square miles) be added
as additions and as new reserves. This added land was valued at
$444,838.80 or $5.10 an acre. The commission recommended that a
total of 47,058 acres (74 square miles) be "cut-off" from existing
reserves. This land to be cut off was almost entirely land regarded as
highly desirable by white farmers, ranchers, developers, speculators,
and municipal officials. It was mostly on the south coast and in the
southern interior. Its value was appraised at between $1.2 and $1.5
million or upwards of $26.52 an acre.[5]

While it could be, and was, contended that Indians in general would
be gaining more reserve land than they were losing, it could not be
denied that the land to be cut off was worth much more than that to be
added. There was, however, no attempt to balance losses and gains for
each Indian community; most of those to experience cut-offs (some
twenty-two communities were principally affected) were to gain little or
no land in return. With the registered Indian population now less than
twenty-four thousand, the commission's recommendations provided for
a province-wide average reserve allocation of just over 150 acres for
each family of five. But the average meant little, for there remained
marked disparities among communities and tribal groups. The Kamloops band, for example, would have 688 acres for each family, while
some other communities would have less than one-tenth that amount.
In 1916, however, federal officials still maintained that no cut-offs would
occur without the consent of the band affected.

Fortunately, or so it must have seemed to the Indians, the governments took no immediate action to implement the report. Premier
McBride had retired in 1915, and H.C. Brewster and his Liberals came
to power in September 1916. Ignorant of Indian matters and aware of
white complaints about some of the proposed new reserves, Brewster
resisted Duncan Campbell Scott's attempts to arrange a secret agreement in which both governments would approve and implement the
commission's recommendations.[6] Brewster died in 1918 and was
replaced as premier by John Oliver. Oliver and his minister of lands,
Duff Pattullo, who was from Prince Rupert on the north coast, remained
in charge of provincial policy on land and Indians over the next decade.
While both would prove "hostile to Indians,"[7] their early actions were
cause for some optimism within the Allied Tribes.

One of Pattullo's first acts was to write to Arthur Meighen, the Conservative minister of Indian affairs, to see whether Indian consent would
indeed be required for the cut-offs. Meighen replied that it would, but
he expressed confidence that his department would be able to obtain
it.[8] In March 1919 the provincial legislature passed the Indian Affairs

Settlement Act. Section 3 authorized the provincial government to "carry on such further negotiations and enter into such further agreements, whether with the Dominion Government or with the Indians" as were necessary to implement the report. Oliver seemed to take the provision seriously, for he proceeded to ask the Allied Tribes for its views on the commission's report. Scott took great exception to section 3 and to Oliver's request. He regarded the province as trespassing onto the exclusive right of the federal government to deal with Indians, and as events would soon make clear, he did not want any suggestion that Indians would have any say in the fate of the commission's proposals. In response, the deputy attorney-general of the province informed Scott that section 3 could be repealed if the dominion did not intend to obtain Indian consent to the proposed cut-offs.[9]

In responding to Oliver's request the Allied Tribes held a general assembly at Spences Bridge in June 1919. Although Peter Kelly, Andrew Paull, and other members of the executive committee had been actively lobbying against the proposed cut-offs, there had been no assembly since the founding of the organization in 1916. At Spences Bridge the Allied Tribes confirmed Peter Kelly as chairman of the executive committee, elected Andrew Paull as "recording secretary" of the organization, and authorized the committee (of which James Teit remained secretary) to prepare the statement requested by Oliver. As part of its preparation the committee held "various large inter-tribal meetings . . . in different parts of the Province."[10] It was through these meetings, rather than general assemblies, that local support for the Allied Tribes and its goals could be gauged, both by the leaders themselves and by Department of Indian Affairs officials in the various agencies.

Having approved a statement drafted by Kelly and Teit, the executive committee presented it to Oliver in a meeting with him in December 1919. The statement, some six thousand words long, was both a comprehensive claim to aboriginal title and a detailed rejection of the McKenna-McBride Commission's report. In the view of the Allied Tribes, the commission's terms of reference ignored the title question, the added lands were worth little while the cut-offs were valuable, inequities between tribes were not addressed, and the commission had ignored important matters, such as water rights, which were within its terms of reference. The statement was widely distributed among British Columbia Indians and appears to have superseded the Nisga'a petition of 1913 as the authoritative statement of British Columbia Indian claims. Like the Nisga'a petition, the statement affirmed that British Columbia Indians would "continue pressing our case in the Privy Council."[11]

In Ottawa matters had now taken an ominous turn. In November Scott had recommended to Meighen that the Conservative government seek authority from Parliament to override the Indian veto, and in January 1920 Scott provided his detailed rationale.

It is just possible that in some instances the Indians might, through some influence or prejudice, refuse to give the necessary consent. I think we should provide against such a contingency in our legislation confirming that all reductions and cut-offs should be effected without the consent of the Indians. I do not see that any injustice would be done to any band by such a provision. These reductions or cut-offs are recommended only where the Indians held more land than they required. When these cut-offs are sold, half of the proceeds will go to the Indians of the band and will be of more real benefit to them than would the land which they do not use.[12]

Meighen agreed. Bill 13, as it was labelled, was soon introduced. The Allied Tribes promptly turned its attention back to Ottawa, lobbying MPs and submitting a petition to the government pointing out the unfairness of cancelling the much vaunted and so frequently reaffirmed promise that Indian consent would be required for cut-offs. Opposition MPs were highly critical of the bill, but Meighen pressed ahead, repeating Scott's rationale.

Bill 13 was signed into law on Dominion Day 1920 as The British Columbia Indian Lands Settlement Act. It authorized the federal cabinet to implement the McKenna-McBride Commission recommendations by ordering "reductions or cutoffs to be effected without surrenders of the same by the Indians, notwithstanding any provisions of the Indian Act to the contrary." The government and Parliament of Canada thus broke repeated official promises. The act also authorized the federal government to proceed to "the full and final adjustment and settlement . . . respecting Indian lands and Indian affairs in the Province." No mention was made of the Indian concerns of title, treaties, and self-government, which Scott and Meighen clearly intended to ignore.

Meighen, who soon became prime minister, allowed Scott to move against Indian interests on several additional fronts. One assumption underlying the federal policy of Indian assimilation had been that the more intelligent, able, and educated Indians would wish to give up Indian status and leave the reserves in order to acquire the rights of full British subjects, that is, to accept "enfranchisement." By 1920 it was abundantly evident that few Indians wanted to take the step. Scott's answer was Bill 14, which was introduced and passed as the companion piece to Bill 13. It allowed the government to enfranchise any Canadian Indian without his or her consent. Enfranchised Indians could neither live on nor be buried on reserves. The bill also strengthened government powers to take custody of Indian children in order to compel school attendance.[13] British Columbia Indians regarded Bill 14 as even more offensive than Bill 13. The Allied Tribes spokesmen complained strenuously. Scott and Meighen remained adamant that compulsory enfranchisement was in the Indians' own best interest.

Although it had been in place since 1884, the anti-potlatch provision of the Indian Act, section 140, had been enforced only sporadically. After Scott became deputy superintendent, it was amended in 1914 and 1918 to expand the definition of prohibited activities and to make prosecution easier. Now the prohibition applied to "any Indian festival, dance or other ceremony of which the giving away or paying or giving back of money, goods or articles of any sort forms a part." The definition was so broad that it could apply to virtually any gathering organized by Indians themselves, including not only the traditional potlatch but also, in the hands of zealous missionaries or Indian agents, meetings to discuss land claims. The penalty for violating the potlatch prohibition did not include the option of a fine; it was jailing for at least two months and a maximum of six.[14]

It was in January 1920, precisely as Bills 13 and 14 were being developed, that Indian agents and police commenced the major wave of potlatch arrests, charges, prosecutions, convictions, and jailings in British Columbia.[15] In some cases agents or missionaries were local justices of the peace and were able to expedite legal proceedings. The Kwagiulth, under the thumb of an especially zealous anti-potlatch Indian agent, were at the forefront of the resistance to the law and its enforcement.[16] A number of prominent chiefs, Kwagiulth as well as others, were convicted and brought to Oakalla Penitentiary to serve their sentences. The jailings added fuel to the political opposition to Bills 13 and 14 and left a legacy of shame and bitterness evident decades later among the children and grandchildren of those imprisoned.[17] One immediate effect, however, was the decision of a number of the Kwagiulth chiefs to participate in the Allied Tribes.

In 1921 there occurred in London an event having critical relevance to aboriginal title throughout the British Empire, but especially in places, such as British Columbia, where title had not been explicitly extinguished. In a case arising in Southern Nigeria, Viscount Haldane affirmed, on behalf of the Judicial Committee of the Privy Council, that aboriginal title was a pre-existing right that "must be presumed to have continued unless the contrary is established by the context or the circumstances."[18] Should the British Columbia land claim get to the Judicial Committee, there was now a substantial possibility that the committee would rule that Indian title had not been extinguished. It is highly unlikely that either Arthur O'Meara or Scott remained unaware of Haldane's ruling or its implications. Scott, as the 1914 order-in-council had shown, was already aware of the danger of allowing the claim into the courts unless the government kept tight control of Indian actions. Now the Haldane ruling would cause Scott and the federal politicians to resolve at all costs to keep the British Columbia claim from getting into the courts and on to the Judicial Committee.

Despite the possible encouragement provided by Haldane's ruling in London, matters were not going well for the Allied Tribes. One persistent problem was the shortage of adequate and accurate information. Inevitably, it was government officials who controlled the most valuable documentary evidence. In their internal correspondence federal officials at times discussed the benefits of withholding information from Kelly and Paull,[19] and the two were in fact prevented by Scott and others from obtaining a copy of the vitally informative *Papers Connected with the Indian Land Question*, the compilation of documents published in 1875 that provided the authoritative record of the land question's early years.[20]

Kelly and Paull could point to no success whatever in their attempts to influence Scott and Meighen in Ottawa, and in Victoria, Oliver and Pattullo were now ignoring the Allied Tribes. In London the British government seemed oblivious to the issue. On the British Columbia coast the enforcement of the potlatch law was inhibiting the holding of local meetings to demonstrate support for the Allied Tribes, and during 1921 Indian opposition to Kelly, Paull, and O'Meara came into the open.

The third assembly of the Allied Tribes was held in January 1922 in North Vancouver; that an assembly was called in mid-winter, the most awkward time for travel, was itself an indication of difficulties. Later, Kelly and Paull described the meeting as having been "a general meeting of all B.C. Indians" at which the Allied Tribes joined with unaffiliated or "independent" Indians to form "a larger alliance."[21] An examination of an attendance list, prepared five years after the event by Paull,[22] shows that only ten or so tribal groups were represented— compared to the sixteen at the founding meeting in 1916. The Nisga'a, Tsimshian, Gitksan, Carrier, Tahltan, Kaska-Dena, and Kootenay were not represented, perhaps more because of the time of year than because of discontent. In any event, the meeting can hardly have been in any position to form a "larger alliance."

The 1922 meeting appears, rather, to have been an attempt to prevent secession from the Allied Tribes by interior Indians. Chillihitza was present and acted as the main dissident spokesman, or so later events would suggest. Possibly the Interior Salish sentiments were affected by the absence of James Teit[23] or by hostility to O'Meara. But outright lack of support for Kelly and Paull was also evident. To counter the dissent, they agreed to reconstitute the executive committee to "consist of Indians and others deemed acceptable by Interiors."[24] While Kelly later stated that the meeting did herald a lesser role for white advisers, there is no evidence that the executive was reformed to the satisfaction of Chillihitza and his followers. Moreover, the only new support claimed after this time by Kelly and Paull was on the coast.[25]

Accounts of the 1922 meeting suggest not only declining unity but also a declining role for tribal groups. In describing the meeting Kelly and Paull enumerated those present not in terms of tribal groups, as they had done for the 1916 meeting, but in terms of bands or local communities.[26] There were some fifty Indians at the meeting, representing about half that number of communities.[27] From 1922 onward tribal groups as such do not appear to have been important elements within the Allied Tribes, nor do the bands and communities seem to have played any active part. Undoubtedly, most Indians endorsed the goals of the organization, but for practical purposes Kelly, Paull, and O'Meara were the organization.

In late 1921 the defeat of Meighen and the Conservatives by Mackenzie King and the Liberals brought about a slightly more sympathetic outlook in Ottawa, even though Scott continued as the senior appointed official in the Department of Indian Affairs. The legislation resulting from Bill 14, however, was soon repealed, and in 1923, with Scott's approval and support, a longstanding grievance was resolved with the granting to Indians of the right to hold commercial ocean-fishing licences. In British Columbia, some of the coastal fishermen soon became financial backers of the Allied Tribes.

The Allied Tribes executive committee resumed its lobbying, sending letters to King and obtaining meetings in 1922 and 1923 with both Scott and Charles Stewart, the minister of Indian affairs. The principal meeting with Scott occurred in August 1923, just after the provincial government had provided for its half of the final implementation of the McKenna-McBride recommendations. Kelly and Paull put forward the 1919 Allied Tribes statement as still valid and urged Scott to recommend that the federal cabinet not proceed to finalize the recommendations. Scott was surprised to find the Indians still committed to the pursuit of aboriginal title. He gave them no assurances.[28]

In 1924 the federal cabinet passed the order-in-council implementing the McKenna-McBride recommendations. The cut-off lands thus ceased to be part of Indian reserves in British Columbia. The action of the government gave an ironic twist to the common white phrase "Indian giver," meaning one who takes back something which has been given to keep. Among British Columbia Indians the cut-off lands remained a major symbol of white injustice.[29]

Defeated on the reserve question, the executive committee redoubled its efforts to get to the Judicial Committee in London. Now there was no ambiguity as to the meaning of "privy council." Kelly and Paull wanted it to rule on the legality of ignoring aboriginal title, and they did not want the federal authorities to block their way to London. In late 1925 the executive committee approved a petition to the Canadian Parliament, drafted by Kelly, asking that it establish a special committee as the first step in getting the proceedings underway. W.G. McQuarrie, MP for New Westminster, submitted the petition in June 1926, but it received little attention for the rest of the year as the King-Byng Affair unfolded and the Liberals again defeated the Conservatives in a general election.

In February 1927, H.H. Stevens, Conservative MP for Vancouver Centre, raised the matter again, asking King and Stewart if the government would not approve a "select committee to hear the representatives of the Indians and give the [land] question study." While he had "not much sympathy with some of the views entertained by those who are agitating," he did think it "desirable to satisfy and quiet the Indians" and so was "anxious to co-operate in giving them every opportunity to have the question settled" and not to have it "drift any longer."[30] On 8 March Stewart introduced, and the House passed, a motion that a special joint Senate-House committee be established "to enquire into the claims of the Allied Indian Tribes of British Columbia as set forth in their petition."[31] In going ahead with the motion, Stewart acted against Scott's advice, but he did so with the "covert intention" that the committee would in fact serve to keep the British Columbia land claim from getting to court and so to the Judicial Committee.[32]

The hearings of the special joint committee, which took place exactly forty years after the north coast enquiry,[33] finally gave Kelly and Paull the opportunity they had been seeking to present their case. The hearings also forced politicians and officials to make some sort of response. The Indians and the federal government had both hoped that the British Columbia government would send a spokesman to take part in the hearings, but Premier Oliver refused the federal invitation to do so.[34] Perhaps the Indians were optimistic that a favourable response was more likely since the committee was federal rather than provincial and since it had a Liberal rather than a Conservative majority. As matters turned out, however, the committee did not divide on partisan lines, and the outlook of white British Columbians was well represented on the committee by H.H. Stevens, by Senator Hewitt Bostock, the Kamloops rancher who was Senate co-chairman of the committee, and by three other senators from the province (G.H. Barnard, R.F. Green, and J.D. Taylor). Also among the fourteen members were Charles Stewart and future prime minister R.B. Bennett. The committee commenced immediately and completed its hearings on 6 April.

During the initial closed meeting of the committee it was agreed that Scott would testify first, allowing him to argue against the case of the Allied Tribes before Kelly and Paull were given a chance to present it. Stevens went so far as to propose, unsuccessfully, that the Indians and other witnesses be excluded during Scott's testimony and thus be prevented from knowing the government's argument.[35] At the start of the open sessions, Scott presented a lengthy statement. He did not deny the existence of aboriginal title, but he argued that awarding reserves and spending federal money on Indian health, welfare, and education, which by that time totalled $10.8 million in British Columbia, was adequate compensation and that no further claim need be entertained. Nor did he believe that the Indians had come to the demands on their own or that their motives were to be respected:

A few interviews with the advisers of the Indians convinced me that they were in possession of erroneous ideas about the nature of the Indian title and exaggerated views of the value of title, and had in fact not fully grasped the conditions under which the Crown had made treaties with the Indians in other parts of the Dominion. I became convinced that the expectation of receiving compensation of very large value either in money or privileges was influencing to a great extent the strength of the pressure being brought to bear on the Government, and I found the idea prevailing that the improvements made by white citizens to provincial lands . . . had enhanced the value of the Indian title.[36]

The only other federal official to take any major part was W.E. Ditchburn, the Indian commissioner for British Columbia. In his view, the matter of aboriginal title was "a canker in the minds of the Indians today. If it were removed . . . it would go very far towards a more satisfactory working out of the administration of the affairs by this Department." When a committee member asked, "Do the young people still harbour the thought that the land ownership will ultimately be vested in them?" Ditchburn replied, "They read as they run, of course, and their idea of the aboriginal title is much more exaggerated than that of the old people."[37]

Paull, Kelly, and O'Meara appeared for the Allied Tribes. They laid out the principles of the Royal Proclamation of 1763; they described accurately and in detail the course of events in British Columbia; they explained patiently and consistently their belief that British Columbia Indians should be dealt with on the same basis as had others in Canada.

Aboriginal title was, in Kelly's words, the "fundamental issue" separate from but underlying all the particular grievances, such as those relating to reserves.[38]

While holding fast to the principle that the dollar amount of compensation for lands taken from Indians must be a matter of negotiation, Kelly amply confirmed the consistent Indian position that the whole point of payment was to acknowledge original Indian ownership and not to make Indians rich. It was also clear that the Indians agreed that suitable treaties would serve to extinguish aboriginal title forever.[39] Simple fairness was raised several times by Kelly: "Why not keep unblemished the record of British fair dealing with native races? Why refuse to recognize the claim of certain tribes of Indians in one corner of the British Dominions, when it has been accorded to others in another part of the same Dominion?"[40]

Throughout the hearings H.H. Stevens was particularly vehement in badgering witnesses, especially O'Meara, whom he blamed for the whole issue. At one point when Kelly was testifying, Stevens referred to the claim as a bone that Kelly would not let go of; when Kelly objected, Stevens made fun of him in asides to other members of the committee.[41] Stevens also asserted that Indians were not farming effectively and were allowing orchard diseases to spread onto white farms. Ditchburn refuted the allegations.[42] Stevens believed that enfranchisement was the only appropriate path for Indians, and he rejected claims to aboriginal title, which, he insisted, were a recent invention, thought-up not by the Indians but by O'Meara:

That is one thing I never did agree to in the last twenty years, or the nineteen years since I heard Mr. O'Meara first moot this claim for an aboriginal title. I never admitted it, and I never could bring my mind to see any solid ground for the aboriginal title. I do say this, that the Indians deserve, and we ought to accord them, the most generous treatment that we possibly can, and I have always advocated that we should try to bring the Indians to the position of independent citizenship as quickly as we can. That is my position, and has been throughout my whole life in British Columbia; but I have never yet been able to see any sound ground for admitting the existence of an aboriginal title, and the evidence we have received here up to the moment, has only confirmed my views.[43]

"Generous treatment" was a stock phrase among white politicians of the period when discussing Indian affairs. In practice the phrase meant allowing Indians full and equal rights providing they ceased to be Indians. It obviously did not mean generosity in such matters as initial reserve acreage or allowing Indians a say in the cut-off issue.

Nor were the Indians to have "generous treatment" in access to vital information about the fate of their aboriginal title. O'Meara attempted to present quotations from the instructions to Governor Douglas of 1858, in which Sir Edward Lytton alluded to treaties and to the Indians' possession of the land. Stevens objected to quotations from documents not placed in evidence and told O'Meara that "I have had twenty years of your nonsense, and I am tired of it."[44] The chairman informed O'Meara that he must produce the original document. Kelly interjected that O'Meara had been striving "to support his contention by making quotations from this authority and from that authority" as lawyers ordinarily did, and asked, "Why is it objected to in this case?" Stevens promptly replied, "Because he does not quote correctly."[45]

At that moment Stevens himself had in his hands a copy of the *Papers Connected with the Indian Land Question*,[46] which he had just sought to prevent O'Meara from quoting on the grounds that it was not available to the committee. Paull now interrupted: "There is a book that has been published many years ago, which contains all the dispatches in colonial days with the Imperial Government. All of those dispatches are contained in that book and we have been trying all the time since I have been associated with this matter to get a copy of it. I have been to the Department, and Dr. Scott could not let me have it. I have been to the Library, and they have not got it there. I know that Commissioner Ditchburn has that book; and I would ask to have access to it." Stevens again stated that O'Meara "ought to know, as your counsel, that he should not quote from something which he cannot produce."

Charles Murphy, one of the Senate members, asked the pivotal question. "Is the book in this room?" Scott replied, "I have no copy of this book, but this one for myself. I have no objection to allowing them to look at this book. I thought Mr. O'Meara was referring to something original from the Imperial Government." Ditchburn also had a copy with him, but he felt it would be more useful where it was than as evidence for the committee (in which case the Indians would have access to it). "I do not want this book to be put in and impounded. It is my personal copy and I do not know where to get another copy of it." Stevens, seeking to keep the cat in the bag, now suggested that Ditchburn do what Stevens had prevented O'Meara from doing. "Read the section into the record, then you will have it," said Stevens.

The committee chairman could at this point have had the book put in evidence, but instead he agreed only that O'Meara, not Ditchburn, should read the relevant section. "We want you to read what you are referring to now, Mr. O'Meara, into the record, because the book from which you are taking it belongs to the Indian Department, and they have only one copy of it, and they cannot let it go."[47] The Indians were thus once again, and for the Allied Tribes for the final time, denied access to the documents which they knew were important to their case. White politicians and officials, in contrast, including Stevens, Scott, and Ditchburn, could routinely possess copies and found it useful to carry them for ready reference.

Chief Chillihitza appeared before the committee, along with a lawyer, stating that he represented some thirty interior chiefs of the Okanagan, Shuswap, and Nlaka'pamux tribal groups. Chillihitza and Basil David, the Shuswap chief, who also spoke, provided a marked contrast to Kelly and Paull. They were still very much the traditional leaders, speaking their own languages through interpreters and showing little interest in legal or political details. At times Chillihitza rambled on about his conversations with G.M. Sproat and with the King in London in 1906, and he even complained about the presence of an unwanted individual on a particular reserve. While both Chillihitza and David sought more land for their peoples, they stressed reserve issues more than "aboriginal title"; indeed, the interpreters did not use the phrase, and the lawyer expressed his view that aboriginal title was not of concern to the interior Indians. In fact, however, Chillihitza did assert aboriginal title in asking, as he had before the McKenna-McBride Commission, that the governments live up to their promise to pay the Indians for lands not included in reserves.[48] Chillihitza and David also made clear that the Allied Tribes did not speak for the interior tribal groups.

After the two old interior chiefs had spoken, Kelly was asked by Stevens, "Supposing the aboriginal title is not recognized? Suppose recognition is refused, what position do you take then?" Kelly's response was prophetic:

Then the position that we would have to take would be this: that we are simply dependent people. Then we would have to accept from you, just as an act of grace, whatever you saw fit to give us. Now that is putting it in plain language. The Indians have no voice in the affairs of this country. They have not a solitary way of bringing anything before the Parliament of this country, except as we have done last year by petition, and it is a mighty hard thing. If we press for that, we are called agitators, simply agitators, trouble makers, when we try to get what we consider to be our rights. It is a mighty hard thing, and as I have said, it has taken us between forty and fifty years to get to where we are to-day. And, perhaps, if we are turned down now, if this Committee see fit to turn down what we are pressing for, it might be another century before a new generation will rise up and begin to press this claim.[49]

Kelly was too pessimistic. It would be only four decades until a new generation rose up and began again to press the claim.

In its report, which was submitted five days after the completion of its hearings and which was immediately concurred in by both Commons and Senate, the committee unanimously rejected all the claims of the Allied Tribes. The committee went beyond the enquiry of 1887 by presenting six reasoned arguments for the rejection. The committee argued, first, that British exploration of the territory and subsequent exertion of sovereignty were evidence that Britain recognized "the lands as belonging to the Crown."[50] The committee ignored completely the acknowledgement of Indian title by colonial secretaries, by James Douglas, and by the island legislature. It did not even consider whether Indian title had existed prior to the advent of colonial government. It took for granted that extension of British sovereignty was in itself evidence that no prior title could have continued or been acknowledged. It did not discuss why the assumptions and procedures that had applied east of the Rockies did not apply in British Columbia. In this first and most basic argument, the committee essentially accepted the views prevailing among British Columbia Whites.

In its second argument the committee turned to revising history by asserting that the Hudson's Bay Company had achieved the "conquest" of "the territory of British Columbia." In support of this assertion, the committee noted that company posts were "fortified and the officers and servants of the Company were prepared to resist hostile attacks." The committee, however, chose to mention only two "attacks." In one, a band of Cowichan Indians "seized and slaughtered several animals belonging to the whites"; in the other, supposedly an aftermath of the first, a Songish group attacked Fort Victoria but was "easily over-awed by artillery."[51]

James Douglas would have been astounded to learn that a military conquest had occurred under his administration, as would he have been to know that it had been achieved by means of a dispute over straying livestock. Wisely, the committee did not dig itself deeper by trying to deal with such questions as how the *defensive* actions of the Company could amount to conquest or how even the "defeat" of two local Indian communities, had it occurred, could be taken to wipe out the land ownership on the rest of Vancouver Island. An even more serious question was how any action involving the company on Vancouver Island, to which its jurisdiction was confined, could be taken as affecting Indian title on the Mainland, which was not yet a colony. Absurd though it was, the conquest argument did have one slight redeeming feature; it contradicted the first argument by implicitly assuming that the prior inhabitants had existed in units recognizable in international law and that the units were in possession of land whose ownership could be transferred by conquest.

As its third argument the committee pointed out that "the Indians were not in agreement as to the nature of their claims" and asserted (wrongly, as has been suggested) that "the representatives of the Indian Tribes in the interior of British Columbia did not make any claim to any land of the Province based on an aboriginal title."[52]

Fourth, in rejecting the aboriginal title claim of the Allied Tribes, the committee went beyond historical exaggeration into falsification and misrepresentation:

Early in the proceedings it developed that the aboriginal title claimed was first presented as a legal claim against the Crown about fifteen years ago. The claim then began to take form as one which should be satisfied by a treaty or agreement with the Indians in which conditions and terms put forward by them or on their behalf must be considered and agreed upon before a cession of the alleged title would be granted. Tradition forms so large a part of Indian mentality that if in pre-Confederation days the Indians considered they had an aboriginal title to the lands of the Province, there would have been tribal records of such being transmitted from father to son, either by word of mouth or in some other customary way. But nothing of the kind was shown to exist.[53]

This was the falsification. There was abundant evidence that Indians had claimed title from the beginning and had demanded treaties as early as 1887 in the north coast hearings. The *Papers Connected with the Indian Land Question*, which the officials had kept away from the Indians, showed that both Douglas and colonial secretaries had considered the Indians to have title. The despatch from Edward Lytton, which Stevens had sought to keep out of the proceedings, confirmed this fact, as did the Douglas treaties, one of which Kelly had read into the record. The *Papers* also provided evidence of numerous instances before 1875 in which Indians had considered themselves to have title. The transcripts of the 1887 hearings contained explicit examples of transmission of title. Even Scott had told the committee that "from the year 1875 until the present time there has been a definite claim, growing in clearness as years went by."[54]

The committee went on to assert that the Indians had, prior to the supposed fifteen-year period, consented to the denial of aboriginal title and that this consent had been demonstrated by their complete acceptance of the governments' reserve policies. "The evidence of Mr. Kelly goes to confirm the view that the Indians were consenting parties to the whole policy of the government both as to reserves and other benefits which they accepted for years without demur."[55] This was both falsification and misrepresentation. It even contradicted Scott's opening statements to the committee that from the earliest times British Columbia

Indians "had complained constantly of the insufficiency of land allotments for reserves."[56]

Fifth, the committee blamed white agitators.

The Committee note with regret the existence of agitation, not only in British Columbia, but with Indians in other parts of the Dominion, which agitation may be called mischievous, by which the Indians are deceived and led to expect benefits from claims more or less fictitious. Such agitation, often carried out by designing white men, is to be deplored, and should be discountenanced, as the Government of the country is at all times ready to protect the interests of the Indians and to redress real grievances where such are shown to exist.[57]

Finally, the committee argued that the Indians had given up the right to serious consideration, since they had rejected the conditions set out in the 1914 order-in-council and had continued to take up the time of the government and of Parliament with "irrelevant issues."[58]

The arguments of the special committee are easily characterized. They were quick and casual, displaying no concern for reasoned explanation that could withstand serious scrutiny. It is noteworthy that the committee did *not* raise two particular arguments. It did not suggest that the Proclamation of 1763 had not extended westward to the Pacific, and it did not assert that the passage of legislation in the colonies prior to 1871 had served to extinguish any aboriginal title that might have existed.[59]

The committee made two main recommendations. First, although it recognized no need for treaties in British Columbia, it suggested that the Indians should receive an annual allotment of $100,000 "in lieu of" treaty payments.[60] (The committee made no mention of other treaty benefits, such as greater reserve acreage.) The government implemented the $100,000 allocation, which became known as the "B.C. special."

The other, more sinister, recommendation has already been referred to; it was that land claim agitation should be "discountenanced." As early as 1924 Scott had proposed prohibiting Indians from paying lawyers to pursue claims without government approval.[61] Now Scott prepared an amendment to the Indian Act which Stewart introduced, and it was quickly passed by Parliament. Appropriately, it was inserted as section 141, next to section 140, the anti-potlatch provision. The amendment stated that

Every person who, without the consent of the Superintendent General expressed in writing, receives, obtains, solicits or requests from any Indian any payment or contribution or promise of any payment or contribution for the purpose of raising a fund or providing money for the prosecution of any claim which the tribe or band of Indians to which such Indian belongs, or of which he is a member, has or is represented to have for the recovery of any claim or money for the benefit of the said tribe or band, shall be guilty of an offence and liable upon summary conviction for each such offence to a penalty not exceeding two hundred dollars and not less than fifty dollars or to imprisonment for any term not exceeding two months.

The committee's recommendation had emphasized agitation by Whites, with persons such as O'Meara obviously in the thoughts of committee members. Section 141, however, applied to "every person," Indian or non-Indian. Had Scott and Stewart sought merely to prevent outside agitation, the amendment could easily have been phrased to apply only to persons who were not Indians. But their intent was to prevent all land claims activity and, above all, to block the British Columbia claim from getting to the Judicial Committee of the Privy Council. Striking at monetary exchanges, actual or promised, was chosen as the most expedient legal means to this end; monetary support was essential to land claims activities, and monetary exchanges could be identified and proven in court.

Without the minister's approval, no Indian or other person acting for the Allied Tribes or the Nisga'a Land Committee, for example, could now request or receive from any registered Indian any fee for legal or other services or any money for postage, travel, advertising, hall rental, refreshments, research expenses, legal fees, or court costs. The amendment quite simply made it impossible for any organization to exist if pursuing the land claim was one of its objectives.[62]

The addition of section 141 to the Indian Act evoked little discussion in Parliament or among white Canadians. It was taken for granted that Parliament had the right to curtail the rights and freedoms of Indians in ways that would not have been tolerated by Whites themselves. Much later, well after its repeal in 1951, the amendment was commonly looked back upon by British Columbia Whites, or at least by the few with reason to have heard of it, as having been merely intended to protect misguided Indians from conniving white lawyers.[63] Among British Columbia Indians the amendment is remembered much more intensely, and mention is often made of it in discussions of Indian political history. In Indian memories section 141 is usually linked with the potlatch prohibition, and the combination of the two produces the still common belief, which presumably existed from 1927 until 1951 as well, that any gathering of Indians or any discussion of land claims was illegal without the permission of a missionary, Indian agent, or police official.[64]

There is no certainty that the Allied Tribes would have survived 1927 even without the prohibition of claims activity. Section 141, however, was the hammer blow which abruptly ended the life of the organization. Nor is there certainty about the outcome had British Columbia Indians been free to pursue their claim through the courts. There was, however, some chance that the Judicial Committee of the Privy Council would have ruled that aboriginal title remained unextinguished in British Columbia, thus compelling the provincial and federal governments to negotiate agreements as stipulated in the Royal Proclamation of 1763. With the new amendment in place, however, it was illegal for the Indians to provide for any of the necessary steps to get their claims into court. From the white perspective, the Indian land question in British Columbia had been resolved.

CHAPTER NINE

Coastal Politics: The Native Brotherhood and Tribal Councils, 1931–58

Following the outlawing of claim-related political activity by Parliament in 1927 and the subsequent collapse of the Allied Tribes, the only Indian organization still existing was the Nisga'a Land Committee. It was quiescent, preparing no petitions, sending no delegations, and seeking no common action with neighbouring tribal groups. However, it remained a real entity within the Nass Valley; its name was still in use, and its leaders still had much influence among the Nisga'a.[1] The men who had been prominent within the Allied Tribes were no longer politically active. The aged Chief Chillihitza died in the 1930s, and no successor from the interior assumed his prominence (and none would do so until the 1950s). On the coast Peter Kelly returned full-time to the ministry,[2] travelling the coast in the mission boat *Thomas Crosby*, while Andrew Paull became a sports writer for the *Province* newspaper and a promoter of Indian activities from beauty pageants to lacrosse.[3]

Government Indian agents throughout the province were now at the height of their influence and control over the local Indian communities. The great majority of Indian children were now in the religious schools. In Ottawa, Duncan Campbell Scott approached retirement after a long and successful career. In British Columbia over the next half century, Whites growing up in the province or emigrating into it remained immersed in their own society's comforting myths and learned virtually nothing of Indian issues or past white policies towards Indians. Among white provincial politicians Indians and Indian issues now seemed either irrelevant or federal responsibilities. In 1927 the provincial government had still not even carried out the promise it had made upon entering Confederation to convey title of Indian reserves to the federal Crown (it finally did so in 1938 "after sixty-seven years of irresolution and vacillation").[4]

Thus, with aboriginal land claims suppressed, Indian political activity appeared at an end. Yet, a new political organization soon emerged on the north coast. It would provide both continuity and transition in British Columbia Indian political activity over the next three decades.

On the north coast the drawing of the Canadian-United States boundary south from the 60th parallel to form the Alaska Panhandle had divided the traditional territories of the Tlingit, Tahltan, Nisga'a, Tsimshian, and Haida. Neither the Tahltan nor the Nisga'a, however, had wintering villages on the Alaska side; while the one small Tlingit community in British Columbia, the Taku Tlingit, no longer had close ties with the coastal Tlingit in the northern portion of the Panhandle. Only the Haida and the Tsimshian had populations which remained in touch across the border. The main Tsimshian community in Alaska had been founded in the 1880s by the exodus from Metlakatla in British Columbia; the new village, also called Metlakatla, was some eighty miles by water from the old. The Haida were the only tribal group to have substantial populations on both sides. The Alaskan Haida, who occupied the southern portion of the Panhandle, were separated from those on the Queen Charlotte Islands by the forty-mile wide Dixon Entrance.

Except at Metlakatla, where one had been specially arranged by American authorities, there were no Indian reservations in Alaska. Everywhere else Whites could settle in Indian villages, and Indians could live among Whites. In this setting, hastened by the effects of government residential schools and of missionary activity (especially Presbyterian), assimilationist pan-Indianism appeared on the Panhandle by the turn of the century. Intriguingly enough, it was the Tsimshian from British Columbia who provided the single and notable exception; they did not participate in the pan-Indian outlook or in the resulting political organization in Alaska.[5]

The Alaska Native Brotherhood was founded in 1912 by a group of "highly acculturated individuals," most of whom were town dwellers who had attended the Sitka Training School and who were "inclined toward adoption of white standards and values."[6] The ANB's structure rested on local village branches called "camps," and its style resembled that of white "fraternal orders and similar groups."[7] Many ANB members were commercial fishermen and the organization's journal was called the "Alaska Fisherman." During its first decade the organization worked toward full citizenship rights (including the right to vote, which was attained), better education, and "abolition of aboriginal customs, or at least of those popularly regarded by Whites as 'savage' and 'uncivilized'."[8] As Philip Drucker observes, "both 'becoming civilized' and getting an education were thus necessary to achieve recognition of the Indian's claim to citizenship, the major landmark on the road to complete cultural assimilation."[9] Land claims were not an initial concern of the ANB, although by the 1930s the ANB and its leaders did support the formation of the Land Claims Association formed by Tlingit and Haida.[10]

The events in British Columbia leading to the formation of the Allied Tribes occurred simultaneously with the founding and early growth of the ANB. Yet, despite the continuing travel and communication across the border between Haida and Tsimshian, the political developments on the two sides were unrelated. The goals of the ANB and of the Allied Tribes were fundamentally different. As Drucker notes, with the Allied Tribes land claims "campaign running full blast," the British Columbia Indians did not "develop much interest in the A.N.B."[11]

After 1927, with land claims no longer possible in Canada and with the ANB regarded in Alaska as an effective vehicle for expressing Indian concerns, the ANB model appeared more relevant than it had previously to the British Columbia Haida and Tsimshian who were familiar with Alaska developments.[12] One of these was Alfred Adams, a commercial fisherman and lay minister within the Anglican church. His home village was Masset, on the north coast of the Queen Charlottes within sight of Alaska. Adams maintained contact with relatives in Alaska, and he had attended several ANB conventions.

In the autumn of 1931 Adams invited the leading Canadian Tsimshian chiefs, almost all of whom were commercial fisherman, to come to Port Simpson in December to discuss forming a new Canadian organization. The meeting formed the Native Brotherhood of British Columbia, which was seen by its founders as a vehicle for continuing the ideals of the Allied Tribes while avoiding any explicit pursuit of the now-prohibited land claim. The founding meeting approved a petition "as representative of our grievances" that included requests for better schooling, for increased recognition of aboriginal rights in hunting, fishing, trapping, and timber-harvesting in off-reserve traditional lands, and for a meeting with Ottawa officials.

As Drucker notes, "these requests resemble and in some cases duplicate the demands made by the Allied Tribes in 1926."[13] But he quite fails to observe that the Native Brotherhood had to cope with being prohibited from devoting any of its activities or resources to pursuing the land claim.[14] Nevertheless, there is no evidence that Native Brotherhood leaders or supporters ever waivered in their belief in aboriginal title, which remained the unspoken premise in the brotherhood's early efforts to gain increased recognition of the right to carry on aboriginal activities on non-reserve lands. Thus, the principles of the Native Brotherhood of British Columbia were the opposite of the those of the Alaska Native Brotherhood. The British Columbia leaders opposed assimilation and favoured "retention of the native's identity, racially and culturally."[15]

The basic units in the structure of the British Columbia organization were village "branches" composed of dues-paying members, with each branch entitled to send equal numbers of delegates to the annual convention, at which the executive body was elected.[16] The executive, however, included a number of vice-presidents, each representing a tribal group. The role of vice-presidents was more than symbolic, as is indicated by James Sewid's comments about being chosen Kwagiulth vice-president: "I was glad to be elected because I always liked to work for my people and I felt they should be represented. It was a big area that I represented and the grievances of my people must be heard truly. I felt that was the only way we could get what we wanted . . . I had to carry all the load of the tribes of the Kwakiutl nation."[17]

Expanding the Brotherhood thus involved setting up branches in new villages as well as attaining the support of chiefs prominent within their tribal groups. Following the 1931 meeting two prominent Tsimshian chiefs, Heber Clifton of Hartley Bay and Edward Gamble of Kitkatla, served as the major organizers. Both were commercial fishermen with their own boats. Clifton, in particular, "put his seine boat at the disposal of the officers of the Brotherhood on numerous lengthy proselytizing trips."[18] By 1936 the Brotherhood was well established on the central and north coasts among the Tsimshian, who seemed to provide the strongest reservoir of support, and the Gitksan, Heiltsuk, Nuxalk, and Haisla.

There were two north coast holdouts. Despite the strong support given by Masset to the Brotherhood and to Adams, who was now president, no support was forthcoming from Skidegate, the other major Haida community, or from its most prominent citizen, Peter Kelly. Nor was there any support from the Nass. The Nisga'a Land Committee refused to allow the Nisga'a villages to participate in any organization that would not take a stand, however futile, on aboriginal land title.[19]

During its first decade the Brotherhood developed several major policy positions. It continued to advocate greater acknowledgement of aboriginal rights; it supported legalizing the potlatch; it favoured replacing the residential schools with day schools in the villages; and it opposed the singling out of Indians for prohibition against alcohol consumption. Brotherhood leaders gave advice and assistance to individual Indians, often commercial fishermen, having problems with government, and annual conventions became important forums for communicating with government officials. Federal officials, especially those responsible for fisheries and Indian affairs, seemed to welcome the opportunity to give speeches and to respond to questions from the audience. In this way the Brotherhood came to play a major role in keeping officials and Indians informed about one another's concerns and in maintaining an atmosphere of some cordiality between the two groups.[20] The prominence of prayers and hymns in the conventions did not detract from the respect the officials evinced toward the Brotherhood and its leaders, nor did the fact that convention delegates were invariably well dressed in suits and ties.[21]

Major changes occurred within the Brotherhood during the early 1940s. The federal government's decision to start imposing income tax on Indian commercial fisherman was seen as an attack not only on income but also on the principle that fish belonged to Indians and not to the government. Seizing upon the issue, Andrew Paull returned to politics and joined the Brotherhood; at the 1942 convention he was appointed to the new position of business agent. Turning his abundant energies to the task and capitalizing upon his own great popularity among the Coast Salish and his close friendship with some of the Kwagiulth leaders (especially Dan Assu of Cape Mudge), Paull quickly organized a number of Brotherhood branches on the south coast. For some years the Kwagiulth had had their own Pacific Coast Native Fishermen's Association. In effect, the association merged with the Brotherhood, bringing commercial fishing concerns even more to the fore. Eventually, the Brotherhood itself assumed the role of fishermen's union, acting as bargaining agent for Indian commercial fishermen. While this role came to be the one most visible to outside observers, the Brotherhood continued to concern itself with the full range of Indian issues. As James Sewid said of Brotherhood conventions, "We were able to talk to the government about the old age pensions, the fish prices, the liquor rights for Indians, and the land question."[22] Hugh Braker has shown, indeed, that more than half the resolutions in conventions dealt not with fishing but with general aboriginal issues.[23]

It was also in 1942 that the Nisga'a Land Committee relented and a Brotherhood branch was established at Greenville. Arthur Calder, now in his mid-seventies, attended the meeting, as did several others who had been active in the committee in its early years. Coming onto the political stage at this time was twenty-nine-year-old Frank Calder, who was appointed secretary of the Greenville branch. Frank was the adoptive son of Arthur and his wife Louisa. As the eldest of six sisters in the leading family in their clan, Louisa would bequeath high chiefly rank to a son. When Arthur and Louisa's own son died in childhood, the couple had followed Nisga'a custom by adopting the son of Louisa's youngest sister, Emily. Much of young Frank's political education had taken place during summers home from school on Arthur Calder's fishing boat, where politics was a frequent conversational topic among the men and where Arthur and other elders had instructed him in his future obligations as a Nisga'a leader. In 1937 he had graduated from Coqualeetza school; among his many school friends from the north coast was Alfred Adam's son Oliver.[24]

Over ensuing years and decades the Native Brotherhood remained a strong and stable organization. In 1946 the monthly *Native Voice* began publication. While it was initially owned and managed by a white woman, Maisie Hurley,[25] the paper was always closely linked with the Brotherhood. Brotherhood membership now included an automatic subscription to the *Native Voice*, and this fact brought the Brotherhood increased membership on the coast and a sprinkling of members in the interior.

Peter Kelly came into the Brotherhood in the mid-1940s, after Alfred Adams' death. The new position of chairman of the legislative committee was created specifically for him. Henceforward, the three main positions of influence within the Brotherhood would be president, secretary, and chairman of the committee. Kelly brought new prominence to the Brotherhood, as the organization did to him. He remained active as chairman of the committee almost until his death in 1966, often outshining the Brotherhood president. At about the time of Kelly's entry, Frank Calder, now a graduate from the Anglican School of Theology at the University of British Columbia, became secretary of the organization.[26] During the 1950s and 1960s William Scow, the best-known Kwagiulth chief, and Guy Williams, the leading Haisla, each served active and lengthy terms as president.

Despite sporadic and half-hearted forays into the interior, the Brotherhood did not ever expand beyond its coastal base; nor, on the coast, did it ever receive from the Salish or Nuu'chah'nulth in the south the degree of commitment it could rely on from groups on the central and north coasts. The Brotherhood's founding base on the central and north coasts linked the organization most firmly to that part of the province, and Protestantism cemented the linkage. The Brotherhood's opposition to residential schools provided an early indication of the role of religion and geography in affecting political outlook. As Drucker observes, the Brotherhood's position was seen by Catholic Indians "and by their missionaries as well, as an attack on the Roman Catholic residential school system" and this perception "completely prevented organization of the interior Indians" by the Brotherhood.[27] In George Manuel's words, "The Native Brotherhood never did become as strong in the interior as the Allied Tribes had been because of their identification with commercial fishing and with Protestantism."[28]

Nevertheless, the Native Brotherhood was, and remained, a highly successful organization. No other aboriginal organization in the country could match its strength and stability. While a few organizations existed elsewhere in the country at the time of its founding, none survived continuously. By the 1960s it was the longest-lived aboriginal organization in Canada, and it still remains vigourous.

Andrew Paull and Dan Assu travelled to Ottawa in 1943 on behalf of the Brotherhood to take part in a fisheries conference sponsored by the federal government. The two went on to Montreal to attend a meeting organized by non-treaty Indians interested in forming a national Indian organization to seek changes in the Indian Act. Paull emerged from the meeting as president of the Brotherhood of Canadian Indians. One year later, at a convention in Ontario, Paull was re-elected for a five-year term, and the name of the organization was changed to North American Indian Brotherhood (NAIB). The NAIB had an extremely loose structure, based on individual members, who did not have to pay dues.[29] The lack of structure allowed maximum freedom, and maximum publicity, for Andrew Paull. As E.P. Patterson states, "the NAIB was not a group for which Paull spoke—it was the means which made it possible for him to be heard,"[30] and as George Manuel confirms, "there was no doubt that the North American Brotherhood was always a support group for Andy Paull's own powerful and unique personality."[31]

Meanwhile, relations between Paull and the north coast leadership of the Native Brotherhood were not going well. He had opened a Native Brotherhood office in Vancouver in 1942, which shifted emphasis to the south coast and kept him from close contact with the leadership. Being in Vancouver allowed Paull to deal with government officials in the name of the Brotherhood and gave him ready access to trains to the interior and to eastern Canada. He continued to write for the *Province*. (Paull had always been friend and mentor to many other Indians; from 1942 to 1946 his Brotherhood and newspaper offices served as a meeting place for other politically inclined Indians, including Frank Calder while he was attending the University of British Columbia.) In 1945 matters came to a head with allegations that Paull could not account for Brotherhood funds. He was dismissed as business agent and quit the Brotherhood.[32] He was replaced by Guy Williams, then in his late thirties.

Paull now turned his attention to the Indians of the interior, primarily the Nlaka'pamux and the Shuswap, the two Salish tribal groups most easily reached by rail from Vancouver. Over the next decade he became the main political spokesman for interior Indians. Most, if not all, of his speeches and other activity took place in Kamloops, which was both an established meeting place and an especially convenient location for him, since he could arrive on the afternoon train, give a speech in the evening, and take the night train back to Vancouver. Calder made some of these trips with him. One of Paull's first actions was to arrange the formation of an organization called the Confederacy of the Interior Tribes of British Columbia.[33]

Like the NAIB, the Confederacy had only a tenuous formal structure; it existed principally in the form of meetings at which speeches were made. The NAIB continued to exist, with Paull making periodic trips to the east to give it publicity and also making speeches on its behalf in Kamloops. Within British Columbia the NAIB did not expand beyond its Salishan base in the interior and on the south coast. Henry Castillou, a white Williams Lake lawyer, served as legal and political adviser to Paull and the NAIB. Catholicism was an element of the NAIB, with clergy often present at its meetings.[34]

The rivalry between the Native Brotherhood and the NAIB/Confederacy became explicit in 1947 over two issues. Under pressure from the federal government, which was seeking a favourable international image, especially in the new United Nations, the provincial legislature was considering repeal of the legislation that prohibited voting in provincial and municipal elections by persons of Chinese, Japanese, and Indo-Pakistani descent. Neither the federal government nor native Indians themselves had proposed that the same prohibition against Indians' voting be repealed, but the idea now occurred to various white politicians.

Believing that the provincial franchise could not threaten existing Indian rights and privileges, which were a federal matter, the Native Brotherhood promptly endorsed the proposal.[35] Andrew Paull and the NAIB just as promptly rejected it on the grounds that it would open the door to assimilation and loss of rights and privileges. After several weeks of public disagreement between the Native Brotherhood and Paull, the legislature removed all racial restrictions from the provincial franchise, thus granting Indians the vote.[36] (The prohibition against Indian pre-emption of crown lands still remained in effect; it was repealed in 1953 when the action was of little practical consequence since most of the available land had already been pre-empted.)[37]

In 1947 a special joint parliamentary committee in Ottawa was considering amendments to the Indian Act. Since the Native Brotherhood was the only Indian organization the committee was aware of in British Columbia, it invited it to send a spokesmen to the committee hearings on behalf of all Indians in the province. Guy Williams appeared before the committee in Ottawa on 2 May. One month later, on 3 July, Frank Assu (a Kwagiulth from the coast and brother of Paull's close friend Dan Assu) held a meeting of the Confederacy of Interior Tribes in Kamloops. It was attended by twenty-four persons, most of whom were Shus-

wap and eight of whom were band chiefs. They signed a petition objecting to the Native Brotherhood's having been accepted as British Columbia spokesman. "We wish to say that the Native Brotherhood of B.C. did
not represent our views or opinions and that their delegates did not
have our permission to speak for us and that Guy Williams . . . did not
speak for us, and that we repudiate everything he said."[38]

The Confederacy of the Interior Tribes continued to hold sporadic
meetings, and Paull continued to give occasional speeches in Kamloops
into the mid-1950s, but neither the Confederacy nor Paull's NAIB took
any important political action. Paull, however, retained a wide following
among interior Indians and undoubtedly played a major role in educating and inspiring many of them concerning their history and their
aboriginal rights.

In the provincial election campaign of 1949 Frank Calder ran successfully as a Co-operative Commonwealth Federation candidate in the
Atlin riding, in which Indians were a majority of the population. He was
the first Indian elected to any post-Confederation Canadian legislature.[39] In the campaign, in gratitude for the Indian franchise, the Native
Brotherhood had endorsed the governing Liberal-Conservative coalition rather than Calder's CCF. Before the election of 1951, Guy Williams
attempted to form the Indian Non-Partisan Party among brotherhood
supporters.[40] Calder and the Nisga'a would have nothing to do with the
idea, and nothing came of it. Williams' attempt was a new departure,
one pointing to the opportunities and pitfalls opened by the provincial
franchise. As it turned out, Indians chose to work within the established
political parties and no further attempt was ever made to form an
Indian political party.

Parliament amended the Indian Act in 1951 to remove the prohibi-
'tions against the potlatch and against claims-related activities. Federal
officials apparently assumed that British Columbia Indians had by this
time realized the futility of pursuing the land claim. In one sense, the
prohibitions were removed because it was thought they had had their
effect and were no longer needed. Another motive was to remove a
potential cause of embarrassment in the liberal post-war international
climate of racial tolerance. It was also the case that the Judicial Committee of the Privy Council had ceased to be Canada's highest appeal court
in 1949; there was now no danger from the judicial committee should
the Indians go to court.

Frank Calder's membership in the legislature[41] gave him a platform to
speak out on Indian issues across Canada. He made several speaking
trips across the country in the early 1950s and also travelled in the
United States, gaining knowledge of the tribal councils existing among
some of the larger tribes. During these years the *Native Voice* contained

many articles on Indian political and other organizations in Canada and the United States. In 1953 and 1954 Calder devoted some effort to forming a "National Congress of Canadian Indians,"[42] but when he was unsuccessful, he turned to reforming the political organization of his own Nisga'a people.

Only someone of Calder's stature among the Nisga'a could have succeeded in uniting the four clans (Eagle, Wolf, Raven, and Killer Whale) and the four communities (Kincolith, Greenville, Canyon City, and Aiyansh). The Nisga'a Land Committee was no longer functioning and for years there had been no effective Nisga'a tribal authority.[43] Calder eventually gained the consent of the four clans and the four villages to form a tribal council. He stressed two points: the tribal council would be a continuation of the land committee, and it would work towards resolving the Nisga'a land claim.[44]

The tribal council differed from the land committee in being an organization of the Nisga'a people themselves and not merely of the leaders; every individual had one vote in council assemblies. Popular equality was not yet something widely approved of among the Nisga'a; Calder had his work cut out for him in gaining its acceptance. In the end it was agreed that the executive would consist of president and several other executive officers elected by the assembly, along with five vice-presidents, one chosen by each of the villages and one by Nisga'a who resided in Prince Rupert. Calder was elected president. In the first constitution a number of social, economic, and political objectives were listed, including the negotiation of "a settlement of the Nishga Land Question." In 1963 the tribal council formally incorporated itself under the provincial Societies Act. The request for incorporation was signed by James Gosnell (Aiyansh), Hubert Doolan (Prince Rupert), Roy Azak (Canyon City), William McKay (Greenville), and Jeffrey Benson (Kincolith). Each listed his occupation as "fisherman."[45]

Arthur Calder had played the leading part in forming the Nisga'a Land Committee, which had had a profound impact on the political outlook and activities of British Columbia Indians. But the land committee, along with the Allied Tribes, had failed to change the outlook of government. Frank Calder now led the Nisga'a into the next major stage in their political evolution. The new Nisga'a institution would come to have as great an impact as its predecessor among British Columbia Indians, and it would ultimately cause a fundamental change in the federal policy concerning aboriginal title in non-treaty areas of the country.

The *Native Voice* published articles about the formation and activities of the Nisga'a Tribal Council, while Native Brotherhood conventions enabled members of other coastal tribal groups to discuss the new body with leading members of the council. The Nuu'chah'nulth formed their tribal council in 1958. For some years they had held annual assemblies arranged by the chiefs at which the "B.C. special" grant in lieu of treaty moneys was distributed to members. In 1958 an Indian sports festival, financed by grants from the provincial government to commemorate the centenary of the creation of British Columbia, was held in Port Alberni as part of the annual assembly and for this reason it was especially well attended.

During the proceedings Jack Peter, a chief and a Native Brotherhood vice-president for the Nuu'chah'nulth tribal group, proposed the formation of a tribal council. In the resulting discussion one of the speakers was thirteen-year-old George Watts, who raised questions about the financing of the new organization. The proposal was approved and the tribal council was named the Allied Tribes of the West Coast. Its structure and goals were similar to those of the Nisga'a Tribal Council. Peter was elected president and William Tatoosh was elected vice-president.[46]

The Nisga'a Tribal Council and the Allied Tribes of the West Coast (which eventually changed its name to Nuu'chah'nulth Tribal Council) both proved to be stable and permanent organizations; both had important effects on Indian outlook and political activities throughout the province; and both produced leaders of province-wide and nation-wide reputation and influence. Compared to the Nisga'a communities, however, those of the Nuu'chah'nulth were more numerous and more dispersed, and political unity among them took longer to attain.

Each of the new coastal tribal councils was formed exclusively by Indians themselves and for their own purposes. They were not responding to any parliamentary enquiry, to any government initiative, or to any other outside exigency. They were seeking political forms which reflected their own understandings and perceptions about their identity, and it was the tribal group which they accepted as the basis of that identity. The two tribal councils thus marked a departure from the Indian Act and from Department of Indian Affairs administration, neither of which acknowledged the existence of tribal groups. Both tribal councils emerged under the umbrella of the Native Brotherhood, which manifested a pan-Indianism based on traditional groupings, and both were returning to the tribalism which had been the original foundation of Indian political organization in British Columbia.

CHAPTER TEN

Interior Politics and Attempts at Province-Wide Unity, 1958–68

Only two dominating political figures have emerged among the Indian peoples of the British Columbia interior. One was the Okanagan Chief Chillihitza, who played the leading part in the Okanagan-Shuswap "confederacy" that so alarmed Whites in the 1870s, who went to London in 1906 as part of the delegation of Salish chiefs, and who opposed Peter Kelly and Andrew Paull before the special parliamentary committee in 1927. He was unable or unwilling to extend his influence beyond the Salish groups in the southern interior, and his upbringing had not provided him with the fluency in English or, apparently, a close understanding of Canadian law and politics. He was very much the traditional leader. Duane Thomson observes that Chillihitza was one of the few interior chiefs to avoid becoming "pathetic figureheads" dependent upon white officials and missionaries, but that even "with his strong sense of traditional authority," he was "eventually destroyed by the twin forces of Indian agent and federal bureaucracy."[1]

George Manuel became the pre-eminent leader of the peoples of the interior.[2] In the history of British Columbia his place is equal to those of the three great leaders who emerged on the coast, Peter Kelly, Andrew Paull, and Frank Calder. In a sense, however, Manuel's personal accomplishment is greater than theirs, for he had neither their tribal political traditions nor their formal education to build upon, and, unlike them, he began his political efforts at the community level, where, like Chillihitza, he had to contend with the pervasive control of government officials. Within British Columbia, Manuel's influence never extended beyond the interior and south coast; on the wider Canadian and international stages, however, his influence and accomplishments remain unrivalled among Indians in all of Canada.[3]

Manuel was born in 1921 in the Shuswap community of Neskainlith, across the South Thompson River from the village of Chase, some thirty-five miles east of Kamloops on the Trans-Canada Highway and the main line of the Canadian Pacific Railway. In his early years he was raised more by his grandparents than by his own parents.[4] He was taken at the age of seven to the Kamloops Indian Residential School, where he was bitterly unhappy. His memories are of having to speak English and of seeing other children being beaten.[5] When he developed mastoiditis, he was held without anaesthetic over a table and operated on by a priest using a knife; the operation left permanent disfiguring scars. Subsequently, when he developed tuberculosis in the bones of his legs, he was transferred to the Methodist "preventorium" at Coqualeetza in the Lower Fraser Valley.

Manuel's formal schooling was never resumed, although the preventorium staff, whom he found friendly and supportive, did make some effort to improve his reading and writing. His formative years were thus spent away from his home and family in confinement with children from all parts of the province. The Coqualeetza preventorium was one of the very few settings, if not the only one, in which children from the Catholic zone were placed in the care of Protestant missionary personnel and in which children from both zones were brought together. He came to regard the tuberculosis, which left him with permanently weakened legs, as having saved him from an obsequious passivity that would have been inculcated by the Kamloops school.

Back home in the late 1940s and early 1950s, Manuel proved far from obsequious or passive. He became chief of his band and sought better links between his people and the local white community. Among his activities was coaching a junior ice hockey team with white and Indian players. Although no great skater himself, Manuel was a popular and effective coach. Local Whites regarded him as a forthright and friendly man, and he formed lasting friendships with some of them.[6]

The absence of adequate health services for Indians became Manuel's special concern. The Department of Indian Affairs paid for only some of these services, and the Neskainlith people had to travel to Kamloops for medical attention and there go to one particular physician, on contract with DIA, whom both the Indians and local Whites regarded as second rate. Manuel was the only chief in the agency ready to criticize DIA officials openly; he did so first over the medical issue and subsequently over others. White agency officials labelled him a marxist.[7] On the other hand, the Conservative MP for Kamloops, Davie Fulton, admired Manuel and often sent him governmental and other material relating to Indian affairs. (Fulton was the grandson of Alex Davie, the provincial attorney-general and foe of aboriginal title in 1887.) Manuel assumed that Fulton was the anonymous sender of a Conservative party membership card, which he was rather pleased to receive.[8] The "Marxist" was thus, in fact, a Conservative party cardholder.

Manuel hitchhiked to other Indian communities to examine the adequacy of their medical services. Realizing that all had the same problems, he organized Indian demands for better services. He soon came to believe that the best political vehicle for Indian interests would be a province-wide Indian organization. He knew something of the Allied Tribes and was critical of Chillihitza's attitude toward Peter Kelly and Andrew Paull. While they never actually met, Manuel was a great admirer of Paull. As he would later state, "Although Peter Kelly's name became a household word in every Indian home on the coast, it was Andy Paull whom we came to know and love in the interior."[9] Unlike Paull, Manuel was a thorough organizer, aware that any effective organization had to be built upon strength at the community level. Among the most influential of those advising Manuel by this time was Henry Castillou, the white Williams Lake lawyer who had previously advised Andrew Paull; from him Manuel gained his knowledge of the legal side of the land question. In 1958 Manuel and the Native Brotherhood agreed to promote coastal-interior co-operation,[10] and the idea emerged of holding the 1959 Brotherhood annual convention in Kamloops.

John Diefenbaker's Conservatives had now replaced the Liberals in Ottawa, and Davie Fulton was federal minister of justice. Another joint parliamentary committee was formed to consider Indian policy. In the autumn of 1958 Manuel began hitchhiking throughout the central and southern interior and the Lower Fraser Valley persuading people to attend the Brotherhood convention and getting their ideas as he prepared a brief he hoped to present to the joint committee.

Manuel was joined in his efforts by Oscar Peters, chief of the Hope band. Peters was a vice-president of the Native Brotherhood and one of the few Coast Salish leaders active in that organization. As the easternmost Coast Salish community, Hope had many contacts and much in common with the neighbouring Interior Salish peoples, especially with Nlaka'pamux bands of the Fraser Canyon. Manuel and Peters organized several intertribal meetings, and at one of these, in late 1958, the "Aboriginal Native Rights Committee of the Interior Tribes of British Columbia" was formed, with Peters elected as chairman. The committee held a large meeting at Hope in early 1959. Besides Manuel and Peters, those who brought supporters to this meeting were Clarence Joe of Sechelt, Genevieve Mussell of the Skwah community at Chilliwack,[11] William Walkem of Spences Bridge, and Charles Brown of Lytton.[12] The meeting was thus composed of Salish people—Nlaka'pamux and Shuswap from the interior and mainland Salish from the coast.

The Hope meeting discussed the outline of the brief to be presented to the special joint committee and also considered whether a new organization should be constituted. Andrew Paull was now seriously ill, and nothing had been heard for some time of his North American Indian Brotherhood. Some speakers at the Hope meeting wanted to revive the NAIB; others, including Manuel, disagreed. Manuel later explained, "if we were ever again to bring Indian people together in our own province, we must do so under a banner that had not yet become identified with any leader, faction, or position."[13] It was decided to continue using the name "Aboriginal Native Rights Committee." The term "committee" was now seen as a compromise, intended to indicate something less than a full-blown organization. The term "tribe" appears to have been generally used to mean "band" or "community."

The term "interior" was a cause of confusion, if not at the time, then among later students of the events, for it was now used to include the Lower Fraser Valley. During the following decade the same usage continued among the political leaders of the areas involved, with the Coast Salish areas of Hope, Chilliwack, and even Vancouver being included within the meaning of the term. This usage was both a recognition of the common outlook of Salish peoples and a response to the association of the word "coastal" with the Protestant and more politically active Native Brotherhood and tribal groups of the central and north coasts. In any case, Manuel and other spokesmen now included the Coast Salish peoples of the Lower Fraser Valley when they used such terms as "interior tribes" or "interior peoples."

The 1959 convention of the Native Brotherhood in Kamloops proved to be of pivotal political significance.[14] In fact, the meeting was more than a convention of one organization; it was the most substantial and representative Indian gathering yet held in the province, having as its only predecessors one or two assemblies of the Allied Tribes. It revealed above all that the aboriginal land claim was still the primary political concern of British Columbia Indians. Some of those present, including Manuel and Frank Calder,[15] were aware that the assembly presented the first opportunity since 1927 to revive the goals of the Allied Tribes. The attempt was personified, or so it initially appeared to both Manuel and Calder, in Peter Kelly, now seventy-four years old and the dominating Native Brotherhood leader.

Three groupings were evident: the Native Brotherhood, led by Kelly; the Nisga'a Tribal Council, with eight chiefs present, led by Calder; and the Aboriginal Rights Committee, led by Manuel. Although the Nisga'a were also members of the Brotherhood, they regarded themselves as a distinct entity and were accepted as such by the others. Manuel and Calder each came to the assembly expecting that the Native Brotherhood would revise its own goals and structure to transform itself into a truly province-wide organization, and Manuel was prepared to merge the Aboriginal Rights Committee into the Brotherhood. The immediate aim of both Calder and Manuel was to have the Native Brotherhood appear before the parliamentary committee on behalf of all British Columbia Indians in order to demonstrate that political unity had been attained.[16] The principal goal of both Calder and Manuel, however, was to have the expanded Native Brotherhood resume the pursuit of the land claim that had been interrupted in 1927.

Assembly discussion soon made clear that Kelly and other Brotherhood leaders were unwilling to welcome Manuel and his interior group as equal partners within a restructured organization. To their disappointment, Calder and Manuel also realized that Kelly was not prepared to lead the Brotherhood in renewed pursuit of the land claim. At several points during the heated discussion the Nisga'a came close to walking out of the meeting and thus out of the Brotherhood itself. None of the three groups was satisfied with the assembly. The only agreement was Kelly's promise to return to the interior to consult with Manuel and to travel to the Nass to consult with the Nisga'a before making the Brotherhood's presentation to the parliamentary committee. Kelly did travel to Aiyansh, but he further angered the Nisga'a by refusing to commit the Brotherhood to the land claim. Kelly did not consult with Manuel or communicate with him in any way after the assembly.

The 1959 assembly had two outcomes: it led the Nisga'a to develop their own independent land claim, and it led Manuel to form a new interior political organization.

Manuel redoubled his hitchhiking efforts, and with the help of Castillou and others, he began preparing the final version of the brief to be presented to the joint committee in Ottawa in the spring of 1960. Following Andrew Paull's death later in the year, Manuel regarded himself as having taken Paull's place in the interior. He organized a meeting at Kamloops in early 1960 that resolved to reconstitute (or, in the view of some of those present, to carry on) the North American Indian Brotherhood. As Manuel later explained, "we felt we should organize into the North American Indian Brotherhood, which was Andy Paull's organization, because we did not wish to see it die."[17] The group elected Manuel as president.

Although some of those active in the new NAIB believed that Andrew Paull had on his deathbed named Manuel as his successor,[18] there is no evidence of any direct organizational link, aside from the continuing role of Henry Castillou, between Paull's NAIB and Manuel's NAIB. In his biography of Paull, E.P. Patterson makes no mention of Manuel, and states that he could find no evidence of "the continuance of Paull's organization."[19]

Manuel's NAIB was the first substantial Indian organization of the interior. It was composed of individual members; it had no local or branch structure. It was the first British Columbia Indian political organization to have women (Guertrude Guerin, of Musqueam, and Genevieve Mussell) in executive positions. Its strongest initial membership support was among the Shuswap, Nlaka'pamux, and Lillooet in the interior and among the Coast Salish along the Lower Fraser River. Andrew Paull's Squamish community and those on the Sechelt Peninsula seem to have avoided the new NAIB completely. There was scattered support among the Chilcotin and several of the Carrier groups, but none was sought among the coastal groups supporting the Native Brotherhood.

Leonard Marchand, twenty-seven years old in 1960, was one of the few Okanagans who was active in the new NAIB. He had attended the Kamloops residential school before transferring to the Vernon public high school, which was near his home reserve. He went on to the University of British Columbia, where he studied agriculture and became, in 1959, the first interior Indian to graduate from a university. Subsequently, he obtained his master's degree from the University of Idaho. He played a major part in preparing the Ottawa brief. In early 1960, despite his qualifications, he was unemployed.

In presenting the brief to the parliamentary committee in Ottawa, Manuel adopted Chillihitza's 1927 strategy; he listed the bands he had consulted that had given support to his brief. On his list were twelve of the twenty Coast Salish bands along the Lower Fraser, eleven of the seventeen southern Carrier bands, every Chilcotin and Lillooet band, fourteen of the eighteen Shuswap bands, nine of the fifteen Nlaka'pamux bands, and every Kootenay band. He had not done well among the Okanagan; he claimed partial support among three of the six bands.[20] As Manuel spoke, he noticed Frank Calder in the audience and invited him to sit at the witness table "to help us on the question of Indian lands, because he is quite familiar with it."[21] Calder accepted the invitation.

Manuel's presentation was lengthy and detailed. He discussed social and economic needs of interior Indians, commented on various aspects of the Indian Act and of DIA administration, and pointed out that interior Indians lacked the sort of economic base that the fishing industry provided to coastal Indians, which allowed them to organize politically. He gave the greatest emphasis, however, to aboriginal title and the need to resolve the issue in a way satisfactory to Indians and to federal and provincial governments. In preparing the sections on aboriginal title, Manuel, Castillou, and Marchand had used the *Papers Connected with the Indian Land Question, 1850-1875*, which H.H. Stevens and the special committee had kept from Paull and Kelly in 1927.[22] Manuel stated:

The Indians of the Interior still feel strongly about the Indian land question in British Columbia, both as to the allocation of land to the reserves by the Provincial and Dominion governments, and as to compensation for British Columbia lands which they consider are not as yet constitutionally surrendered with commensurate compensation to their peoples . . . The gist of the claims is as follows: That the various nations or tribes have aboriginal title to certain territories within the province, which, to perfect the Crown title in the right of the province, should be extinguished by treaty providing for compensation for such extinguishment . . . The British Columbia Interior Indians who submit this brief affirm that we wish to keep our chiefs and councillors, our lands and our hereditary privileges of hunting, trapping, and fishing, also our water and grazing rights. That is, as a group, we wish to live as Indians with our separate identity, and our traditional way of life. But we are eager to cooperate with other people of Canada where our mutual interests naturally merge. We believe that this statement, coming from us directly, will clear away any misunderstanding that may exist.[23]

After his presentation, Manuel gave well-informed answers to questions from committee members, none of whom was at all knowledgeable about the Indian land question. Manuel mentioned Marchand's unemployment as an example of the difficulties facing even well-qualified Indians. Fulton learned of Manuel's comment, and Marchand soon obtained a position at the federal agricultural research station at Kamloops.

In 1960 Parliament passed a government bill granting status Indians the right to vote in federal elections. The legislation was a product of Diefenbaker and Fulton's view that Indians should have political equality without reduction in status or aboriginal rights. Subsequently the government let it be known that it was considering the creation of some mechanism or procedure to deal with Indian land claims.

For the next three years the new North American Indian Brotherhood was active under Manuel's leadership. There were meetings at various localities throughout the year and there were well-attended annual conventions. Manuel continued to state his preference for common political action by all British Columbia Indians. He made the need for common action the theme of his address to the NAIB's convention at Chilliwack in March 1963, and he pressed the point in the following months.

In 1963 Lester Pearson's Liberals replaced the Conservatives in Ottawa and promised to establish an Indian claims commission. This promise generated much discussion, and even some optimism, within the NAIB, the Native Brotherhood, and the Nisga'a Tribal Council. Apparently Manuel, Calder, and Guy Williams, who had become Native Brotherhood president in 1960, agreed that their three organizations would consult each other before taking any action on land claims.

Then, in the early autumn of 1963, Manuel stunned his followers by resigning abruptly from the presidency and from the NAIB itself. At the same time he joined the Native Brotherhood, stating that "I have decided to join the ranks of those Indians who have the desire to see provincial unity for all the Indians of B.C." He also said: "Our most pressing needs are the Indian Land Question and the settlement of Indian claims. These questions are of equal concern to all Indians of our province, regardless of our cultural background, regardless of whether we live in the Interior, along the Pacific Coast, or in the timberlands of the north."[24] There seems now to be no adequate explanation for Manuel's action.[25] There is no indication that he was losing support within the NAIB or that there was any personal or policy disagreement between him and other executive members. His resignation did come when plans were well advanced for an NAIB delegation to travel to Ottawa and to the United Nations headquarters in New York to seek further recognition of aboriginal rights. The delegation did make the trip, under Castillou. Williams and Calder each sought to undermine the delegation by sending telegrams to Pearson pointing out that Manuel had resigned, that the delegation was not led by an Indian, and that the NAIB was in breach of the earlier agreement to refrain from unilateral action.[26]

Manuel's move to the Native Brotherhood did not prove successful or of consequence.[27] Much weakened by Manuel's departure, the NAIB continued to exist under the successive presidencies of Benjamin Paul of the Lower Fraser Valley and Gus Gottfriedson of Kamloops. Marchand remained an active member. Manuel was politically inactive for a year or so, at least outside his own band, and then began re-establishing his political contacts. His resignation seems not to have affected his personal popularity in the southern interior.

Under the stimulus of federal government interest in establishing an Indian claims commission, the period commencing in 1964 was a time of hectic and unprecedented political activity among British Columbia Indians, or at least among the leaders of the organizations. New leaders appeared and new organizations formed, including a new tribal council among Coast Salish on Vancouver Island, the Southern Vancouver Island Tribal Federation. Caught up in the frenetic round of events, the leaders, old and new, at times found themselves making hasty statements or quick commitments that they, or, more often, their supporters, came to regret.

In early 1965 the federal government introduced Bill C-123 to establish the Indian Claims Commission and to provide for financial assistance to Indian groups in preparing and presenting their claims. Guy Williams and Frank Calder responded with distrust and criticism, believing that the government was seeking to impose terms of settlement unilaterally. In July the Nisga'a Tribal Council executive proposed that "the recognized Indian organizations consider the advisability of a federation of their executive committees to form the British Columbia Indian land question committee."[28] Similar sentiments were by now evident among NAIB supporters.

In Ottawa DIA officials felt that the Indians had no cause for alarm, but they were finding it more and more difficult to keep abreast of the accelerating twists and turns in British Columbia Indian politics. Agency officials were by this time required to hold meetings of chiefs, but these meetings, which came to be called "district councils," were not proving useful to senior officials as a source of information about what was really going on among Indians.[29] In 1965, to provide a direct channel of information to Ottawa, Len Marchand was appointed special assistant to J.R. Nicholson, the Vancouver MP who was minister of Indian affairs. Marchand was the first Indian ever appointed to the staff of a federal minister; he retained the position when Arthur Laing, another Vancouver MP, became minister the following year. Over the ensuing two decades, as British Columbia Indian politics gave no sign of becoming easier for outsiders to comprehend, the practice of appointing a young Indian from the province to the minister's Ottawa staff was continued.

The Confederation of Native Indians of British Columbia (CNIBC) was formed in March 1966 at a meeting at Musqueam. Most of those in attendance were Salish from the Island, the mainland coast, or the interior. Those who took an active part in the meeting were already members of the Southern Vancouver Island Tribal Federation (SVITF) or of the NAIB. A committee was struck to meet with representatives of the Native Brotherhood, the Allied Tribes of the West Coast, and the Nisga'a Tribal Council. The CNIBC was intended to be a co-ordinating forum which would neither replace nor supplant existing organizations, but would serve their common interests. It was the first such body in the province and it was given much publicity in the *Native Voice*.

The first full meeting of the CNIBC took place in November 1966. The NAIB, the Native Brotherhood, the SVITF, and the Nuu'chah'nulth leaders were all present, as were spokeswomen of the Homemakers, the home improvement clubs sponsored by DIA at the community level. The Nisga'a Tribal Council was not officially represented, but Calder and other Nisga'a leaders continued to be active in the Native Brotherhood. The meeting showed that the CNIBC was not a clearly structured confederation. Any person present was allowed a say and, apparently, a vote. Some of the DIA-organized district councils, which had as yet little life of their own, were also acknowledged as members of the CNIBC.

The meeting agreed to a policy statement that demanded that the federal government negotiate directly with Indians rather than with a claims commission as intermediary. The statement also asserted: "We have confidence that with the formation of the Confederation, the Indians of British Columbia have attained unity and are now in a position to speak with one voice on the main matters of concern starting with the land question." The statement was signed by the representatives of each of the twelve organizations present, including the nascent district councils.[30]

Indian affairs minister Laing accepted the demand for direct negotiation, on condition that the Indian spokesmen could demonstrate that they represented at least 75 per cent of status Indians in the province. The critically important assumption held by both Indians and Laing at this time was that there would be "one big claim" on behalf of all British Columbia Indians who had not signed treaties. The Allied Tribes had proceeded on this same assumption prior to 1927, but with the important proviso that each tribal group would negotiate particular details relevant to its own situation and territory. There was no mention of any such proviso in 1966. While little attention was given to it at the time, there was still the matter of the province's part in any final settlement. Since the province claimed ownership of the lands in question, the province would still have to be dealt with even if the Indians and the federal government came to an agreement. The main issue in Indian politics, however, was whether the CNIBC, with its loose structure and its Salish base, would be the "one big voice" in presenting the one big British Columbia claim.

Peter Kelly died in 1966. At the February 1967 annual convention of the Native Brotherhood, Calder was elected to replace him in the prestigious post of chairman of the legislative committee. Calder proposed to the convention that the leaders of all the Indian organizations meet to draw up a firmly and clearly structured "constitutional basis for provincial Indian unity," and he listed off the organizations. The mere fact that he was making the proposal was hardly an expression of confidence in the CNIBC, and his list favoured the Native Brotherhood's portion of the province.[31] South coast and interior groups would have at most three delegates (from the SVITF, the NAIB, and the Sunshine Coast Tribal Council), while the west/central and north coasts would have seven or eight (from the Native Brotherhood, the Nuu'chah'nulth Allied Tribes, the Nisga'a Tribal Council, and five or six of the DIA's nascent district councils). Under Calder's proposal, which was approved by the

Native Brotherhood convention, the CNIBC itself would likely be ignored on the grounds that it was not an organization.[32]

The years 1967 and 1968 were a time of accelerating instability. Only the Nisga'a Tribal Council seems to have avoided internal stress and provided firm support to its leaders. The CNIBC next met in September 1967; those present were again almost exclusively Salish. An executive was chosen, and the youthful Philip Paul from Vancouver Island was elected president. The CNIBC was thus showing signs of becoming an organization itself; there was no suggestion, however, that the two pre-existing Salish organizations, the SVITF and the NAIB, would cease to operate. The CNIBC, indeed, now resembled the Native Brotherhood in that its geographic area of support contained regional or tribal organizations to which its members also belonged. At the September meeting of CNIBC a draft constitution was approved for further discussion by supporting bands and organizations.[33]

The SVITF annual convention at Duncan in December 1967 was attended by the presidents of the other four established organizations: Gus Gottfriedson (NAIB), Guy Williams (Native Brotherhood), Jack Peter (Allied Tribes of the West Coast), and Calder (Nisga'a Tribal Council). Philip Paul was present in his role as SVITF secretary. Wilson Bob, the SVITF president, and Paul were both defeated in the SVITF elections, in part, it would seem, because they both opposed Calder's unity constitution. Ross Modeste, the new president, supported it.[34]

Gottfriedson, Williams, Calder, Peter, and Modeste now became known among Indians as "the big five." They all supported the unity constitution. On 3 February 1968 a meeting was held at Musqueam under their auspices; they hoped that it would approve Calder's proposal. The CNIBC was one of the groups sending representatives. Not having brought copies of the constitution for distribution, Calder read it out, explained that its main purpose was to create "the Indian Land Claims Committee," and asked the meeting to approve it. Both the big five and the unity constitution met strenuous opposition from the audience. All the critics were Salish.[35] Benjamin Paul, past-president of the NAIB, stated that the big five represented at most seven thousand Indians, that Gottfriedson was not reflecting the views of NAIB members, and that for effective land claim action, "we must have a mandate from the people" rather than self-generated action by the big five leaders acting independently of their organizations. No one had suggested before that the Indian people might have a voice in affecting actions on their behalf. Guertrude Guerin of Musqueam, a former NAIB vice-president and now representing the CNIBC, said: "My voice is not for organizations, my voice speaks out for my people in little villages, unorganized people in isolated areas who must have area representation. The organizations here represent coastal areas. In other areas the needs are different and they must have a voice."[36] The meeting eventually voted not to approve the constitution but it did agree that it could be sent to bands and organizations for further discussion.[37]

Exactly one week later Calder, Williams, and Gottfriedson took the ferry from Vancouver to Ross Modeste's home town of Nanaimo for a meeting with him and some other members of the SVITF executive. Such a meeting had not even been hinted at one week earlier. On the same day (whether before or after the meeting remains a matter of some debate), Calder and Williams issued a press release stating that at the Nanaimo meeting "the constitution of the new organization known as the B.C. Indian Claims Committee was accepted. They will now meet with the Minister of Indian Affairs to settle the B.C. Indian Land Claims."[38]

The press release caused both despair and amusement in Ottawa, where Marchand was able to put it in proper context for DIA officials. It caused outrage among Indians. Even the Native Brotherhood's long-established internal unity fell apart. Williams and Calder were privately called to task by other Native Brotherhood executive members. The editorial staff of the Brotherhood's *Native Voice* laid their jobs on the line with news stories and editorials that accused Calder and Williams of engaging in self-aggrandizing actions that were destructive of unity; Calder's role was described as "dictatorial"; and those taking part in the Nanaimo meeting were called "a splinter group."[39] In response, the executive shut down the newspaper, thus removing the only Indian news medium in the province.

In response to the Nanaimo press release, the CNIBC sprang into life, organizing a protest meeting which took place at Musqueam the next week. The sentiments of the meeting were expressed by Philip Paul: "Every chief and band councillor in B.C. should be heard by the Land Claims Commission. And they should be allowed to elect leaders who will not manipulate them to serve their own ends. The elected leaders . . . should not commit themselves to any political party. At the present time we are victims of politicians."[40] Paul was alluding to Calder and Williams, implying that their personal interests and ambitions as members of political parties were diverting them from genuine dedication to Indian concerns.[41]

The frantic pace of Indian politics now subsided. The Cowichan band, the largest band in the province and the only large band in the SVITF, withdrew from it in protest over the Nanaimo meeting. Modeste resigned as president of the SVITF and was replaced by Philip Paul. Don Moses, a Nlaka'pamux and recent graduate of the Kamloops school, replaced Gottfriedson as president of the NAIB. The CNIBC itself faded from sight. The only political innovation during 1968 was the formation of the Indian Homemakers' Association from among the forty Homemakers Clubs that DIA had established among women on the larger reserves in the province. The new association formed initially to protest the intended firing of white DIA employee Ray Collins, who had implemented reforms in off-reserve Indian education. The association's first executive and board of directors were composed exclusively of Salish women, but the organization later expanded into all parts of the province.

There was one further notable political event in 1968. Len Marchand returned from Ottawa to run as the Liberal candidate against Davie Fulton in Kamloops. Marchand did not emphasize Indian issues, nor did he criticize Fulton, for whom he retained a strong respect. He presented himself as knowledgeable in the ways of Ottawa and as loyal to the new Liberal leader and prime minister, Pierre Trudeau, who came to Kamloops to speak glowingly of the candidate. Marchand defeated Fulton, becoming the first Indian elected to the Canadian House of Commons. Bill Mussell, son of Genevieve Mussell and also an NAIB member, replaced Marchand as special assistant to the minister in Ottawa.

The failed attempts at province-wide unity during the 1958–68 period revealed and re-emphasized the dual pan-Indianism among British Columbia Indians.[42] There was the pan-Indianism of the west/central and north coasts within which Protestantism, commercial fishing, and the clans and other lineages were unifying elements. This pan-Indianism was characterized by clearly structured organizations with stable leadership. For the most part the young had to inherit their influence or serve a long political apprenticeship before attaining prominence. The residential schools, especially Coqualeetza, had played a major part in developing the pan-Indian leadership. The Native Brotherhood was the long-lived dominant organization; tribal councils represented an emerging new element, but one that was based upon traditional identities.

There was also the separate and distinct pan-Indianism of the south coast and southern interior. This was essentially a Salish pan-Indianism; its roots lay in the Salish intertribal co-operation that had been demonstrated in the assembly and petition of 1874, in the confederacy of the 1870s, and in the assembly and delegation to London of 1906. But it was a pan-Indianism that lacked any firm political base in contemporary religion and did not have the clans or lineages to provide internal strength; moreover, its leaders had no strong economic base, let alone one facilitating common action. In this pan-Indianism, young men of ability and education had much political opportunity, however little their political experience. Equality of individuals and of communities was an underlying value that was strongly expressed, but by its very nature it inhibited the deference to leaders and the willingness to compromise that were generally evident within the coastal organizations. For all these reasons the political organizations of the interior were less stable than those of the coast.

As the pace of Indian politics subsided, the focus of Indian political effort in the province turned to responding to various policy initiatives of the federal government. The failed attempts at unity, however, left a legacy of mistrust, misperception, and, in a number of cases, bitter personal antagonisms that would colour the next two decades of British Columbia Indian politics.

CHAPTER ELEVEN

Federal Government Initiatives, 1960-9

Within the federal Department of Indian Affairs during the 1960s there emerged a half-dozen policy initiatives that came to have important but quite unintended effects upon Indian political organization in British Columbia. The various policy initiatives were conceived, planned, and implemented separately within DIA, and there was little co-ordination among them. Each was rooted in the longstanding small "L" liberal ideological view that individual Indians desired to be and should be assimilated as equals into the larger Canadian society. This view ignored the attachment of Indians to their ancestral communities and tribal groups.

One of the initiatives, which has been discussed in the previous chapter, involved taking some steps towards settling the British Columbia land question. It was the only one which had its origin in explicit demands of Indians. The other five initiatives were applied to Indians across Canada. Four of these were quite specific; they concerned education, local community development, Indian advisory bodies, and consulting Indians about amendments to the Indian Act. The final initiative, conceived as the culmination of the others, was the great federal attempt of 1969 to produce a final Indian policy.[1]

After the Second World War the department allowed Indian parents on reserves to send their children to public schools if they wished to, and a small number did. There was also an increasing number of Indian parents living off reserves who wanted their children to have a regular education. The widowed Ethel Wilson of the Cape Mudge Kwagiulth community was one example; she was living in Comox and her children attended public school. As a result, by the early 1960s there was a small number of Indian high school graduates, including Ethel's son Bill.

By this time the curricula, teaching methods, and general atmosphere in the Indian residential schools had changed considerably, and these schools were also producing a small flow of graduates who had received a relatively good education. The overall quality of Indian education remained low, however, and the dropout rate was high. It was clear that the residential schooling was still not leading to assimilation, and white public opinion seemed to be turning against the notion of racially segregated schools, especially with the news media filled with accounts of black school desegregation in the United States. For these reasons DIA decided to phase out the residential schools and began to do so in the early 1960s. The department established primary schools on larger reserves, but it relied on the public school system to absorb Indian high school students.[2] Where distance was a factor, the children would be bused to school or boarded in school dormitories with white children.

Indian education in British Columbia thus changed fundamentally during the 1960s. Integration replaced segregation, religious control vanished, and separation of children from parents and home locality was largely eliminated. The school system ceased to be a factor in pan-Indianism, since children from distant points and different tribal groups were no longer collected together. Fortuitously, the province was establishing community colleges at the time that Indians were beginning to graduate from high schools in some numbers. Within the sphere of education the colleges and the three universities now became the major influence on pan-Indianism. The pan-Indian impetus was now province-wide, with much attention as well to Canada-wide and international aboriginal identity.

The new high school graduates were the first generation of British Columbia Indians to have extensive first-hand familiarity with day-to-day details of white society. They had a range of skills, including literacy and the ability to deal with bureaucratic routines, that had formerly been the preserve of a very few Indians. The young high school graduates were the counterparts of the United States Indians who, at the turn of the century, had been led by their off-reserve and integrated upbringing to choose assimilation for themselves and their people. It was the assumption of federal and provincial officials in Canada in the 1960s that the Indian graduates of integrated schools would make the same choice. In British Columbia they did not.

As the events of 1969 and the following decade would make clear, the Indian high school graduates of the 1960s had not lost their Indian identities and loyalties. They felt themselves to be fully British Columbian and fully Canadian, but they knew they were Indian and they wanted to be Indian. They were bicultural. The skills and attitudes that gave them the option of assimilation also equipped them for effective political action. Forty years earlier, at the close of the special committee hearings of 1927, Peter Kelly had expressed the hope that a future generation would one day take up the land claim were his generation to fail. The graduates of the 1960s became the leaders of that future generation.

The Indian community development program, or "CD program," as it became known, began on Indian reserves in 1964. Its official purpose was to develop local government skills and attitudes comparable to those existing in white communities. Its deeper purpose was to make Indian bands acceptable to the provinces as candidates for regular municipal status under provincial jurisdiction. The program brought to the reserves an influx of "CD workers," most of whom were young Whites coming directly from university studies in social sciences or humanities with little practical experience. While the department was willing to hire Indians as CD workers, the very fact that the program was needed was an acknowledgement that rather few Indians were thought qualified for the task. Indians who were hired were in most cases assigned as assistants to white CD workers.[3]

About a dozen Indian CD workers were employed in British Columbia. One was George Manuel, who was hired in 1966 and assigned with Noel Bayliss to the Cowichan Band near Duncan on southern Vancouver Island.[4] Bayliss was about Manuel's age, and thus older than most CD workers. Manuel's work with the Cowichan people, who had the same broad Salishan identity as his own Shuswap people, was highly successful. He was popular with the Indians, made a favourable impression on the leading Whites in the area, and made use of the time away from his own people to improve his knowledge and skills. Although remaining more at ease in spoken than in written English, he went over material provided by Bayliss and discussed with him such topics as social change and policy-making within DIA. On Bayliss's advice he joined the local Toastmasters' Club to improve his public speaking.[5] In 1968 he was transferred to a Nuu'chah'nulth area on the west coast.[6] Here, among people of a very different culture who were resistant to outside advisers, he was not successful. He soon left DIA and moved with his family to Edmonton to work for the Alberta Indian Association under Harold Cardinal.[7]

In most cases the white CD workers had little in common with regular DIA staff. Many of the workers came straight from the university classroom and had little thought for future career security. A good many were idealists who were as optimistic about promoting social change among Indians as they were about inducing new attitudes in the department.[8] Many of the workers became dedicated secular missionaries. Very often they brought with them, or soon developed, the explicit goal of encouraging Indian assertiveness towards white society, towards gov-

ernment in general, and towards DIA in particular. They lived on the
reserves, where they did impart new skills, knowledge, and awareness
directly to band leaders and ordinary band members. In a number of
cases the workers gave home-tutoring to Indian high school students,
thus contributing to the quality of Indian education.

The CD program increased political awareness and instilled new confidence at the band level. One indication of the program's success was
the unsettling effect it had within the department. Sally Weaver observes
that the program was thought "a roaring success" by the "social activists" but that it "created chaos" within the department.[9] As a result the
program was eliminated by 1969. Many of the CD workers obtained
other positions within DIA, bringing to the department a new level of
awareness of Indians and Indian concerns. Over the next decade this
factor contributed to the ability of DIA staff in British Columbia to
respond effectively to the new Indian political organizations. Former CD
workers, white and Indian, also played important roles within the new
Indian political organizations that began to appear in 1969.

By the early 1960s the federal-provincial relations division had been
established in DIA to facilitate the transfer to the provinces of Indian
programs and responsibilities.[10] From the division the idea merged in
1963 of creating "advisory" bodies of Indians at the regional and
national levels in order to give the department direct information about
Indians and to allow it to influence Indian opinion. There was no
thought that Indians should, or would, provide independent advice to
which the government should respond. There is no evidence that the
origin of the idea had anything to do with the fact that Indians were
now federal voters,[11] nor was there any direct connection with the set-
ting-up of district councils,[12] which began at the agency level a few years
later.

The minister of Indian affairs approved of the advisory bodies in
January 1964 and presented a policy statement on the topic to the
Federal-Provincial Conference on Indian Affairs in October 1964.[13]
Implementation began in December 1964. Each DIA region was to have
an advisory council of about ten members, while at the national level
there was to be an advisory board composed of several members from
each region. At both levels the term of office would be three years.

DIA officials took for granted that the advisory bodies would be composed entirely of Indians, but they initially assumed that the department would choose them. In early 1965 it was decided that Indians
themselves should do the selecting, with existing organizations appointing some members and reserve-level Indians selecting others.

The advisory body for DIA's westernmost region, which still included
the Yukon, was officially styled the "British Columbia-Yukon Regional

Indian Advisory Council." J.V. Boys, the Indian commissioner for the region, decided that the two existing political organizations, the Native Brotherhood and the North American Indian Brotherhood (NAIB), would each select one member, while a third member would be chosen by the Indian Homemakers' Clubs.[14] To choose the remaining members Boys grouped the province's agencies into five zones and left the Yukon as the sixth. Within each zone each band council could nominate one or two persons as candidates and, in the later election, vote for one of the candidates. The candidate who came second in the voting would serve as an alternate. The zone selection process was carried out in the spring of 1965. Those elected were Philip Paul (Vancouver Island), James Gosnell (north coast), George Manuel (southern interior), James Antoine (central/northern interior), and Richard Malloway (lower mainland). In the southern interior zone election Manuel defeated Gus Gottfriedson, of the Kamloops Band, who was president of the NAIB.[15]

Since the Yukon bands had not responded to the DIA request for nominations, Boys appointed Clara Tizya, a Yukon Indian living in Vancouver, to represent them. For British Columbia the Native Brotherhood and NAIB each appointed their presidents, Guy Williams and Gottfriedson, while Laura Williams (no relation to Guy Williams) represented the Homemakers. The only politically prominent Indian not on the council was Frank Calder. Subsequently, he sought to have his Nisga'a Tribal Council represented on the advisory council, but Boys rejected the attempt on the ground that undue enlargement would result.

The first meeting of the council, in June 1965,[16] was attended by Boys and two senior DIA officials from Ottawa, R.F. Battle, the assistant deputy minister of Indian affairs, and L.L. Brown, the head of the federal-provincial relations division. Since James Gosnell was at sea fishing, his zone was represented by the alternate delegate, Ken Harris. The three officials spent some time explaining the purpose of the council, after which Boys turned to the election of a council chairman (for a one-year term) and of three delegates to the national advisory board (for three-year terms). Boys had the eight members[17] hand their written votes to him. The results were indicative of the lack of familiarity and cohesion among the members; three of them received two votes each, while two others received one vote each. Boys did not indicate who had received the votes, and the delegates accepted his suggestion that selection of chairman for the first year be held over to the next meeting.

The Indians decided that the national advisory board delegates should be chosen to ensure that one came from the southern half of the coast, one from the northern half, and one from the interior. Paul, Harris, and Manuel were chosen, respectively, to represent the three areas. At the next meeting Manuel was elected chairman of the council, but at the end of the first year, when he accepted the position of CD worker at Cowichan and had to move from the southern interior, he resigned. However, he retained his position on the national board. Gottfriedson was elected as the next chairman.

The council met several times each year and subcommittees met more frequently. All the meetings were held in DIA regional headquarters in Vancouver. They appear to have been amicable enough. Among the members there was little overt sign of the patterns of hostility that were evident in their public political activities during the same period.[18] Paul and Williams, for example, worked together as a subcommittee at the time of the public animosity between the Confederation of Native Indians and the big five and produced a comprehensive report at the height of the conflict in February 1968. Presumably, the council amity could be maintained because meetings were held privately under the aegis of DIA and because the matters under discussion could not easily be seen as benefitting one group over another.

Council meetings often took the form of lengthy study sessions in which senior Ottawa officials provided detailed advice about legislation, regulations, policies, and the inner workings of the department. While the verbatim minutes suggest that the officials at times became exasperated with the plodding questions of the Indians, the meetings appear on the whole to have been open and cordial. Nevertheless, unanimous Indian opposition to various DIA activities or proposals soon became a feature of the meetings.

Although nothing of its formal purpose was achieved, since no federal Indian responsibilities were transferred to the province, the advisory council served the completely unintended purpose of dramatically increasing political communication among British Columbia Indians and between them and others in Canada. Each council member had access to information about Indian matters throughout the province and in every other region. Verbatim minutes were taken of each advisory council meeting across the country, and in each region each council member was given copies of the minutes of all the other councils. At the national level the advisory board not only provided extensive information to Manuel, Paul, Harris, and its other members, but it also gave them a network of contacts with other Indians and with Ottawa officials and politicians.

Gosnell, Gottfriedson, Manuel, and Paul were the leading and most active members of the British Columbia-Yukon Council. Their membership allowed them to become better known and to have greater prestige both in their own zones and among Indians throughout the province. Through their membership on the national board Manuel and Paul, as well as Harris, became well known to Indian leaders across Canada. (Harris was less prominent within British Columbia, since, as an alternate member, he could attend council meetings only in Gosnell's absence.) Manuel was elected as chairman of the national board, thus attaining his first national recognition, while Harris became the board's secretary. Had DIA in fact intended to lay the foundation for province-wide and Canada-wide Indian political organization, it could scarcely have done a better job than it did. In particular, had it not been for the zone elections and the national advisory board, George Manuel would not have obtained his start in national Indian politics.

From the first meeting of the advisory council there was a low-key but persistent disagreement between the Indians and DIA officials over the proper role of council members. In the spring of 1965, as Brown and Battle travelled west attending advisory council meetings in the various provinces on their way to the first meeting in Vancouver, they wrote ahead to Boys indicating their disquiet over the general desire of the council members in the other provinces to consult and take directions from those who had elected them. Battle and Brown had most definitely not expected this development. Presumably they realized that it threatened to transform the advisory bodies into active lobbies over which DIA would have little control. Perhaps even worse, the development would stand as an affront to the white assumption that the Canadian Indian population was composed of individuals without any serious desire to survive as members of Indian communities or tribal entities.

In his opening remarks to the first Vancouver meeting, Battle told the Indians that it was "important for the government in discussions with advisory councils to get collective personal views" and that the minister was "seeking the personal views of a group of competent, experienced leaders as guidance in planning for the future."[19] Battle emphasized the word "personal," and the DIA stenographer underlined it when she typed the minutes of the meeting.

Unfazed by this admonition, some council members immediately "wanted to know what provisions had been made for expenses to enable council members to report back to the bands they represent." In reply, Battle "emphasized again that it was the personal view of the council members that the Department was seeking" and that "it should not be necessary to meet with band representatives either before or after council meetings." Still undeterred, and with Battle and Brown still present, the council proceeded to resolve unanimously "that the Government appropriate funds for travelling expenses and compensation for loss of salary by Regional Advisory Council delegates for reasonable and essential consultation with the Indian people they represent." Here was another unanticipated turn of events. The officials had apparently not even considered the possibility that an advisory council would pass resolutions; apparently the British Columbia-Yukon council was the first to do so.

Brown remained upset at the Indian refusal to give "personal" views. From Ottawa he later wrote to Boys:

There have been attempts at most of the meetings to bring up all sorts of local matters; discussion about the need for Council members to visit their bands to explain what is taking place in the Council and a reluctance to give personal views . . . If the Council members refuse to give their personal views and insist that they must first consult with their bands, then the original concept of the Councils is meaningless. I think we have to . . . find out whether the Council members are prepared to give their personal views . . . If not, I can see no alternative but to recommend to the Minister that we drop the whole idea . . . The major problem to overcome may be, of course, the misconception held by Indians generally. Obviously, many of the bands believe they elected their representatives to give the band's opinion. It is perhaps too much to expect that elected representatives can go back to the bands and explain that this is not the case. Nevertheless, this may have to be done effectively to enable Council members to feel free to express personal views . . . I think we will have to . . . if necessary, try and come up with some scheme to re-educate the bands if this appears necessary in British Columbia to achieve the effective operation of your Council.[20]

The British Columbia Indians persevered, however, continuing to raise the matter in advisory council and national advisory board meetings over the next two years. In the end they proved more consistent than did DIA officials on the point. In the third year the department agreed to provide travel funds for the British Columbia-Yukon council members to consult with the bands in their zones. This outcome confirmed the council members' own view of their role as representative in dealing with DIA. In effect, the DIA officials acquiesced to the Indian view that representatives were to be the delegates of those who had chosen them and that to carry out their role they must report back to their constituencies and receive guidance from them. DIA officials in British Columbia never again presumed that Indian spokesmen could be induced to be the eyes and ears of the department. While the outcome was only a small victory for the council members, it did demonstrate the strength of the Indian convictions on the issue. It also demonstrated that persistent insistence could be a fruitful strategy to use in dealing with DIA.

Unlike Indians in other provinces, British Columbia Indians regarded the advisory council process as a worthwhile endeavour. Weaver's general observation that "the regional and national Indian Advisory

Boards . . . ended in 1967 when Indian spokesmen withdrew from the meetings, resentful of the limited power they were granted and uncertain of their support from Indian communities"[21] was not reflected in British Columbia, where the council continued meeting until the end of its three-year term. Its last meeting took place in April 1968, with its members expecting that new elections would be held.

Boys did call for nominations from the bands for zone representatives, and some were received, but no new election was held. While it does not appear that Boys was actually instructed not to proceed, his superiors would have no reason to wish one advisory council to continue without the others. British Columbia Indians accepted the demise of the advisory council because by early 1968 a new advisory process was being arranged by the department.

Under its new minister, Jean Chrétien, the department was setting out to consult the Indian people about amendments to the Indian Act. The new process, which fitted in with the "participatory democracy" then much in favour with the Liberal Party and Prime Minister Trudeau, was presented by Chrétien as allowing Indians to have a real influence on Indian policy. The "consultation process," as the exercise became known, remains the most comprehensive of any such efforts ever undertaken in Canada, among Indians or any other groups.

In March 1968 the department mailed a booklet entitled "Choosing a Path" to every status Indian household, to every band council, and to every Indian organization in the country. The booklet presented the main provisions of the Indian Act, posed a series of questions about how the act could be amended, and provided alternate possible amendments. Each band was asked to hold public meetings to discuss the questions and to choose one delegate to attend a zone meeting. Each zone meeting was to select one of its participants to attend the national consultation meeting in Ottawa. Each province-wide Indian organization would also send a delegate to the national meeting. The zone meetings took place across the country from July 1968 to January 1969; in British Columbia the zones used for the advisory councils were used again. The national meeting was scheduled for May 1969.

In British Columbia the Native Brotherhood and the North American Indian Brotherhood were the two organizations eligible to select delegates.[22] The Native Brotherhood appointed Guy Williams; the NAIB appointed its new president, Don Moses, who was now a student at Simon Fraser University. James Gosnell, Gus Gottfriedson, and Philip Paul, now a student at the University of Victoria, were elected to be the national delegates from their zones. Nick Prince, the young chief of the Necoslie band, was elected to represent the northern interior, and Joe Mathias, the equally young chief of the Squamish band, was elected to

represent the lower mainland. Mathias, a grandson of Chief Joe Capilano, one of the three Salish chiefs to travel to London in 1906, was now
attending the University of British Columbia. Thus, a majority of the
seven delegates had been members of the advisory council; four of
them were young high school graduates, and three of these were now at
university.

According to the procedure laid out by Ottawa officials, the band
delegates to each zone meeting were to meet for one or two days by
themselves before the formal meeting, which would be attended by the
department's "consultation team." The team for British Columbia consisted of Ottawa officials and Walter Dieter of Saskatchewan, the president of the fledgling National Indian Brotherhood. The extent to which
Indians made use of the initial closed meetings provides an indication
of the degree of political development in the zone and of the degree to
which neighbouring tribal groups were able to co-operate.[23] One
extreme was illustrated in the northern interior meeting at Prince
George. Here Commissioner Boys was allowed to run the meeting, and
Manuel, an outsider and a DIA employee, was accepted as co-chairman
at Boys's suggestion.[24] During the meeting the discussion was random
and delegates showed little knowledge of the Indian Act. Clearly there
had been no prior discussion or planning by the Indians.

The other extreme was evident in the north coast meeting at Terrace.
Here the public meeting was a smoothly orchestrated performance that
gave prominence to hereditary clan chiefs, who had not even been
considered in the Department's plans. The Indians ran the meeting
from the start, and in the beginning did not even refer to the presence
of the commissioner and the consultation team. After announcing that
the hereditary chief who owned the land on which Terrace was located
would be honorary chairman of the meeting, James Gosnell led the
singing of "Oh Canada" and the recitation of an Anglican prayer. Only
then were the commissioner and the team acknowledged; they were told
that the Indians would not proceed until the leader of the team had
signed a statement confirming that the meeting would not prejudice the
land claims. The official signed the statement.

The Indians remained in charge of the meeting. On the fifth and
supposedly last day they refused to elect a national delegate because
they had not yet discussed all the items in "Choosing a Path." Instead,
they adjourned the meeting with the demand that the department
arrange a continuation. The department subsequently did hold a second meeting at Terrace, which was one of the two in British Columbia
that Chrétien attended. The other meeting that he attended was at
Kelowna. There he sought to reassure the Indians. "We do not want to
assimilate the Indian population . . . In the society that we want to

develop, it will be possible for groups like you or my own group to keep our identity and be good citizens of the land."[25]

Among British Columbia Indians the consultation process served to reinforce the principles of representation previously embodied in the advisory council and to confirm Paul, Gosnell, Gottfriedson, and Williams in their leading roles. At the same time the process brought Prince, Mathias, and Moses into prominence, adding them to the small group of leaders whose reputation extended beyond their own localities. The zone meetings made band delegates more aware of the relative state of Indian political organization in the province. Members of the consultation team often alluded to the lack of political unity among British Columbia Indians, and Dieter always took some opportunity to speak about his National Indian Brotherhood and usually mentioned the greater unity among Indians in other provinces. As 1969 began, British Columbia was the only province west of Nova Scotia not to have a province-wide political organization able to speak for all status Indians.

At the Ottawa meeting in May 1969 the British Columbia delegates pressed in unison for recognition of the unique position of British Columbia Indians in never having surrendered title to their lands. They sat together in the meeting and caucused both during and after the daily sessions. They played the leading part in diverting the meeting from the department's object of discussing the Indian Act to the Indian concern to resolve the questions of land claims and aboriginal rights. In several of their evening caucuses they agreed that new efforts must be directed to forming an organization which could speak for all British Columbia Indians.[26]

The federal government's grand design for Indian assimilation and equality came suddenly to a head in June 1969 when Chrétien issued the "Statement of the Government of Canada on Indian Policy." Ostensibly, the policy statement was the outcome and culmination of the consultation process. The government proposed the abolition of Indian status, the elimination of DIA itself within five years, the ending of the special responsibility of the federal government for provision of services to Indians (Indians would thus receive the same services from the provinces as would other Canadians), and, generally, the elimination of Indian status as a legal concept. Reserves would be turned over to Indians as private land holdings.[27]

Ordinarily, in keeping with federal government terminology and for reasons having nothing to do with race, the standard governmental term "white paper" would have been applied to the policy statement. Chrétien and his officials were astute enough to take steps to avoid the term. They themselves refrained from mentioning it and misleadingly presented the policy statement as a "green paper." In fact, the copy mailed out to Indian bands across the country did have a green cover. The steps failed. The policy pronouncement was promptly and properly labelled "the white paper."[28] The white paper of 1969 became "the" white paper, thus precluding the use of the term for any future policy pronouncement in Indian affairs.

Most Indian leaders were astounded by the fact that the white paper made a mockery of the whole consultation process by proposing not the amendment but the abolition of the Indian Act. They were angered by the treachery of the government in obviously having prepared the white paper even before the Ottawa consultation meeting had taken place. Within months, in response to the white paper, an organization had been formed in British Columbia that could indeed speak for all status Indians. However, the white paper was merely the final stimulus in the formation of the new organization. It was a product of the existing political organizations in the province, of the principles and structures resulting from the workings of the advisory council and the consultation meetings, and of the new Indian awareness and confidence brought to the surface at the band level by the community development program and the reforms in the schooling of Indian children.

CHAPTER TWELVE

The Formation of the New Organizations, 1969–71

Among British Columbia Indians 1969 is remembered not only as the year of the federal white paper, but also as the year in which the "big organizations" were formed. Status Indians created a new province-wide organization to resume pursuit of the land claim that had been interrupted by the collapse of the Allied Tribes and the outlawing of claims activities in 1927. Non-status Indians and Métis became politically active for the first time and created their own organization to pursue social betterment and assimilation. The fact of the separate organizations accorded both with the Indian Act's division of Indians into status and non-status categories and with the resulting division between reserve dwellers and those who formed minorities in towns and cities.

In response to the white paper of June 1969, several of those who had been consultation spokesmen, especially Philip Paul and Don Moses, resolved to keep alive the political network that had developed in the consultation process. They were seriously handicapped, however, by the absence of any Indian newspaper, for throughout 1969 the *Native Voice* remained shut down (as a result of the earlier dispute between the editorial staff and the Native Brotherhood executive). They approached senior Department of Indian Affairs officials in Vancouver, who agreed to their request to provide one or two clerical staff to keep open the Indian Communication Office in DIA regional headquarters, which had served as clearing house and message centre during the consultation process. During the critical period from July to November 1969 the communication office continued in its previous role.

The first to propose holding a province-wide conference was Dennis Alphonse, the young chief of the Cowichan band, the largest band in the province and the one in which George Manuel and Noel Bayliss had served as community development workers. Until this time Alphonse had assumed no prominent position outside his own community. In June and July he wrote letters to many chiefs and to the tribal councils and political organizations proposing a conference of band representatives. Almost certainly the same proposal would have emerged soon in any case, but Alphonse's was the first.

At this time there were three tribal councils (the Southern Vancouver Island Tribal Federation and those of the Nisga'a and the Nuu'chah'-nulth) and three political organizations (the Native Brotherhood of British Columbia, the North American Indian Brotherhood, and the Indian Homemakers' Association) existing in the province. The Island Tribal Federation, the NAIB, and the Homemakers Association were based in the southern portion of the province among Salish peoples. Their presidents—Philip Paul, Don Moses, and Rose Charlie—responded promptly to Alphonse's proposal[1] while neither the Native Brotherhood nor the Nisga'a or Nuu'chah'nulth did so at all. The response pattern suggested that the legacy of dual pan-Indianism (Salish and Roman Catholic on the one hand, Protestant and west/central and north coast on the other) still affected Indian politics. At the time, however, the legacy seemed irrelevant, for band chiefs in every part of the province responded enthusiastically to the conference proposal.

Moses, Paul, and Charlie, aided by other young people from various parts of the province, proceeded to organize a conference to be held in Kamloops in November. They applied to the provincial First Citizens' Fund[2] for money to allow the planning committee to operate, and Dan Campbell, the minister in charge, approved a grant of $13,000. Alphonse became chairman of the planning committee.[3] It is not clear how the principle that each band was to be represented by its chief (or alternate) emerged, for it had not been in effect for the consultation meetings, to which many bands sent delegates other than their chiefs. However the new principle was accepted by the committee.

Included in the federal white paper had been a promise that the federal government would provide funds to Indian bands and organizations to allow them to consider programs and policies relevant to the Indian people.[4] The leaders of the Salish organizations now had very good contacts with the Liberal government in Ottawa. Len Marchand was Liberal MP for Kamloops, while Bill Mussell, son of Genevieve Mussell, was special assistant to Jean Chrétien, the minister of Indian affairs. Both Marchand and Mussell had been active in the NAIB. The department agreed to provide $6,500 for planning the conference and $60,000 for the conference itself.

The Kamloops conference of 17–22 November 1969 was more broadly representative than any previous Indian assembly held in British Columbia.[5] It outdid by a substantial margin the assembly that

George Manuel and the Native Botherhood had held in the same city ten years earlier. One hundred and forty bands were represented; they contained 85 per cent of the status Indian population. All areas of the province were well represented. Ardyth Cooper, an alternate representing her Sooke band, was the youngest delegate. Most of the executive members of the three political organizations were present, as were the leaders of the three tribal councils. In addition, there were some two hundred Indian observers, including a number of students whose way had been paid by an additional grant from the First Citizens' Fund. The conference took place in the Kamloops Indian Residential School, then in the final stages of being phased out.

Conference proceedings were orderly, discussion was for the most part well informed and to the point, differences of opinion were expressed diplomatically, and in the few decisions that were not unanimous, the dissenters were few. The consultation spokesmen and the organization leaders played their part, but no person or group dominated the conference. Federal government officials were noticeably absent. Walter Dieter, president of the National Indian Brotherhood, was present and reminded the conference that any resulting new organization would become the British Columbia component of the NIB. Dan Campbell represented the provincial government and took a leading part in conference discussions during the first several days. He was the first provincial official ever to participate so actively in an Indian meeting or assembly. His presence, his favourable attitude, and his having granted money for the conference were seen as auspicious omens by most of the Indians in attendance.

The numerous opening speeches emphasized the themes of Indian unity and pursuit of aboriginal rights. As Dennis Alphonse stated: "The main purpose of us here today as official delegates of Bands throughout British Columbia and representatives of organizations [is] to discuss our aboriginal rights in regards to the British Columbia land." A few spokesmen regretted the complete rejection of the white paper, seeing it as a step towards equality, but even these few were intent on settling the land claim. Clarence Jules, Sr., chief of the Kamloops band, said, "Let the Government guarantee that our land claims will be fairly dealt with, and let us immediately embark on a program that will ensure our people other rights and privileges enjoyed by all Canadians."

In general, the speakers believed that the white paper's promise of equality meant simply the denial of aboriginal rights and of the right to legislative protection. Philip Paul summed up the reasons for rejecting the white paper, stating that the Liberal government "will not recognize the aboriginal rights of Indian people," that the Indian Act was to be "done away with, removing all legal obligations of the Federal Government to the Indian people," and that the white paper was "nothing much more than a version of the policy designed to assimilate the American Indian into the mainstream of the American society." Paul undoubtedly expressed the concerns and hopes of the conference when he stated, "The history of disunity in this Province gave birth to this Conference . . . and depending on the outcome of this Conference is the future of your children and mine."

After the speeches the conference elected George Manuel as chairman[6] and, at the planning committee's suggestion, agreed to hire Davie Fulton, then practising law in Kamloops, as conference legal adviser.[7] One whole day was devoted to discussion, led by Fulton, of legal aspects of the land claim. There was a general assumption by most of the participants that the best strategy would be to have Fulton seek to approach provincial and federal governments with one general land claim on behalf of all non-treaty status Indians in the province.

By this time the Nisga'a had already embarked on a different strategy. Even before the release of the white paper they had decided to wait no longer for governments to become receptive to their land claim. The Nisga'a Tribal Council had hired lawyer Thomas Berger (then New Democratic Party leader in the province) to take their land claim to court, or, more specifically, to seek a court declaration that aboriginal title to the Nass Valley had never been extinguished. As on previous occasions the Nisga'a were acting alone as they set out upon an untrod path.

Contrary to what came to be believed many years later, the Kamloops conference did not reveal any friction between advocates of the two strategies, nor was there even any debate on the issue. The Nisga'a chiefs did not make any major statement on the subject, but when a motion was made that the conference approve the one general claim, they abstained, as did Musqueam, Squamish, and Native Brotherhood representatives.[8]

Subsequently, the conference agreed unanimously to form a new organization, and it elected a committee, of which Don Moses became chairman, to recommend a name and structure.[9] After a day's deliberation the committee proposed the name "Union of British Columbia Indian Chiefs" and a three-level structure. The first level would be the annual meeting of chiefs, which would debate resolutions and set policy. Second, there would be a board of directors, called the "chiefs' council," composed of representatives chosen by the chiefs in the various zones.[10] Third, there would be an "executive committee" made up of three members of the chiefs' council chosen by the council. The conference committee suggested also that there be a small staff consisting of an administrator, a secretary-treasurer, and possibly a few experts, such as "lawyer, anthropologist, etc."

The conference committee envisioned the Union as a co-ordinating body and pressure group on behalf of British Columbia's status Indians that would confine its activities to pursuit of the land claim; there was no thought that the Union would become heavily staffed or that it would have any service-delivery role. Implicit in the report was the hope that unity or "union" would manifest itself in the common action of the chiefs.[11] In assuming that decision-making would be collegial at each level, and by not making a recommendation that there be a Union president, the committee was seeking to avoid the difficulties the organizations had experienced when presidents had acted autocratically and in isolation from the members.

The committee gave little attention to financing the new organization, but this subject received much attention in conference discussion. It was assumed that the federal government would contribute an annual amount equivalent to one dollar for each registered Indian in the province, as it was already doing in the case of province-wide organizations in other regions. During the discussion the hope emerged that Dan Campbell and the province would be willing to make a regular contribution of 10 per cent of the First Citizens' Fund's proceeds, which would mean about $175,000 annually for the Union. Campbell had left by the time the matter arose, and knew nothing of the new expectation. By the time the conference ended, however, a firm conviction that the province was obligated to provide the money had emerged among the Indians.

At the close of the conference a chiefs' council was selected, and it chose Heber Maitland of Kitamaat, Victor Adolph of Lillooet, and Philip Paul as members of the executive committee.[12] The three were chosen to ensure that the committee had members from the north coast, the south coast, and the interior. In later months Paul became the acknowledged chairman of the committee, and he was at times referred to as "chairman of the Union of B.C. Indian Chiefs,"[13] although no such position formally existed. The executive committee appointed Moses as administrator, and, assured of receiving the $46,000 per capita funding from DIA, it rented office space in Vancouver in early 1970 and hired a small staff.

The committee soon applied to the First Citizens' Fund for the annual 10 per cent grant. Dan Campbell offered $53,000, somewhat less than 3 per cent, and, in the first instance, for only one year. At a time when a good annual salary was about $8,000 and when there were many applicants seeking money from the fund, the amount was considerable. Moreover, it was a historic turn of events that the provincial government was now willing to finance an organization dedicated to attaining a land claims settlement. The chiefs' council, however, bitterly rejected Campbell's offer as a snub of the Union and its ideals. Members of the council became contemptuous of Campbell, whom they had hitherto regarded as a friend and ally. The incident was the turning point in Union attitudes towards the provincial government and the ruling Social Credit Party.

In April 1970 Moses hired several Indian university students for the summer. One of these was Bill Wilson, now in his mid-twenties. He had graduated from the University of Victoria, majoring in English and political science, and was now enrolled in law school at the University of British Columbia. (At this time only one other British Columbia Indian, Alfred Scow, also a Kwagiulth, had obtained a law degree.) Wilson worked with Fulton, first on completing the Union's draft constitution, and then on the formal land claim statement, which they entitled "Claim Based on Native Title to the Land now known as British Columbia and the Waters Adjacent Thereto."[14]

During the summer the Union acted as host to the National Indian Brotherhood's annual assembly, which was held in Vancouver. With the aid of some procedural manoeuvring by the Union staff and leaders, the position of NIB president was opened for re-election, and George Manuel defeated Walter Dieter. At the end of the summer, buoyed by encouraging word from their contacts in Ottawa concerning the possibility of substantial federal funding, the staff and executive optimistically prepared a budget of $3.6 million for the 1971-72 fiscal year.

The Union's second assembly took place in Vancouver in November 1970. Attendance was somewhat greater than in 1969, with 142 bands represented. In the opening speeches there was much confidence that province-wide Indian unity had at last been attained. The unity was symbolized in the new practice of having one co-chairman from the coast (in this case, William Scow, the pre-eminent Kwagiulth) and one from the interior (Gus Gottfriedson). The internal accord was matched by feelings of amity towards the larger society. When one of the guest speakers, Frank Howard, the New Democratic MP for Skeena, who had long taken an active interest in Indian concerns, mentioned the tactics of Quebec terrorists who were then much in the news, he was promptly rebuked by Scow: "I am sure that my people will never entertain or even mention the idea of F.L.Q. We know that our people are sensible people. We have selected our able leaders who are now able to converse with the powers that be." The only entity receiving any serious criticism in the assembly was the Social Credit government for its First Citizens' Fund decision.

In preparing the draft constitution, Fulton and Wilson had followed the instructions of the Kamloops assembly in having the membership of the Union consist of the chiefs of bands. However, Wilson (who presided over the portions of the 1970 assembly dealing with the constitution) himself believed that the membership should consist of the Indian people. He put this belief to the meeting on the first day and was supported by a number of speakers, including Philip Paul, who said that "every Indian should be a member of this Union." The change in composition would be of major philosophical significance, indicating a grass-roots orientation rather than the local elitism that could be inferred from having only chiefs as members. Although the fact is not now well remembered, the Vancouver meeting did follow Wilson, Paul, and others in approving the principle that the Union's membership consist of individual Indians rather than the chiefs.[15] The change in principle necessitated a change in name. "Union of British Columbia Indians" met with general acceptance. It was clear however, that most of the chiefs were willing to accept a union only of status Indians. Wilson, in contrast, made clear his conviction that all Indians, status and non-status, should be included.

Before the assembly ended, the change in principle was reversed. Fulton reported that the provincial registrar of societies would not approve the name "Union of British Columbia Indians," on the grounds that the term "British Columbia Indians" was "already incorporated in [the name of] some organizations."[16] In other words, he said, the provincial Societies Act precluded the possibility that "membership be open to all Indians of B.C.," and so, he concluded, the logical thing to do would be to have membership consist only of the chiefs.[17] The advocates of popular membership reluctantly accepted defeat. The chiefs would retain their exclusive membership. The stage was set for much future conflict concerning the orientation of the Union.

Fulton outlined to the Vancouver assembly the approach that he and Wilson were taking on the land claim. There would be one general claim on behalf of all British Columbia status Indians, which would be presented to the federal and provincial governments and then negotiated with them. The Nisga'a, through Bill McKay, questioned Fulton about whether the general approach would be jeopardized by a favourable outcome for the Nisga'a in their court case, which was now before the Supreme Court of Canada (the Nisga'a having lost in the lower courts in the province). Fulton said that it would not. In the Vancouver assembly, as had also been the case at Kamloops, there was no inclination by speakers to see the land claim process as more than preparation by non-Indian experts of a historical-legal assertion of entitlement, and there was no thought expressed by members of any other tribal group that they might emulate the Nisga'a by proceeding to prepare their own case.

Those who drew up the proposed Union budget of $3.6 million for 1971–72 did so on the assumption that the Union would not only immediately take over DIA's major activities but that it would also receive the funds necessary to do so from the federal government. The assumption was criticized by those who believed, as had the organizing committee at the Kamloops meeting, that the Union should remain a co-ordinating body and not seek major administrative responsibilities. The critics believed that replacing DIA with the Union would merely change the colour of the bureaucracy, leaving its role and behaviour unchanged. Wilson was the most outspoken critic of "brown bureaucracy." "If you want to turn [the Union] into a bureaucracy like the Department of Indian Affairs, fine. We have a lot of Indian candidates who are willing to be bureaucrats." His comments brought a standing ovation.

Following the Vancouver assembly the Union's new chiefs' council again selected Paul, Adolph, and Maitland as the executive committee. At its meeting in May 1971 the chiefs' council approved the final draft of the constitution and by-laws that Fulton and Wilson had prepared. Formal incorporation under the name "Union of British Columbia Indian Chiefs" took place in June 1971.

The formation of the British Columbia Association of Non-Status Indians, or "BCANSI,"[18] as it was universally called, was very much the work of one man, H.A. (Butch) Smitheram.[19] Smitheram had been born in 1918 near Penticton. His mother was Okanagan, and his father was English; their marriage had deprived wife and children of Indian status. After quitting high school well short of graduation, Smitheram had worked at various jobs and started his own family before joining the Department of Indian Affairs in 1950. He was the first Indian in western Canada to become an assistant Indian agent, holding that position in the Kamloops Agency. In the late 1950s he left the department, enrolled in the private Shur-Pass school in Vancouver, quickly passed the provincial high school equivalency examinations, and entered the University of British Columbia to study English literature. Illness and shortage of money to support his family compelled him to withdraw before obtaining his degree and to take a job in Vancouver with the Department of Manpower and Immigration. By 1968 he was responsible for promoting Indian training and employment; his duties required him to travel widely in the province as well as to Ottawa. By this time also time he was an active and leading member of the Indian-Eskimo Association of Canada, a largely white group formed to support native causes.[20]

"In 1968," he later wrote, "after a meeting with other Provincial Métis leaders, and with the encouragement of Ernie McEwan [executive director] of the Indian Eskimo Association, I decided to direct my time and energy toward the organization of the unregistered, or non-status Indian people of B.C. and the Yukon."[21] In March 1969, in Vancouver, Smitheram and four others (one non-status Musqueam[22] and three Métis originally from outside the province) officially formed BCANSI. Smitheram became interim president. These first efforts to organize non-status Indians in the province occurred while the consultation process was being held for status Indians. Thus, BCANSI was actually founded before the release of the white paper in June 1969 and also before the founding of the Union of British Columbia Indian Chiefs. BCANSI, however, did not become a vigorous organization until 1971, well after the Union had done so.

The founders intended BCANSI to appeal equally to non-status Indians and to Métis. The Métis were members of the ethnic and cultural group of mixed Indian-European origin that evolved during the fur trade era on the prairies and in the North West Territories, but not in British Columbia. After the Second World War thousands of Métis had migrated into British Columbia. While the distinction between non-status Indians of British Columbia origin and persons of Métis ethnic identity was clear enough, the terms "non-status Indian" and "Métis" were not completely distinct, since Métis individuals are also non-status Indians in that they have Indian ancestry but do not have Indian status under the Indian Act.[23] The founders of BCANSI had decided against the name "association of non-status Indians and Métis," on the grounds that the more inclusive single term "non-status Indians" would imply greater unity of purpose.

BCANSI was intended to be a grass-roots organization in which "locals" in the communities would carry out the major activities and be relatively independent of the provincial organization. In March 1969 only the Vancouver local existed, composed of the five BCANSI founders. Over the next two years Smitheram played the major part in organizing additional locals. He focused his efforts on the towns and cities having the greatest numbers of potential members. He distributed a draft local constitution, gave talks to meetings of potential supporters, and oversaw the organizing of the first province-wide meeting in Burnaby in November 1969.

The draft constitution was typically adopted without major change by the locals as they were formed. Membership in a local was open to "any unregistered person of native Indian descent, who is one quarter or more Indian blood, but does not have . . . Indian Treaty Rights."[24] (The "one-quarter or more" provision was the same as that in the constitutions of the major prairie Métis associations.) Membership was open as well, however, to spouses of those eligible; this provision allowed persons without any Indian ancestry to become full members of a local.

The BCANSI provincial constitution of March 1969 provided that the locals would be the component units in the provincial structure. At provincial meetings each local would have at least one vote, with one additional vote (to a maximum of four) for each twenty-five members of the local. The annual meeting would elect the twelve provincial directors (electing four each year to serve three-year terms). The directors would in turn elect six executive officers: a president, four vice-presidents, and a secretary treasurer. The directors would be responsible for giving direction to the executive officers in accord with policies established by the annual meeting. The directors and officers would have no vote in the annual meetings.

Several themes were evident in Smitheram's speeches and interviews with the press during the founding period.[25] He viewed the non-status Indians and Métis as suffering the same social and economic discrimination as status Indians but as lacking the benefits in housing, post-secondary education, occupational training, economic development grants, and reserved lands accorded to status Indians. Thus, the general purpose of BCANSI was "to advance the level of education, training and opportunity among Non-Status Indians and Métis people in B.C."

Smitheram very clearly held out Métis history, identity, and achievements as worthy of admiration and emulation by non-status Indians. Indeed, the first BCANSI annual meeting had Métis culture as its theme, and it paid tribute to the ideals of the Métis leader Louis Riel. The meeting was given the name "Riel Days," and the major guest speakers were Adam Cuthand of the Canadian Métis Association and Stan Daniels, president of the Alberta Métis Association. Smitheram did not seek to have the non-status Indians recognize and revive aspects of Indian culture, although he often mentioned the common need of all BCANSI members to have pride in their cultural background.[26]

Smitheram gave great emphasis to individual personal improvement and education. "Our main purpose in organizing is to bring about the acceleration and *upward social mobility* of our people."[27] At times he would give examples of notably successful persons said to have some Indian ancestry—Sir James Douglas, Jack Dempsey, Joe Louis, George Armstrong, Johnny Cash, Wayne Newton, Roy Rogers, Paul Newman, and Winston Churchill.[28]

If we are to rise above the mediocrity of the common herd, we must widen our view, develop our inherent curiosity, bolster up our courage, exercise our self-discipline, and wrap the whole lot with enthusiasm. There is no doubt that there are future lawyers, doctors and teachers sitting at your table every day . . . Your children are the wealth of our nation—give them the opportunity and the inspiration and they will build on the foundations that you have laid for them.

The ultimate success, he would say, would be to have the child of a BCANSI member become prime minister of Canada. Nothing could be achieved, however, without the aid of government. Government could be persuaded to help non-status Indians and Métis if three initial steps could be achieved: first, unity through BCANSI; second, alliance with status Indians; and third, unity at the ballot box.

We must organize ourselves along ethnic lines, or in other words, bring in all non-status Indians for regular membership, and all others who wish to help us as associate members. As a second stage of organization we must form a political alliance with the registered Indian associations or the B.C. Union of Chiefs.

When we reach the stage of unity where we can predict the political action of all people of Indian ancestry in a given area, we will see the wisdom of building a solid organization. When we can go to the polls holding the balance of power in our hands, then we will, for the first time in the last two hundred years, realize equality in the land of our birth. We will have a bargaining power that we can use for the benefit of all poverty stricken people.

Smitheram would state explicitly that "our organization is not trying to establish an ethnic group." His desire to "organize ourselves along ethnic lines" was thus apparently a means to bring personal identity and confidence to non-status persons in order to equip them to seek their own individual future.

The need for non-status Indian associations will exist until the people feel confident that they can cope with the problems found in society, on both an individual and community level. When the people have regained their pride and identity they will integrate into society at their own speed, at which time the non-status Indian Association will exist as a social club or will be dissolved.

We must develop our people in all facets of modern living in an urban area. We must not only train our young people in the trades and skills that are in demand on the labour market,—but we must train them in the *social skills* that will make it easier for them to cope with their non-Indian friends of the middle class . . . Music, painting, ceramics, sculpture, and creative writing, as well as Indian crafts, must be offered to our young people. [Emphasis in original]

On balance, then, it would seem that the Métis were put forward not so much as an example to be emulated by non-status persons who were not already Métis, but more as an example of non-status success in obtaining recognition and benefits from government. The ultimate good fortune of non-status and Métis persons would be individual assimilation into the larger society, at which point a non-status political organization could cease to exist.

BCANSI's early growth was slow. About forty people attended the meeting held in Burnaby in 1969; only about a dozen of them were from outside the Vancouver area. Eighty attended the second annual meeting in Victoria in November 1970.[29] By this time no more than half a dozen locals had been formed and only those in Dawson Creek, Chetwynd, and Prince George appear to have been active. During this period Smitheram was often mentioned in the *Indian Voice*[30] and the *Native Voice*—but as government official and organizer of fund-raising events (of benefit to status as well as non-status Indians) rather than as president of the little-known BCANSI.

The slow start was a reflection of government actions, or, more accurately, lack of them. The non-status and Métis population had been affected by neither the Indian Advisory Council nor the consultation process, and the white paper was no threat to them. Government funds were difficult to obtain. The federal Department of the Secretary of State did provide a small grant for the 1969 "Riel Days," but the provincial government rejected Smitheram's application for $40,000 on the grounds that only status Indian groups were eligible for First Citizens' Fund grants.

BCANSI's fortunes improved dramatically in late 1970 and early 1971. The provincial policy was reversed, and BCANSI was granted $56,000 from the First Citizens' Fund (about the same amount that the Union of British Columbia Indian Chiefs had rejected). At this time the secretary of state's department embarked upon a program of encouraging "multiculturalism" and granted BCANSI $40,000 for the period ending 31 March 1971 and a further $77,000 for the next fiscal year. After the 1970 annual meeting a full-time executive director and six full-time organizers were hired, and a head office was opened in Vancouver.

In this same period a commitment of $400,000 was obtained from the federal government's Central Mortgage and Housing Corporation for construction of houses for non-status persons in Chetwynd (recipients would repay the costs through long-term mortgages), and a number of smaller federal and provincial grants were obtained by BCANSI or its locals. BCANSI reported an income of $19,382.97 in the calendar year 1970 and $179,711.59 in 1971.[31]

The leaders of the Métis organizations of the three prairie provinces attended the 1970 annual BCANSI meeting. At Smitheram's initiative, they and the BCANSI leaders agreed to establish a national non-status and Métis organization as the counterpart to the National Indian Brotherhood. Out of this agreement, following further meetings in Edmonton and Ottawa, came the Native Council of Canada. Smitheram drafted its constitution and by-laws.[32]

The newly hired BCANSI organizers, or "field workers" as they were called, found fertile ground, especially among the Métis. Thirty-five locals were fully established by the time of the third annual meeting in November 1971. The largest and most active were in the interior boom towns: Dawson Creek, Fort St. John, Chetwynd, Prince George, Williams Lake, and Kamloops. These localities were on the main transportation arteries from Alberta and had the highest concentrations of Métis in the province. Métis now composed more than half the membership of BCANSI and held the majority of positions on the board of directors.

While the board had re-elected Smitheram as president after the 1970 meeting, friction soon became evident. Against his wishes the board hired three of the Métis directors (including Fred House of Dawson Creek) as full-time employees. Smitheram, in contrast, was receiving no salary as president and had to remain a government employee.

House, hitherto best known as an entertainer and country-western singer, challenged Smitheram in the 1971 annual meeting. He and his supporters succeeded first in having the meeting contravene the BCANSI constitution by giving the directors votes in the meeting; then they used their resulting narrow edge in voting power to have the constitution amended to eliminate staggered terms for directors, to provide for direct election of the president by the annual meeting, and to pay the president a full-time salary. In the election of the new board the House forces won almost all the seats, and House then defeated Smitheram as president. Had it not been for the additional directors' votes, Smitheram would likely have retained the presidency even under the new procedures.[33] As it was, however, the Métis component had taken control of BCANSI.

For all aboriginal peoples in British Columbia the 1969-71 period was a time of unprecedented political development. By 1971 the old pattern of dual pan-Indianism seemed completely eclipsed, for both organizations had active supporters in all parts of the province. In neither of the big organizations was there more than a remnant of the turn-of-the-century pattern of tribalism, in which the various tribal groups, such as the Nisga'a, had been the basic elements of wider political organization. The Nisga'a were proceeding on their own in keeping their land claim before the courts, but no other tribal group seemed inclined to act alone.

Despite their different memberships and goals, the Union of British Columbia Indian Chiefs and BCANSI did share one important feature.

Their creation and early growth had been almost entirely dependent upon government funding. The willingness of governments, both provincial and federal, to provide large amounts of money was a crucial new factor. Dependency on government funding would now affect virtually every aspect of aboriginal political activity, including the attempt of the Union to prepare one big land claim covering most of British Columbia.

CHAPTER THIRTEEN

Big Money and Big Organizations, 1972-5

By 1972 the political environment for British Columbia Indians was radically different from what it had ever been in the past. The British Columbia Association of Non-Status Indians and the Union of British Columbia Indian Chiefs were now the dominant elements in Indian politics, each having some two hundred full-time employees and an annual budget well in excess of $2 million. There was now a thriving set of Indian publications. The Native Brotherhood's *Native Voice*, the Homemakers' *Indian Voice*, the Union's *Nesika*, and BCANSI's *Non-Status News* provided much political information, not only about organizations, issues, and the leaders within the province, but also about events and developments elsewhere in Canada and in the United States. Newspapers and periodicals of the National Indian Brotherhood and the Native Council of Canada were also readily available. For the first time political ideas and information circulated widely and quickly among British Columbia Indians. For the first time also, the non-Indian public began to receive regular news about Indians. Ron Rose of the *Vancouver Sun* became the first non-Indian journalist to specialize in British Columbia native issues.

British Columbia Indians themselves now had a substantial presence in Ottawa. Len Marchand continued as a Liberal MP and became a junior cabinet minister; Guy Williams was now a Liberal senator; and George Manuel remained president of the National Indian Brotherhood, which had a large staff in offices not far from the Parliament Buildings. The three men had direct access to the most senior officials in the federal departments, and they could readily bring matters to the attention of the cabinet.

The federal government continued its policy of providing substantial amounts of money to aboriginal political organizations, almost giving the impression of trying to make amends for the prohibition of political fund-raising from 1927 to 1951. In other policy spheres there was a notable absence of federal policy initiatives, especially from the Department of Indian Affairs, which was demoralized and "experiencing a general policy vacuum"[1] in the aftermath of the white paper.

On 6 July 1972 the leaders of the Union of British Columbia Indian Chiefs met with federal officials in Ottawa. George Manuel sat in on behalf of the National Indian Brotherhood. Manuel, Philip Paul, Victor Adolph, Delbert Guerin, and other chiefs sat on one side of a large table; Prime Minister Trudeau and his officials sat on the other. The meeting was regarded by both sides as simply a polite, although important, political gesture. The Union leaders outlined the Indian claim to the non-treaty portions of British Columbia; they made no formal presentation. The prime minister was courteous and obviously willing to be seen as taking Indians seriously, but he was noncommittal. No negotiation occurred.

The Indian newspapers in British Columbia gave great prominence to photographs and reports of the meeting. At the time, and for months afterwards, stories in the Indian papers referred to the British Columbia land claim as having been "presented"[2] at the meeting. Some writers assumed that actual negotiations had started at the meeting; almost all left the impression that a major and decisive step had been taken to advance the claim. The meeting, or at least the way in which it was depicted, created substantial Indian optimism. The Union leaders did not go out of their way to dampen it.

A few weeks later, in August 1972, the Social Credit provincial government was defeated. A New Democratic Party majority was elected under the leadership of Dave Barrett. The party of Frank Calder and Tom Berger was now in power. (Berger himself had been appointed by Prime Minister Trudeau to the Supreme Court of British Columbia and was no longer in politics.) Calder was appointed to the new provincial cabinet. Many Indians took it for granted that the provincial government would now recognize aboriginal title and proceed to negotiate a settlement. Indian optimism thus grew even stronger. Indian confidence increased further in early 1973 when the Supreme Court of Canada went against the British Columbia courts and sided with the Nisga'a in ruling that aboriginal title had existed in British Columbia.

The rapid growth of the organizations and the favourable developments in Ottawa and Victoria led to unprecedented levels of hope and enthusiasm, even euphoria, among Indians. These feelings were especially evident in the annual assemblies of BCANSI and the Union. Largely for social reasons the two assemblies had been held simultaneously in the same city in 1971,[3] and the practice was continued. The assemblies of 1972, 1973, and 1974 provided the settings for huge Indian gatherings of a sort quite unknown previously in the province. They were giant festivals allowing direct personal and social communication across every dividing line that had hitherto characterized Indian society and political organization in British Columbia. Cultural and political slogans were everywhere—on banners in the assembly halls and along the streets outside and on bumper stickers, badges, buttons, hats, T-shirts, and bead work. Many of the slogans affirmed tribal identity, such as in "Haida All the Way," and another frequent slogan was "Proud to Be Indian." The festivals were a very evident manifestation of a new pan-Indianism, one marked by personal pride and revitalization of tribal identity. The challenge to BCANSI and the Union was to meet the expectations of this new pan-Indianism.

The majority of Union employees worked in the head office in Vancouver or in the Land Claims Research Centre established in Victoria under the direction of Philip Paul. Relatively little emphasis was placed upon grass-roots activity. The band chiefs who composed the Union's membership were not expected to act as local activists or publicists for the Union; their role was seen as local representatives at the centre. The structure of the Union, resting on pre-existing local leadership rather than a voluntary membership, did not encourage innovation at the local level. Most chiefs, especially the older and less-educated ones, saw their new role as requiring little more than attendance at meetings. For these reasons the Union served to reinforce the Indian Act's chief and council structure, and the Union had little effect on most ordinary Indians living on the reserves.

BCANSI, in contrast, faced neither inertia nor other constraints arising from existing political institutions at the local level, for there had been no such institutions among non-status Indians or Métis in British Columbia. By 1974 there were BCANSI locals in seventy-five cities and towns. About half of BCANSI's employees lived and worked outside Vancouver. Most of these were "field workers" with the explicit task of publicizing BCANSI and recruiting new members. This task followed naturally from the fact that BCANSI, unlike the Union, was based on voluntary membership. By 1974 there were some two thousand members. Most locals included a core of able and energetic activists who dedicated themselves wholeheartedly to BCANSI and its ideals. They organized policy discussions, prepared resolutions to take to annual assemblies, and arranged a multitude of social activities, including highly popular dances and bingo games, which drew participation from well beyond the formal list of BCANSI members. BCANSI was able to reach out to bring new meaning and fulfilment into the everyday lives of many of its supporters. Moreover, local delegates to BCANSI assemblies were selected by competitive election, with the result that the more informed and energetic members were usually chosen. Overall, BCANSI was a dynamic organization with the potential of creating and pursuing new ideals.

The most important funding agencies for BCANSI and the Union were the provincial First Citizens' Fund and three federal departments: the Department of the Secretary of State (DSS), the Department of Indian Affairs, and the Canada Mortgage and Housing Corporation. In 1971 DSS established its "core and communications" funding program for ethnic minorities and classified both status and non-status Indian organizations as eligible recipients. Core funds were intended to cover the basic, or core, aspects of operating an organization, including the payment of full-time salaries to executive officers; communications funds were intended to provide for publication of the newspapers, purchase of audio-visual equipment, and salaries of field workers engaged in community development.

DSS policy was to fund only one status and one non-status organization for each province and to allocate funds to each organization in proportion to the size of the status and non-status populations. Status population sizes were known exactly but non-status population sizes could only be estimated. For British Columbia the fiction was adopted that the non-status population was equal to that of status Indians, and so BCANSI and the Union were granted identical combined core and communications allotments. The first annual grant to each organization was $448,000; later grants were somewhat larger. DSS committed itself in the beginning to provide grants over a five-year term. Financial security and certainty were thus attributes of both organizations during the 1972–75 period.

Program funds came from a variety of federal and provincial agencies, and there is now no way to determine their total amount.[4] CMHC was the largest single source of program funds for BCANSI, while DIA was the largest source for the Union, with each providing in excess of $1 million annually within British Columbia. The First Citizen's Fund, now in the hands of the New Democratic Party government, provided close to $400,000 to each organization in some years for various training and other programs. Altogether BCANSI and the Union each received at least $2 million annually in program funds during the period.[5]

In the fall of 1972 Fred House was able to say of BCANSI, "We have grown quite enormous and have quite a few different departments."[6] BCANSI now had newly rented and spacious headquarters in Vancouver. There were six departments: education, health and welfare, communications and publications, human resources, housing, and citizenship training. Bill Wilson, now in his final year of law school, was BCANSI's director of citizenship training, with the task of encouraging Indians to vote and participate in politics in greater numbers. As a status Indian he was ineligible to be a member of BCANSI, but he could be one of its employees. He was spending as much time at BCANSI headquarters as he was at his studies.

For the most part the two organizations remained separate in carrying out their programs. The exception occurred in their joint sponsorship of the Native Courtworker and Counselling Association,[7] which trained Indians to provide para-legal assistance and other forms of counselling to Indians in court or in jail. Among all the attempts by either of the two organizations to develop and implement programs for Indians during the 1972-5 period, only this one was successful. The training and experience of the courtworkers and counsellors gave them political awareness and confidence; many of them went on to become politically active.

The Union used its core and communications grants from DSS to set up its headquarters, hire staff, commence publishing *Nesika*,[8] and send some community development workers out to the districts. Land claims research funds were provided by DIA to enable status Indian organizations to prepare statements of claim; DIA policy, like that of DSS, was to provide funds to only one organization in a province. By 1974 land claims research funds were the largest amount being received by the Union, with most of it devoted to the research centre in Victoria.

During most of the period Union leaders themselves conceived of the land claims process as consisting of two stages: first, preparing documents demonstrating in historical and legal terms that Indians had owned and used the land before contact; and, second, negotiating with governments for extinguishment and compensation as anticipated in the Proclamation of 1763. Philip Paul later characterized this view: "If we look at land claims settlement purely on the basis of a real estate proposition there is really no need to consult too many people, just prepare a position paper through computers and expert academics and negotiate with the Government for the best deal."[9] One big claim on behalf of all non-treaty Indians in the province seemed the best way to proceed.

In 1974 the Union established seven new senior staff positions, with the appointees responsible for developing programs in housing, social services, education, economic development, culture-linguistics-crafts, Indians and the law, and local government. DIA and other federal departments were already providing services to bands in each of these areas. The Union's aim was not only to attain greater influence over the government programs but also, or at least some in the Union still believed, to have the Union replace DIA within British Columbia.

Matters did not go well for Frank Calder in the NDP cabinet. He was merely a minister without portfolio and had little prestige or influence, while Norman Levi, the minister in charge of social services, served as government spokesman on Indian matters. Calder, a proud man keenly desirous that Indians receive their political due, found his position demeaning. He attempted to establish good relations with the Union leaders, whom he had formerly criticized,[10] and he sought to facilitate BCANSI's dealing with the various ministries. But he had a difficult time explaining his own role. Soon after taking office he spoke to the Union's annual assembly. He "explained that his job as Minister without Portfolio was to go out and make a complete survey of the Indian matters, but said that he would not do one because of the many surveys already done on Indian people."[11] His attempts to be helpful to the organizations were not appreciated. Fred House was contemptuous, stating that when BCANSI officials went to Calder, "he'd sort of lecture us on how to approach other ministers, how to come in the door, and that kind of b.s."[12]

In April 1973 Calder was held by the Victoria City Police for a brief time after being found drunk in a public place. Charges were laid against his companion, but not against him. The incident took several months to find its way into the news media, which treated the matter circumspectly. *Nesika* reported that Premier Barrett had first heard of the matter two months after it occurred, and that he was unable to get Calder to admit that the event had occurred or to come to his office to discuss the matter.[13] As a result, Calder was dismissed from the cabinet.[14]

The Calder affair was a minor scandal which had no effect upon the course of provincial Indian policy or upon the activities of the big organizations. Until well into 1974 there was a widespread belief among Indians that BCANSI and the Union were either meeting their goals or were well on their way to doing so. The leaders of both organizations publicly encouraged this belief. In reality neither organization was meeting any of its major goals. This fact was at the root of the internal disputes that existed within each organization by 1973. These disputes, which became ever more debilitating, centred upon three aspects: policy initiation and orientation, relations between elected officials and appointed staff, and the personal conduct of leaders.

The most common criticism in each organization was that the leaders were out of touch with the grass-roots concerns of ordinary people on reserves and in local communities. It was made in every annual assembly during the period and, beginning in mid-1973, in the newspapers. In August 1973 Butch Smitheram wrote:

I am of the opinion that the native movement is getting distorted . . . [Our leaders] have become polished politicians who spend a great deal of time and energy on political campaigns and mutual backscratching and not enough time in training, organizing, and encouraging the leaders back in the small communities . . . They are proposing and implementing programs that originate in the heads of well meaning leaders, but the proposals lack the support and input from people who live on bannock and beans.[15]

Smitheram also pointed to the growth of the women's organizations as a sign that the two big organizations were not orienting their policies towards a major segment of the Indian population.[16]

Within the Union the issue of policy orientation was at the heart of the controversy that resulted in the first defection from the Union, that of the Nisga'a in 1973. In the Nisga'a view the Union's only mandate was to proceed with the land claim. The difference of approach, with the Nisga'a preferring to use the courts and the Union preferring direct negotiations with government, was not at issue. James Gosnell and other Nisga'a chiefs had attended each Union annual assembly up to, and including, that of 1972 without ever criticizing the Union's approach. What the Nisga'a objected to was the Union's taking on programs and activities not directly related to land claims. Statements such as "the Union was told to go after land claims and they got into everything else"[17] and "the union [became] another department of Indian affairs and refused to support our land claims"[18] were typical among the Nisga'a at the time and later.

The Supreme Court of Canada's decision in the Nisga'a case in January 1973 brought matters to a head. The court acknowledged that the Nisga'a had held title to their land before colonial government was established, but the judges divided evenly on whether the title still existed.[19] Jubilant over the court's acknowledgment that aboriginal title had existed in British Columbia and at Prime Minister Trudeau's public comments showing he recognized the significance of the court's action, Calder had Senator Guy Williams arrange a meeting in Ottawa between the prime minister and the Nisga'a chiefs. The meeting was scheduled for the afternoon of 7 February. Shortly before the meeting the Nisga'a were infuriated to discover that George Manuel and Union leaders had learned of the meeting and arranged to meet with the prime minister earlier on the same day. Convinced that Manuel and the Union, as well as Len Marchand, were attempting to deflect credit from the Nisga'a by making it appear that the Union and Manuel's National Indian Brotherhood had supported and fostered the Nisga'a case, Calder and Williams informed the prime minister's office that they would not attend. The meeting was re-scheduled to allow the Nisga'a delegation to meet with Trudeau before Manuel and the Union leaders did so. Trudeau told the Nisga'a that his own thinking had been changed by the Supreme

Court's recognition that the Indians had owned their land before contact and by the opinion of three judges, for whom he had an especially
high regard, that the Nisga'a still did own their land.[20]

As a result of the Nisga'a decision, Trudeau redirected federal policy
to allow the Nisga'a and other non-treaty groups to negotiate directly
with the federal government. The Indian Claims Commission was
replaced by the Office of Native Claims within DIA, and land claims
negotiations were started. Those with the Nisga'a began in 1976. The
federal government had returned to its historic position on aboriginal
title.

It was because of the actions of Manuel and the Union leaders in
attempting to share credit for the Nisga'a decision[21] that the Nisga'a
withdrew from the Union. No Nisga'a chief attended the 1973 Union
assembly or those which followed. The Nisga'a withdrawal was the first
explicit and public defection from the Union. It drew attention to the
fact, however, that support for the Union was already declining among
central and north coast groups. The proportion of bands in those areas
sending delegates to Union assemblies had been decreasing, and it
continued to decline. The old dual pan-Indianism was reappearing.
The Union was becoming a Salish organization.

In both BCANSI and the Union attaining harmonious and effective
relations between elected officers and senior staff proved impossible. In
both there were well-publicized resignations and firings accompanied
by name-calling and bitter accusations.[22] In both organizations there
was much criticism of the deportment of leaders. They were said to be
avoiding their duties, getting drunk, spending organization funds on
high living, and misreporting their expenditures. One of the most active
BCANSI members later observed that

A regular entourage flew to every annual meeting and founding meeting of
every non-status and Métis association in Canada. It would not have been so bad
if only the Pres. or the Vice Pres. made the trip, but [the president] usually took
about six of his friends along. The pay-off was when the Native Council of
Canada held a Board meeting . . . in Mexico City. Most of the BCANSI Board
members and their wives or girlfriends went along too and a great time was had
by all.[23]

One of the most prominent staff members later described his time with
BCANSI as "a continuous cross-country social foolaroundathon."[24] In
both organizations the payment of travel and living expenses for all
assembly delegates, as well as per diem honorariums to directors and
chiefs' council members, facilitated attendance by a minority without
serious intent. Within BCANSI Fred House continued to gain election as

president, but after 1972 Indians rather than Métis held a majority of positions on the board of directors. The board was often critical of House's tardiness and absences. The board and House remained at odds.

At the Union's second assembly, in 1970, Bill Wilson, Philip Paul, Delbert Guerin, and other young Indians had expressed the ideal of uniting status and non-status Indians in one organization. The ideal seemed forgotten as BCANSI and the Union gained momentum. The separate and massive funding of the two organizations dampened any desire for unity; a merger would necessitate a reduction in the number of leadership positions and a diminution of the prestige, perquisites, and power that the two sets of leaders were enjoying. BCANSI leaders were hoping for better services for non-status Indians and Métis; they had no interest in the land claim. The Union leaders sought to focus on the land claim and on the needs of status Indians; they had no interest in non-status Indians or Métis. The place of the Métis in any scheme of Indian unity remained cloudy; no mention of them had been made in the 1970 discussions at the Union assembly.

While working for BCANSI in 1972, Bill Wilson[25] prepared at his own initiative a short paper entitled "Aboriginal Title." He presented it at BCANSI's annual assembly that autumn.

It is the purpose of this paper to point out to the members of the B.C. Association of Non-Status Indians that they have a legitimate interest in the area of Aboriginal Title. It must be recognized, however, that because of political considerations, organizational jealousies, and other factors dividing Native people, the B.C. Association of Non-Status Indians' claim will not be satisfied without a great deal of effort on the part of the Association . . . Unless the members of the B.C. Association of Non-Status Indians pursue the claim based on aboriginal title then no benefits will be forthcoming for approximately half of those people who have an ancestral right to the land in the province of British Columbia.

Wilson's paper and his speech urging status/non-status co-operation were supported by the assembly; it promptly endorsed the principles of unity and of sharing by all British Columbia Indians in claims for aboriginal title. While they did not expressly oppose the action, the Métis members, having no ancestral interest in lands in the province, did not indicate any particular interest in the issue. Presumably they did not take seriously Wilson's suggestion that Métis and non-status Indians from outside the province could be adopted by groups of British Columbia Indians and so share in land claims settlements. The members of BCANSI who gave enthusiastic support to Wilson and the unity ideals were the Indians of British Columbia ancestry.

After the assembly the BCANSI board created the new position of director of land claims research and appointed Wilson to it. Wilson and his supporters now attempted to gain the co-operation of the Union. They were rebuffed. Victor Adolph, the dominant member of the Union executive, said that the "first obligation" of the Union was "to our Indian people."[26] He seemed to be saying that non-status Indians were not Indian people.

In the 1973 Union assembly at Penticton the chiefs from his Kwagiulth district chose Wilson as their alternate delegate on the council of chiefs. In January 1974, when the regular delegate resigned, Wilson became a full member of the council and gave up his BCANSI position. During the next months he sought to have the Union's land claims negotiation committee expanded to include representatives of the Native Brotherhood, the Homemakers, BCANSI, and the Nisga'a Tribal Council. His efforts met strong opposition from other council members.

Wilson and other young Indians had already been giving practical evidence of their ideals. British Columbia Indians had mounted no major political protests since the 1920s when the Kwagiulth and others had held public potlatches. In 1973 the contemporary era of British Columbia Indian political protest began.[27] The timing was in part influenced by events in the United States. For several years Indians in Washington State had been protesting violations of their fishing rights, and the spring of 1973 brought much attention in the Indian newspapers to the action of armed members of the American Indian Movement in occupying Wounded Knee, South Dakota, the site of the final massacre in the Indian wars of the previous century.

During the summer of 1973 young Indians, mostly BCANSI and Union staff, and including Wilson, occupied regional DIA headquarters in Vancouver and demanded government action on land claims. There was no thought of violence or damage to property; the protesters vanished as soon as the police were summoned. On the Island young Cowichans built a traditional weir and caught salmon in contravention of government regulations. Nine fishermen were arrested. The news media, Indian and white, gave much attention to the Indian actions.

At the same time Indian dissatisfaction with the NDP provincial government was growing. Some Indian hope remained that Norman Levi would succeed in persuading the government to recognize aboriginal title, but there was no sign of his doing so. In June 1974 the staffs of BCANSI and the Union, along with several district and tribal councils and a number of bands and BCANSI locals, organized a protest march on the legislature. Placards were carried and flyers were handed out dealing with land claims, cut-offs, education, unemployment, Indians in prison, and the NDP's emphasis on welfare rather than economic development.

Elated by the high turnout and with its enthusiasm raised by a series of Indian speakers, the crowd gave a friendly reception to Levi when he came out of the legislative building to speak. The enthusiasm turned to booing and shouting when Levi stated that title was a federal matter and that the province would take no action. At the front of the crowd Wilson and others hurled obscenities at the departing Levi. The NDP government was seen as having reneged on an initial promise to recognize title. As Wilson put it, "They lied. The whole thing of dealing with land claims was bald-faced, bloody lie."[28]

On one major Indian issue the NDP government did prove willing to reverse provincial policy. Persuaded by the Union leaders and their research material that the cut-offs had been made unfairly, the NDP attorney-general, Alex Macdonald, agreed on behalf of the government to consider their return. The federal government had already indicated its readiness to do so. Preparations got underway, but negotiations had not begun by the time the NDP was defeated in the election of December 1975.[29]

Confrontations between Indians and government officials occurred in British Columbia and other parts of Canada during the summer of 1974. DIA offices were occupied in Alberta and Ontario. In British Columbia the Nisga'a confronted Canadian National Railway surveyors and were successful in stopping possible railway development. Providing a new departure in the province was the prolonged blockade of a provincial highway by armed members of the Bonaparte Band near Cache Creek. The major demand was for better housing, but statements were made about aboriginal rights and Indian ownership of the land under the highway. An RCMP officer negotiated with the Indians for a number of days while a police force waited nearby. The blockade ended with the officer's promising to convey the Indians' demands to the government. In October several hundred British Columbia Indians travelled by car in a "Native Caravan" to Ottawa to demand more definite action on land claims and greater attention to other issues. On Parliament Hill the peaceful and unsuspecting demonstrators were suddenly set upon and driven back by a club-swinging RCMP squad in full riot gear.

In November 1974 the Union's council of chiefs met in Terrace to discuss what was by now the obvious lack of progress in preparing a formal statement of land claim to present to the federal government. At the insistence of some of the younger members who were in favour of Indian unity, the other major organizations—the Native Brotherhood, the Nisga'a Tribal Council, the Indian Homemakers, and BCANSI—had representatives at the meeting. The meeting was acrimonious and inconclusive.[30]

Wilson now became the first to indicate a comprehensive view of reform. In a lengthy interview published in January 1975 in the Home-makers' newspaper, the *Indian Voice*, he laid out four principles or elements he regarded as essential in achieving the reform. One element was all-Indian unity:

What bothers me about the whole status, non-status situation is: there are so many non-status Indians that are non-status through no conscious fault of their own, yet are victims of the bigotry of status leaders. Indians discriminating against Indians because government has made this arbitrary distinction. They are listening to white people who are telling them who is an Indian and who is not, instead of following the dictates of their own common sense.

A second element was the decentralization of power to the grass-roots level. "The Union of B.C. Indian Chiefs is operated like a secret society, the grass root level of the Indian people have no access to and receive no information from the Union . . . The Union council does not believe in the democratic process and they don't have faith in their own people." By the grass-roots level he meant tribal groups as much as the bands and communities on which the Union was based. He gave as examples the Salish, Haida, and his own Kwagiulth. Leadership of the tribal groups would be close to the people and would not be encumbered by large bureaucracies. Each tribal group should be able to proceed along its own "separate way."

A third principle was the use of Indian history and tradition as the source of ideals and examples for the present. While this ideal was not discussed explicitly in the interview, it had already been presented in a number of Wilson's speeches and published comments, and it was implicit in the turning back to the tribal groups. Quite unlike the band councils created under the Indian Act, tribal leadership structures could be seen to have existed before contact. The fourth principle was Indian self-reliance.

After I had experience with the Union, BCANSI, and other organizations that are funded by the government I began to realize the inherent worth of that pioneer organization [the Native Brotherhood, which relied solely on its members for financial support] . . . I think the whole [current] philosophy follows through with the core funding initially . . . the core funding robbed us of the kind of leaders we once had. It's robbed us of the Andy Paulls. We have lost the quality of leaders we once had. We now have these welfare recipients who exist on core funding and who would not be in the movement if there were no financial gain . . . [Council of chiefs members] receive $50.00 a day honorarium and all expenses plus $250 a month ... They come to Vancouver every three weeks for a chiefs' council meeting and booze it up.

Because of a deliberate policy of the government ... the core funding is there to involve [Indians] in personal hassles ... men against women, tribe against tribe, different groups are locked in futile disputes ... youth against aged, uneducated against educated ... reserve Indians against urban Indians ... The government has been successful. We are in our fourth year of guaranteed core funding and the Union has done nothing ... absolutely nothing. I think the only solution is to stop the core funding. Get rid of the carpet-baggers, the smooth-tongued orators, and all the other con artists that are involved in the movement. When we get rid of the core funding, people at the grass root level will have to pay the salaries and expenses of meetings. If the grass root people are paying the expenses they are calling the shot. And that is not happening today.

Wilson's vision pointed to a radical transformation of the established state of affairs within British Columbia Indian politics. Two major features flowing from the Indian Act, the distinction between status and non-status Indians and the existence of Indian bands as the only recognized entity at the local level, would be superseded by an all-Indian unity expressed through self-reliant tribal councils at the local level. The tribal councils, some twenty-five in number, would replace the two big central organizations as the vehicles for pursuit of Indian land claims.

That Wilson should emerge as the leading advocate of grass-roots politics was a paradox, for among all the young Indians playing leading roles in BCANSI or the Union, he had the least grass roots experience. He had had no local political or administrative experience in either an Indian band or a BCANSI local. His reputation rested on the prominence of his own family among the Kwagiulth, especially of his mother,[31] on his educational attainments, on his oratory, and on the fact that he was identifying and expressing ideals well established at the grass-roots level within communities and tribal groups. He was now the leading spokesman for these ideals.

By the time Wilson's interview was published, the formal leadership in both big organizations was in disarray. The Union's executive committee was scarcely functioning, while the council of chiefs was a confusion of factions and shifting majorities. There was even some indications that a bare majority of the council might approve the idea of a merger of the two organizations. BCANSI's executive had ceased to function. Fred House had dropped from sight. The BCANSI board was now firmly controlled by Indians of British Columbia ancestry, who were acting on the assumption that a merger with the Union would in fact soon take place. In preparation for the merger, organization charts were drawn and enquiries were made about office space.

The Union's 1975 annual assembly stands as a pivotal event in modern British Columbia Indian political history. It was held in April in Chilliwack.[32] Partly in response to the accumulated frustrations over the failure of the Union leadership to attain the Union's goals, but even more in response to the emergent ideals of unity, the 1975 Union assembly assumed a life of its own. It became a political and cultural revival meeting that had a profound emotional significance for many of those taking part. No one had anticipated such a possibility.

The older members of the executive committee and the chiefs' council drew back, bewildered, as the events unfolded. Formal rules of order were often ignored. Spontaneous performances of traditional songs or dances (notably by the Nuu'chah'nulth) occurred when feelings ran high. Emotions about Indianness went far beyond mere words. The distinctions between status and non-status Indians and between chiefs and ordinary Indians were abandoned in the proceedings. Non-status Indians made speeches to the assembly, and at times everyone present, whether chief or not, voted on motions. Four young Indians dominated the meeting. Bill Wilson and George Watts played the major part in leading the assembly in the new directions. Delbert Guerin and Philip Paul had major roles as well; they were more cautious and more concerned with practical outcomes.[33]

Among the many resolutions passed by the assembly, four were of special importance. One provided that the three-member executive committee would now be elected directly by the annual assembly. This change, which stripped the chiefs' council of its major power, was intended to ensure that the executive would be directly responsible to the delegates of the local communities. Two resolutions opened the way for all-Indian unity. One of them stated that henceforth a primary purpose of the Union would be "to provide a central organization for uniting together the Indian people of the Province of British Columbia for the purpose of settlement of Land Claims and Aboriginal Rights." The other provided that all persons having at least one-quarter British Columbia Indian blood were to share in the land claims settlement. The Union thus accepted the ideals that Bill Wilson and other young Indians had proclaimed during the Union's founding and that had more recently been accepted within BCANSI. The Chilliwack assembly, however, paid virtually no attention to the actual steps that would need to be taken "to provide a central organization for uniting together the Indian people." Scarcely noticing this fact, the leading BCANSI activists were ecstatic, believing merger of the two organizations was actually at hand.

The assembly is best remembered, however, for another motion. In their speeches Wilson, Watts, and others contrasted the jet-set lifestyle of BCANSI and Union leaders with the poverty on reserves and among BCANSI members, and they pointed to the failure to produce a land claim statement despite the millions of dollars ostensibly spent on research and preparation. Wilson's initial intent was to have the assembly vote to reject government funding of the Union itself in order to compel the leadership to rely on the grass roots for support and contributions. However, as the speeches and dances proceeded, the desire to be free of government grew apace, as did faith in the ability of Indians to be fully self-sufficient.

Part way through the assembly a telegram arrived from George Manuel on behalf of the National Indian Brotherhood. Contrary to what he had intended, the wording of Manuel's telegram could be, and was, taken as suggesting that bands as well as the political organizations should free themselves of government financial control. As a result, the motion that was eventually put to the assembly asserted not merely that the Union would accept no more government money, but also that British Columbia Indians rejected government funds of every sort. The motion passed overwhelmingly.

The decision to reject all government funds was an astounding turn of events; no one had even thought of it before the assembly. Without having consulted the grass roots, the advocates of grass-roots control were now demanding that Indian communities and individuals give up all government financial support, including local administration grants, educational financing, and welfare payments.[34]

At the close of the Union assembly the delegates elected Wilson, Watts, and Paul as the members of the new executive committee. Several weeks later, in a special assembly called for the purpose, BCANSI voted to reject government funding and to proceed to merge with the Union.

In accordance with the expressed wishes of the organizations, the Department of Indian Affairs and the Department of the Secretary of State cut off funds to them, and DIA began to phase out payments at the band level. With their funding stopped, BCANSI and the Union closed their head offices and laid off all their employees. At the band level among status Indians fear and confusion reigned. The grass-roots outpouring against the rejection of band funding was unprecedented and unambiguous. Among status Indians at the local level there was also evident a hostility to BCANSI and non-status activists, who were viewed as responsible for triggering the rejection of funds.

The summer of 1975 brought a new round of Indian protests. Placard-carrying Indians marched down main streets. Indians took fish in defiance of federal regulations. Indians occupied DIA offices in Wil-

liams Lake and Kamloops. There were several road blockades; the most
sustained was mounted by the Mount Currie Band, with active supporters present from across the province.

Wilson, Watts, and Paul were unable to act with any coherence as the
Union's executive; Watts and Paul soon resigned. Wilson and the chiefs'
council called a special assembly in Kamloops for the autumn, but it was
poorly attended. Wilson argued unsuccessfully in favour of continuing
the rejection of funds. Within the Union there was now little support for
merger with BCANSI or for allowing non-status Indians to share in land
claims. DIA officials, no longer viewing the Union as credible, began to
restore band-level funding.

The Kamloops assembly elected a new executive, consisting of Wilson
and two other equally young men, Stephen Point (Sto:lo) and Robert
Manuel (Shuswap, son of George Manuel). Without funds, without staff,
and without explicit grass-roots support, the new executive was no more
effective than the last. The Union now had neither the desire nor the
ability to consider any merger with BCANSI. Also without funds and staff,
the remaining BCANSI leaders were no more able to function than were
the Union office holders. BCANSI and the Union had collapsed, and with
them, it seemed, the reform ideals. The big organizations had failed to
meet the expectations of the new social and political confidence among
British Columbia Indians.

CHAPTER FOURTEEN

Tribalism Re-Established, 1976–9

The growing strength of tribalism was a major cause of the simultaneous collapse of the British Columbia Association of Non-Status Indians and the Union of British Columbia Indian Chiefs in 1975. The collapse of the two big organizations allowed tribalism to grow more rapidly and spread more widely among British Columbia Indians. Tribalism involved political thought and action centring upon the historic language or culture groups, which have been referred to in this book as "tribal groups."[1] Tribalism showed itself in several ways. Individuals came to re-emphasize their tribal group as the focus of their personal Indian identities and loyalties.[2] The tribal groups themselves established their own political organizations and sought to promote their fundamental Indian interests through these organizations. At the provincial level the tribal groups replaced the bands or local communities as the basis of political representation.

Tribalism was nothing new; it had been a basic element in the early Indian attempts to resolve the land question and in the formation of the Allied Tribes. It had diminished with the prohibition of claims-related actitivities in 1927 and had been further discouraged by deliberate policies of the Department of Indian Affairs, especially through the Indian Act's exclusive focus on bands and band councils. The formation of tribal councils by the Nisga'a and Nuu'chah'nulth in the 1950s had signalled a renewing tribal vitality. Both BCANSI and the Union, however, had sought to ignore tribal groups in their structure and activities.

The ideals and beliefs that led to the collapse of the big organizations were intimately related to tribalism. Accepting the notion that the tribal group was the fundamental unit for Indian identity and loyalty went hand in hand with the ideal of unity and equality among all members of each tribal group, whatever their status under the Indian Act. Among British Columbia Indians in the 1970s the adjective "tribal" came into common use for the first time, as did the term "tribal group."[3] Besides connoting the various language or culture groups, the adjective "tribal" also denoted "Indianness" and suggested a turning towards group self-reliance. Tribalism was thus marked by a rejection of the forms and values of large, centralized, bureaucratic entities, whether government departments or Indian organizations.

Everywhere tribalism rested on the principles of popular equality and popular participation. Had modern tribalism been an elitist phenomenon restricting power and influence, it could not have flourished among contemporary Indians well versed in the principles and practices of liberal democracy. Among the coastal peoples, especially on the north coast, one-person-one-vote principles thus signified an addition to tradition.[4] Within every tribal group the formal creation of a "tribal council" was the sign that the principle of tribalism had been accepted. Tribal councils consisted of the people of the group gathered together in assembly, with each person having one vote. Members of the various bands or local communities thus came together as individuals, with each person ordinarily having an equal vote in the election of tribal council chairman and other executive members. In tribal council operations, however, the bands or communities did retain a recognized place; typically having equal representation on a board of directors. In this sense, tribal councils could be regarded as federations of the bands or communities making up the tribal group. The whole tribal council, however, meeting in assembly, remained the governing body of the tribal group.[5]

During the 1970s Department of Indian Affairs' control was still pervasive at the band level. Reducing this control, that is, attaining more self-government, was a major goal of those who favoured tribalism. District and tribal political organization was in every case motivated in good part by the benefits of common action on the part of communities in seeking more local control. There was no thought that tribalism would cause communities to fade in importance or to have diminished self-government. Everywhere demands for greater local autonomy accelerated along with tribalism.

Effective land claims preparation was regarded as a major goal of tribalism, and in most cases overall responsibility for such preparation was regarded as belonging exclusively to the tribal councils. Yet, even land claims preparation was regarded by most tribal leaders as intimately dependent upon the health and vitality of the local communities. For this reason not all tribal groups hurried to follow the Nisga'a in presenting their land claims to the federal government. Most tribal group leaders deliberately chose to wait until their peoples attained renewed unity and their communities were more self-sufficient, and for this reason the leaders devoted much effort to social and economic development. Preparation of land claims, however, remained the ultimate goal. As the years proceeded, more and more tribal groups did prepare and present their claims formally to the federal Office of Native Claims or, as it was later called, the Comprehensive Claims Branch.[6]

Two factors were important in facilitating the spread of modern tribalism and the formation of tribal councils prior to 1975. One of these was the continuous example provided after 1955 by the tribal councils of the Nisga'a and the Nuu'chah'nulth. The other was the establishment throughout the province of "district councils." By the late 1960s agencies were styled "districts," and the Indian agents, now called "district managers," were under instructions to call periodic meetings of the chiefs. While the intended purpose of these "district councils" was to counter the widespread lack of support among Indians for departmental actions and policies, one of their effects of was to increase communication among the chiefs and communities within a district. In a number of cases the districts were coterminous, or nearly so, with tribal group areas; in these cases the district councils served as incubators of tribal councils. In other cases districts included portions of several tribal groups, and in some of these the differing groups did form single tribal councils, but the motive in such cases was almost always to present a common front to DIA and not to prepare land claims.[7] Eventually, however, the general tendency was for each tribal group to have its own tribal council and to ignore any conflicting district boundaries.

The collapse of the big organizations in 1975 provided a further major stimulus to the growth of tribalism. The collapse cleared the political centre stage, giving more visibility and more room to tribalism, which the big organizations had ignored and obscured. At the same time the disintegration of the big organizations left their leaders and staff unemployed. Some four hundred people, the most informed and experienced Indian political actors in the province, were suddenly at loose ends. Some took jobs with government or private companies, some went back to school, some hung out in Vancouver, but many went home to their own communities and tribal groups. This sudden infusion of new political talent at the local and tribal level was a crucial development; it was one of the major beneficial legacies of the big organizations. After 1975 the young veterans of the big organizations played key roles in the development of every tribal council except that of the Nisga'a. In effect, British Columbia Indians were now providing their own community development workers.

The emphasis upon tribalism was at first much more evident on the coast than in the interior. Among the coastal peoples the age-old tribal identities and institutions remained in place to a substantial extent, and so the return to tribalism was in good part a matter of dusting-off and renovating; the process was already underway in 1975, and it was substantially complete by 1980. Among the interior peoples, whose tribal institutions and loyalties were less developed, the turn to tribalism required innovation and creativity, and it often engendered internal controversy. In the interior the process had scarcely begun by 1975, and it was a decade before most interior groups had functioning tribal councils. After 1975 it was the major coastal tribal councils (those of the Nisga'a, the Nuu'chah'nulth, and the Gitksan-Wet'suwet'en) that stood out as the most active, strong, and stable. They became the models for tribal political development in the rest of the province.

The Alliance of British Columbia Indian Bands, formed in 1974, shared features of both a tribal council and a political organization. It was initially composed of the Squamish, Sechelt, and Musqueam bands, which were alike in having progressive leaders intent on taking advantage of their closeness to Vancouver for purposes of economic development. Joe Mathias, chief of the Squamish, and Delbert Guerin, chief of the Musqueam, remained the main Alliance spokesmen as it expanded during the late 1970s to have a membership of nine bands, including Nanaimo on Vancouver Island and Westbank in the Okanagan Valley. The Alliance could be, and was, taken as a new provincial political organization, similar in structure to the Union. Yet the Alliance had tribal aspects as well, for all of the member bands were part of Salish tribal groups. This feature of the Alliance drew attention both to the fact that support for the Union of British Columbia Indian Chiefs was continuing to shrink back to the Salish areas in the south of the province and to the fact that even in these areas there was less than unanimous support for the Union. Opposition to the Union was a major factor in the growth of the Alliance, for each of its bands had quit the Union and regarded the Alliance as something of a replacement. The leaders of each of the Alliance bands were supportive of tribalism and of eliminating the status/non-status distinction.

One final observation may be made about tribalism and the political conflicts it engendered after 1975. At the time many Indians and outside observers viewed the Indian political leaders as so obsessed with their personal standing and so touchy about criticism that they were failing to respond to the real needs of ordinary Indians. Undoubtedly, there were personal interests involved (to lose an election or to suffer a reduction in government funding could mean losing prestige, salary, and travel funds), and certainly there were some whose judgement was clouded by alcohol, ill-health, advancing years, or uncritical advice from sycophants. For the most part, however, the personal conflicts did relate to real and fundamental issues that had to be settled before tribal groups could act effectively in setting and pursuing their own goals. Furthermore, the annual assemblies and board meetings of the tribal councils and of the provincial organizations were characterized by open debate, in which pointed criticism of leaders was often made. Leaders who proved unresponsive could be removed, as the Nisga'a and Gitksan-Wet'suwet'en Tribal councils showed in removing presidents. Most of the political leaders could have obtained secure jobs, and higher incomes, in non-Indian sectors.[8] Given the choice, they chose Indian politics.

During the era of the big organizations a distinct political pattern had emerged in the use of meeting and drinking places by Indians in Vancouver. Leaders, employees, and members of BCANSI preferred places along the southern reaches of Granville Street, the area of the downtown closest to BCANSI's head office; their favourite spot was the Nelson Place Hotel. Leaders, staff, and supporters of the Union favoured the area around their head office on West Hastings Street; their favourite meeting place was the Marble Arch Hotel. Forays would on occasion be made into the bars or beer parlours of the other camp, often with jocular bravado or feigned deference, as though enemy territory were being penetrated. Before and after the collapse of the two organizations, some of the advocates of Indian unity demonstrated their sincerity by frequenting establishments of the other camp.

Thus it was on the evening of 6 January 1976 that George Watts, chairman of the Nuu'chah'nulth Tribal Council and recent member of the Union's executive committee, sat alone in the bar of the Nelson Place Hotel.[9] To his delight he was soon joined by three Indian women; two had just returned from a southern holiday and were staying at the hotel en route to their homes in the interior. Before Watts had time to savour his good fortune he felt a hand on his shoulder. It belonged to Bill Wilson, one of the two persons whom Watts most intensely disliked. "Let me buy you all a drink," said Wilson. In fact he had already ordered the drinks, which were arriving as he spoke. Watts cursed silently at Wilson's intrusion and thought to himself, "Here's the biggest jerk[10] in the province offering to buy me a drink. What's he going to do? Put cyanide in it?" Wilson sat down. As the evening progressed, Wilson and Watts found their forced cordiality giving way to real amity and agreement. From the evening emerged a lasting personal friendship and the beginnings of an important political partnership between the two men.

BCANSI and the Union each revived to some extent after 1975. Each sought and received renewed government funding. They responded very differently, however, to the growing presence of tribalism. One welcomed it and flourished with it; the other fought it and declined in face of it.

Bill Lightbown and a few others guided the affairs of BCANSI in preparing for the 1976 annual assembly. They kept in touch with Wilson. Seeing themselves as having been rebuffed by the Union in their attempts to merge with it, they now decided upon the alternative of opening BCANSI membership to status Indians. They accepted the principles of tribalism and intended that BCANSI would promote the political development of the tribal groups. Over considerable opposition, they persuaded the assembly (which was held in June, on the cheap, in the Totem Park student residences at the University of British Columbia)[11] to make three fundamental constitutional amendments. First, the membership provision was changed to allow anyone with one-quarter or more Indian blood, and only such persons, to belong. The distinction between status and non-status Indians was thus erased, and spouses having no Indian blood could no longer be members. Second, the role of locals in choosing assembly delegates was eliminated; all members could now attend assemblies and vote. Third, since the old name was now inaccurate, a new one was chosen. It was "United Native Nations." "Nations" meant "tribal groups." The new name signified that the organization, like the United Nations, would serve the interests of the separate nations while respecting their rights and identities.[12]

Wilson was present throughout the conference, even though, as a status Indian, he could not be a member until the change in eligibility was approved, at which point he joined. With Lightbown's support, he was then elected as first president of the United Native Nations, or "UNN," as it was called. Wilson held the office for the next six years, making full use of it as a platform, and remaining the most prominent and influential proponent of tribalism and of doing away with status/non-status distinctions in order to achieve political co-operation and harmony among all British Columbia Indians. In good part as a result of Wilson's advocacy, the term "Indian unity" emerged as a major symbol and slogan. Its use affirmed the conviction that status and non-status Indians should come together as political equals and that provincial Indian organizations should pool their political efforts.

Until this time BCANSI had been the British Columbia component unit of the Native Council of Canada, the national organization of Métis and non-status Indians. Butch Smitheram had been one of those principally responsible for the NCC's formation, and Gloria George, as NCC president, had been the only woman to lead a national aboriginal organization. The opening of membership to status Indians placed the UNN in violation of the NCC's membership provisions, and there was no inclination at the national level to change those provisions. Wilson led a delegation of UNN delegates consisting of eight status and nine non-status Indians to the next NCC annual meeting. They walked out just before they were formally excluded from the meeting and from the NCC. The exclusion remained in force until 1982. The isolation of the UNN from national aboriginal politics during this period spared Wilson and the other UNN leaders from the seductive and enervating distractions of national aboriginal politics, thus leaving them free to focus their political energy fully within British Columbia. The inclusion of status Indians did not affect funding from the Department of Secretary of State; the UNN continued to receive its major funding from the department.

Unlike BCANSI, the Union continued with the same membership structure as before, but it did change its executive structure. The three-member collegial executive was replaced by a president and four vice-presidents (to represent four geographic divisions), all elected by the annual assembly. The change was a response both to the previous organizational difficulties and to the impending retirement of George Manuel as president of the National Indian Brotherhood. Manuel came home to British Columbia in 1977 and was elected as the Union's first president.[13] Manuel's unrivalled stature as a national Indian spokesmen continued, and through him the Union now had an even more effective set of contacts with NIB staff and with federal officials in Ottawa. The Union remained the only status Indian organization in British Columbia receiving core funding from DSS and also the sole recipient in the province of DIA land claims research funding.

Composed of band chiefs, and thus naturally committed to the primacy of bands as the basis of Indian political organization, the Union had little incentive to embrace tribalism or to cooperate with non-status Indians. The Union activists considered the non-status issue to have been settled by the Union's decision not to unite with BCANSI.[14] In 1977 the question of tribalism had yet to arise directly, and some advocates of tribalism remained active in the Union. The most prominent of these were Ray Jones (Gitksan) and Ernie Willie (Kwagiulth); both were Union vice-presidents.

Nevertheless, tribalism was already eating away at the Union. The pattern was clear on the coast. There was still considerable Union support where tribal councils were not yet strong, as among the Kwagiulth, Skeena River Tsimshian, Nuxalk, Haisla, Island Salish, and Sto:lo. Wherever active and well-organized tribal councils (or, among the Salish tribal groups, the Alliance) were present, many of the bands had withdrawn from the Union. George Watts took the remaining Nuu'chah'-nulth support with him when he broke with the Union over what he viewed as efforts to weaken the Native Courtworkers Association. The territories of the Nisga'a, Haida, Tsimshian, Heiltsuk, and Nuu'chah'-nulth were becoming devoid of Union support. These were the tribal groups that provided the bulk of Native Brotherhood membership.[15]

Brotherhood spokesmen intensified their opposition to the Union, criticizing it publicly for its lack of co-operation with other organizations,
for its monopoly on status Indian funding, and for its continued failure
to produce a land claim.

The leaders of the Brotherhood, the UNN, and the Alliance were in
frequent communication. A number of them, including Wilson, Joe
Mathias, George Watts, and Edwin Newman (a prominent executive
member of the Brotherhood), were close personal friends. All of them
shared the same ideals and the same antipathy towards the Union
leaders for rejecting those ideals. They believed that the weakness of the
Union would be used increasingly by the federal government as an
excuse to avoid any serious response to land claims. Their three organizations held a conference of supporters in Vancouver in April 1977;
there was criticism of the Union, and fear was expressed that governments would increasingly ignore Indian concerns. Senator Guy Williams said that it would be wise to "forget the UBCIC; they have failed the
Indians badly." Mathias said that Indians were "losing ground in the
courts and in the cabinet rooms, and we are losing time."[16]

Mathias and Wilson believed that a new voice was needed for those
who supported unity and tribalism. Wilson proposed that the word
"coalition" be used, "because it describes an emergency situation, like
war-time coalition governments."[17] The Brotherhood, UNN, and Alliance
agreed to the formation of the British Columbia Coalition of Native
Indians; they invited Union bands to participate. Philip Paul spoke for
the Union in rejecting the suggestion, saying that those who had failed
to destroy the Union from within were now seeking to destroy it from
without.[18]

In turn, the Coalition spokesmen stated that the Union no longer
represented either a majority of Indians or of bands. Soon they were
demanding that DIA and DSS funds for status Indian organizations no
longer be allocated exclusively to the Union, but that they be distributed
instead to the Union and other organizations, including tribal councils,
in proportion to popular support by the status Indian population.[19] The
question of proportionate funding remained a major issue over the next
four years, with the Union continually on the defensive.

The Coalition's founders intended it to foster and co-ordinate Indian
land claims activity, to promote unity and tribalism, and to put pressure
on both federal and provincial governments to respond seriously to
land claims. A further purpose was to provide a forum in which groups
and interests not represented by the Union could attain publicity for
their concerns. The founders did not intend it to be a new organization,
much less one that would replace or supersede existing organizations.

The Coalition could thus be termed a "co-ordinating forum." In this respect it was similar to the Confederacy of Native Indians of British Columbia that Philip Paul and others had formed a decade earlier.

In 1976 the federal cabinet, in good part as the result of pressure from George Manuel and the NIB, had issued a directive to all federal departments that Indian organizations (that is, status Indian organizations) were to be consulted on all policy matters affecting Indians. Upon his return to British Columbia, Manuel had pressed the new DIA regional director-general, Fred Walchli,[20] to arrange a formal method of consultation with the Union. The regional "secretariat" was the result.[21] It was to consist of periodic meetings between Union representatives and senior DIA regional officials. Before the first meeting, in July 1978, the Indian Homemakers' Association, the Native Women's Society, the Alliance, and the Nuu'chah'nulth Tribal Council separately approached either DIA or the Union asking to be able to participate along with the Union. Walchli, to his later regret, left the matter to the Union. Manuel took the position that the Union represented all status Indians in the province. The question of whether the Union was the legitimate representative of all status Indians was the second major issue dominating Indian politics over the next four years, with the Union, again, on the defensive.

Federal officials in Vancouver and Ottawa were caught in the cross-fire. Walchli and his staff were uneasy over the exclusion from the secretariat of groups not supporting the Union. Max Beck, the regional director-general in DSS, was equally concerned over the funding issue. Walchli was lobbied by the Brotherhood and the Alliance; Beck, by the UNN as well. (At this time the UNN still had no dealings with DIA and was not yet seeking them.) The Indian spokesmen were well informed and forceful. Walchli and Beck had no real reply to the complaints, except that policy made in Ottawa could only be changed in Ottawa. Both men were also in frequent touch with Manuel and other Union leaders, who were pressing their views with equal force. Ottawa officials, less aware of the circumstances, seemed willing to go along with the position taken by Manuel. Yet, there was some unease among Ottawa officials as well, in particular among DIA officials, who were willing to consider alternatives to the secretariat. The 1976 cabinet directive, after all, had not anticipated the existence of separate status Indian organizations competing for the ear of government in the same region.

Little came of the British Columbia Coalition of Native Indians. It gained no standing with DIA and it attained no identity separate from its founding organizations, whose leaders continued to believe that tribal land claim preparation required coordination at the provincial level, and that groups not represented by the Union were entitled to have a formal voice with DIA. Wilson, Mathias, Watts, and Newman concluded that reform would result only from grass roots pressure. The idea emerged of holding a province-wide conference of tribal group representatives. Mathias and John Clifton, president of the Brotherhood, approached DIA officials in Ottawa and found them willing to provide the necessary funding. In the names of their three organizations, Mathias, Clifton, and Wilson then wrote a joint letter to all "aboriginal tribal groups," as they referred to them, inviting each to send two delegates to Prince George in September. They suggested that in each case one delegate should be a status Indian, the other, non-status.

No thought had been given to inviting the Union, since it was not a tribal group and was not in favour of land claims preparation by tribal groups. The Ottawa officials, however, wanted the Union to be included. The three organizers agreed that the Union could send two delegates. The officials went further; one of them wrote to Manuel urging him and the Union to step forward to act as co-sponsor. Manuel refused and at the next meeting of the secretariat, held in Vancouver on the day the Prince George conference opened, he gave his reasons.

The conference is being organized on a tribal basis and there isn't any recognition of Bands and Band Councils as the governing structures with authority. The UBCIC structure recognizes status Indians by way of their chiefs, and our goal is to strengthen Band Councils. What concerns us is that the delegates to this conference are not going to be chiefs, they are just going to be Band members. A Tribal negotiating structure is being proposed and this appears to be a strategy to break down the authority of Band Councils. The Government's funding of this conference indicates a shift in the Minister's position because he is suddenly recognizing tribes rather than Band Councils. This is in direct contradiction to the structures recognized in the Indian Act, and is in complete opposition to the UBCIC's goals. Strong Band Councils are going to be at the heart of our land claims and we are very concerned that our work not be undermined by this tribal structure.[22]

The role and motives of the DIA officials in funding the conference and trying to include the Union remained matters of disagreement among Indians. Manuel and other Union leaders saw the officials as having actively promoted the conference in order to weaken the Union. (During the ensuing years, Union spokesmen would continually attribute responsibility and blame to DIA officials for the innovations made or demanded by Indians who supported unity and tribalism. Thus, ironically, those who wished to maintain the principles originating in the Indian Act sought to condemn the advocates of a return to tradition as following the dictates of government.) Those who organized the conference saw the DIA officials as having at last begun to respond to the realities of British Columbia Indian politics, but as still seeking to shore up the Union by putting it in a position to influence and claim credit for the new developments. For his part, Manuel clearly perceived the basis of the threat to the Union. His statement in the secretariat was a forthright and accurate depiction of the differences between the Union and its opponents on the fundamental questions of unity and tribalism.

Speakers at the Prince George meeting, both government and Indian, evinced some optimism at the progress of land claim negotiations. An official from DIA's Office of Native Claims reported that the 1973 federal claims policy was proceeding satisfactorily and the Nisga'a claim was being negotiated. Of the greatest significance, however, was his report that the provincial government was in fact participating in the Nisga'a negotiations. Some members of the audience were excited by this news; others were sceptical. In any case, the official's optimistic assertions proved ill founded.[23]

The Prince George conference agreed to form the "Aboriginal Council of British Columbia." It would be a province-wide co-ordinating forum consisting of two delegates, one status, one non-status, from each tribal group. Its purpose would be to foster tribal political development and to encourage and co-ordinate preparation of land claims. The founding meeting of "AbCo" was set for May 1979 in Prince Rupert. Shortly after the Prince George conference the Union held a special general assembly to discuss, among other matters, the question of whether Union bands should allow their tribal groups to participate in AbCo. A motion that the Union endorse such participation was put forward. Manuel and others spoke strongly against the motion, and it was defeated:

When this resolution was put forward on the floor of the assembly, there was a long and earnest discussion and debate as to our participation. Concern for our own future was paramount. When the final vote was called there was one vote in favour, two abstentions, and the rest against.[24]

The Prince Rupert meeting proved a lacklustre start to the Aboriginal Council. Twenty-two tribal groups were nominally represented, each by a status and non-status Indian. However, only two tribal councils, the Nuu'chah'nulth and the North Coast, sent their leaders.[25] Many of those present had been selected by the meeting's organizers rather than by their own tribal groups. With the exceptions of Joe Mathias and George Watts, the political leaders of the tribal groups seemed unwilling to align themselves with any new province-wide body.

The United Native Nations grew rapidly under Wilson's leadership. Some twelve hundred people attended the 1977 assembly, while twenty-two hundred attended the following year. George Watts was now playing an active role in the UNN and serving as a prominent reminder not only that his Nuu'chah'nulth tribal group had, like others, withdrawn from the Union, but also that it had aligned itself with the hitherto non-status organization in support of unity and tribalism. Yet, not all supporters of unity and tribalism felt impelled to choose either the UNN or the Union. Sophie Pierre, chief of her band and leader of the Kootenay Area Council,[26] was one of these; she was a close friend of Wilson's and she attended UNN assemblies, but she also participated in Union activities and was a member of the Union's council of chiefs. There were undoubtedly many Indians who believed that the UNN and Union should co-exist, with overlapping support and differing policies.

The leaders of the Union and the UNN did not share any such belief. They saw each other as self-interested toadies of DIA dedicated to destroying the real interests of Indians.[27] Between members of the two organizations there was now almost none of the personal and social contact that had existed between BCANSI and the Union; instead, a clear pattern of hostility and lack of communication divided politically active Indians into two camps. In one camp was the Union, supported by the Indian Homemakers. In the other was the UNN, together with the Native Brotherhood, the Alliance, the active coastal tribal councils, and, eventually, the Native Women's Society.[28] Each camp came to be personified by one person: Manuel in one case, Wilson in the other. On the street, individuals would ignore persons from the other camp. Manuel, Wilson, and Ed Newman, now the president of the Native Brotherhood, made some attempts to restore personal contacts with the other side, but they felt rebuffed and became even more hostile.

The advocates of unity and tribalism continued their demands for proportionate funding and for a formal channel to DIA equivalent to the Union's secretariat. DIA and DSS officials in Vancouver and Ottawa had no objective way to gauge Indian support for the two camps. Some bands withdrew from the Union simply by ceasing to participate; others did so formally through a resolution passed by the band council. By the summer of 1978 such resolutions had been passed by at least 25 bands in the province,[29] most of them larger bands and most of them members of the Alliance or of coastal tribal councils. Some 30 additional bands, many of them very small, had taken no part in Union activity since before 1975. At most, then, some 140 bands could be said to support the

Union. About 130 bands had been represented at the 1977 annual assembly.[30] Attendance was not a fully accurate measure of unequivocal support, however, for the Union provided chiefs with travel and hotel expenses. (The UNN, in contrast, having a much larger number of assembly delegates, provided minimal travel funds and only tent accommodation.)

The Union leaders claimed more support than they had. Their annual report to the provincial registrar of societies for 1977 went so far as to state a membership of 213, or 15 more than the number of bands in the province. In secretariat meetings in 1978 Union spokesmen referred several times to "our 186 member bands,"[31] and in a letter to the minister in 1980 Manuel still claimed the support of 179 bands.[32]

The Union's main strategy was to convince MPs and senior federal officials that the Union did have substantial popular Indian support and that Fred Walchli and his officials were manipulating, if not creating, the anti-Union groups in order to squelch progressive reforms demanded by the Union. Particular effort was devoted to the three opposition Progressive Conservative MPs from British Columbia who were members of the Commons Committee on Indian Affairs. Each of them, as it happened, represented an interior riding in which Union support did remain strong. Frank Oberle and Lorne Greenaway were the most partial to the Union and most hostile to Walchli. (The NDP members of the committee who were from British Columbia all represented coastal ridings and were well informed about the activities of the Brotherhood, the Alliance, and the UNN. There were no Liberal MPs from the province at this time.) The Union's Ottawa efforts further embittered feelings in the anti-Union camp. Wilson, Watts, Mathias, Newman, and others intensified their pressure on DIA for access and on DIA and DSS for proportionate funding. Several of them went to Ottawa and met with John Munro, the minister of Indian affairs. Munro's special assistant at the time had previously been the Union's senior staff official and had been suggested to Munro by Manuel. Wilson and the others believed that Munro had been brainwashed in favour of the Union.

Fred Walchli felt the dilemma more and more acutely. He believed that the 1976 cabinet directive required him to consult all groups on a formal basis and that if DIA continued to support the Union's monopoly, it would simply be continuing and reinforcing the old pattern of white interference in Indian politics, and also increasing the department's unpopularity among a growing number of British Columbia Indians. Yet if he attempted to add other groups to the secretariat the Union would object, the non-Indian news media would go to Manuel and Union officials for their stories, and the three Conservative MPs would almost certainly take up the Union's cause in the House of Commons, embarrassing the Liberal government and criticizing him personally (as they were already doing in letters to the minister). Walchli was well aware of the attempts to unite organizations in the Coalition and to bring tribal groups together in the Aboriginal Council. He thought there might be some way of building on the two attempts.

In the early summer of 1979 Walchli instructed the DIA district managers throughout the British Columbia region to consult the bands in order to assess support for the various provincial Indian organizations. The managers' reports showed that 102 of 194 bands,[33] containing 48 per cent of the status Indian population in the region, expressed support for the Union. However, 14 of these 102 bands also supported the Native Brotherhood, and 7 also supported the UNN. Thus, Walchli felt it reasonable to conclude that at most 81 bands, or 42 per cent of the total, containing less than 40 percent of the population, would favour continuing the Union's monopoly on formal access to DIA through the secretariat.

Upon reaching this conclusion, Walchli invited a small number of prominent band chiefs and administrators to meet with him and his senior officials in December.[34] He informed George Manuel and other Union officials of his intentions, asking if they wished to participate; they replied that they did not and stated that they intended to continue with the secretariat.[35]

At the meeting Walchli explained his intention to introduce "one more regional mechanism which we are calling a provincial forum." It would bring together regional DIA officials and representatives from each of the tribal councils (or, where none yet existed, from the district councils) and also from "the provincial organizations not affiliated with the secretariat." The organizations he named as likely participants were the Alliance, the Homemakers' Association, the Native Women's Society, and the Native Brotherhood.[36] He did not mention the United Native Nations, since he and his officials had decided that to include it in their own proposal would be to invite too much criticism from the Union and the MPs. He did assume, however, that once the forum got off the ground the participants themselves would wish to include the UNN. He summed up his general intentions in saying to the meeting, "Once this forum is in place we will have established a framework for consultation and involvement of the Indian leaders throughout the region."[37] The Indians at the meeting supported the proposal.

Walchli next wrote to nineteen district/tribal[38] councils and the four organizations inviting them to send representatives to a meeting in Vancouver on 30 January 1980. The Alliance, the Native Women's

Society, and the Brotherhood sent representatives, as did eight coastal and three interior district/tribal councils. No Indian prominently and exclusively associated with the Union attended. Those present resolved unanimously to accept the principle of the forum and agreed to meet again at the end of February for its official launching.

CHAPTER FIFTEEN

Forums and Funding, Protests and Unity, 1980-9

The February 1980 meeting was taken as the official founding of the Tribal Forum.[1] It was attended by the leaders of the Native Brotherhood, the Alliance, the Native Women's Society, and by representatives of fifteen district/tribal councils.[2] One of the first acts of the Forum was to invite the United Native Nations to participate. The invitation to the UNN, the organization seen as representing non-status Indians, meant that non-status Indians were now, for the first time, accepted by status Indian leaders as full political participants at the province-wide level. The Forum played a crucial role in British Columbia Indian politics during the early 1980s. Together with the already established Aboriginal Council, it proceeded to serve as both catalyst and active agent in attaining fuller recognition of tribalism by government and by Indians. The Forum's success, however, fuelled an intense opposition movement. As a result, the early 1980s were a time of unprecedented political acrimony among political activists.

The Union of British Columbia Indian Chiefs, which regarded the Forum supporters as sell-outs to the Department of Indian Affairs, quickly suffered three major defections. Two of its four vice-presidents, Ray Jones (Gitksan) and Ernie Willie (Kwagiulth), left the Union because of disgreements with George Manuel; each became the leader of his tribal group and represented it in the Forum. At this same time the Indian Homemakers' Association severed its ties with the Union and began to send representatives to Forum meetings.[3]

Those most influential in guiding the Forum were Delbert Guerin, Joe Mathias, Ed Newman, George Watts, and Bill Wilson.[4] They maintained an easy camaraderie and kept in close touch with the leaders of the major tribal councils, especially with James Gosnell of the Nisga'a, whom they regarded as the elder statesman among Indian politicians.[5] They all shared an animosity towards Manuel, who they believed was out of touch with tribalism and the majority of British Columbia Indians; they all respected Fred Walchli for what they saw as his demonstrated willingness to seek out and respect Indian views.

Several major goals were pursued within the Forum and by those who supported it. First, the tribal leaders pressed their band councils to pass resolutions indicating support for the Forum. By the end of 1980 more than half the bands in the province, containing considerably more than half the status Indian population, had produced such resolutions. Many of the resolutions stated explicitly that the bands were rejecting the Union as their spokesman. With the UNN firmly supportive of the Forum, there could now be no doubt that the Forum represented the majority of both status and non-status Indians in the province.

Second, the Indians took control of the Forum itself and used it as a vehicle to press their views upon government. Initially Walchli and his staff suggested meeting times, prepared the agendas, co-ordinated travel and hotel arrangements, and regarded themselves as full participants, just as they were in secretariat meetings with Union leaders. Walchli himself chaired the Forum meetings. A visit of the minister of Indian affairs, John Munro, to Vancouver in May 1980 provided an early turning point. Munro and Walchli had a morning meeting with Manuel and other Union leaders, who criticized the Forum at length, delaying Munro's departure for his afternoon meeting with the Forum. Meanwhile, as the well-attended Forum meeting waited in the Musqueam Band hall, Walchli's assistant attempted to begin the meeting as acting chairman. Wilson, Watts, and Mathias promptly objected, proposing that Guerin, as host chief, chair the meeting. Had Walchli been present, no thought of replacing him would have arisen at this time. As it was, Guerin was in charge to welcome Munro and Walchli, and the practice of having an Indian chairman of Forum meetings was retained.

Munro, whose opening comments showed that he was ill-informed about the Forum, now heard more than two hours of forthright statements. The Forum participants lectured him on the nature of British Columbia Indian politics, warned him of the dangers of relying on his Ottawa bureaucrats, scolded him for believing the Union's claims of support, and demanded that he recognize the Forum as the major voice of British Columbia Indians. Munro admitted to having difficulty in knowing what was "going on west of the mountains," agreed to take the Forum seriously, and promised that "you can see me whenever you need to." Until the summer of 1984, when the Liberal government was defeated, Forum spokesmen did have ready access to Munro and his senior officials. They regarded the Musqueam meeting as a turning point in their relations with the Ottawa officials.

After the Musqueam meeting, the Forum's Indian leaders took

charge of preparing and conducting meetings. They came to regard Walchli and his officials not as part of the Forum, but as guests to appear only when invited. To reinforce this point, they at times kept DIA officials waiting needlessly (in particular those whom they disliked) and would on the spur of the moment call for in-camera sessions, thus compelling all non-Indians to leave the meeting room. The Indians relished turning the tables on the officials. Great care was taken to avoid having the Forum seen as another organization. No executive positions were created; rather, a four-member "steering committee" was set up and George Watts was appointed "co-ordinator." Aside from a stenographer, no staff was hired.

The third goal pursued by the Forum, the one seen as most significant by the Indians themselves, was to have DIA and the Department of the Secretary of State alter their funding policies concerning status Indian organizations in the province. The Union was still the sole recipient of DIA land claims preparation funds and the major recipient of DSS core funding for status Indians. Tribal councils received neither category of funding. The aim of the Forum was to have the funding allocated to organizations and tribal councils according to popular support. Forum spokesmen lobbied senior DIA and DSS officials in Vancouver and in Ottawa.

After much consultation with tribal councils and the organizations, both departments eventually acquiesced. Each agreed to allocate funds on the basis of popular support as demonstrated annually through band council resolutions. Thus, if a particular organization or tribal council received the support of say, nine bands having 13 per cent of the status Indian population, it would receive 13 per cent of the funding. The new procedure was first applied by DIA in allocating its "policy, research and consultation" funds for the 1981–2 fiscal year. Each band council was asked to indicate its preference as to which organization or tribal council should receive such funds. The Union was supported by bands having 24 per cent of the population. The various tribal councils were supported by bands having 49 per cent of the population.[6] The outcome was a massive shift of funding, amounting to some $300,000 annually, from the Union to the tribal councils. A similar reallocation of core funding resulted from DSS's consulting the bands. Again, district and tribal councils found themselves with a new supply of funds, while the Union faced a sudden and substantial loss.

A fourth goal of the Forum leaders was to strengthen the other co-ordinating Forum, the Aboriginal Council. The two entities had similar structures, with AbCo consisting only of tribal group representatives, while the Forum included organization representatives as well. The two shared the same leaders and the same office address in Vancouver.

Often sequential meetings were arranged, allowing participants to meet first as one entity, then as the other. As the Forum became established, AbCo gained in stature and in participation. Roles were kept distinct, however, with the Forum dealing with such matters as program administration by bands and tribal councils, while AbCo dealt with tribal political development and land claims preparation.

Before 1980 the majority of tribal groups knew little of the affairs of other tribal groups and had taken few actual steps towards preparing their land claim statements. Now, during 1980 and 1981, AbCo became both active agent and clearing house in promoting formation of additional tribal councils and preparation of land claims. The more advanced tribal councils served as guides and teachers. The Nisga'a prepared a documentary film, which they showed at AbCo meetings and sent around the province; the Gitksan-Wet'suwet'en, now led by Neil Sterritt, presented workshops at AbCo meetings and lent staff members to help new tribal councils get underway.

The years 1980 and 1981 also marked the height of activity and influence for Bill Wilson and the United Native Nations. Unaffected by the funding controversy, since it remained the sole recipient of non-status core funding, the UNN maintained a vigorous presence and gained increasing support from status Indians and tribal groups. Wilson campaigned strenuously in favour of tribalism and integration of status and non-status Indians, and he constantly urged the tribal groups to get on with their land claims. The Nuu'chah'nulth, the Heiltsuk, and the Kootenay remained UNN supporters, while the Nisga'a, the Gitksan-Wet'suet'en, and the North Coast Tribal Councils now proceeded to affiliate and to send their leaders to UNN assemblies. The Nisga'a were the prize addition, with the attendance of James Gosnell and the other Nisga'a leaders symbolizing to many UNN members the merger of status and non-status identities. A number of those present wept with emotion as Gosnell spoke at his first UNN assembly.

Major leadership changes occurred within both the Union and the UNN in this period, and there were also changes in national political participation by British Columbia Indians. Wilson stepped down as UNN president in July 1981. George Manuel, his health declining, retired as Union president three months later and was replaced by his son Robert. Del Riley was now president of the National Indian Brotherhood, having defeated Robert Manuel for the position. Riley spoke at several meetings of both the Forum and AbCo. For several years previously many British Columbia chiefs, including most of those in the tribal groups supporting the Forum, had been ignoring the NIB. Riley's leadership, as well as their concern over the proposed new Canadian Constitution, induced a number of them to return to the NIB. The

Union, however, was still regarded officially by the NIB as the voice of British Columbia, and it remained responsible for selecting the British Columbia vice-chief of the NIB.

The Native Council of Canada, the national association of Métis and non-status Indians, had become more amenable to co-operation between status and non-status Indians, and it had readmitted the UNN to membership in 1980. In 1982 Bill Wilson was elected as the vice-president of the NCC, becoming the first status Indian to hold office in the organization. The British Columbia advocates of tribalism and of merging of status and non-status interests thus gained a national spokesman.

Within British Columbia the changes in federal funding policies further exacerbated the hostility between the Union and the UNN. Although material interests were important, since salaries, prestige, and influence were at stake, there were also sharply contradictory perceptions about what had happened, and why. Those who supported the Forum saw it as resulting from the Union's refusal to give up its monopoly on formal access to DIA through the secretariat; they believed that funding should accord with popular support and that tribal groups had historic and contemporary importance. They even came to regard the Forum as their own creation, especially after they had taken over its operation. Union leaders and supporters, in contrast, simply could not believe that substantial numbers of Indians would desert the Union of their own volition. For the most part, having little tradition of tribal politics themselves, Union leaders had difficulty in acknowledging tribalism as a political force motivating other Indians. Nor did the Union leaders appreciate the strength of the desire among other Indians to eliminate the Indian Act's distinction between status and non-status Indians.

The Union explanation for the Forum's growth and the Union's decline came to be not only that Fred Walchli had created the Forum in order to curb the growth of the Union, but also that he continued to control it and was using it to buy off those Indians who were venal enough to accept the funding which had been diverted from the Union. Extreme views came to be held by a number of Union supporters. Walchli was seen as personifying the bureaucratic evil associated with a century of DIA manipulation of Indians. Indian supporters of the Forum were frequently stereotyped as wealthy fishermen or land developers who had no interest in the plight of ordinary Indians. Leaders of the major Alliance bands (Musqueam, Squamish, Sechelt, and Westbank), who had so publicly split from the Union, were viewed with special animosity. Sechelt efforts to attain self-government through a special act of Parliament were interpreted as treacherous collaboration with government. Sechelt chief Stan Dixon was a scathing critic of the Union, as was Ron Derrickson, the wealthy chief of the Westbank Band, who was also a prominent Liberal. Union supporters saw the two as Walchli's cronies and collaborators.

The general Union view was given a veneer of objectivity in a report prepared for the secretary of state in 1980 by Walter Rudnicki, a former employee of DIA. Rudnicki presented the Union as an organization with a "signed-up membership" of "about 133 bands" that sought to serve "the whole native community in the Province."[7] He dismissed tribal councils as "structures being fostered by DIAND to facilitate consultation." He depicted the UNN, the Alliance, and Native Brotherhood as groups with "highly circumscribed memberships" that had created the Aboriginal Council as "a strategem" to gain "access to the whole native community." He portrayed the Forum as "very much a product of DIAND's aim to create a compatible native institutional system." He concluded that Forum supporters, in contrast to the Union's, were so lacking in integrity and commitment to Indian values that they were willing "to serve as auxiliaries to government agencies."[8]

The three British Columbia opposition Conservative MPs on the Commons Indian affairs committee, Frank Oberle, Lorne Greenaway, and Fred King,[9] apparently accepted the Union's, and Rudnicki's, views of Walchli and the Forum. During the spring of 1982 the committee met in Vancouver. Rather than following the traditions of parliamentary and cabinet government by attacking the department through the minister, the three MPs publicly criticized Walchli in his personal role as an individual public servant.

Union leaders pressed John Munro to fire Walchli.[10] Ed Newman, Joe Mathias, George Watts, and James Gosnell informed Munro of their support for Walchli, and they spoke out publicly in his defence. Their efforts blunted the attempts to remove Walchli from British Columbia, but they also served to confirm the beliefs held by his critics. The Union leaders and the Conservative MPs then demanded a public enquiry, alleging that Walchli had mismanaged DIA funds and had displayed favouritism to bands who supported the Forum, in particular the Westbank band. Munro ordered an internal review, which was conducted without serious effort to consult Walchli or his regional officials, and the resulting report was not shown to Walchli, although it was given to members of the Indian affairs committee.[11] In 1983 Walchli was removed as DIA director-general and, having declined an offer to spend a year studying French at government expense, was demoted to the position of senior federal negotiator for land claims in British Columbia.

When the Conservatives' came to power in 1984, the vilification of Walchli intensified. Greenaway charged that Walchli had been involved in fraud with the Westbank band, and the new minister, David Crombie, established a public enquiry. Greenaway and the other Conservative

MPs declined to provide any specific information to the inquiry commissioner, whose report, released in 1987, found no evidence to support
Greenaway's accusations. Although Walchli's career had been permanently damaged,[12] a denouement of sorts did take place. George
Manuel, in very poor health and confined to a wheelchair, had himself
brought to Walchli's office, where he stated that he had been wrong and
expressed his regret for the whole affair.

The controversy and intrigue between Indians and the federal government during the early 1980s served to obscure a major turn of events
in relations with the provincial government. In 1976, when the Social
Credit Party returned to power, the attorney-general, Allan Williams,
carried forward his NDP predecessor's pledge to work toward return of
the cut-off lands.[13] Tri-partite negotiations, involving the province, DIA,
and the Indian bands affected, finally began in 1981. The Union and
the Alliance played major roles, each giving legal assistance and guidance to their affiliated bands. The principles accepted were that cut-off
lands that remained vacant should be reinstated as reserve land and
that compensation, at current market value, should be paid to the bands
for developed cut-offs that could not be returned. In the first settlement,
reached in 1982, the Penticton band regained hundreds of acres and
was paid $14 million compensation for the remainder. Settlements fol-
lowed with other bands. The process proved satisfactory to the bands
and to both governments. (There were only a few instances of white
public complaint; one of these arose in Williams' own riding over
return of West Vancouver's Ambleside Park to the Squamish Band.)

Aboriginal title was not involved in the cut-off lands issue. Nevertheless, one major part of the Indian land question in British Columbia
had been resolved. The province had acknowledged a past injustice and
accepted a present-day responsibility to remedy it. The device of tri-
partite negotiations was exactly what the Indians and the federal government wanted the province to agree to in order to settle the issue of
aboriginal title. On the title issue, however, the province remained adamant, refusing to acknowledge the possibility of aboriginal title and
refusing to respond to Indian land claims.

The antagonism between the Union and the advocates of tribalism
faded somewhat in the fall and winter of 1982. The departure from their
respective presidencies of Wilson and the elder Manuel served to
remove from each camp the main political target of the other and thus
to ease the relations between the Union and other organizations. The
principal factor impelling some interaction, however, was the common
perception that the new Canadian Constitution presented dangers to
aboriginal title and other Indian interests. Once again, the device of the

"co-ordinating forum" provided the vehicle for renewed political unity.

The two Manuels and other leading Union activists, including Wayne Christian (Shuswap) and Saul Terry (Lillooet), had been the first British Columbia Indians to perceive that the new Constitution would destroy the direct and special relationship that they believed existed between the British monarch and Canadian Indians. They had also been concerned that the draft constitution provided no clear protection for aboriginal rights and did not recognize unextinguished aboriginal title. The Union quickly became more active than any other organization in Canada in opposing the Constitution;[14] it mounted campaigns for support in Ottawa, Europe, London, and at the United Nations in New York. The Union's efforts, although unsuccessful, brought it renewed support among Indians in all parts of the province.

In late 1982, when the text of the Constitution had been finalized, Ed Newman, George Watts, and James Gosnell went to the Union's office to meet with Robert Manuel and other Union officials to discuss British Columbia Indian participation in the required first ministers' conference on aboriginal rights, which was to be held in March 1983. They agreed to call an immediate assembly.

The January 1983 assembly, officially called the "British Columbia Aboriginal Peoples' Constitutional Conference" (APCC), was a remarkable success. Every district or tribal council, each provincial organization, and some 125 bands, including almost all those of substantial size, were represented. Some five hundred Indians were present. Non-status Indians were represented through tribal councils and through the UNN. The only comparable previous assembly had been the Union's 1969 founding assembly in Kamloops, but it had included neither tribal nor non-status representation. The 1983 assembly dealt almost exclusively with the Indian land question and other aboriginal rights. Although the participants from the Forum side played the major part in the guiding the proceedings and proposing motions, harmony and unity were maintained. As Robert Manuel said, "B.C. Indians have matured and we are prepared to work with each other to fight a common adversary."[15]

The assembly adopted a motion that "the position of the British Columbia Indian People before the First Ministers' Conference be that Aboriginal Title must be immediately entrenched in the Constitution and protected with a consent clause."[16] At the end of the assembly Joe Mathias and Ed Newman moved that James Gosnell, of the Nisga'a Tribal Council, be appointed "as our Spokesman for the entrenchment of Aboriginal Title in the Constitution."[17] Approval was unanimous. A historic step had been achieved. For the first time ever one leader could truly speak for all British Columbia Indians.

In accepting the position, Gosnell stressed the equality of all Indians and all tribal groups and explained the enduring nature of tribal identity and aboriginal title.

This is the principle upon which the Nishga people are united, that we are all the same. No one is greater than the other . . . No one tribe is greater than the others . . . Down through the history of the Government of British Columbia, they have refused to recognize our title. Neither have they extinguished it. On that basis, the title is here and now. The title is you and me. It's a living title . . . God gave us our title and our rights . . . Only God can change that.[18]

Gosnell participated in the March 1983 first ministers' conference as part of the National Indian Brotherhood delegation. Bill Wilson took part as the main spokesman for the Native Council of Canada. Each spoke eloquently; each pressed his points in repartee with Prime Minister Trudeau; each was singled out for attention by the national news media. The conference, however, was a failure. The British Columbia government was among those most opposed to acknowledging aboriginal title.

Meanwhile, among the tribal groups across the province land claims preparation went ahead. The federal guidelines for the submission of land claims were straightforward. The government would consider claims only for land which had traditionally been, and still was, used and occupied by the claimant group. Thus, claims for lands that were now used and occupied by others ("third parties," as they were called) would not be considered. The actual formal statement of claim document had merely to indicate the boundaries of the area in question, supply basic information about the claimant group, and provide evidence for the continual use and occupancy. While the guidelines required that claims be submitted to both provincial and federal governments, this requirement in no way compelled any province to respond to the claims.

The negotiation of each claim would focus on the question of how much of the claimed land the Indian group would retain. As was explained in Chapter 1, a claim was not to be seen as a demand for present and future ownership and control of all the land in question. A claim, rather, was a demand for acknowledgement of pre-contact land ownership and, equally, a demand that a new arrangement be achieved through negotiation. This new arrangement would involve Indian ownership and control of only a portion of traditional territory. Once the amount of retained land was agreed upon, questions such as the amount of compensation for surrendered lands, the degree of control the Indian group would exercise over the land, and the form of relations with provincial and federal governments would be negotiated. According to its own policy, the federal government would negotiate only one claim at a time in each province or territory.[19] While the federal government hoped and assumed that provincial governments would participate in negotiating claims in their provinces, it had not consulted them in devising its policies concerning claims submission and negotiation.

Despite the simplicity of the guidelines, several factors made claims preparation a time-consuming process, at least if it was taken seriously. A credible claim had to be supported by detailed evidence concerning both the extent of pre-contact territory and the subsequent use and occupancy. To justify the amount of land to be retained, the groups had to consider their own future social and economic development and give careful thought to how the land and its resources would be managed. Success in actual negotiations would depend upon having confident and knowledgeable negotiators supported by an informed and united membership.

For these reasons the process of claims preparation was as much a matter of education, community development, and leadership preparation as it was of producing an actual document to submit to the Comprehensive Claims Branch,[20] and the act of submitting a claim was in most cases a good indication that a group had evolved to a new level of awareness and internal unity. In almost every tribal group the young veterans of the big organizations played leading parts in this evolution. Claim submission was the practical manifestation of the renewed tribalism among British Columbia Indians. Submitting their claim was for most Indians a solemn and exciting moment; they felt a renewed understanding of their own past, a strengthened Indian identity, a deeper loyalty to their tribal group, and a confidence that they could deal as equals with government negotiators. Submitting a claim thus also signified that the claimant group was in political fighting trim.

The chronology of claims submissions, presented in Table 2, serves to chart the most recent social and political development among British Columbia Indians. The paramount role of tribalism is confirmed in the fact that tribal groups are the entity of choice in advancing claims. Only 7 of the 199 bands in the province have chosen to present claims on their own,[21] and they have done so without rejecting the principle of tribalism. Only coastal groups submitted claims prior to 1980. With the exception of the Tahltan, no group submitted a claim during the next three years while Indian political effort was focused on the new Canadian Constitution and on establishing the Tribal Forum and the Aboriginal Council. The spate of submissions in 1983 resulted in part from the encouragement and guidance provided within AbCo, in part from the opening of a branch office (the only one in Canada) in Vancouver of the Comprehensive Claims Branch, and in good part from the diversion of funding from the Union to tribal councils. As for groups which had not yet submitted claims by 1989, one correlation was evident: all except the Squamish were groups which had given strong support to the Union; they had turned to their own claims preparation only after 1982, when it was utterly clear that the Union itself would not be preparing any claims.

TABLE 2: British Columbia land claims, 1974–89*

CLAIMS SUBMITTED[a]

(coastal		(interior)	
Nisga'a	1974		
Kitwancool Band	1977		
Gitksan-Wet'suwet'en	1977		
Musqueam Band	1977		
Haisla	1978	Tahltan	1980
Nuu'chah'nulth	1983	Nazko-Kluskus Bands	1983
Haida	1983	Kaska-Dena	1983
Heiltsuk	1983	Carrier-Sekani	1983
Nuxalk	1983	Alkali Lake Band	1983
Kwagiulth	1984	Taku Tlingit	1984
Sechelt Band	1984		
Homalco Band	1985		
[Coast] Tsimshian	1987	Nlaka'pamux	1987
[Skeena] Tsimshian	1987	Kootenay	1987

CLAIMS IN PREPARATION

Songish	Chilcotin
Sto:lo	Lillooet
Squamish	Okanagan
	Shuswap

CLAIMS IN NEGOTIATION

Nisga'a

*Derived from information supplied by DIA, Comprehensive Claims Branch, BC
  Operations, December 1989.
[a]Submitted by tribal groups unless "band(s)" indicated.

By late 1989 the federal government had accepted nineteen of the twenty-two submitted claims as being suitable for negotiation; it was delaying acceptance of three south coast claims (those of Sechelt, Homalco, and Musqueam) because it considered most of the claimed lands to be fully used and occupied by other parties.[22] However, under the federal policy of negotiating only one claim at a time in any province, only the Nisga'a claim, the first submitted, was being negotiated.

Federal officials and the Nisga'a had been negotiating since 1976, getting as far as they could without provincial participation.

Optimism had been much in evidence among the groups as they prepared the claims. By 1983 there was frustration and cynicism as they waited in line, knowing that the line would not even begin moving until the province agreed to participate in a settlement of the Nisga'a claim. Increasingly, the provincial government became the focus of resentment and hostility, especially since provincial ministers made combative statements and asserted that the province would never recognize Indian title.[23]

Commencing in 1983 Indians and their supporters mounted a series of protest blockades. In the first, the Kaska-Dena hindered the activities of a timber company. In 1984 the Nuu'chah'nulth blocked logging access to Meares Island. In 1985 the Haida obstructed logging on Lyell Island. In 1986 Kwagiulth protested logging on Deere Island, and the Nlaka'pamux and Lillooet took action to halt railway-widening that would damage salmon spawning beds in the Thompson River. By this time, too, the Nlaka'pamux were engaged in a sustained effort to deter the logging of the Stein Valley. The Nisga'a again took action to resist new railway construction. On a number of occasions the Gitksan-Wet-'suwet'en halted logging in their land claim area. They also confronted federal fisheries officers, becoming the first Indians in more than a century to take offensive action—they hurled marshmallows at the officials. In 1987 the McLeod Lake Band of Sekanis closed a logging road, and in 1988, in a reversal of tactics, they defied provincial regulations by cutting trees in their claim area.[24]

Resource company executives and provincial politicians expressed puzzlement over the protests, in part because of their sudden emergence and in part because Indians were now objecting to activities which had not elicited complaint in the past. The explanation lay in land claims preparation. In virtually every case the protesting groups had prepared and submitted their land claim, and they were now seeking to protect the lands and their resources until the claim was settled. The political fighting trim developed for negotiating the claims was now being put to direct use.

Most of the protests of the 1970s had been carried out by individual bands and had related to fishing rights or to reserve matters. Blockades had closed roads in order to inconvenience Whites, especially local Whites, against whom there was often a general resentment. Usually there had also been specific grievances against DIA and the federal government. Support of white groups had not been sought, nor was it offered. The Indians had made little use of the non-Indian news media, and they had not initiated court action. The RCMP had played a firm and authoritative role in responding to the blockades of the 1970s, as at Cache Creek and Mount Currie, with reinforcements on call and a senior officer acting as government spokesman.

Most of the protests of the 1980s were carried out by tribal groups, not by individual bands or communities, and related to land outside reserves on which claims had been submitted. Blockades were used almost exclusively to stop construction or resource exploitation by private corporations, and they were justified by the Indians in terms of aboriginal title and the refusal of the province to recognize the validity of the land claims. Even though the resource companies were the immediate targets of protest, Indian spokesmen in each case emphasized that their quarrel was with the province, which had authorized the companies' activities. The province was now very much the focus of resentment, with the federal government receiving only minor criticism, usually for its policy of negotiating only one claim at a time. The RCMP deliberately played a minor role, trying to avoid becoming government spokesmen. In the major protests RCMP officials and Indian leaders kept in personal contact; when protestors were arrested, the timing was no surprise to either the Indians or the waiting television crews.

In most cases the Indian groups went to court, seeking injunctions to halt the logging or other activities until their land claims were settled. They failed in a few cases but obtained notable successes in others; the courts were now willing to curb the province's authority over non-reserve lands pending land claim settlement.[25] Both the Gitksan-Wet'suwet'en and the Nuu'chah'nulth Tribal Councils also took their actual land claims to court, seeking, as the Nisga'a had done, to obtain judicial declarations that their aboriginal title had not been extinguished. The Gitksan-Wet'suwet'en case was taken first, occupying several years in the British Columbia Supreme Court and receiving much news media attention.[26]

The support of white groups was sought and provided during the protests. Spokesmen for each of the major churches urged the province to negotiate, as did the interchurch group Project North. Various local and provincial environmental groups raised money for the Indians and lobbied the provincial government. In both the Meares Island and Lyell Island cases important support was given by groups of local Whites, some of whom manned the blockades with the Indians; the proportion of local Whites giving support was highest in the Meares Island case, with even the local municipal leaders (of the village of Tofino) opposed to the logging. The linking of the Indian land question with wilderness preservation and environmental protection, which had strong support among Whites, was a critical new political development.

In the 1980s the protest leaders actively sought the understanding of the non-Indian editors and journalists in order to influence white public opinion. Indeed, skill in making the specific issues clear to journalists, most of whom had little knowledge of the land question, was an important factor in the protests. Journalists, especially those in television from Toronto and Montreal, quickly came on side when chanting Indians in traditional costume confronted white loggers on magnificent coastal islands or in pristine mountain valleys; less attention was paid when Indians in blue jeans and baseball caps did the same thing in the dreary spruce forests of the northern interior. There was, however, substantial and serious television and newspaper coverage. Terry Glavin of the *Vancouver Sun* took the retired Ron Rose's place as the province's leading reporter specializing in aboriginal matters. Besides providing direct coverage for the white public, journalists pressed the provincial officials to defend their refusal to negotiate. In the provincial election campaigns of 1983 and 1986 and in the federal campaigns of 1984 and 1988, the land claims and other aboriginal issues were the subject of major questions put to the party leaders and candidates by reporters and editors.

In November 1985, in the midst of the Lyell Island protests by the Haida, the *Sun* had a public opinion survey carried out on the subject of land claims and protests. To the question "Should Premier Bennett agree to negotiate Indian land claims?" 63 per cent replied that he should, 21 per cent said that he should not, and 16 per cent gave no opinion. On the question of the Lyell Island protest itself, 50 per cent said the Haida were justified in their actions.[27]

In late 1984, during the Meares Island protests, David Crombie appointed a task force, under the chairmanship of Murray Coolican, to review federal claims policy. Crombie appointed Joe Mathias as one of the members. The Coolican report, issued in December 1985, when the Lyell Island blockade was in full swing, recommended that the federal government devote greater effort to claims negotiation, and, in particular, that it abandon the policy of negotiating only one claim at a time in any one province.[28] Crombie soon left federal politics. The Coolican report seemed forgotten. The two governments did, however, allow a victory of sorts to the Haida by agreeing that the southern portion of the Queen Charlotte Islands would become a national park. While this step did not deal directly with the land claim, it did involve the province's agreeing to transfer its interests in the future park lands to the federal Crown.[29] The federal government was thus left free to reach a land claim settlement with the Haida, but negotiations have still not begun.

With the exception of the Native Brotherhood, which continued in its established role, the provincial Indian organizations found themselves with less to do as tribal groups became more prominent during the 1980s. The two women's organizations declined in support and influence. The United Native Nations remained active, especially under the leadership of Ron George and Ernie Crey, but directed its efforts largely towards issues of concern to off-reserve urban Indians. The amendment of the Indian Act in 1985, which allowed most non-status Indians to regain their status, led to some reduction in UNN membership. A number of Indians who had been active in the UNN moved from Vancouver back to their tribal group areas, while a number of Métis left to take part in exclusively Métis organizations, such as the Louis Riel Métis Association. Bill Wilson did not seek re-election as vice-president of the Native Council of Canada; he went home to Comox to live with his family and to work for one of the Kwagiulth tribal councils.

Support for the Union of British Columbia Columbia Indian Chiefs shrank back further within its southern Salish base; it became essentially an extensive tribal council itself, having an active membership of some thirty bands, most of them rather small, and most of them either Lillooet or Shuswap. The Aboriginal Council continued to function as a clearing house for tribal groups. George Watts remained a pre-eminent Indian spokesman, although the Tribal Forum found itself dealing with ever more routine matters and fading in political importance; its last meeting took place in March 1988. The Aboriginal Peoples Constitutional Conference (APCC), founded in 1983, continued to meet; by early 1988, however, its active participants were considering a new role for it.

In 1984 the National Indian Brotherhood had reconstituted itself into the "Assembly of First Nations" (AFN). Hitherto its members had been the chiefs of Indian bands, but now the membership would consist of the bands themselves. (In the terminology of Indians east of the Rockies, "first nations" meant Indian bands and not tribal groups.) Within each province the first nations would choose an AFN vice-chief for that province. Since the APCC was now indisputably the entity representing most of the "first nations" in British Columbia, the AFN transferred the responsibility for selecting the vice-chief from the Union to the APCC. The Union thus lost its special connection with the national organization, and became simply another among the provincial organizations.

Joe Mathias became AFN vice-chief for British Columbia and also chairman of the APCC. He sought to publicize the land claim issue among non-Indians and to press the province to change its policy; he remained active as well in aboriginal politics at the national level. While the APCC continued as the official Indian political voice on the land question, it remained largely unnoticed by the white public and by the provincial government, and it failed to attain a clear role or identity among the Indian public.[30] In 1987, with the ending of the series of required first ministers' conferences, the APCC found itself without an official reason to exist.

Mathias and others took for granted that one principal co-ordinating forum was still needed, but they believed that it would have to differ from the APCC in having a mandate to consider any matter of Indian concern. They also believed that it would need to have a clear identity if it were to gain popular support among Indians and be able to perform the essential tasks of gaining non-Indian support and bringing pressure to bear on the provincial government concerning aboriginal title and claims negotiations. Mathias arranged to have Kathryn Teneese and Stephen Olson, of the private Centre for Indian Training and Research,[31] consult with bands, tribal groups, and provincial organizations concerning some sort of new co-ordinating forum. For several years there had been mention here and there among Indians of a "parliament" or "congress"; Teneese and Olson found widespread support for the idea. They proposed a "parliament"[32] composed of representatives of each "first nation."

"First nation," was not a term yet in common use among British Columbia Indians; in the provincial context it could mean either "tribal group" or "band." It was quite clear, however, that the concept applied only to grass-roots entities; it did not apply to provincial organizations. Teneese and Olson suggested that any group designating itself a "first nation"[33] should be allowed to participate in the "parliament."[34]

The APCC met for the final time in October 1988 at Musqueam. James Gosnell was notably absent; he had died of cancer in August. Representatives of some 130 bands, 22 tribal councils, and each of the provincial organizations were in attendance. Some 250 persons were present. In the political history of British Columbia Indians, only the first APCC meeting, in January 1983, had been better attended or as widely representative.[35] Mathias was re-elected without opposition as vice-chief of the AFN.

The proposal for an Indian "parliament" was debated for three days. Saul Terry, now president of the Union, was opposed to forming any new body, saying "We don't need a new organization."[36] Others from the Lillooet and Shuswap tribal groups expressed the same view. Most speakers, however, supported the proposal. Rod Robinson, one of the Nisga'a hereditary chiefs, argued that "we all need to come together in a new forum."[37] Mathias, Watts, Wilson, Newman, and many others stressed the need for unity in pursuit of the land claims, believing that a new institution would allow Indians a stronger and clearer voice to influence public opinion and urge the province to negotiate.

While most speakers initially preferred "parliament" to "congress," they were persuaded that the term "congress" was the better one; it implied equality among representatives and had few prior connotations. On the last day Robinson moved that "the First Nations here

assembled hereby establish the First Nations Congress."[38] The motion
did not define "first nation"; the preceding debate had made clear that
any grass-roots group calling itself a first nation would be given representation.[39] The motion was approved almost unanimously.[40]

During the assembly it was evident that Mathias had come to be
recognized as the leading political figure among British Columbia Indians. On the last day Robinson and other participants acknowledged
him as the "head" of the new Congress. The new role, which was seen
as separate from Mathias's other role of vice-chief of the AFN, was given
substance when the assembly authorized him to hire staff to serve the
Congress and administer its affairs.

One entity and one leader now represented all British Columbia
Indians and had their mandate to press for land claims negotiations as
the highest priority and also to take up any other matter of aboriginal
concern. The provincial Indian organizations, which had been so dominant after 1969, retained not even a token place in the composition or
conduct of the new body. Direct tribal and community participation was
now firmly established as the basis of province-wide political representation. Although it was anchored in the experience of the preceding
decade, the Congress was more than merely another co-ordinating
forum. It had a leader with authority to act between sessions, and he was
also the British Columbia spokesman in national aboriginal affairs.[41]
Whatever the future of the Congress, its formation was a major attainment in the enduring quest for political unity among British Columbia
Indians.

CHAPTER SIXTEEN

Aboriginal Title in the Courts

There are two main legal questions concerning aboriginal title in British Columbia or, indeed, anywhere in Canada. The first is whether pre-contact use and occupancy endowed the various communities or tribal groups with land ownership. Put in legal terminology, the question is whether there was "pre-existing title" when European colonies were created. If there was no pre-existing title, the colonial governments faced no pre-existing constraints in dealing with the land.

The second question arises only if pre-existing title did exist. This question has to do with the strength and continuity of the title under the new regime. The stark test lies in the means required to extinguish the title. At one extreme, the title may be seen as no more than a minor encumbrance which survives at the pleasure of the new regime. In accord with this view, any contrary action by the authorities, however implicit, serves to extinguish the title. Towards the other extreme, continuing Indian title may be seen as a legal right. In this case extinguishment must be regarded as more difficult and could require explicit action, such as sale or expropriation.

While treaties or other explicit actions do not necessarily prove that title was a pre-existing legal right, they are universally taken as having extinguished title to the affected lands. In British Columbia the two questions thus have relevance only to the non-treaty areas. The questions may be put succinctly: Did British Columbia Indians have pre-existing land title? If they did have such title, is implicit action sufficient to extinguish it, or does it continue until explicit extinguishment occurs?

During the century following 1763, decisions of the Judicial Committee of the Privy Council recognized the "pre-existence" of aboriginal rights and their continuity under the new regime unless explicitly extinguished. The decisions thus remained in accord with the principles of the Royal Proclamation and so also with the view of aboriginal rights held by British Columbia Indians.[1] By the time the province had joined Canada, however, the doctrine of legal positivism, which held that the sovereign was the sole source of rights, had become dominant within British jurisprudence.[2]

In 1888, in an Ontario case which involved the St Catharines Lumber and Milling Company,[3] the committee ruled that aboriginal title had no pre-existence, but was created, through the proclamation, by the British authorities themselves. The proclamation was suddenly distorted.[4] Aboriginal title was abruptly debased. Seen as the creation of the British authorities, that title could now also be seen as remaining in effect only at the pleasure of those same authorities; any contrary action by them, however implicit, would do the trick of eliminating it. Ironically enough, it was shortly after the *St Catharines* decision that British Columbia Indians discovered the proclamation, took it to mean what it said, and proceeded to develop their optimistic faith in British justice.[5]

In the decades following the *St Catharines* decision no cases arose concerning Indian title in British Columbia or other non-treaty areas in Canada. Cases involving aboriginal title in New Zealand, India, and a number of African colonies, however, continued to arise. In deciding them, the Judicial Committee returned to its earlier principles. Two of the committee's rulings would much later prove of special relevance to the land question in British Columbia. In 1919, in a case arising in Southern Rhodesia, Lord Sumner ruled, on behalf of the committee, that there were "aboriginal tribes" who were "so low in the scale of social organization" that their "usages and conceptions" could not be continued under the British regime. "On the other hand," there were "indigenous peoples whose legal conceptions, although differently developed, are hardly less precise than our own"; their systems of land title could continue. Sumner thus endorsed pre-existence and continuity, but he added an important caveat: for title to continue, the traditional land title system had to be based on individual rather than tribal ownership. Sumner could be taken as asserting that what he called "aboriginal tribes" were, by definition, too primitive to have their title continue under the British regime.[6]

Only three years later, however, in deciding a case from Nigeria, the Judicial Committee rejected Sumner's requirement of individual ownership and indicated that pre-existing communal or tribal title should be presumed to continue under the British. Viscount Haldane delivered the ruling:

In interpreting the native title to land, not only in Southern Nigeria, but other parts of the British Empire, much caution is essential. There is a tendency, operating at times unconsciously, to render that title conceptually in terms which are appropriate only to systems which have grown up under English law. But this tendency has to be held in check closely ... The title, such as it is, may not be that of the individual, as in this country it nearly always is in some form, but may be that of a community ... The original native right was a communal right, and it must be presumed to have continued to exist unless the contrary is established by the context or the circumstances.[7]

Both pre-existence of aboriginal title and its continuity unless explicitly extinguished were now re-established in the jurisprudence of the Judicial Committee.[8]

Haldane's ruling came at the very time that the land claims efforts of the Allied Tribes of British Columbia were at their most intense. As was indicated in Chapter 9, it was presumably the Haldane ruling which played a major part in leading Parliament to outlaw claims-related activity in 1927, making it legally impossible for British Columbia Indians to take the steps necessary to get the claim into the courts as the first step on the road to the Judicial Committee. The 1927 amendment seemed to stand as a permanent solution to the Indian land question.

In 1949 the Judicial Committee ceased to be Canada's highest appeal court.[9] No longer was there any possibility that the views of the Judicial Committee could be imposed on Canada. Canadian judges were free to use the Judicial Committee as a source of precedent, but their doing so seemed unlikely, for conventional wisdom among judges, lawyers, academics, and government officials held that aboriginal rights were both insignificant and irrelevant. The thinking embodied in the St Catharines decision of 1888 was now firmly entrenched in Canadian jurisprudence. With the Judicial Committee out of the way and with officials assuming that British Columbia Indians had forgotten about aboriginal title, the federal government had the Indian Act amended in 1951 to remove the prohibition against claims-related activity (the anti-potlatch provision was removed at the same time).[10]

In 1951 two elements were absent from the Canadian legal and political systems. One was Indian political activity in pursuit of aboriginal rights; it reappeared in British Columbia within a few years of the 1951 amendments. The other element was an active judiciary willing to examine aboriginal rights independently of government and from an ethical and legal perspective. Judges began to assume a more important role in the 1960s as a direct result of the actions of British Columbia Indians.

An awakening judiciary was something the British Columbia government could not ignore. Throughout the century following the retirement of James Douglas, there had never been any pressing motive for the province to provide any reasoned explanation for its unchanging denial of aboriginal title. In the 1960s, with Indians in court and judges listening to arguments in support of aboriginal rights, the province was compelled for the first time to prepare arguments in defence of its historic position. Except on Vancouver Island and in the Peace River area, there had never been explicit action intended to extinguish Indian title in the province. There was now the possibility that the courts would accept Indian title as pre-existing and as continuing in the absence of explicit extinguishment. More specifically, the courts might apply the Royal Proclamation and follow Viscount Haldane's reasoning. During the 1960s lawyers hired by the province devised two related arguments to head off these possibilities.

In line with the *St Catharines* decision of 1888, the lawyers assumed that any aboriginal title could have been created only by the Royal Proclamation. They therefore argued that the proclamation had not applied to British Columbia. This was a lawyers' argument contrived retrospectively. No one associated with any aspect of the Indian land question had previously read the proclamation as not extending to the western edge of the continent. There had been no such suggestion in 1927, for instance, when H.H. Stevens and other members of the special parliamentary committee were seeking so intently to discredit the Indian claim. Had there been any such suggestion, Stevens and the committee would most certainly have seized upon it.

To support their argument, the lawyers pointed first to the present tense in one key phrase in the proclamation. They maintained that the usage "Indians with whom We are connected" meant that the proclamation applied only to Indians with whom the British were in contact in 1763 at the instant the proclamation was issued. Since the British had no relations with Indians west of the Rockies in 1763, it followed that the proclamation did not apply to that territory.

Two observations may be brought to bear in assessing this contention. First, statutes, proclamations, and constitutions are ordinarily taken as continuing to "speak" until they are repealed. The proclamation has never been repealed; it continues to be published along with the regular statutes of Canada.[11] Second, in legal enactments the present tense is often used with a prospective intent. Had the British monarch issued another proclamation stating that a royal biscuit was to be given to "any person with whom We are having tea," it would be ridiculous to argue that the provision applied only to persons at the table with the monarch at the moment of signing and that it did not apply to future tea parties. Today the Canadian Charter of Rights and Freedoms uses the present tense in expressing its guarantees; no sane person would maintain that its guarantees were intended to apply only at the moment the Charter was approved. Thus, the "present tense" argument advanced by the province's lawyers to deflect the proclamation from British Columbia must be rejected as implausible and indefensible.

The lawyers also supported their contention by pointing out that the territory had not been explored by the British in 1763; therefore, they asserted, the British had not intended the proclamation to apply to it. This assertion was simply that; no actual supporting evidence could be provided. To the contrary, as Brian Slattery observes, "Imperial enactments . . . were normally given a prospective application so as to apply not only to colonies and territories held when the legislation was enacted, but also to those acquired subsequently, unless this result was clearly excluded."[12] Otherwise, the British would have had continually to amend colonial proclamations and other legislation to take account of each new colony or territory; this they most assuredly did not do.

The most explicit refutation of the contention, however, is provided in the language of the proclamation itself, which reserves "for the use of the said Indians . . . all the Lands and Territories lying to the West-ward of the Sources of the Rivers which fall into the [Atlantic] Sea from the West and the North West." In 1763 the general outline of North America was well known; the British had long since reached California and the Russians held Alaska; world maps printed in Britain and else-where at the time showed the east coast of the Pacific Ocean. The British officials who drafted the proclamation can hardly have been ignorant of, or uninterested in, the westward extent of the continent. The contention that the proclamation was not intended to extend to the Pacific is thus insupportable in the absence of explicit evidence to the contrary.[13]

The second provincial argument was designed to meet the possibility that the courts would recognize title to have been pre-existing. The argument was simply that implicit extinguishment was sufficient.[14] Given the absence of any explicit extinguishment in the non-treaty areas, no other argument could be put forward. The action advanced as serving to extinguish any continuing title was the colonial legislature's enacting land use legislation that ignored Indian title. Ignoring Indian title was thus to be seen as extinguishing it.

Put another way, the argument asserted that the ordinary operation of a British colonial government had the effect of wiping out the legitimacy of any pre-existing aboriginal arrangements. The argument thus not only took for granted that extinguishment of title could be implicit; it also assumed that extinguishment would be automatic. The argument of implicit extinguishment through ordinary legislation has not been raised in other parts of Canada. In the Yukon and Northwest Territories and in northern Quebec general land laws had been in effect for decades, yet this fact was not taken as having extinguished aboriginal title in the 1970s when modern land claims negotiations began. More-over, neither H.H. Stevens nor Duncan Campbell Scott produced the argument in 1927.

Within British Columbia, however, the notion of implicit and auto-matic extinguishment accorded with the old white myth that Indians had been primitive creatures whose inferior ways and usages must inevitably give way to those of the more civilized Whites. Perhaps for this reason the argument of implicit extinguishment proved highly pop-ular among provincial government politicians; they adopted it as the major tenet in their anti-title doctrine during the 1970s and 1980s. Among judges the argument also had considerable success, although by 1989 there had still been no court decision that dealt decisively with the argument.

Until 1963 no court case arising in British Columbia had involved aboriginal rights in any significant way, and none had involved Indian title. Cases arising elsewhere in Canada had involved aboriginal rights, but few had concerned aboriginal title. Since 1963 the most important aboriginal rights cases in Canada have arisen in British Columbia, and the most notable of these have concerned aboriginal title. The changes were initiated by a number of rifle shots on Vancouver Island in 1963.

Exactly two centuries after the Royal Proclamation came into effect, two members of the Nanaimo Indian band, Clifford White and David Bob, shot six deer on unoccupied land which Governor James Douglas had purchased from their community in 1854. The purchase agreement had stated that the Indians were to be "at liberty to hunt over the unoccupied lands . . . as formerly."[15] Provincial officials arrested the two men for possessing game without a permit and out of season, in viola-tion of provincial law.[16] Maisie Hurley, the white publisher of the *Native Voice*, learned of the arrests and informed Tom Berger, a young lawyer with a new practice.[17] Berger took on the case and argued in court that the purchase agreement was a treaty, that it recognized a pre-existing right in accord with the Proclamation of 1763, and that the proclama-tion stood as a guarantee of aboriginal and treaty rights in British Columbia.[18]

Lawyers hired by the province depicted the agreements as mere pri-vate arrangements between the Hudson's Bay Company and the Indi-ans rather than as treaties agreed to by colonial authorities. They also presented their arguments that the proclamation did not apply to the territory.[19]

In the British Columbia Court of Appeal the case was heard by a panel of five judges. Three of them, including Mr. Justice Tom Norris, ruled that the agreement was indeed a treaty; they thus acquitted White and Bob. Norris, however, was the only one of the three who considered the proclamation as relevant to the case. Agreeing with Berger, he presented a detailed forty-page opinion in which he concluded that "the aboriginal rights as to hunting and fishing affirmed by the Proclamation of 1763 and recognized by the Treaty ... still exist."[20] For the first time a judge, and a well-respected British Columbia judge of conservative leanings at that, had presented a comprehensive opinion endorsing both the pre-existence and the continuing existence of aboriginal rights in British Columbia.

The province appealed the acquittal to the Supreme Court of Canada which summarily confirmed the decision of the Appeal Court, but without going beyond the narrow question of whether the purchase agreement had been a treaty. Norris's views were thus not accepted by the highest court, but neither were they rejected.[21] Berger's arguments and Norris's opinion, together with the acquittal of White and Bob, "had the effect of reviving the aboriginal rights issue" not only in British Columbia but in the Canadian judicial system as a whole.[22]

As a direct result of Berger's success in the *White and Bob* case and keenly aware that the principles of that case could be applied to aboriginal title, the Nisga'a Tribal Council hired Berger[23] to go to court for a judicial declaration that their "aboriginal title, otherwise known as the Indian title . . . to their ancient tribal territory . . . has never been lawfully extinguished."[24] The Nisga'a were thus asking the courts to recognize pre-existing title as a legal right and to declare that extinguishment required explicit action. Going to court for this purpose was at the time regarded by other Indians and by most lawyers as enormously risky. The chances seemed overwhelming that the courts would rule that title had never existed.

In 1969 Berger and the province's lawyers argued the case in the Supreme Court of British Columbia. In its decision the court accepted the province's legal arguments. There had been no Nisga'a title because the Royal Proclamation did not apply and therefore had not created Indian title. However, even if there had been such title it had been extinguished, implicitly, by land legislation passed before 1871.[25] The case then went to the British Columbia Court of Appeal, where Chief Justice H.W. Davey[26] decided to head the appeal panel himself and not to appoint Mr. Justice Norris to the panel. The panel unanimously upheld the initial decision. The chief justice took Lord Sumner's Judicial Committee ruling of 1919 as providing the relevant precedent.[27]

In spite of the commendation by Mr. Duff, the well known anthropologist, of the native culture of the Indians on the mainland of British Columbia, they were undoubtedly at the time of settlement a very primitive people with few of the institutions of civilized society, and none at all of our notions of private property . . . I see no evidence to justify a conclusion that the aboriginal rights claimed by the successors of these primitive people are of a kind that it should be assumed the Crown recognized them when it acquired the mainland of British Columbia by occupation.[28]

Davey viewed the proclamation as the only possible source of aboriginal title and interpreted the proclamation as not applying to British Columbia. He also accepted the notion of implicit extinguishment.[29] Mr. Justice Charles Tysoe's view of the Nisga'a hearkened back to Premier William Smithe's telling the Nisga'a chiefs in 1887 that they had been "little better than the wild beasts of the field."[30] Tysoe said, "The appellants' ancestors fished, hunted and picked berries. The skins of animals were used for clothing. These people knew nothing of the so-called benefits of civilization. Having regard to the size of the territory over which they may have roamed they were comparatively few in number."[31] He also endorsed the notion of implicit extinguishment.[32] Davey and Tysoe added insult to injury by accepting Joseph Trutch as the authority on what had been the practice and the intent in Douglas's early policies.[33]

Things were not going well for the Nisga'a. They were losing their case, and they had given provincial appeal court judges the opportunity to reiterate and revive the century-old white myth that the province's Indians had been creatures too primitive to have recognizable land ownership. Calder and the others felt discouraged and embarrassed, but they instructed Berger to appeal to the Supreme Court of Canada.[34] The real question now was whether judges from elsewhere in Canada would have the same views as most judges whose legal careers had been spent in British Columbia.

Seven members of the Supreme Court of Canada heard the appeal. None was from British Columbia. One of them, Mr. Justice Louis-Philippe Pigeon, decided against the Nisga'a on the procedural ground that they had not followed the provincial Crown Procedure Act's requirement that any party bringing action against the provincial Crown must first obtain the provincial government's permission to do so. British Columbia was the only province in the country still to have such a law in effect, and had the Nisga'a sought permission, they would most likely not have got to court in the first place. Pigeon did not express any opinion on the merits of the Nisga'a claim.

Quite unexpectedly, on the question of pre-existing Indian title the other six judges not only ruled against the province and in favour of the Nisga'a, but they did so unanimously. Three of the judges, led by Mr. Justice Emmett Hall, accepted the proclamation as extending to the Pacific and as affirming pre-existing aboriginal title as a legal right.[35]

The other three, led by Mr. Justice Wilfred Judson, concluded that the proclamation did not apply to British Columbia, but they did not go on to conclude that Indian title could not have existed. As Judson said, "I think that it is clear that Indian title in British Columbia cannot owe its origin to the Proclamation of 1763." He went on: "The fact is that when the settlers came, the Indians were there, organized in societies and occupying the land as their forefathers had done for centuries. This is what Indian title means."[36] Judson thus asserted that there had been Indian title, and that the proclamation was irrelevant on this point, but he did not indicate whether title was a legal right.

The Supreme Court of Canada thus ruled that the Nisga'a had held title to their land when the colonial government came into existence in 1858. Thus, the essential assumption underlying the province's denial of aboriginal title had been declared invalid by Canada's highest court. The Indian land question in British Columbia could no longer be dismissed as frivolous or irrelevant. The Nisga'a had won a major moral victory.

The practical question, however, was whether the Nisga'a still held title in 1973. In the view of the three judges led by Hall, the Nisga'a did indeed still own their land. Hall cited Viscount Haldane in support of the principle that "once aboriginal title is established, it is presumed to continue until the contrary is proven." In Hall's opinion the absence of "clear and plain" extinguishment meant that the Nisga'as' "rights to possession of the lands . . . have not been extinguished by the Province of British Columbia or by its predecessor, the Colony of British Columbia, or by the Governors of that Colony."[37] Thus, in the opinion of three judges, explicit extinguishment was required; implicit extinguishment was not sufficient.

The three judges led by Judson accepted implicit extinguishment as sufficient and as having taken place; like the British Columbia Appeal Court judges, they accepted Joseph Trutch as the authority on what had happened under James Douglas.[38] The result (with Pigeon abstaining from giving any opinion on issues in the case) was a three-three tie. In practical terms the Nisga'a appeal thus failed. On the question of continuing title the ruling of the lower courts was upheld. Still, the fact that three members of Canada's highest court viewed Nisga'a title as still in existence was a major turn of events (and one which soon led the federal government to agree to negotiate where title had not been explicitly extinguished). The province had clearly lost the legal argument over pre-existing title and had almost lost on the issue of continuing title. It now had good reason to fear future court decisions.

The next court case at first seemed to have nothing to do with aboriginal title. In the late 1950s, at the instigation of the local Indian agent, the Musqueam band agreed to the lease of 162 acres of its main reserve to the Shaughnessy Golf Club. The entire transaction was handled by federal officials. In 1970 Delbert Guerin, then chief of the band, learned that crucial information had been withheld from the band by the officials[39] and that the terms of the lease were exceptionally and suspiciously favourable to the Golf Club. In 1975 the band sued the federal government for breach of trust and the Federal Court awarded the band $10 million in damages. The Federal Court of Appeal overturned the award, on the ground that the Indian Act gave the government the authority to do as it wished with reserve land and imposed no legal obligation on the Crown to act in the band's interest. The band appealed to the Supreme Court of Canada, which upheld the appeal and ordered the government to pay the $10 million to the band. The Supreme Court based its decision on aboriginal title. In so doing it revised the previous understandings of the Nisga'a decision and gave new life to land claims activity in British Columbia.

Chief Justice Brian Dickson gave the court's main judgment in November 1984. In the Nisga'a case, he said, "this court recognized aboriginal title as a legal right derived from the Indians' historic occupation and possession of their tribal lands."[40] Hitherto it had been clear that only three judges in the Nisga'a ruling had accepted title as a legal right. Now Dickson had Judson's group doing so as well. Pre-existing aboriginal title as a legal right was suddenly established in Canadian law. Dickson, relying on Viscount Haldane's ruling of 1921,[41] left no ambiguity on this point. "[The Indians'] interest in their lands is a pre-existing legal right not created by Royal Proclamation, by . . . the Indian Act, or by any other executive order or legislative provision. It does not matter, in my opinion, that the present case is concerned with the interest of an Indian band in a reserve rather than with unrecognized title in traditional tribal lands. The Indian interest in the land is the same in both cases."[42] Pre-existing aboriginal title was thus a legal right still having force on reserves and *outside reserves* on "traditional tribal lands."

It was evident almost immediately that the *Guerin* decision had major practical implications in British Columbia concerning the role of the courts and the means by which Indian groups could protect their interests in the land against the efforts of the province. Three weeks after the *Guerin* decision, Nuu'chah'nulth Indians and other protestors blocked the access of the MacMillan Bloedel Company to Meares Island. With small exceptions, Meares Island was not reserve land; the province had always regarded it as provincial crown land and had followed all the proper steps in authorizing the company to begin clear-cut logging. The chiefs of the Clayoquot and Ahousaht bands, Moses Martin and Corbett

George, sought a declaration from the courts that "any authorization purporting to allow logging or to in any other manner interfere with ... aboriginal title on Meares Island" was beyond the powers of the province; in other words, they took their land claim to court.[43] At the same time the chiefs applied to a British Columbia Supreme Court judge for an injunction halting logging until the claim had been resolved "at trial" in court. Central to the Indian application was the desire to preserve evidence of their historic usage, including "culturally modified" trees that had been worked prior to white arrival. The province used its standard arguments against title. The company argued that economic chaos would spread across the province if the injunction were granted.

The judge "refused to believe that Dickson meant what he said about aboriginal title."[44] Still reading the 1973 Nisga'a decision to mean that the British Columbia Indians could have no continuing aboriginal title and so no chance of success with any claim, the judge denied the injunction. He concluded also that halting the logging would have "potentially disastrous consequences" across the province, that clear-cut logging on Meares Island would cause no unacceptable harm to any Indian interest, that money damages could be sought if harm were done, and that the Indians had "slept on the rights they assert" by waiting long past the time they first knew logging was being planned.[45]

The Indians appealed. Departing from the usual practice of not hearing appeals in such injunction cases, the British Columbia Court of Appeal took it up. Chief Justice Nathan Nemetz chose Justices Peter Seaton, W.A. Craig, J.D. Lambert, J.A. Macdonald, and A.B. Macfarlane as the appeal panel. The panel divided three to two, with Seaton, Lambert, and Macfarlane composing the majority; they based their ruling on the split decision in the Nisga'a case. Seaton gave the court's main opinion:

The [BC Supreme Court] judge thought the claim to Indian title so weak that he could safely conclude that it could not succeed. I do not agree with that view ... The proposal is to clear-cut the area. Almost nothing will be left. I cannot think of any native right that could be exercised on lands that have recently been logged ... I am firmly of the view that the claim to Indian title cannot be rejected at this stage of the litigation ... The Indians have pressed their land claims in various ways for generations. The claims have not been dealt with and found invalid. They have not been dealt with at all. Meanwhile, the logger continues his steady march and the Indians see themselves retreating into a smaller and smaller area. They, too, have drawn the line at Meares Island. The island has become a symbol of their claim to rights in the land ... It is important to the Indians' case that they be able to show their use of this forest. I do not mean to suggest that the Indians ought to continue using the forest only as they used it in the past. The importance of the evidence of extensive use is that it may demonstrate a right to continued use . . . It has . . . been suggested that a decision favourable to the Indians will cast doubt on the tenure that is the basis for the huge investment that has been and is being made. I am not influenced by that argument . . . There is a problem about tenure that has not been attended to in the past. We are being asked to ignore the problem as others have ignored it. I am not willing to do that.[46]

The "others" who had not dealt with Indian claims and who had ignored the problem of title were provincial government politicians. Macfarlane was even more definite in indicating what was expected of the provincial government:

The fact that there is an issue between the Indians and the province based upon aboriginal claims should not come as a surprise to anyone. Those claims have been advanced by the Indians for many years. They were advanced in [the Nisga'a case], and half the court thought that they had some substance . . . I think it fair to say that, in the end, the public anticipates that the claims will be resolved by negotiations and by settlement. This judicial proceeding is but a small part of the whole of a process which will ultimately find its solution in a reasonable exchange between governments and the Indian nations.[47]

On the three-two division, the court granted the injunction. The logging was not to proceed. The division in the court, however, was not clear-cut. Although they were opposed to the injunction, Craig and Macdonald each gave some support to the Indians. Craig was of the view that "the Indians have raised a fair question as to the existence of the right which they allege" and that the British Columbia Supreme Court judge "was wrong in concluding otherwise."[48] Macdonald believed that the "issues in dispute" would "be determined through successful negotiations in the future."[49] All five judges[50] thus affirmed that there was substance to Indian claims and believed that the province should negotiate with the Indians.

The British Columbia Court of Appeal had come a long way since Chief Justice Davey had dismissed both the Nisga'a and their claim sixteen years earlier. As he emerged from the court room after the decision, George Watts, the chairman of the Nuu'chah'nulth Tribal Council, broke down and wept with emotion. That evening Brian Smith, the provincial attorney-general, looking grim and displeased, made clear that the government intended no change in its policy. Soon the province requested the Supreme Court of Canada to allow it to appeal; the court denied the request.[51]

After the Meares Island ruling, British Columbia Supreme Court judges proceeded to issue injunctions when approached by Indian groups whose claims had not yet been heard. Logging was halted on Deere Island in Kwagiulth territory. Railway expansion was prevented along the Thompson River. Logging preparation was halted in the Gitksan-Wet'suwet'en claim area. Resource development was stopped in the whole area that the McLeod Lake band was seeking to have recognized as its reserve should its efforts to adhere to Treaty No. 8 be successful. Later, the courts allowed the band to sell the logs produced in its protest cutting in the area.[52] In each of these six cases the courts suspended the ability of province to treat the land as though aboriginal title did not exist.[53] The injunctions prompted the major resource development corporations to begin considering whether their own interests would not be better served by the province's negotiating with the Indians.

The new Canadian Constitution of 1982 introduced major new possibilities affecting aboriginal title. Section 35(1) states that "the existing aboriginal and treaty rights of aboriginal peoples of Canada are hereby recognized and affirmed." (This section had been removed from the draft constitution, with British Columbia officials among those advocating the removal, but then re-inserted in response to public criticism.) The section leaves open for the courts the question of whether unextinguished title is a continuing aboriginal right.

By 1989 no court had applied section 35 to any aboriginal title question. One British Columbia decision, however, had applied it to a related question, that of aboriginal fishing rights in non-treaty areas. The case arose when Ronald Sparrow, a Musqueam, was charged with contravening federal regulations while fishing in the Lower Fraser River. The location was not part of a reserve, nor did any treaty apply. In late 1986 the Court of Appeal ruled unanimously that section 35(1) meant that an aboriginal right to fish for food continued to exist in non-treaty areas of the province.

The Appeal Court based its decision on the fact that the Indians' right "to fish for food in their traditional fishing grounds . . . has always been recognized."[54] For this reason, as Chief Justice Nemetz was at pains to emphasize, the ruling did not affect the question of continuity of land title, in which the unresolved issue is whether or not such recognition is required.[55] Nevertheless, the court's ruling was a further defeat for the provincial government, which had intervened in the case to support its position that no aboriginal right could still exist in British Columbia. The possibility did remain that section 35 could be important in future title cases. However, for this possibility to materialize, the courts would have to accept at the same time that explicit extinguishment was required or that the colony and province had lacked the

power to effect extinguishment by any means. As either of these principles could be accepted without relying on section 35, it seemed unlikely
that the new Constitution would have a direct effect on the outcome of
the Indian land question.

By 1989 the courts had answered one of the two basic legal questions
pertaining to aboriginal land title in British Columbia. The Indians did
have title to their lands before colonial government was established, and
aboriginal title is a pre-existing legal right. The other question, whether
explicit extinguishment is necessary or whether implicit extinguishment
is sufficient, was still to be answered. In 1989 the next major title case,
that of the Gitksan-Wet'suwet'en, was well underway in the British
Columbia Supreme Court,[56] but, should there be an appeal, it would be
several years before the Supreme Court of Canada could provide the
final decision.[57]

The courts were now in a position, were they so inclined, to play the
decisive part in settling the land question. They could do so by declar-
ing that aboriginal title continues in the absence of explicit extinguishment. In this event the courts would almost certainly direct the province
and the Indian claimant groups to come together to devise an appropriate present-day arrangement. In all likelihood the courts would look to
the contemporary land claim agreements in other parts of Canada as
models to be followed in British Columbia.

CHAPTER SEVENTEEN

The Province and Land Claims Negotiations, 1976-89

British Columbia is not the only portion of Canada in which aboriginal title was not extinguished and in which aboriginal peoples have been pressing their land claims in recent times. British Columbia is, however, virtually alone in continuing to refuse to acknowledge aboriginal land claims or to negotiate. Since 1974 major contemporary treaties, called land claims "settlements" or "agreements," have been negotiated in Quebec, Yukon, and the Northwest Territories. In each case the provincial or territorial government has participated in the negotiations and agreed to the aboriginal ownership of lands that had previously been treated as having no aboriginal interest.

Quebec was not originally willing to acknowledge title or aboriginal claims; its hand was forced by a court injunction halting hydro power development. The result was the "James Bay and Northern Quebec Agreement," which received final approval in 1975; it covers 1,050,000 square kilometres. The Inuit and Cree together obtained about 1 per cent of this territory in outright ownership (thus surrendering title to an area almost identical in size to the whole province of British Columbia). They obtained exclusive fishing, hunting, and trapping rights over an additional 14 per cent. In compensation for surrendered lands the Inuit received $90 million; the Cree, $135 million.[1] The payment was thus about $217 a square kilometre, or eighty-eight cents an acre, for the 85 per cent of their territories which they surrendered. Much of the money was paid by the province.

The 1984 Inuvialuit agreement covers 430,000 square kilometres, most of it ocean, in the western Arctic. The Inuvialuit retained outright ownership of 2.6 per cent, and surface ownership (that is, excluding subsurface minerals) of an additional 18.1 per cent of the area. In payment for the surrendered 79.3 per cent they received $84 million ($249.27 a square kilometre, or $1.01 an acre).[2]

The Yukon Agreement, signed in 1988, covers almost all of Yukon's 483,000 square kilometres. Yukon Indians retained outright ownership of 25,900 square kilometres and surface ownership of an additional 15,540 square kilometres. The total Indian ownership of 41,440 square kilometres amounts to 8.6 per cent of Yukon. In compensation for lands given up the Indians accepted $232 million, an amount approximating $526 a square kilometre or $2.13 an acre. In both northern agreements the federal government assumed responsibility for all payments, since the territories remain under federal jurisdiction.[3]

In British Columbia, the hostility to Indian claims and the opposition to negotiations centre within the Social Credit Party, which has governed the province since 1976. The New Democratic Party, the only provincial opposition party with elected members, has come to accept the validity of the claims and has promised to negotiate with the various Indian groups should it form the government. While the worth of the promise remains to be tested (especially since the NDP government of 1972–75 did not agree to negotiate),[4] the mere fact that one of the two main political parties has endorsed provincial negotiation is a major step in the evolution of the Indian land question. The longstanding consensus among white politicians has come to an end.

The differences between Social Credit and NDP on the land question result to a large extent from their differing ideologies and, in particular, from their differing views of groups and group rights. The NDP sees society as composed of unequal groups and classes; it has little difficulty with notions of group rights and group benefits; and it expects government to help underprivileged groups. Social Credit sees free and enterprising individuals as the key element in society, and it rejects the notion that individuals should receive rights or benefits because they belong to a particular group.

Personalities and party history are additional factors. NDP attitudes towards Indians were influenced by the long presence of Frank Calder in party ranks, and later by the personal outlooks of two party leaders, Tom Berger and Robert Skelly, each of whom was exceptionally well informed about Indian concerns before entering politics and each of whom continued to regard land claim negotiations as appropriate and feasible. Social Credit was not influenced by Calder's passing presence, and no Social Credit politician has come to office with any reputation for being knowledgeable about land claims or other Indian political concerns, let alone supportive of them. Political history is another factor. The principal Social Credit spokesmen on Indian land claims were the inheritors of the major assumptions and perceptions held by white politicians and officials during the province's early decades.

Three men were prominent as such spokesmen: Allan Williams,

Brian Smith, and Garde Gardom.[5] When they joined Social Credit in the 1970s, Smith had long been active as a Progressive Conservative; Williams and Gardom had been Liberals. All three were lawyers. Like early government politicians, the three sought more to avoid or ignore the land claims issue than to deal with it extensively; most of their statements were made during the mid-1980s in attempts to shore up public opinion against the Indian protest blockades and as the province took part in the first ministers' conferences on aboriginal rights.[6]

Basic to the early white beliefs had been the conviction that Indians had not originally regarded themselves as owning the land. As time went on, there was a continuing tendency for white politicians to see land claims as having arisen only recently and to dismiss them for this very reason. H.H. Stevens had provided a perfect example of this tendency during the 1927 parliamentary hearings. Gardom did the same in the 1980s: "Indian dissatisfaction grew over the size of the reserves and concern that European settlement was interfering with traditional Indian ways. There was also concern (rightfully) [sic] that federal Indian Agents shackled the Indians' capacity to advance into the mainstream of economic Canada. *Eventually the unrest has manifested itself in the context of assertions of Indian title and demands for land claim settlements*".[7] [Emphasis added]

There was a reluctance by early Whites to accept Indian land claims as relevant to what Whites perceived as the problems facing Indians. Similarly, Social Credit spokesmen saw land claims as a surrogate issue raised in place of what they took to be the real issues that Indians ought to be dealing with. Gardom provided evidence of this view in the quotation just given. Williams expressed the same view (while also implying that Indians had come to believe in title only after contact):

In discussion with some of the bands, it is quite obvious that it ["land claims"] is a convenient tag to give to what are grievances that have gone back over a century or even more. In many cases, the resolution of many grievances which aren't associated with land at all might result in less attention to the so-called land claims . . . some people, quite obviously, are using the popularity of the land claims issue for purposes which are not associated with either the resolution of those land claims or the betterment of the Indian people and the resolution of grievances which they properly have with the rest of us in society.[8]

In the early period white politicians blamed white agitators, especially missionaries, for giving the Indians new ideas and false hopes. Social Credit spokesmen blamed the federal government. Gardom also blamed "legal and academic advisors" for encouraging Indian leaders to pursue impossible goals.[9]

That money was the motive for claims was another early white belief. Smith vigorously perpetuated it in the 1980s. "All they want is dollars. They don't want to throw anybody off the land, they just want billions and billions of dollars."[10] Smith, however, went beyond sarcasm. The most hostile early white view of Indian motives and morality was expressed in the report of the joint federal-provincial Commission of Enquiry which visited the north coast in 1887. Claims were seen not only as deriving from white ideas, but also as being taken up by Indians who were treacherous and disloyal.[11] Smith seemed to hold the same impression. "You start negotiating land claims and you're down the Neville Chamberlain route."[12] As prime minister of Britain, Chamberlain had sought to appease Germany and head off the Second World War by negotiating a non-aggression agreement with Hitler. Smith's none-too-subtle analogy put British Columbia Indians in the same category as the Nazis, the enemy forces who withheld their real intentions and made a fool of Chamberlain through an agreement which they had no intention of following. (Smith's statement was made in an interview with Southam News reporter Ben Tierney, who was so taken aback that he asked Smith to confirm what he had said. Smith did so.)[13] Premier William Bennett apparently had similar impressions about Indian loyalty to Canada; in 1984 he labelled some proposals for Indian self-government as "FLQ-style sovereignty."[14]

Gardom, in particular, professed on a number of occasions an inability to comprehend what was meant by "aboriginal title," "aboriginal rights," and other basic concepts.[15] In the legislature he once asked, rhetorically, "What precisely does aboriginal title mean?" and then promptly raised a quite ludicrous possibility: "If it means that one Indian band owns all of British Columbia, I don't think that would be acceptable."[16] Several years later the following exchange took place with Robert Skelly, then leader of the NDP:

Skelly: This minister . . . in spite of all the advice he has received, claims to
           be ignorant of the issue of aboriginal title and what the Indian
           people are asking for in this province.
Gardom: Can you define it? Can you define it? No.
Skelly: I can tell you the process by which it could be defined, and that
           process is the process of negotiating in good faith.[17]

Notably absent from the public statements of Smith and Gardom was any discussion of the modern Canadian land claims negotiations that had been concluded or were well underway by the mid-1980s. British Columbia Indian leaders tended to assume that the other agreements would reassure the Social Credit government. Despite these agreements, however, and despite the absence of evidence, Smith persisted in his view that Indians were mainly intent on gaining enormous amounts of money. Ten billion dollars was one of his estimates, which, as he pointed out, would mean "payouts the equivalent of, or larger than, the amount of money in the entire budget of the province of British Columbia."[18]

Gardom went even further in taking the expectations of the Indians to be radically different from what their spokesmen were asserting and from what was being agreed to by aboriginal peoples in the north and in Quebec. He depicted the Indians as seeking nothing less than the actual present-day ownership and control of all their traditional territories. He raised the specter of Indian control of the provincial economy and of Indian "pre-eminence" over white and other non-Indian British Columbians.

Many of our first citizens are pursuing not only ownership of land, which they generally define as "aboriginal title," but also various "aboriginal rights" over lands, water, and resources—natural assets that most British Columbians believe should be controlled for the benefit of *all* British Columbians . . . "Aboriginal rights," broadly defined, include the Indians' desire for constitutional authority to substitute Indian laws for any federal or provincial laws that they may now, or in the future, consider unsatisfactory to them . . . These new laws could regulate the use of natural resources within what Indians describe as their "traditional territories." They could, in effect, govern B.C.'s vast fishing, mining, forest, and wilderness-based tourism industries, as well as range lands and salt and fresh water resources . . . It appears that B.C. Indian leaders, encouraged by their legal and academic advisors and by the federal Department of Indian Affairs, have been genuinely led to anticipate that about 60,000 people, less that two per cent of B.C.'s population, may achieve . . . legal pre-eminence over 2.8 million people.[19]

In this statement Gardom declined to recognize that the very essence of every historic treaty and every modern agreement in Canada has been the giving up by aboriginal peoples of claim to the vast majority of their traditional lands and most certainly of control over the surrendered lands. The modern agreements provide for community or tribal self-government, but it would be preposterous to suggest that the agreements in Quebec, Yukon, or the Northwest Territories give aboriginal peoples the sort of control over other peoples that Gardom depicted for British Columbia. His statement was straightforward demagoguery.

Gardom was unable or unwilling to accept the possibility, borne out in every Canadian treaty and claims agreement, that claims to historic ownership were, in the Indian view, both basic justification and starting point in the process of negotiation. Were there no historic claims, there would be no reason for the contemporary land claims and therefore no reason to negotiate. In responding to criticism on this point, Gardom demanded that Indians, in effect, abandon their view of title, claims, and negotiations by promptly and publicly explaining "their position concerning suggestions that some of their demands may be exaggerated for negotiation purposes."[20] As a pre-condition to being taken seriously by the province, the Indians were being invited to confess to falsifying their own history, as Gardom quite apparently believed them to have done.

Smith and Gardom provided classic examples of white North Americans whose perceptions suggest a generalized and pejorative image of native Indians. While their public remarks indicated none of the racism and bigotry evident among earlier provincial leaders,[21] they did imply a perception of Indians that was remarkably similar to that evident among white politicians during the province's early decades. Implicit in Smith and Gardom's statements was an image of Indians who were: *insincere*, if not *devious* and *hypocritical*, in falsely claiming pre-contact ownership; *unsophisticated*, in accepting misleading guidance from Indian politicians and outside advisers; *ignorant*, in leaving aside important social and economic problems in order to pursue the futile land claims; *venal*, in being concerned with money rather than historical truth and fairness; *underhanded*, in disguising their real intentions; *untrustworthy*, in being unlikely to live up to agreements; and *selfish* and *unrealistic*, in seeking extensive control over provincial resources and over non-Indian British Columbians.

The Indian leaders were intensely aware of the image that was being perpetuated, and they were highly resentful of the government's tactics. Indeed, their view of the Social Credit government was virtually identical to its view of them. They regarded the government as deceptive, hypocritical, venal, ignorant, untrustworthy, and demagogic.

In 1985 Vaughn Palmer, the province's leading political columnist, summed-up the strategy on aboriginal title and negotiations being pursued by the Bill Bennett Social Credit government:

Its first position is that aboriginal title never existed. The second holds that if it ever existed, it was extinguished. Then the government will argue that even if title still exists it has little meaning in terms of compensation . . . The next fallback is that even if the natives are entitled to substantial compensation, the federal government must provide it under the terms that brought B.C. into Confederation. And the fifth and final position, though seldom articulated, is that the public will never stand for the level of compensation expected by native leaders, and therefore little risk attaches to the effort to defeat the claim in court.[22]

Palmer observed that the government believed the courts "will clarify the issue in the government's favor, while the outcome of negotiation based on prior recognition of aboriginal title would be far more expensive and politically risky. Attorney-General [Brian] Smith in particular believes the native claim will fail, and his reputation is on the line after many public statements to that effect."[23] In part, then, the government's refusal to negotiate was based on a straightforward weighing of alternatives. Undoubtedly it was also based on the Smith-Gardom image of Indians, for that image simply precluded the treatment of Indians as legitimate participants in the political process. In addition, however, Smith and Gardom repeatedly asserted the existence of legal and constitutional provisions that, they maintained, served to prevent the province from negotiating and that compelled the federal government to be the sole negotiator and the sole provider of compensation.

Gardom claimed that "only the government of Canada has the historic and legal responsibility to negotiate and conclude treaties"[24] and that "anyone who suggests that the B.C. government has the authority to negotiate treaties for ownership of and sovereignty over land by Indians is totally incorrect."[25] Immediate and commonsense refutation of Gardom's claim is provided by Quebec's full participation in negotiating and signing the James Bay and Northern Quebec Agreement. There is no judicial support for his claim, nor do any other legal opinions appear to exist supporting it. Certainly the Constitution contains no provision such as Gardom implied. Perhaps Gardom was seeking to imply, quite falsely, that the Indians or the federal government expected the province to negotiate all on its own without federal participation.

In the same context Gardom stated that "Our B.C. Indians' lawyers and academics . . . rarely, if ever, demand that the federal government go to the table—as it rightfully and constitutionally should."[26] The statement was bizarre; the federal government had then been at the table with the Nisga'a for ten years, had recently concluded the Inuvialuit agreement, and was then at the table in both northern territories.

One of Smith's basic arguments was that "In accordance with s 91(24) of the *British North America Act*, Canada has responsibility for Indians and lands reserved for Indians. The negotiation of Indian claims is therefore, principally a federal responsibility."[27] The same argument had been raised by the province at the first stage of the Nisga'a land claim case in 1969. The British Columbia Supreme Court had rejected it then, on the obvious grounds, first, that the lands at issue had not been reserved for Indians and, second, that title involves the status of land not the nature of the persons interested in it.[28] The province's lawyers had not raised the argument again in court.

The most vehement argument put forth by Smith and Gardom, however, related to Article 1 of the terms of union: "Canada shall be liable for the debts and liabilities of British Columbia existing at the time of union." Smith and Gardom asserted that the provision required the federal government to assume the payment for any title extinguished *after* British Columbia joined Canada. As Smith put it: "[If] Indian title existed when British Columbia entered Canada in 1871 . . . aboriginal title represented a liability or charge upon the colonial government to which [sic] the government of Canada alone is responsible."[29]

And Gardom:

Any unextinguished aboriginal title at the time of union would be just such a debt and just such a liability.[30]

If unextinguished aboriginal title exists in B.C., if there is any liability or charge upon the colonial government, Canada is fully responsible for that, and not B.C.[31]

Gardom and Smith both expressed puzzlement at the federal government's failure to read their meaning into Article 1. Gardom called the federal action "constitutional impertinence."[32]

Both ordinary insight and legal reasoning serve to refute the relevance of article 1 to *unextinguished* aboriginal title. Property which the province did not own at the time of union, and for which no purchase arrangement had been made, could not engender any provincial debt or liability at the time of union. Presumably this point would be incontrovertible in case of, say, steamships or buildings owned by private white citizens at the time of union; any subsequent purchase or expropriation by the province would not involve a debt or liability at the time of union. On the other hand, had the province obtained ownership of the boats or buildings at union but not yet paid for them, there would have been a provincial debt or liability and so a federal obligation to pay.

There is no reason why the principles should differ for aboriginal title. If the title was unextinguished at union, that is, in Indian ownership, there was no government debt or liability related to it. Only if Indian title had been extinguished *before union*, but not yet paid for, would there have been a debt or liability *at union*. As Douglas Sanders observes, "If aboriginal title was not extinguished before 1871 there was no 'liability' of the province in 1871. There was a fact of Indian ownership, but that fact does not, itself, give rise to a government liability. Liability would only arise on a taking of the property right."[33]

Smith and Gardom were apparently unable to conceive of aboriginal title as similar to other property rights or to regard continuing title as compatible with the existence of the province. They were, again, immune to contrary examples, as in the Quebec case, and also in earlier Ontario instances, in which the province itself did pay for surrender of aboriginal title.[34] The Constitution and the terms of union are, in fact, both silent on whether the province should pay any part of compensation for aboriginal title.

The Social Credit administration of Premier William Vander Zalm, which began in 1986, gave increased attention to Indian issues, and with the departure from politics of Smith and Gardom, and of several senior officials associated with them, a more moderate provincial stance emerged. The Ministry of Native Affairs assumed a new prominence under Bruce Strachan, the first minister assigned to it in the new government. He adhered firmly to the province's established position on title and negotiations, but he was, unlike any previous provincial minister, willing to meet with Indian groups in order to discuss and defend it, and he did so frequently. For the first time, the two sides were able to communicate on the land question without serious antagonism. Strachan's approach was continued in the ministry, especially by Jack Weisgerber, who continued as minister through 1989, and by Eric Denhoff, who was responsible for dealings with Indian groups (and who became deputy minister in early 1990). In other policy areas, new and better relations were developed with Indian communities, tribal groups, and political organizations, all of which were now generally accepted as legitimate interest groups within the provincial political process.[35] Bud Smith, the new attorney-general, initially opposed negotiations, but he too was willing to discuss the issue with Indian leaders and, unlike his predecessor, he was willing to be guided by current realities rather than old images.

After 1986, knowledge of Indian claims increased and resistance to negotiations decreased among the province's major interest groups. The Indian protest blockades did not engender any general non-Indian antagonism to the land claims. The efforts of Brian Smith and Garde Gardom had failed to create any new public hostility. Through the news media and in numerous public forums Indian leaders were now able to communicate directly and continually with their fellow British Columbians. The principal Christian churches, both individually and through the inter-denominational Project North, had for more than a decade been urging the province to negotiate and they continued to do so. The

British Columbia Federation of Labour, in which forestry, fishing, and mining workers are prominent participants, held a series of conferences with tribal groups and Indian political organizations in the mid-1980s and then gave its unanimous support to negotiations. In the same period the Union of British Columbia Municipalities held meetings and workshops on aboriginal issues and a number of mayors became advocates of negotiations.

Of perhaps the greatest portent, however, were two conferences in which tribal group representatives from across the province met privately with senior officials of the province's largest forestry, fishing, and mining companies. The meetings (at Whistler and Penticton in 1989) were organized by Bill Wilson, on behalf of the First Nations Congress, and Tom Waterland, representing the British Columbia Mining Association.[36] The British Columbia Council of Forest Industries and the Fisheries Council of British Columbia also gave their support. The first conference was designed mainly to educate the industrial representatives about the claims, and to enable the two sides to make personal contacts; the second dealt more with current policy issues. At both conferences the discussions were full, frank, and cordial.[37] The attendance of some of the executives was motivated by concern about the court injunctions that were blocking resource development in a number of land claim areas, but there was also a pronounced willingness to consider the land question from an ethical rather than an economic viewpoint, and there was substantial sentiment among the executives that the province should proceed to negotiate.

In 1989 the premier established a native affairs advisory council, which included several Indians (none of them of any previous political prominence) and which he accompanied on visits to the major tribal groups. The fact that the Nisga'a were visited first, and that senior provincial officials were perfectly aware beforehand that the Nisga'a would talk almost exclusively about their land claim, suggested that the government was preparing to take land claims more seriously. By late 1989 the advisory council had visited some half dozen tribal groups and in every case the principal Indian demand had been for land claim negotiations. Unlike any of his predecessors, the premier was willing to take part in public meetings with the tribal groups and to state in reply to Indian questions that it might be appropriate for the province to negotiate. By this time several of the advisory council members had indicated their support for negotiations, and it appeared likely that the council's eventual report to the premier would recommend that the province proceed to negotiate.

The Vander Zalm government continued to lose every by-election to the NDP. Clearly the NDP's support of land claims negotiations was not impairing its success, even in hitherto safe Social Credit ridings. One of these was the Cariboo constituency, in which both parties initially considered that the local saliency of the land claims issue, as well as the prominence of Indian complaints about the justice system, might be factors contributing to retention of white voting support by Social Credit. Moreover, David Zirnhelt, the NDP candidate, was well-known as an advocate of negotiations. However during the campaign, which took place in 1989, opinion polls by both parties indicated that white voters were unconcerned about the position of the NDP on aboriginal issues, and in the election several thousand former Social Credit supporters switched to Zirnhelt, giving him a decisive victory.

By this time officials in the ministries of native affairs and of the attorney-general had arrived at a new provincial outlook concerning the Indian land question. They believed that the province's major interest groups would continue to expect negotiations, and they were mindful that the NDP might win the next election. They knew that further court injunctions would likely follow upon any new Indian protest blockades, and a growing number of the officials expected that the British Columbia Supreme Court would affirm some degree of continuing aboriginal title in the Gitksan-Wet'suwet'en land claim case. Above all, they understood the futility of seeking to thwart or divert the Indian determination that the land question be resolved. By the end of 1989 most of the senior officials had concluded that the province's refusal to negotiate was no longer politically or legally defensible.[38] As 1990 began, however, the government politicians had yet to make any public moves towards negotiations. Officially, as it had throughout its history in Canada, British Columbia still remained faithful to the views and policies of Joseph Trutch.

Notes

NOTES TO THE PREFACE

1 BC, *Papers Connected with the Indian Land Question, 1850–1875* (Victoria: Government Printer 1875; reprinted, Victoria: Queen's Printer 1987).
2 As I explain in Ch. 4, the volume's origins are quite different from those that have been assumed in this century.
3 See Ch. 8.
4 George Shankel merits mention at this point. His 1945 doctoral dissertation, "The Development of Indian Policy in British Columbia" (University of Washington) has been of much use to later scholars.
5 *The Indian History of British Columbia, Vol. 1, The Impact of the White Man*, Anthropology in British Columbia, Memoir No. 5 (Victoria: Provincial Museum of British Columbia 1964).
6 (Vancouver: University of British Columbia Press).
7 (Vancouver: New Star Books).
8 Ibid., 271 n 16.
9 *A Narrow Vision: Duncan Campbell Scott and the Administration of Indian Affairs in Canada* (Vancouver: University of British Columbia Press 1986).
10 (Lantzville: Oolichan Books; and Halifax: Institute for Research on Public Policy 1988).
11 Today Métis and other aboriginal peoples have immigrated into the province; my point is that they are not aboriginal *to British Columbia* and make no claim to aboriginal land title in the province.
12 "Pakeha" literally means "having a different odour."

CHAPTER ONE: ABORIGINAL PEOPLE AND ABORIGINAL CLAIMS

1 Wilson Duff's 1964 estimate was "at least 80,000, and probably somewhat

more" (*The Indian History of British Columbia, Vol. I, The Impact of the White Man*, Anthropology in British Columbia, Memoir No. 5. [Victoria: Provincial Museum of British Columbia 1964]. 39).

2 In 1987 Richard Inglis, curator of ethnology, Royal BC Museum, estimated a pre-contact population of 500,000 on the entire coast from California to Alaska, (*Vancouver Sun*, 21 November 1987).

3 The classification is based upon Duff, *Indian History of British Columbia*, 15 ff., and M. Dale Kinkade and Wayne Suttles, "New Caledonia and Columbia [Linguistic Families]," in R. Cole Harris, ed., *Historical Atlas of Canada, Vol. I* (Toronto: University of Toronto Press 1987), 66. In several cases (e.g., the Babine) I have consulted members of the groups.

4 "Tribal group" as used here must not be equated with "tribe" as used by anthropologists.

5 The most common error among non-Indian observers in BC is to confuse tribal groups with Indian bands.

6 In BC usage and in this book, "west coast"refers exclusively to the west coast of Vancouver Island.

7 Lillian Howard, pers. comm.

8 "From the custom of widows carrying the ashes of a deceased husband in a bag" (Douglas Hudson, "Carrier," *Canadian Encyclopedia*, 2nd ed. [Edmonton: Hurtig 1988), 366–7]).

9 Morton Fried, *The Evolution of Political Society* (New York: Random House 1967). See also Stuart J. Fiedel, *Prehistory of the Americas* (Cambridge: Cambridge University Press 1987), Ch. 6, "Chiefdoms and States: The Emergence of Complex Societies."

10 Philip Drucker, *Indians of the Northwest Coast* (Garden City, NY: Natural History Press 1963; first published 1955), 121.

11 Ibid., 132.

12 D. Duane Thompson, "A History of the Okanagan: Indians and Whites in the Settlement Era, 1860–1920" (PH.D. diss., University of British Columbia 1985), 68–9.

13 Daniel Raunet, *Without Surrender, Without Consent: A History of the Nishga Land Claims* (Vancouver: Douglas and McIntyre 1984), 5.

14 Cf. Duff, *The Indian History of British Columbia*, 18–37. The major examples are provided by some of the larger coastal communities, such as Masset, Skidegate, Squamish, Port Simpson, and Cowichan.

15 The administration entity has existed continuously since before Confederation, usually as a division within a ministry, such as the Department of Indian Affairs and Northern Development. Because of its common use in BC, the name "Department of Indian Affairs" or "DIA" is used throughout this book.

16 See below, Ch. 4, for further details. In 1986 the Indian Act was amended

to eliminate the marriage factor. Persons who had lost their Indian status as a result of marriage could regain it; henceforward, any child who had at least one parent who was a registered Indian would be registered.

17 There is no exact census of non-status Indians. In addition to BC women who have "married out," the number includes their children and and a good number of immigrants from elsewhere in Canada.

18 The total number of bands is at times stated to be less than 199, either because the very smallest bands are omitted, or because the total is being given for the BC administrative region of the federal Department of Indian Affairs. This region is not quite coterminous with the province of BC, since the northernmost strip of the province, which contains the Atlin, Dease Crossing, and Liard River bands, lies within the DIA's Yukon administrative region.

19 The proclamation continues to be published along with the revised statutes of Canada ("Appendix No. 1; The Royal Proclamation, October 7, 1763," *Revised Statutes of Canada 1970* [Ottawa, Queen's Printer 1970], 123–9 (cited hereafter as Proclamation).

20 Proclamation, 127. The rivers coming from the west are those, from Quebec to Florida, which flow directly into the Atlantic; the ones coming from the northwest are those, principally the Mississippi, which flow into the Gulf of Mexico.

21 Ibid., 128.

22 Brian Slattery, "The Hidden Constitution," in Menno Boldt and J. Anthony Long, eds., *The Quest for Justice: Aboriginal Peoples and Aboriginal Rights* (Toronto: University of Toronto Press 1985), 122, 121.

23 See below, Ch. 16, for discussion of the government's assertion that the proclamation did not extend to BC.

24 In return for land title, the treaties east of the Rockies also granted certain new rights; these "treaty rights" included annual payments, provision of medical care and education, and exemption from taxation.

25 The judicial treatment of the principles of pre-existence and of continuity is examined in Ch. 16, below.

26 Slattery, "The Hidden Constitution," 118.

27 The BC claims are dealt with in later chapters, especially 5, 8, 15, 16, and 17. The modern Canadian land claims agreements outside BC are described in Ch. 17.

28 Aside from the treaties arranged by James Douglas on Vancouver Island and Treaty No. 8 arranged by the federal government in northeastern BC. See Chs. 2 and 5, below.

29 *Globe and Mail*, 30 April 1984.

30 Gosnell made this statement in a letter to the editor of the *Vancouver Sun*, 12 December 1985.

31 Interview, CBC Radio, 5 March 1984.
32 Barbara Williamson, "The Pizza Syndrome," *Project North B.C. Newsletter* (Fall 1989):1–2.
33 The province's legal arguments are examined in Ch. 16, below; while the contemporary views of provincial government politicians are dealt with in Ch. 17.

CHAPTER TWO: THE DOUGLAS TREATIES
AND ABORIGINAL TITLE

1 Captain James Cook arrived four years later. In later white mythology his coming became celebrated as the discovery of British Columbia.
2 Robin Fisher, *Contact and Conflict: Indian-European Relations in British Columbia, 1774–1890* (Vancouver: University of British Columbia Press 1977), 42.
3 Margaret Ormsby, "James Douglas" *Canadian Encyclopedia*, 2nd ed. (Edmonton: Hurtig 1988), 614.
4 Archibald Barclay to Douglas, December 1849. Original in Provincial Archives of British Columbia; quoted in Derek Pethick, *James Douglas: Servant of Two Empires* (Vancouver: Mitchell Press 1969), 77–78. The term "waste" presumably meant simply "uninhabited, uncultivated."
5 16 May 1850. Original in Provincial Archives of British Columbia (AC 20 Vi2); quoted in Wilson Duff, "The Fort Victoria Treaties," *BC Studies* 3 (Fall 1969):7.
6 Ibid., 9–10. This text was copied by Duff directly from the original hand-written copy in the Public Archives of BC. The texts, with altered punctuation and differing upper and lower case, are reprinted in BC, *Papers Connected with the Indian Land Question, 1850–1875* (Victoria: Government Printer, 1875), 5–11. (Cited hereafter as BC, *Papers*.)
7 James Hendrickson, "The Aboriginal Land Policy of Governor James Douglas, 1849–1864" (paper presented at BC Studies Conference, Simon Fraser University, 4–6 November 1988).
8 As Duff points out, the chiefs did not in fact sign their names or make their marks. At the foot of each document the names of the chiefs are listed in a neat column obviously written by an experienced clerical hand. The x's, all equal in size and form, lie to the right in a neat vertical column, with each x precisely in line with the name of a chief. They were almost certainly made by the same clerical hand. Perhaps, as Duff suggests, each chief placed a fingertip atop the pen as his x was made ("Fort Victoria Treaties," 17–18).
9 Hendrickson, "The Aboriginal Land Policy of Governor James Douglas," 6. Hendrickson concludes that Douglas was already familiar with the New Zealand text and had its contents in mind when meeting with the Indians.

Duff identifies the handwriting of the documents as that of Douglas ("Fort Victoria Treaties," 17).

10 *Regina* v. *White and Bob* (1964), *50 Dominion Law Reports (2d)* [1965], 613–66 [BC Court of Appeal]. *Regina* v. *White and Bob* (1965), *52 Dominion Law Reports (2d)* [1965], 481 [Supreme Court of Canada].

11 Cf. Fisher, *Contact and Conflict*, 66–7.

12 This meaning could be taken from Pethick's comments (*James Douglas*, 79).

13 A map is presented in Duff, "Fort Victoria Treaties," 10.

14 A family was taken as having five members; if there were more than five, additional acres were awarded. Individual families, however, were not awarded blocks of land; rather, the formula determined the acreage of reserve land for the band or community.

15 Fisher, *Contact and Conflict*, 58.

16 James Hendrickson, ed., *Journals of the Council, Executive Council and Legislative Council of Vancouver Island, 1851–1871. Vol. 1: Minutes* (Victoria: Provincial Archives of British Columbia 1980), 1 March 1860.

17 *Colonist*, 30 June 1860.

18 Douglas to Newcastle, 25 March 1861, in BC, *Papers*, 19. While no treaties were arranged after 1854, Fisher has located an 1859 "deed of land purchase" from Indians in the Barclay Sound by one of Douglas's officials (*Contact and Conflict*, 151). The existence of this deed is not well known; the suggestion that it might have the status of a treaty appears not to have been put forward.

19 Contrary to what Robert Cail states in his *Land, Man, and the Law: The Disposal of Crown Lands in British Columbia, 1871–1913* (Vancouver: University of British Columbia Press 1974), 172, Douglas did not in fact request the loan to extinguish title to "all" remaining lands on Vancouver Island, but only title to the three areas.

20 19 October 1861 (BC, *Papers*, 20).

21 *Colonist*, 1 April 1862.

22 Hendrickson, *Journals*, 566.

23 Ibid., 1 November 1864. By "their just claims" Kennedy was referring to Indian expectations of compensation and adequate reserves.

24 *Colonist*, March 1861.

25 Ibid., 8 March 1861.

26 Ibid., 21 March 1862. De Cosmos distorted Newcastle's use of "trifling"; Newcastle had applied the term to the amount of money, not to the principle of the extinguishment.

27 Ibid., 30 July 1862

28 Ibid., 17 December 1862.

29 Ibid., 12 May 1863.

30 Ibid., Cf. Fisher, *Contact and Conflict*, 108, 110–11.

31 Ibid., 153.

32 Ibid.

CHAPTER THREE: THE DOUGLAS "SYSTEM"

1 Robin Fisher, *Contact and Conflict: Indian-European Relations in British Columbia* (Vancouver: University of British Columbia Press 1977), 153; Robert E. Cail, *Land, Man, and the Law: The Disposal of Crown Lands in British Columbia, 1871–1913* (Vancouver: University of British Columbia Press 1974), 16.

2 Margaret Ormsby, "James Douglas," *Canadian Encyclopedia*, 2nd ed. (Edmonton: Hurtig 1988), 614.

3 Fisher, *Contact and Conflict*, 86.

4 31 July 1858 (British Columbia, *Papers Connected with the Indian Land Question, 1850–1875* [Victoria: Government Printer 1875], 12). (Cited hereafter as BC, *Papers*.) Cf. also Fisher, *Contact and Conflict*, 147; he does not allude to the mention of treaties.

5 Cf. Fisher, *Contact and Conflict*, 147, 151.

6 30 December 1858 (BC, *Papers*, 15).

7 Ibid.

8 14 March 1859 (ibid., 16–17).

9 Ibid., 17.

10 Ibid. By "self-government" Douglas plainly meant that of the individual, not of communities.

11 Ibid., 17.

12 20 May 1859 (ibid., 18).

13 James Hendrickson, ed., *Journals of the Council, Executive Council and Legislative Council of Vancouver Island, 1851–1871. Vol. 1: Minutes* (Victoria: Provincial Archives of British Columbia 1980), 19 March 1862. Hendrickson has taken the text from the *Colonist*, 20 March 1862.

14 The cut-offs are described in Ch. 8, below.

15 C. Good to R.C. Moody, 5 March 1861 (BC *Papers*, 21).

16 Moody to Cox, 6 March 1861 (ibid., 21).

17 Capt. R.M. Parsons to Sapper Turnbull, 1 May 1861 (BC, *Papers*, 22).

18 27 April 1863 (ibid., 26–7).

19 Fisher, *Contact and Conflict*, 154, also 155–66.

20 Cail, *Land, Man, and the Law*, 179.

21 Wilson Duff, *The Indian History of British Columbia, Vol. 1, The Impact of the White Man* (Victoria: Provincial Museum of British Columbia 1965), 61.

22 20 May 1859 (BC, *Papers*, 18).

23 "Petition from lower Fraser Chiefs . . . 6 December 1868," quoted in Robin Fisher, "Joseph Trutch and Indian Land Policy," *BC Studies*, 12 (Winter 1971–72): 16.

24 Duff, *Indian History in B.C.*, 61.

25 Cf. BC, *Papers*, 20 ff.
26 Ibid., 26.
27 Fisher, *Contact and Conflict*, 165.
28 C. Brew to Wm. McColl, 6 April 1864 (BC, *Papers*, 43).
29 Hendrickson, *Journals*, 21 January 1864.
30 Young to Moody, 26 June 1862 (BC, *Papers*, 25).
31 Ibid., 20-9.
32 16 May 1864 (BC, *Papers*, 43).
33 Douglas to I.W. Powell, 14 October 1874, quoted in Fisher, *Contact and Conflict*, 165.
34 George Shankel, "The Development of Indian Policy in British Columbia" (PH.D. diss., University of Washington 1945), 53-4; Duff, *Indian History of B.C.*, 61; Cail, *Land, Man, and the Law*, 175. See, in contrast, Fisher, *Contact and Conflict*, 165.
35 Vancouver Island, *Proclamation No. 4*, 19 February 1861. BC, *Proclamation*, 4 January 1860, contained in BC, *List of Proclamations for 1858 . . . 1864* (New Westminster: Government Printing Office n.d.).
36 Moody to W. Young, 11 June 1862 (BC, *Papers*, 25).
37 Moody to Douglas, 28 April 1863 (ibid., 27).
38 Cf. Young to Moody, 11 May 1863 (ibid., 28).
39 Hendrickson, *Journals*, 21 January 1864.
40 Lytton to Douglas, 31 July 1858 (BC, *Papers*, 12).
41 This interpretation of Douglas as policy maker differs from the conclusions of Shankel, Duff, Cail, and Fisher. Duff's conclusion is that Douglas's "main concerns, in addition to maintaining law and order, were to purchase the Indian ownership rights to the land and to set aside adequate reserves for their use" (*Indian History of B.C.*, 61).
42 Clarence Karr, "James Douglas: The Gold Governor in the Context of His Times," in E. Blanche Norcross, ed., *The Company on the Coast* (Nanaimo: Nanaimo Historical Society 1983), 77.

CHAPTER FOUR: SEGREGATION AND
SUPPRESSION, 1864-87

1 Robin Fisher, "Joseph Trutch and Indian Land Policy," *BC Studies* 12 (Winter 1971-72):3-10.
2 Robin Fisher, *Contact and Conflict: Indian-European Relations in British Columbia* (Vancouver: University of British Columbia Press 1977), 161. The quoted words are Fisher's.
3 Wilson Duff, *The Indian History of British Columbia, Vol. 1, The Impact of the White Man* (Victoria: Provincial Museum of British Columbia 1965), 42.
4 Ibid., 62.
5 British Columbia, *Papers Connected with the Indian Land Question, 1850-1875*

(Victoria: Government Printer 1875), appendix, 11 (cited hereafter as BC, *Papers*).

6 Ibid.

7 Ibid.

8 BC, "An Ordinance further to define the law regulating acquisition of Land in British Columbia," 31 March 1866. A further amendment in 1870 extended the prohibition to "any of the Aborigines of this continent." Individual Indians were not prohibited from purchasing land from non-Indians.

9 BC, *Papers*, 29ff.

10 Ibid., 47.

11 Ibid., 29–33.

12 Ibid., 42.

13 Ibid., 53.

14 Cf. Fisher, "Joseph Trutch," 20.

15 Fisher, *Contact and Conflict*, 176.

16 BC, Legislature, *Sessional Papers*, 1871, 12.

17 Fisher, "Joseph Trutch," 26.

18 BC, *Papers*, 152.

19 BC, Qualification and Registration of Voters Amendment Act, 1872, s. 13.

20 Indian Act, 1880, s. 4.

21 See Ch. 1, above.

22 1880, ss. 99ff.

23 E. Brian Titley, *A Narrow Vision: Duncan Campbell Scott and the Administration of Indian Affairs in Canada* (Vancouver: University of British Columbia Press 1986), 13.

24 Ibid.

25 Duncan to minister of the interior, May 1875 (BC, *Papers*, 13–15).

26 Although the Indian Act prohibited pre-emption by registered Indians, there was little inequity so long as Indians had access to reserve land of the same amount and quality as was available to settlers in the same region. Such was often the case east of the Rockies.

27 Fisher, *Contact and Conflict*, 18off.

28 BC, *Papers*, 107ff.

29 Emphasis is original. Powell to provincial secretary, 15 August 1874 (ibid., 139).

30 Ibid., 118ff.

31 Ibid., 153.

32 Memo, 2 November 1874 (ibid., 151–5).

33 Keith Ralston, "William Smithe," *Canadian Encyclopedia*, 2d ed. (Edmonton: Hurtig 1988), 2017.

34 *Colonist*. 9 May 1875.

35 Cf. Fisher, *Contact and Conflict*, 187.

36 *Colonist*, 14 April 1875.

37 Ibid., 9 May 1875.

38 21 April 1875.

39 28 April 1875.

40 21 April 1875.

41 28 April 1875.

42 BC, *Papers*. As is apparent and contrary to what has often been assumed, the *Papers* were not published by the government at its own initiative.

43 Spokesman of the Allied Indian Tribes of BC were denied access to the document during the 1927 parliamentary hearings on the BC land claim. See below, Ch. 8.

44 15 May 1875.

45 And, two decades later, there was an entirely unpredicted federal action in the form of Treaty No. 8 in northeast BC. See below, Ch. 5.

46 George Stewart, *Canada under Administration of the Earl of Dufferin* (Toronto: Rose-Belford 1878), 492-3.

47 Fisher, *Contact and Conflict*, 188.

48 Cf. Gilbert M. Sproat, *The Nootka: Scenes and Studies of Savage Life*, edited and annotated by Charles Lillard (Victoria: Sono Nis 1987).

49 Fisher, *Contact and Conflict*, 199.

50 Some of this dissatisfaction is illustrated in Ch. 5, below.

51 Fisher, *Contact and Conflict*, 180ff.

52 1880, s. 72.

53 An Act to Amend the Indian Act, 1884, s. 3.

CHAPTER FIVE: DEMANDS FOR TITLE, TREATIES AND SELF-GOVERNMENT, 1887-99

1 Robin Fisher, *Contact and Conflict: Indian-European Relations in British Columbia, 1774-1890* (Vancouver: University of British Columbia Press 1977), 117.

2 Ibid., 107, 158-68, 183-90; Wilson Duff, *The Indian History of British Columbia, Vol. 1, The Impact of the White Man* (Victoria: Provincial Museum of British Columbia 1965), 63-7.

3 Enlarged to wall size, the photo was prominent feature in the Royal British Columbia Museum in the 1980s.

4 Peter Ayessik to Lieutenant-Colonel Powell, 14 July 1874, in BC, Legislature, *Journals*, 1885, 4:674.

5 Ibid.

6 Fisher, *Contact and Conflict*, 178ff.

7 Sproat to superintendent general, 10 November 1879, NAC, RG10, vol. 3669, file 10,691.

8 D. Duane Thompson, "A History of the Okanagan: Indians and Whites in

the Settlement Era, 1860–1920" (PH.D. diss., University of British Columbia 1985), 53, 68–73, and 127ff.

9 Sproat to superintendent general, 26 July 1879, NAC, RG10, vol. 3696, file 15,316.

10 *Colonist*. 21 August 1879.

11 Ibid.

12 BC, Commission Appointed to Enquire into the Conditions of Indians of the North-west Coast, *Papers relating to the Commission* . . . (Victoria: Government Printer 1888), 32–3, 48 (cited hereafter as North Coast Enquiry, *Papers*).

13 Fisher, *Contact and Conflict*, 205.

14 Information and inferences about these meetings may be gleaned from North Coast Enquiry, *Papers*.

15 Twelve years earlier Smithe had played a major part within the legislature in advocating larger Indian reserves. Now, as premier, Smithe had adopted the policies he had formerly criticized. See above, Ch. 4.

16 The government stenographer recorded him as "Burton" from Kincolith; my assumption is that he was the Kincolith chief Charles Barton, later to be prominent in Nisga'a politics.

17 BC, Legislature, *Sessional Papers*, 1887, 254ff.

18 Ibid., 254. In the Nisga'a language the group's own system of norms or laws may be referred to as a protective covering (James Gosnell, pers. comm.); thus alien laws could be taken as a smothering stratum.

19 BC, Legislature, *Sessional Papers*, 1887, 259–60.

20 Ibid., 255.

21 Ibid., 256.

22 Ibid., 259.

23 Ibid., 262.

24 See above, Ch. 3. However, Davie's grandson, E. Davie Fulton, would, much later, play a prominent role in support of Indian title. See Ch. 12, below.

25 BC, Legislature, *Sessional Papers*, 1887, 264.

26 Ibid., 257.

27 Ibid.

28 George Shankel, "The Development of Indian Policy in British Columbia" (PH.D. diss., University of Washington 1945), 152.

29 North Coast Enquiry, *Papers*, 2.

30 The Metlakatlan departure is a well-known event in BC history. Whites tend to see William Duncan as the leader of the exodus and as motivated by disagreement with his Anglican superiors. Indians see Duncan as having followed the Metlakatlans, who decided on their own to flee Canada because they were denied the title to their land.

31 North Coast Enquiry, *Papers*, 18–19.

32 Ibid., 19.

33 Ibid.

34 Ibid., 20.

35 Ibid., 24. In Nisga'a the literal meaning of "Nass" is "purse" or "basket."

36 Ibid., 47–49; a more extensive account of the Nisga'a testimony is contained in Daniel Raunet, *Without Surrender Without Consent: A History of the Nishga Land Claims* (Vancouver: Douglas and McIntyre 1984), 8off.

37 North Coast Enquiry, *Papers*, 33, 35–6.

38 Ibid., 45.

39 Ibid., 38.

40 Ibid., 6.

41 The upriver Nisga'a were among the last Indians to convert; when they did, the majority became Anglicans; even Greenville, the former hotbed of Methodism, switched to Anglicanism. The Nisga'a, however, did not abandon their land claim, and Kincolith supported it as strongly as did the other three communities.

42 Although Duncan had by that time split with the Anglican authorities.

43 North Coast Enquiry, *Papers*, 8–9.

44 Ibid., 11.

45 Ibid.

46 Canada, Privy Council, PC No. 2749, 6 December 1898.

47 Ibid.

48 E. Brian Titley, *A Narrow Vision: Duncan Campbell Scott and the Administration of Indian Affairs in Canada* (Vancouver: University of British Columbia Press 1986), 138, 158–9.

49 Duff, *The Indian History of British Columbia*, 70–1. G. Brown and R. Maguire, *Indian Treaties in Historical Perspective* (Ottawa: Research Branch, Department of Indian Affairs and Northern Development 1977), Ch. 1.

50 In the 1980s the federal government acceded to the demands of the excluded communities that treaty negotiations take place with them. The province refused to acknowledge any obligation, although it did eventually agree to transfer land for some new reserves.

CHAPTER SIX: THE POLITICS OF SURVIVAL

1 Hazel Hertzberg, *The Search for American Indian Identity: Modern Pan-Indian Movements* (Syracuse: Syracuse University Press 1971); R.K. Thomas, "Pan-Indianism," in *The Emergent Native Americans: A Reader in Culture Contact*, ed. D.E. Walker, Jr. (Boston: Little, Brown 1972), 739–46. Thomas is one of the best known of the anthropologists who are United States Indians.

2 A.F.C. Wallace, "Revitalization Movements," *American Anthropologist* 58, no. 2 (1956):264–81.

3 In many cases even their tribes of origin were no longer intact, for in

many cases reservation populations consisted of mixed tribal remnants forced together by American authorities. For example, the Kootenay who live in the United States share their reservation with Salish.

4 Hertzberg, *The Search for American Indian Identity*, 300.

5 Ibid., 300–7. The Alaska Native Brotherhood, formed in 1912 by Tlingit and Haida on the Alaska Panhandle, was a nearby example of a regional pan-Indian organization whose goals involved considerable acculturation, if not assimilation, at least according to Philip Drucker, *The Native Brotherhoods: Modern Intertribal Organizations on the Northwest Coast*, Smithsonian Institution, Bureau of American Ethnology Bulletin 168 (Washington: Government Printing Office 1958), 32ff.

6 Hertzberg, *The Search for American Indian Identity*), 307ff.

7 Such organizations had only mixed success, nor was theirs the only type of pan-Indianism in the United States. Later, during the 1960s, "pan-Indianism" came to denote the identity derived from expanding the symbols and image of the plains Indian to apply to Indians throughout the United States. BC Indians of the central and southern interior and of the south coast adopted some of these symbols (such as holding powwows and rodeos and wearing western clothing), while Indians of the west/central and north coasts did not.

8 The only exception, a partial and temporary one which occurred in the late 1960s, is dealt with in Ch. 12, below.

9 It was not until the 1970s that there did emerge among British Columbia Indians a cohesive group having a degree of contact with Whites comparable to that of the first United States pan-Indians. This group did not choose assimilation but chose instead to pursue the same goals that Indian political leaders had been seeking for a century. See Ch. 11, below.

10 During the 1960s and 1970s the BC government did commence a substantial program of apprehending Indian children and placing almost all of them in white homes. In its extent the program was unique in Canada. The episode is known among Indians as the "sixties scoop." Some four thousand children were apprehended.

11 Michael M'Gonigle and Wendy Wickwire, *Stein: The Way of the River* (Vancouver: Talonbooks 1988), 39–41.

12 The phrase was often used in political speeches. In the 1980s a popular wall poster in the offices of tribal councils and political organizations was emblazoned with a phrase from a speech of Frank Calder: "The Nishga are not on trial. British Justice is on trial!"

13 The fact that pan-Indian mass movements did not appear in the province provides one indication that anomy was not sufficient to erode traditional identities.

14 Whites had used cars for decades, but they tended to avoid giving rides to Indians.

15 *Indians at Work: An Informal History of Native Indian Labour in British Columbia, 1858-1930* (Vancouver: New Star Books 1978), 33. Knight provides a comprehensive treatment of the subject.

16 Much relevant information is contained in James Spradley, *Guests Never Leave Hungry: The Autobiography of James Sewid, a Kwakiutl Indian* (New Haven: Yale University Press 1969).

17 Drucker, *The Native Brotherhoods*, 124.

18 Ibid., 124.

19 Allan Smith, "The Writing of British Columbia History," *BC Studies*, 45 (Spring 1980):90.

20 Stephanie Hudson, "The Role of Indian Agents in British Columbia" (unpublished student paper, Department of Political Science, University of British Columbia 1987).

21 See Ch. 3, above.

22 Edwin Lemert, "The Life and Death of an Indian State," *Human Organization* 13, no. 3 (1954):25.

23 Ibid., 26.

24 Ibid. The case, and the Roman Catholic missionaries' use of corporal punishment more generally, are discussed in D. Duane Thomson, "A History of the Okanagan: Indians and Whites in the Settlement Era, 1860–1920" (PH.D. diss., University of British Columbia 1985), 90ff.

25 Drucker, *The Native Brotherhoods*, 147–8. Drucker was apparently unaware that the ban on the potlatch had been lifted in 1951, before he arrived on the scene.

26 Ibid., 147.

27 John Veillette and Gary White, *Early Indian Village Churches: Wooden Frontier Architecture in British Columbia* (Vancouver: University of British Columbia Press 1977) contains numerous photographs allowing comparison of Catholic and Protestant churches.

28 Lemert, "The Life and Death of an Indian State," 27.

29 Cf. Thomson, "A History of the Okanagan," 59.

30 European family names remain good indicators of which of the two parts of the province Indians are from, and a good many names remain specific to particular tribal groups. In BC there was almost none of the literal translation of Indian names into English that there was on the Prairies, and little of the assigning of unconventional names as was done in Yukon.

31 Thomson provides an insightful examination of Indian schooling in the southern interior ("A History of the Okanagan," 96–110).

32 E. Brian Titley, *A Narrow Vision: Duncan Campbell Scott and the Administration of Indian Affairs in Canada* (Vancouver: University of British Columbia Press 1986), 18, 93.

33 First-hand accounts of Indians who attended the Kamloops school are presented in Celia Haig-Brown, *Resistance and Renewal: Surviving the Indian*

Residential School (Vancouver: Tillacum Library 1988).

34 Thomson, "A History of the Okanagan," 106.

35 During the 1980s there were several court cases, and convictions, relating to substantial and long-term sexual abuse of male children by teachers or staff in Protestant and Catholic schools during the 1960s. Several very prominent educators were among those convicted. These cases revealed that the majority of men of the relevant age group in particular villages were still suffering emotional effects and disabilities.

36 George Manuel was one of those who vehemently blamed the schooling for creating political passivity. The term "passive" is his (interview, 18 March 1980, Vancouver). For an account of Manuel's own school experience, see below, Ch. 10.

37 The view that BC Indians wanted to assimilate was common among Whites, perhaps especially between 1927 and 1969. In his *Roar of the Breakers: A Biography of Peter Kelly* (Toronto: Ryerson 1967), Alan Morley uncritically and enthusiastically accepts this view, using as his criterion of assimilation the proportion of Indians taking up a contemporary lifestyle and living off reserves (152). Morley, who makes numerous factual errors, ignores the evidence indicating that Indian political leaders desired continuation of a distinct Indian identity. Among such evidence was Peter Kelly's own hope that the struggle for land rights would be continued by future generations should his generation fail (113ff.).

CHAPTER SEVEN: FROM INTERTRIBAL TO PROVINCE-WIDE POLITICAL ACTION

1 BC, Commission Appointed to Enquire into the Conditions of the Indians of the North-west Coast, *Papers relating to the Commission* . . . (Victoria: Government Printer 1888), 15–17.

2 George Shankel, "The Development of Indian Policy in British Columbia" (PH.D. diss., University of Washington 1945), 193.

3 Rolf Knight, *Indians at Work: An Informal History of Native Indian Labour in British Columbia, 1858–1930* (Vancouver: New Star Books 1978), 59.

4 Ibid.

5 Ibid.

6 One of the elders I spoke to in 1981 animatedly described watching "whole villages" walk the winter ice of the Nass to attend a revival meeting.

7 Frank Calder, pers. comm., 22 February 1990.

8 Ibid.

9 Philip Drucker, *The Native Brotherhoods: Modern Intertribal Organizations on the Northwest Coast*, Smithsonian Institution, Bureau of American Ethnology, Bulletin 168 (Washington: Government Printing Office 1958), 90ff.

10 Frank Calder, interview, 11 June 1981, Victoria; Hubert Doolan, interview,

13 May 1980, Aiyansh. Doolan was able to name and give the clan and community affiliations of members of the Land Committee shown in photographs on display in the Nisga'a Tribal Council office.

11 Cf. photographs on display in Nisga'a Tribal Council office, Aiyansh. Ultimately, among south coast and interior Indians, who preferred blue jeans and plaid shirts, the three-piece suit became a symbol of north coast snootiness.

12 E. Brian Titley, *A Narrow Vision: Duncan Campbell Scott and the Administration of Indian Affairs in Canada* (Vancouver: University of British Columbia Press 1986), Ch. 8, gives a thorough account of the relations between the two governments on Indian issues during the 1908–27 period.

13 Just after formation of the land committee, the Nisga'a had made similar, but unsuccessful, initiatives towards the Tsimshian (Drucker, *The Native Brotherhoods*, 91).

14 Edwin May, "The Nishga Land Claim, 1873–1973" (MA thesis, Simon Fraser University 1979), 69ff.

15 Ibid., 70ff.

16 There is some later confusion of the two organizations, beginning with Forrest LaViolette's erroneous implication that the name of the coastal organization was "Indian Tribes of BC" (*The Struggle for Survival: Indian Cultures and the Protestant Ethic in British Columbia* [Toronto: University of Toronto Press 1961], 127). Oddly, LaViolette gives no attention to the Indian Rights Association (cf. 131).

17 *Province*, 2 June 1910; quoted in May, "The Nishga Land Claim," 73–4.

18 Titley, *A Narrow Vision*, 139.

19 May, "Nishga Land Claim," 70ff.

20 Canada, House of Commons, Special Committees of the Senate and House of Commons . . . to inquire into the Claims of the Allied Indian Tribes of British Columbia . . . , *Proceedings, Reports and the Evidence* (Ottawa, King's Printer 1927), xx (cited hereafter as Special Committee [1927], *Proceedings*).

21 May, "Nishga Land Claim," 75.

22 21 July 1911, quoted in ibid., 78.

23 It was provincial intransigence on these two points which had most concerned Department of Indian Affairs officials, since the province had been able to prevent DIA itself from having full control over use and disposal of reserve lands (Titley, *A Narrow Vision*, 161). "Disposing of reserve land for the benefit of Indians" was, for the most part, a euphemism for an element of the assimilation process in which reserves were reduced by transferring segments to the private ownership of Indians who had relinquished their status.

24 A copy of the agreement is contained in BC, Royal Commission on Indian Affairs, *Report, Vol. 1* (Victoria: Acme Press 1916), 10–11. The commission is cited hereafter as McKenna-McBride Commission.

25 McKenna was one of the federal appointees; McBride was never a member.

26 E.P. Patterson, "Andrew Paull," *Canadian Encyclopedia*, 2nd ed. (Edmonton: Hurtig 1988), 1630.

27 May, "Nishga Land Claim," 166.

28 Ibid., 168-73, contains the text of the petition.

29 Ibid., 168.

30 May, "Nishga Land Claim," 168; Titley, *A Narrow Vision*, 218.

31 The actual British privy council, that is the King's (or Queen's) Privy Council, was by 1913 a purely honorific body, no longer giving advice to the monarch or even meeting for any making of decisions. The Judicial *Committee* of the Privy Council, the highest appeal court in the United Kingdom and the British Empire, was nominally a committee of this body. Ostensibly, however, the monarch continued to act mainly on the advice of the Privy Council, as in making "orders in *council*." The cabinet, or government of the day, was in practice the active part of the Privy Council, and with documents going before it commonly referred to as going before the Privy Council.

32 For example, among others, Titley, *A Narrow Vision*, 142; May, "The Nishga Land Claim," 81ff.; Drucker, *The Native Brotherhoods*, 95. The fact that present-day scholars can be confused over the meaning of "privy council" also suggests that Indians could have been in earlier periods.

33 Cf. note 31, above.

34 Darcy Mitchell, "The Allied Indian Tribes of British Columbia: A Study in Pressure Group Behaviour" (MA thesis, University of British Columbia 1977), 40, 59.

35 The report of the 1927 special parliamentary committee implied that Arthur O'Meara should be held responsible for the Indians' misguided perceptions (Special Committee [1927], *Proceedings*, ix).

36 Titley, *A Narrow Vision*.

37 Ibid., 50.

38 Ibid., 142, 153.

39 May, "Nishga Land Claim," 88.

40 PC 751, 20 June 1914.

41 Drucker's discussion of this point is marred by his failure to take account of government motives and of the role a government lawyer would have played. He concludes that the Indians "would certainly appear to have been ill-advised" in refusing "to take advantage of" the order-in-council (*The Native Brotherhoods*, 98).

42 Edwin May considers the Allied Indian Tribes to have been formed at the assembly ("The Nishga Land Claim," 92-5). See note 47 below.

43 *Native Voice*, April 1968, contains a photograph of the delegation and lists the chiefs' names and bands.

44 Titley, *A Narrow Vision*, 144.
45 May, "Nishga Land Claim," 96-7.
46 "Exhibit No. 4, from Andrew Paull," Special Committee (1927), *Proceedings*, 175.
47 The Spences Bridge assembly of the previous year is sometimes taken as having formed the Allied Tribes. In 1927, however, Pauli claimed that the June 1916 assembly had been the founding meeting ("Exhibit No. 4, from Andrew Paull," Special Committee [1927], *Proceedings*, 175). Wilson Duff (*The Indian History of British Columbia, Vol. 1, The Impact of the White Man*. Anthropology in BC, Memoir No. 5. [Victoria: Provincial Museum of British Columbia 1964], 69) also accepts 1916 as the founding date. Although Paull's claim was perhaps not devoid of self-interest (as he could take no credit had the organization been founded in 1915), the fact remains that the Vancouver assembly was the more representative.
48 May, "Nishga Land Claim," 96-7.
49 Special Committee (1927), *Proceedings*, 31.

CHAPTER EIGHT: CUTOFFS, CLAIMS PROHIBITION,
AND THE ALLIED TRIBES

1 The origins of the commission are described in the previous chapter.
2 BC, Royal Commission on Indian Affairs for the Province of British Columbia, *Evidence* (Victoria: Acme Press 1916), hearings of 18 October 1913 at Douglas Lake, 1-2. (Cited hereafter as McKenna-McBride Commission, *Evidence*.)
3 Kuldoe and Kisgegas no longer exist, having merged with other communities.
4 McKenna-McBride Commission, *Evidence*, hearings of 13 July 1915 at New Hazelton, 4-5.
5 BC, Royal Commission on Indian Affairs for the Province of British Columbia, *Report* (Victoria: Acme Press 1916), 1:177.
6 E. Brian Titley, *A Narrow Vision: Duncan Campbell Scott and the Administration of Indian Affairs in Canada* (Vancouver: University of British Columbia Press 1986), 145. Titley presents a comprehensive treatment of the actions of the two governments after 1916 (145-61).
7 Ibid., 145.
8 Darcy Mitchell, "The Allied Indian Tribes of British Columbia: A Study in Pressure Group Behaviour" (MA thesis, University of British Columbia 1977), 42.
9 Ibid., 43.
10 Canada, House of Commons, Special Committees of the Senate and House of Commons . . . to Inquire into the Claims of the Allied Indian Tribes of British Columbia . . . , *Proceedings, Reports and the Evidence* (Ottawa, King's

Printer 1927), 38. (Cited hereafter as Special Committee [1927], *Proceedings*).

11 Allied Tribes, "Statement of the Allied Indian Tribes of British Columbia for the Government of British Columbia [December 1919]." The full text is presented in Special Committee (1927), *Proceedings* 31–8.

12 NAC, RG10, vol. 3820, Scott to Meighton, 9 January 1920, quoted in Darcy Mitchell, "The Allied Indian Tribes," 49. See also Titley, *A Narrow Vision*, 147ff.

13 Titley, *A Narrow Vision*, 49–51.

14 There were two further prohibitions contained in section 140. One was aimed specifically at the sundance of plains Indians. The other was more general; without the permission of the minister, no Indian in any of the four western provinces could participate "in any show, exhibition, performance, stampede or pageant in aboriginal costume" or "in any Indian dance outside the bounds of his own reserve."

15 Daisy Sewid-Smith, *Prosecution or Persecution* (Campbell River: Nu-Yim-Baleess Society 1979).

16 Forrest LaViolette, *The Struggle for Survival: Indian Cultures and the Protestant Ethic in British Columbia* (Toronto: University of Toronto Press 1961), 83ff.

17 The jailings are often mentioned today, even by young Indians.

18 *Amodu Tijani* v. *Secretary, Southern Nigeria* (1921) 2 AC, 409–10, quoted in *Calder* v. *Attorney-General of B.C.* (1973), *34 Dominion Law Reports (3d)* [1973], 208 [Supreme Court of Canada]. The ruling is further discussed in Ch. 16, below.

19 Edwin May, "The Nishga Land Claim, 1873–1973" (MA thesis, Simon Fraser University 1979), 110.

20 Special Committee (1927), *Proceedings*, 225–6. The compilation is BC, *Papers Connected with the Indian Land Question, 1850-1875* (Victoria: Government Printer 1875) (cited hereafter as BC, *Papers*). For explanation of the origin of the *Papers*, see above, Ch. 4.

21 Special Committee (1927), *Proceedings*, 175–6. Cf. Titley, *A Narrow Vision*. 151.

22 Special Committee (1927), *Proceedings*, 175–6.

23 Teit was ill at this time; he died in October 1922. Kathleen Mooney, "James Alexander Teit," *Canadian Encyclopedia*, 2nd ed. (Edmonton: Hurtig 1988), 2121.

24 Special Committee (1927), *Proceedings*, 176.

25 Ibid.

26 Cf. Mitchell, "The Allied Indian Tribes," 64ff.

27 Special Committee (1927), *Proceedings*, 175–6. The numerous misspellings of both personal and place names as well as several errors in linking persons with places suggest that the list presented by Paull to the Special Committee in 1927 was not an original list filled out at the time of the meeting or by those who actually attended.

28 Titley, *A Narrow Vision*, 148.

29 Fifty years later both governments did agree that the cut-offs had been unjust, and arrangements were made to return the lands or to compensate the Indians for them. See below, Chs. 13 and 15.

30 House of Commons, *Debates*, 9 February 1927, 174, quoted in Mitchell, "The Allied Indian Tribes," 80–1.

31 Ibid., 8 March 1927, 985, quoted in Mitchell, "The Allied Indian Tribes," 82.

32 Titley, *A Narrow Vision*, 154.

33 Cf. above, Ch. 5.

34 Special Committee (1927), *Proceedings*, 2.

35 Ibid., 4.

36 Ibid., 12–13. In fact, as Kelly soon confirmed to the committee, the Allied Tribes had avoided presenting any dollar figure and continued to insist that any monetary aspect of settlement would be modest.

37 Ibid., 187.

38 Ibid., 146.

39 Ibid., 153–69.

40 Ibid., 160.

41 Ibid., 15.

42 Ibid., 155, 184.

43 Ibid., 161.

44 Ibid., 223.

45 Ibid., 225.

46 BC, *Papers*.

47 Special Committee (1927), *Proceedings*, 225–6. There is some suggestion in the committee discussion that O'Meara had been able to examine the *Papers* in the Parliamentary library before they were borrowed or removed.

48 Ibid., 141ff.

49 Ibid., 160.

50 Ibid., viii.

51 Ibid.

52 Ibid.

53 Ibid.

54 Ibid., 6.

55 Ibid., viii.

56 Ibid., 6.

57 Ibid., viii-ix.

58 Ibid., ix-xi.

59 These were arguments advanced by the province in the 1960s as it sought to defend its denial of title. See Ch. 16, below.

60 Ibid., xviii.

61 Titley, *A Narrow Vision*, 59.

62 Organizations relying on white support were not affected but Scott and

Stewart had no worries that such support would be significant. O'Meara did appear to be continuing to raise funds among the Nisga'a, and Scott considered prosecuting him, but his death in 1928 ended any concern in Ottawa (Titley, *A Narrow Vision*, 157). The amendment was not restricted to land claims. Except with the minister's approval, no chief or band council could now use funds contributed by band members to pursue claims of the everyday sort that might arise against persons harming band property, persons doing business with the band, or the department itself.

63 I base this observation upon the responses of white lawyers and government officials whom I interviewed or discussed the matter with during the 1980s.

64 Daniel Raunet, relying on his Nisga'a informants, writes that "There was a time, before the fifties, when the mere mention of the land issue was unlawful" (*Without Surrender Without Consent: A History of the Nishga Land Claims* [Vancouver: Douglas and McIntyre 1984], 15). In 1988 the editor of *Kahtou* wrote that "the federal government passed legislation prohibiting the right for chiefs to gather for the discussion of the settlement of land issues in BC" (7 November 1988).

CHAPTER NINE: COASTAL POLITICS

1 Frank Calder and Hubert Doolan, interviews, 3–5 April 1980, Kincolith.

2 In the United Church, which had been formed in 1925 by the union of his Methodists with Presbyterians and Congregationalists.

3 Frank Calder, interview, 11 June 1981, Victoria.

4 E. Brian Titley, *A Narrow Vision: Duncan Campbell Scott and the Administration of Indian Affairs in Canada* (Vancouver: University of British Columbia Press 1986), 160.

5 Philip Drucker, *The Native Brotherhoods: Modern Intertribal Organizations on the Northwest Coast*, Smithsonian Institution, Bureau of American Ethnology Bulletin 168 (Washington: Government Printing Office 1958), 17–33.

6 Ibid., 33.

7 Ibid., 31. The organization was an example of what Hazel Hertzberg calls "fraternal pan-Indianism" (*The Search for American Indian Identity: Modern Pan-Indian Movements* [Syracuse: Syracuse University Press 1971]).

8 Drucker, *The Native Brotherhoods*, 41.

9 Ibid.

10 Ibid., 56. Having left their land behind in British Columbia, the new Metlakatlans could make no land claim in Alaska.

11 Ibid., 104.

12 Jacqueline O'Donnell, "The Native Brotherhood of British Columbia, 1931–1950: A New Phase in Native Political Organization" (MA thesis, University of British Columbia 1985).

13 Drucker, *The Native Brotherhoods*, 106.

14 Drucker is singularly insensitive to the legal aspects of the BC land claim. Nowhere in his detailed survey of events leading to the formation of the Native Brotherhood does he mention, or indicate that he is aware of, the 1927 amendment to the Indian Act which prohibited receipt of funds for claims-related activities and precipitated the collapse of the Allied Tribes. Drucker is disdainful of the attempt by the Brotherhood to gain increased protection for aboriginal rights, comparing it to attempting to have one's "cake and eat it too" (ibid., 141).

15 Ibid., 137, 147.

16 "Constitution: Native Brotherhood of British Columbia, 1931–32," reprinted in ibid., 178–9. As in Alaska, a Native Sisterhood was formed in BC, but it existed essentially as local ladies auxiliaries to the Brotherhood branches, and in contrast to the Alaska Sisterhood, it had no strong central organization and did not affect policy-making.

17 James Spradley, *Guests Never Leave Hungry: The Autobiography of James Sewid, a Kwakiutl Indian* (New Haven: Yale University Press 1969), 191.

18 Drucker, *The Native Brotherhoods*, 106.

19 At least this was the view among Nisga'a elders whom I interviewed in the 1980s. Drucker's view is that the committee feared it would be supplanted by the Brotherhood (ibid., 109, 121).

20 Ibid., 120–48. See also Spradley, *Guests Never Leave Hungry*, 173.

21 In the reports they made to the Indian commissioner for BC in the 1940s and 1950s, regional DIA officials were invariably complimentary about the organization and the conduct of Brotherhood conventions (DIA, Regional Archives, Vancouver, "B.C. Native Brotherhood" files).

22 Spradley, *Guests Never Leave Hungry*, 173.

23 "Native Brotherhood Policies" (unpublished student paper, Department of Political Science, University of British Columbia 1982).

24 Frank Calder, interviews, 5 April 1980, Kincolith, and 11 June 1981, Victoria.

25 She was the only White ever prominently associated with the Brotherhood. She had come to her interest in Indian matters through her well-known lawyer husband, Tom Hurley, who had represented Indians in a number of cases and who was often turned to by Brotherhood leaders for legal advice (Tom Berger, pers. comm., 7 October 1988).

26 Calder was the second BC Indian to graduate from the University of British Columbia or one of its schools; the first was Percy Gladstone, a Haida, who obtained his BA and MA in economics.

27 Drucker, *The Native Brotherhoods*, 120–21.

28 George Manuel and Michael Posluns, *The Fourth World* (Toronto: Collier-Macmillan 1974), 97.

29 E.P. Patterson, "Andrew Paull and Canadian Indian Resurgence" (PH.D. diss., University of Washington 1962), 225–52.

30 Ibid., 249.

31 Manuel and Posluns, *The Fourth World*, 97.

32 Frank Calder and Guy Williams, interviews, 3–5 April 1980, Kincolith.

33 H.B. Hawthorn et al., *The Indians of British Columbia* (Toronto: University of Toronto Press 1960), 47, attribute the formation of the Confederacy to Basil Falardeau, a Shuswap, but Calder affirms that Paull, with Calder in attendance, formed the organization, with the first meetings likely occurring in 1945. Falardeau was a member and chaired a number of meetings (Calder, interview, 11 June 1981, Victoria).

34 H.A. (Butch) Smitheram, interview, 12 March 1982, Vancouver. Smitheram attended some of the NAIB meetings while he was assistant Indian agent in Kamloops.

35 The Native Brotherhood continued to oppose seeking the right to vote in federal elections.

36 Drucker, *The Native Brotherhoods*, 139.

37 BC, Land Amendment Act, 1953.

38 Canada, Parliament, Session 1947, Special Joint Committee [to consider] the Indian Act, *Minutes of Proceedings and Evidence*, 2050–1. Assu's covering letter stated, misleadingly, that the Confederacy had been "organized" at the 3 July meeting. For Guy Williams' presentation and the committee's questioning him about the state of Indian organization in BC, see 781ff.

39 The Métis Louis Riel had been elected to the House of Commons shortly after Confederation; Calder was thus the second aboriginal person elected to a legislature after Confederation (Bennett McCardle, "Frank Arthur Calder," *Canadian Encyclopedia*, 2nd ed. [Edmonton: Hurtig 1988], 314).

40 Leslie Kopas, "Political Action of the Indians of British Columbia" (MA thesis, University of British Columbia 1972), 132–3.

41 He remained a member of the opposition until 1972, when his party, by then called the New Democratic Party, took office and he was appointed to the cabinet.

42 *Native Voice*, January 1954.

43 Department of Indian Affairs files by this time contained a number of letters from individual Nisga'a complaining bitterly about the actions of other Nisga'a, especially relating to use or occupancy of land.

44 This and the following information was obtained in interviews with Calder, James Gosnell, and Hubert Doolan, all whom were key participants in forming the tribal council.

45 "Nishga Tribal Council-Nass River, BC—Constitution & By-Laws," 25 January 1963 (typescript copy on file in Nisga'a Tribal Council office, Aiyansh, 21 June 1981).

46 William Tatoosh, interview, 14 May 1980, Port Alberni; George Watts and Hugh Watts, interviews, 21 February 1981, Vancouver.

CHAPTER TEN: INTERIOR POLITICS AND
ATTEMPTS AT PROVINCE-WIDE UNITY

1 D. Duane Thomson, "A History of the Okanagan: Indians and Whites in
   the Settlement Era, 1860–1920" (PH.D. diss., University of British Columbia
   1985), 73; see also 53, 68–73, and 127ff.
2 H.A. (Butch) Smitheram, a non-status Okanagan Indian, played a role in
   BC Indian politics equal to that of Manuel, but Smitheram's role was province-wide, and he was never regarded as a spokesman for interior Indians
   as such. Smitheram's role is discussed in Ch. 12, below.
3 He was president of the National Indian Brotherhood from 1970 to 1977,
   and after 1975 he was a major figure as well in the World Council of Indigenous Peoples. He died in 1989.
4 Manuel, interviews, 4 February and 18 March 1981, Vancouver.
5 Manuel was forever troubled by his memories of witnessing a teenage run-
   away being whipped to unconsciousness with a length of hose in front of
   the assembled students; the whipping would have stopped had the boy
   cried out, but he refused to do so.
6 Harold and Betty-Lou Linville, pers. comm., 5 June 1984.
7 H.A. (Butch) Smitheram, pers. comm., 3 March 1981. Smitheram was assistant agent in Kamloops in the 1950s.
8 Manuel, interview, 18 March 1980, Vancouver.
9 George Manuel and Michael Posluns, *The Fourth World* (Toronto: Collier-
   Macmillan 1974), 84.
10 My interviews with three of the major participants in these events, Manuel,
   Frank Calder, and Guy Williams, left unresolved the question of who first
   approached whom.
11 A White who had married into her community, she was the first woman to
   be elected chief of a Canadian Indian band.
12 Manuel and Posluns, *The Fourth World*, 120.
13 Ibid., 121.
14 According to Manuel the assembly had two unintended side effects. It stim-
   ulated a number of interior Indians, especially younger ones, to take a
   greater interest in politics, and it caused white civic and business leaders in
   Kamloops to think better of all Indians once they had encountered the
   well-spoken and well-dressed Indians from the coast. Manuel felt at the
   time that his own interior people were "like country cousins" compared to
   the polished Native Brotherhood members (interview, 18 March 1980, Vancouver).
15 The following material on the Kamloops assembly is based on interviews
   with Calder and Manuel.
16 Manuel was aware of the difficulties involved. In responding to my ques-

tions about the 1959 meeting, he made several asides about the much earlier differences between the Allied Tribes of the coast and Chief Chillihitza of the interior (interviews, 4 February and 18 March 1980, Vancouver).

17 Canada, House of Commons, Special Joint Committee ... to [consider] the Indian Act, *Minutes of Proceedings and Evidence*, No. 7 (26 May 1960), 621. (Cited hereafter as Special Committee [1960], *Proceedings*.)

18 I have heard this belief expressed by several of those who were active in the new NAIB.

19 E.P. Patterson, "Andrew Paull and the Canadian Indian Resurgence" (PH.D diss., University of Washington 1962), 373.

20 Special Committee (1960), *Proceedings*, No. 7 (26 May 1960), 619–21.

21 Ibid., 621.

22 Cf. above, Chs. 4 and 8.

23 Special Committee (1960), *Proceedings*, No. 7 (26 May 1960), 593, 594, 602.

24 *Native Voice*, November 1963.

25 He himself declined any comment on the matter during my interviews in 1980.

26 Copies of the telegrams are contained in the file "B.C. Native Brotherhood," DIA Regional Archives, Vancouver.

27 Years later neither Frank Calder nor Guy Williams even remembered that Manuel had joined the Brotherhood (interviews, 3–5 April 1980, Kincolith).

28 *Native Voice*, July 1965.

29 There was also in existence at this time a regional advisory council, and subsequently a major consultation process was developed. These are dealt with in the following chapter.

30 *Native Voice*, December 1966.

31 It was also at this time that Calder and the Nisga'a Tribal council were preparing to take their own land claims to court. See below, Ch. 16.

32 Leslie Kopas, "Political Action of the Indians of British Columbia" (MA thesis, University of British Columbia 1972), 152.

33 *Native Voice*, September-October 1967.

34 Southern Vancouver Island Tribal Federation, "Minutes of Convention of December 9 and 10, 1967, Duncan, B.C." (typescript copy in "South Island Federation," file, DIA Regional Archives, Vancouver, March 1981).

35 *Native Voice*, February 1968.

36 Ibid.

37 Ibid. In this case the intent was to bury the proposal.

38 Ibid.

39 Ibid.

40 Ibid., April 1968.

41 Calder's best-known role continued to be that of New Democratic Party member of the legislature, while Williams had been a federal candidate first for the Conservatives and then for the Liberals.

42 See above, Ch. 6.

CHAPTER ELEVEN:
FEDERAL GOVERNMENT INITIATIVES

1　The authoritative examination of the development of the policies is presented in Sally M. Weaver, *Making Canadian Indian Policy: The Hidden Agenda 1968–1970* (Toronto: University of Toronto Press 1981).

2　The arrangement required the agreement of the provincial government, which was reimbursed by the department for the costs of educating each status Indian pupil.

3　Department of Indian Affairs and Northern Development, BC Region, "British Columbia-Yukon Regional Indian Advisory Council . . . Vancouver B.C. [Minutes]," 3 June 1965, remarks of R.F. Battle, assistant deputy minister of Indian affairs. (DIA Regional Archives, Vancouver, in "Regional Advisory Council" files) (cited hereafter as British Columbia-Yukon Advisory Council "Minutes").

4　Cf. George Manuel and Michael Posluns, *The Fourth World* (Toronto: Collier-Macmillan 1974), Ch. 6.

5　The information in this paragraph was obtained in interviews with Manuel (4 February 1980, Vancouver) and conversations with Bayliss (May and June 1980, Vancouver). Bayliss remained with DIA, eventually becoming director of public information services in the BC region.

6　Apparently the motive was simply to bring Manuel's experience to a group of Indians seen as needing community development.

7　Manuel had met Cardinal while both were members of the National Indian Advisory Board. See below.

8　My observations are based on conversations with a number of Indians and with some of my students who became CD workers.

9　Sally M. Weaver, "Recent Directions in Canadian Indian Policy" (paper presented at the annual meeting of the Canadian Sociology and Anthropology Association, London, Ontario, May 1978), 2.

10　Unless otherwise indicated, this section is based on material from "Regional Advisory Council" files in DIA Regional Archives, Vancouver, which was examined in May and June 1980.

11　Nowhere in the extensive internal DIA correspondence relating to developments in BC is there any hint that officials thought of Indians as groups of voters who might be important in federal elections.

12　"District" was the new term for "agency" (agents were now styled "district managers"). The district councils were meetings of the chiefs and DIA officials within each district. These councils were important precursors of tribal councils. See Ch. 14, below.

13　Department of Indian Affairs and Northern Development, Federal-Provincial Relations Division, "Regional Advisory Committee on Indian Affairs-National Indian Advisory Board" (memorandum, 24 September 1964).

14 These were women's home-improvement groups that had been set up by DIA in a number of bands; the more active members were by now being brought together in annual province-wide conferences sponsored by DIA.

15 Manuel's Neskainlith band voted for Gottfriedson, while Gottfriedson's Kamloops band voted for Manuel. Perhaps this voting was seen as the gentlemanly thing to do, for there was no other sign of lack of support for either man in his own band.

16 British Columbia-Yukon Advisory Council "Minutes," 3 and 4 June 1965.

17 Laura Williams was absent.

18 See above, Ch. 10.

19 British Columbia-Yukon Advisory Council "Minutes," 3 and 4 June 1965.

20 Chief, Federal-Provincial Relations Division, to Indian Commissioner for BC, 21 September 1965.

21 Weaver, "Recent Directions in Canadian Indian Policy," 3.

22 The Homemakers Clubs were not eligible because, unlike the other two, they were not formally registered under the provincial Societies Act.

23 The information on the BC meetings is obtained from the extensive minutes of each meeting. (Department of Indian Affairs and Northern Development, "Report of . . . Indian Act Consultation Meeting," published separately by the department for each meeting: Prince George, 14–18 October 1968; Terrace, 24–8 October 1968 and 27–8 January 1969; Nanaimo, 30 October-2 November 1968; Kelowna, 12–16 November 1968; and Chilliwack, 18–22 November 1968).

Manuel, still a community development worker on Vancouver Island, took no part in the meeting in his own southern interior area. At the Vancouver Island meeting he was elected chairman by the delegates even though he was not a delegate himself.

24 At Boys's request Manuel had accompanied the DIA officials to the Prince George meeting.

25 Department of Indian Affairs and Northern Development, "Report of the Indian Act Consultation Meeting [Kelowna, November 12–16, 1968]," 62.

26 James Gosnell, interview, 14 May 1980, Aiyansh; Guy Williams, interview, 4 April 1980, Kincolith; Joe Mathias, interview, 26 May 1982, Vancouver.

27 Weaver, *Making Canadian Indian Policy*, 3–4, 166–8.

28 The *Oxford English Dictionary* defines "white paper" as a "report issued by Government to give information" and a "green paper" as a "tentative report of Government proposals, without commitment." The 1969 pronouncement gave information and as a "policy statement" was presented as neither tentative nor without commitment.

CHAPTER TWELVE: THE FORMATION OF THE NEW ORGANIZATIONS

1 Rose Charlie's account of these events is given in *Native Perspective* (July-August 1977):29. See also *Indian Voice*, June 1971.

2 The First Citizens' Fund had been established not long before this time by the Social Credit government of W.A.C. Bennett. While the government ignored the land question, it was willing to support Indian cultural and economic development activities and to adopt the term "first citizens." Bennett seems to have been sympathetic towards Indians, but presumably he also recognized that Indians could be a significant voting bloc in some ridings and that they tended to vote for Calder's New Democratic Party. The fund consisted of a $25 million endowment; its proceeds were disbursed by a committee of cabinet ministers. Hitherto the grants had been awarded mainly for recreational and cultural activities.

3 BC Chiefs Conference Planning Committee, "First Meeting of BC Chiefs Conference Planning Committee, October 18 and 19, 1969, Kamloops" (mimeo).

4 Department of Indian and Northern Affairs, *Annual Report 1969-70*, 163.

5 Except where otherwise noted, information in this chapter about the conference is obtained from Union of BC Indian Chiefs, "Indian Chiefs of British Columbia Conference; Kamloops, November 17-22, 1969." These minutes contain a verbatim report of the first day's proceedings and an abridged report of the remaining proceedings. The copy on file in the Union's head office in April 1980 contained an unattached insert listing the official delegates to the Kamloops meeting.

6 Manuel was not a delegate, but he had been sent from Alberta by Harold Cardinal to assist at the conference. He obtained 79 votes, defeating Gottfriedson (39 votes) and Ross Modeste (22).

7 There was some questioning of Fulton's $3,000 retainer, and he was asked if he would pursue the claim "on a percentage basis." As the minutes state, "he indicated that it was not his policy to do business percentage basis."

8 Gosnell, Bill McKay, and Morris Nyce were the Nisga'a leaders present; among those who also abstained were Guy Williams and John Clifton of the Native Brotherhood, Delbert Guerin of the Musqueam, and Joe Mathias of the Squamish.

9 Besides Moses, the members were Dennis Alphonse, Philip Paul, Joe Mathias, Evelyn Paul (active in the Homemakers and wife of Benjamin Paul), Gus Gottfriedson, Heber Maitland, and James Gosnell. Guy Williams was nominated but declined to serve on the committee. At the conference's main banquet, he served as the replacement speaker for Bill Mussell, whose flight from Ottawa was delayed. The speech did not commit the

Native Brotherhood to any particular relationship with, or support for, the new organization. That Williams did give the main banquet speech was well remembered and at times in later years wrongly taken, or used, as evidence that Williams and the Native Brotherhood had played a major part in establishing the new organization.

10 As the constitution was eventually written, membership on the chiefs' council was not restricted to chiefs or even to band delegates; any status Indian could be chosen. In subsequent years this element of flexibility allowed non-chiefs, including Bill Wilson, Ray Jones, and Ernie Willie, to assume important leadership roles at the council and executive levels. The committee proposed that nine zones be created for selecting chiefs' council members; in fact the conference proceeded to use the twelve DIA districts. Later the Vancouver Island district was split into Salish, Kwagiulth, and Nuu'-chah'nulth zones, producing a chief's council of fourteen members.

11 The pronoun "they" (that is, "they" the chiefs) was used rather than "it" in the committee's report to refer to the new entity.

12 Except where otherwise noted, information about the first year of operation of the Union and about the second Annual meeting is obtained from Union of BC Indian Chiefs, "Minutes of the Second Conference, November 1970, Vancouver." (Cited hereafter as UBCIC, "Minutes, 1970").

13 Cf. *Indian Voice*, December 1969.

14 Wilson, pers. comm., 29 October 1988.

15 UBCIC, "Minutes 1970," day 1, 18.

16 Ibid., day 5, 10.

17 The interpretation that the Societies Act, or decisions made by the registrar under authority of the *Act*, would not allow membership to be open to all BC Indians or, more particularly, all BC status Indians is odd. The Registrar had in 1969 approved the name "British Columbia Association of Non-Status Indians" and allowed that association to hold its membership open to all non-status Indians.

18 "BCANSI" was pronounced to rhyme with "the chancy."

19 His given names, which he never used as an adult and kept a virtual secret, were "Henry Arthur." Smitheram provided lengthy interviews and read and commented upon an initial draft of this chapter before his death in 1982.

20 For further details of Smitheram's career, see "H.A. ('Butch') Smitheram," *Native Perspective*, 2, no. 10 (1978): 18-19; also, *Indian Voice*, July 1970.

21 Mimeographed statement by Smitheram, untitled and undated, in BCANSI files. These files, which were by then fragmentary, were located and examined in the head office of the successor organization, the United Native Nations, in 1982.

22 Della Kew, a Musqueam.

23 "Métis" can also be used to mean any person of mixed Indian-white blood,

that is, as a polite synonym for "half-breed." This usage, which has never been common in BC, can add to the ambiguity, since there are mixed-bloods among both status and non-status Indians.

24 Several versions of these drafts survive in the Len and Kitty Maracle Papers, University of British Columbia Special Collections. The versions, which are undated, differ only in minor details.

25 Smitheram's personal scrapbooks, which he allowed me to examine in 1982, contained numerous news releases, press clippings, and memorabilia relating to his organizing efforts. The BCANSI files, such as survived and were held by its successor organization, the United Native Nations, contained the complete texts of two speeches. They are undated but their content indicates that they were composed in late 1969 or early 1971. One is entitled "The BC Association of Non-Status Indians"; the other, "The Non-Status Indian of BC and the Yukon." Also in the files was a set of undated, untitled, typed pages, numbered 5 to 13, that are so similar in style and content to the two speeches as to leave little doubt that they are Smitheram's. The quotations which follow are taken from these three sources.

26 In the copies of his speeches that survive there is no mention whatever of any aspect of Indian history or culture unique to BC.

27 Emphasis in original.

28 Douglas's non-white ancestry was African, not Indian; Churchill's American grandmother was said to have had Indian ancestry.

29 BCANSI, "Second Annual General Meeting . . . Victoria, BC, November 6, 7, 8, 1970." Minutes of the annual meetings are cited hereafter as BCANSI, Minutes.

30 This was the new newspaper published by the Indian Homemakers' Association.

31 BCANSI, annual audited statements submitted to BC Registrar of Societies, examined in office of Registrar of Societies, Victoria, April 1982.

32 Comments of Ernie McEwan in *Native Perspective* 2, no. 10 (1978):18.

33 The House forces likely gained 8 or 9 votes. On the first ballot House obtained 48 votes; Smitheram, 42; and a third candidate, 12. House then won on the second ballot (BCANSI, Minutes [1971], day 2).

CHAPTER THIRTEEN:
BIG MONEY AND BIG ORGANIZATIONS

1 Sally Weaver, *Making Canadian Indian Policy: The Hidden Agenda 1968–1970* (Toronto: University of Toronto Press 1981), 188. However, as mentioned below, the federal government was soon to reorient its policy on Indian claims.

2 E.g., *Nesika*, March 1973.

3 The desire to have simultaneous assemblies was not unrelated to the fact

that a majority of BCANSI delegates were women, while most band chiefs were men. Butch Smitheram, however, hoped that the practice would lead to closer relations between the two organizations.

4 The federal government maintained no centralized record or accounting of the funds going to either organization, while neither the Union nor BCANSI published accurate accounts.

5 These are the standard estimates by those who dealt with the funds.

6 BCANSI, board of directors, "Minutes," meeting of 9 September 1972.

7 Isabel Harrison, "The Native Courtworkers and Counselling Association of British Columbia" (unpublished paper, Department of Political Science, University of British Columbia, 1981).

8 The name, meaning "ours" in the Chinook lingua franca, was suggested by Ardyth Cooper.

9 *Ha-Shilth-Sa*, 17 March 1975. At the time he spoke, Paul was not endorsing this view.

10 In 1970 he had obviously been referring to Union leaders when he had stated in the legislature that some Indian spokesmen had met with government officials while drunk (*Indian Voice*, February 1970).

11 Union of BC Indian Chiefs, "Minutes of 1972 Annual Assembly" (mimeo).

12 *Nesika*, July 1973.

13 Ibid. See also *Native Voice*, August 1973.

14 The other Nisga'a leaders were deeply embarrassed. At the next annual meeting of the Nisga'a Tribal Council, James Gosnell defeated Calder as president. Calder quit the NDP and joined the Social Credit party before the provincial election of December 1975, in which he was re-elected. He retired from provincial politics after being defeated, by one vote, in the 1979 election, but he regained his stature as Nisga'a elder statesman and continued as an active proponent of aboriginal rights throughout the 1980s.

15 *Native Voice*, August 1973.

16 Ibid. Besides the Indian Homemakers' Association, there was now also the BC Native Women's Society. The two had similar goals and policies.

17 Ed Wright, Secretary, Nisga'a Tribal Council, interview, 14 May 1980, Aiyansh.

18 James Gosnell, quoted in the *Province*, 29 November 1981. In context, Gosnell was referring to the BC claims in general, not only to the Nisga'as'.

19 The decision is discussed in Ch. 16, below.

20 Frank Calder and James Gosnell, interviews, 3–5 April 1980, Kincolith.

21 Manuel did in fact make the attempt (George Manuel and Michael Posluns, *The Fourth World* [Toronto: Collier-Macmillan 1974], 223).

22 *Indian Voice*, June 1971, and *Nesika*, April 1973 and July 1973, contain details.

23 Pers. comm., 10 February 1982.

24 Pers. comm., 4 June 1980.

25 As noted earlier, as a status Indian Wilson could be an employee but not a member of BCANSI.

26 Union of BC Indian Chiefs, "Minutes of 1973 Annual Assembly" (mimeo).

27 The first political protest concerning land would appear to be the one which occurred at Fort St. John in 1971 or 1972, when Indians briefly blocked and boarded a train carrying Premier W.A.C. Bennett. Their complaint concerned provincial slowness in fulfilling a promise concerning reserve land (Don Ursaki, pers. comm., 14 June 1989). In 1972 there was an Indian protest demonstration at Williams Lake over the death in RCMP custody of Fred Quilt, a Chilcotin.

28 *Kamloops Daily Sentinel*, 7 August 1975.

29 The policy on negotiating return of the cut-offs was continued by the new Social Credit government, which took office in January 1976; however, actual negotiations with the bands did not start until 1981. See Ch. 15, below.

30 *Indian Voice*, January 1975.

31 Having remarried (in so doing she had lost her status), she was now Ethel Pearson.

32 The BCANSI board had decided to forego a simultaneous assembly in order to allow its own subsequent assembly to respond to whatever action the Union would take on merging the organizations.

33 This and the following observations are based on Union of BC Indian Chiefs, "Minutes of 1975 Annual Assembly" (verbatim transcript), and on interviews and conversations with a number of those taking part in the meeting.

34 Robert Matthew, "Central Interior Tribal Councils: Reaction to the Rejection of Funds in 1975" (unpublished student paper, Department of Political Science, University of British Columbia 1986).

CHAPTER FOURTEEN: TRIBALISM RE-ESTABLISHED

1 Table 1 lists the tribal groups. As was emphasized in Ch. 1, above, the term "tribal groups" refers to the thirty or so groups that had distinct languages, cultures, and identities at the time of contact and that continue their identities today. See note 3, below.

2 For many Indians the turning to tribalism was a matter of discovering or reaffirming their own roots and personal identity, and thus tribalism often raised intense personal and spiritual feelings.

3 The new adjectival uses of "tribal" were not accompanied by any lessening in the ambiguity of the noun "tribe," which continued to be used by both Indians and others in British Columbia to refer variously to communities, clans, or tribal groups.

4 Continued existence of traditional structures need not be incompatible with democratic *procedures*; among the Nisga'a and other north coast groups such procedures are used in both band council and tribal council elections; however, election winners are those who hold high traditional positions in the clans or who have been approved by the clan leaders.

5 A tribal council is thus quite different in principle and structure from a band council. The latter consists of a few persons elected to represent a band; the former consists of all the people composing a tribal group. Tribal councils have executive bodies, which are sometimes mistaken by observers to be the actual tribal council.

6 The claims preparation process is discussed in somewhat more detail in the following chapter, as is the political frustration resulting from the lack of federal and provincial action once claims were presented.

7 Here the term "tribal" implied "Indianness" and autonomy rather than exclusive action by one tribal group. The Caribou, Carrier-Sekani, North Coast, Central Interior, and Gitksan-Wet'suwet'en tribal councils included communities of more than one tribal group. Of these only the Gitksan-Wet'suwet'en and the Carrier-Sekani prepared land claims.

8 Bill Wilson and Joe Mathias, for example, did not proceed to practise law (Mathias, in fact, was diverted from completing law school by his political activities), while a number of the west, central, and north coast leaders often had to interrupt their profitable commercial fishing ventures for their political responsibilities. George Manuel could have done well as a consultant and lecturer. Virtually every leader could easily have obtained a secure job with the federal government, especially with DIA.

9 The following account is based on interviews and conversations with four of the five participants; the fifth denies being present.

10 "Jerk" is my euphemism.

11 Appropriately enough, in light of the course the assembly took, the residence halls are each named after Indian tribal groups.

12 There was at this time no thought given to having the tribal groups as the component units of a province-wide structure. This idea would arise later.

13 Manuel did not return to band politics. The Union president and vice-presidents had to be status Indians, but they did not have to be chiefs.

14 The Union had held a special assembly in Courtenay in early 1976 at which it specifically rejected union with BCANSI.

15 The exception was provided by several of the Gitksan bands, whose support for the Union was symbolized by Ray Jones' position as Union vice-president.

16 *Nesika*, Spring 1977.

17 Ibid.

18 Ibid.

19 *Native Voice* June 1977.

20 Walchli (pronounced "walk-lee") had been appointed director-general in 1976, after a successful period as director-general in the troubled Alberta region.

21 The policy matters to be discussed in the secretariat related mainly to band administration and DIA funding. Land claims were the responsibility not of Walchli and his officials, but of the department's Office of Native Claims, which had at this time not yet established an office in Vancouver.

22 "Union of B.C. Indian Chiefs' Position on the Aboriginal Tribal Council Meeting—as explained by George Manuel at the Secretariat Meeting on Friday, September 22, 1978" (typescript).

23 "Discussion Paper on Indian Land Claims in BC—prepared by the Department of Indian and Northern Affairs for the Conference on Aboriginal Rights, Prince George, September 22–24, 1978," 3–4. The province subsequently took the position that it was willing merely to "discuss" the claim and that its officials were attending the Nisga'a claim negotiations simply as observers.

24 Letter, George Manuel to director-general, Department of Indian and Northern Affairs, BC Region, 19 March 1979.

25 The North Coast Tribal Council was the descendant of a district council that had included the Coast Tsimshian and Haida bands as well as one Nisga'a band, Kincolith; there was no thought that it would prepare a land claim. Its Nisga'a and Haida members also participated in their own tribal councils.

26 The Kootenay and the Taku Tlingit maintain social and political contact with tribal group members who live outside BC (in the United States and in Yukon, respectively). Because the BC Kootenay are only part of their tribal group, they use the term "area council" rather than "tribal council."

27 The Union side saw its Indian opponents as the creatures of DIA officials in Vancouver, while the UNN side saw the Union as dependent upon the paternal support of DIA officials in Ottawa.

28 The Native Women's Society, led by Mildred Gottfriedson of Kamloops (wife of Gus Gottfriedson), had been formed in the early 1970s, in part by women who believed the Homemakers' Association was too much controlled by one family.

29 At this time there were 198 bands in the province.

30 *Nesika*, Spring 1977.

31 For example, Department of Indian and Northern Affairs, BC Region, Secretariat, "Minutes, September 22, 1978."

32 Manuel to minister of Indian and northern affairs, 16 October 1980.

33 The four bands not included in the survey consisted of two very small bands with inactive band councils and the two in northern BC located in DIA's Yukon administrative region, which had been made a separate region in the previous decade.

34 Department of Indian and Northern Affairs, "Minutes of the Regional Management Committee Meeting held at the Empress Hotel, Victoria, BC, December 4, 5 & 6, 1979" (mimeo).

35 Ibid., 23.

36 Ibid., p. J6.

37 Ibid., p. A5.

38 The term "district/tribal" appeared about this time; its use indicated that a district or area could be represented by either a district or tribal council (but not both) and that prior to the maturity of a particular tribal council there could well be ambiguity as to whether it had divorced itself enough from DIA to cease being called a district council. The Kwagiulth tribal council, for example, shifted its name back and forth from "district" to "tribal" council as it gained and lost autonomy.

CHAPTER FIFTEEN:
FORUMS AND FUNDING, PROTESTS AND UNITY

1 The name "Walchli's Forum" lasted only a few months; "Provincial Forum" or "Regional Forum" were used for several years before "British Columbia Tribal Forum" was made the official name.

2 I attended each meeting of the Forum held during 1980 and 1981 and a majority of those held subsequently. During the same period I attended the annual assemblies of the major organizations and meetings of most of the major tribal councils. My analysis in this chapter is based largely on observations, interviews, and conversations at, and following from, these meetings and assemblies.

3 However, the Homemakers later withdrew from the Forum, in good part because of lingering personal animosities between their leaders and the male politicians.

4 As Brotherhood president and the leader of the Heiltsuk, Newman possessed great personal and political stature among coastal Indians. Wilson often compared him to his own father, whom he had lost in childhood.

5 Gosnell's reputation rested less on age (he was now in his late fifties) than on his personable nature, on his skills as orator and political tactician, and on his being the leader of the Nisga'a.

6 More precisely, the percentages refer to population share among bands in the BC region that responded to the DIA survey. The other provincial organizations, and the Forum and the Aboriginal Council, shared the remaining support (Department of Indian and Northern Affairs, BC Region, "1981–82 Policy, Research and Consultation Fund" (June 1981]).

7 Walter Rudnicki, "The Native Core Funding Program: An Interim Review prepared for the Secretary of State Department" (30 April 1980), 69. Rudnicki did not explain "signed-up membership"; perhaps it included bands

that had not formally notified the Union of their withdrawal. He avoided considering "*paid-up* membership."

8 Ibid., 72–3.

9 As mentioned earlier, the three MPs represented interior ridings in which Union support did remain substantial.

10 This and the following information was obtained,while the events were unfolding, through conversations with senior DIA officials in Vancouver, with one member of the Union's chiefs' council, and with most of the Indians named in the text.

11 In 1985 Derrickson obtained the internal report from a person associated with one of the MPs and gave a copy to Walchli.

12 Walchli's conduct during the enquiry as well as the findings did lead to his regaining much of his standing within the department. As of late 1989 he remained in charge of the BC office of the Comprehensive Claims Branch. Derrickson sued his original detractors within his band and was vindicated in 1989 when the British Columbia Supreme Court awarded him the largest libel award in Canadian history (*Vancouver Sun*, 19 October 1989).

13 See above, Ch. 8.

14 For a fuller account, see Douglas Sanders, "The Indian Lobby," in Richard Simeon and Keith Banting, eds., *And No One Cheered* (Toronto: Methuen 1983), 301–32.

15 *Native Voice*, February 1982.

16 BC Aboriginal People's Constitutional Conference [26–9 January 1983], "Isolated Motions," No. 3.4. A "consent clause" was one which would prevent amendment of aboriginal provisions without aboriginal consent.

17 Ibid., No. 4.1.

18 *Native Voice*, February 1982.

19 Federal officials originally assumed that one big claim would be submitted by BC Indians. However, even if there were to be several claims, it made sense to establish precedents and procedures in dealing with one claim before dealing with others. It had not been anticipated that there would be more than twenty claims in BC, nor had much thought been given to the effect of a provincial refusal to participate.

20 In the mid-1980s the Office of Native Claims was renamed the "Comprehensive Claims Branch."

21 This number excludes the two cases, those of the Taku Tlingit and the Haisla, in which tribal groups consist of only one band.

22 At the time, portions of the University Endowment Lands, all of which were traditional Musqueam territory, were in fact vacant and undeveloped. The Musqueam still had the option of taking their claim to court.

23 Statements of provincial officials are examined in Ch. 17, below.

24 The MacLeod Lake claim was distinct in that the band was seeking to "adhere" to Treaty No. 8 and thus to have the province allocate land for a

reserve commensurate with the acreages granted earlier to other bands under Treaty No. 8. Cf. Verne Salonas, "The McLeod Lake Indian Band: Adhesion to Treaty 8 versus Comprehensive Claims" (unpublished student paper, Department of Political Science, University of British Columbia 1985). Salonas was one of the protest leaders.

25 The court injunctions are listed in the following chapter.

26 No decision had been delivered as of early 1990.

27 *Vancouver Sun*, 30 November 1985.

28 Task Force to Review Comprehensive Claims Policy, *Living Treaties: Lasting Agreements* (Ottawa: Department of Indian and Northern Affairs 1985).

29 In the case of the Stein Valley, the province did depart from precedent by having the responsible minister hold a series of meetings with Indian spokesmen. Neither side budged, however, and the meetings ended in late 1988 without resolution. In early 1989 the Fletcher-Challenge forest company announced a one-year moratorium on Stein logging.

30 One major symptom of the APCC's lack of identity was its lack of a clear name. "APCC," which I use here, was not used in practice; nor was the full name, presumably because of confusion with the "real" constitutional conferences, composed of first ministers and dealing with aboriginal rights. It was often referred to as the "all chiefs conference," an inaccurate designation which caused confusion with meetings of the Union of BC Indian Chiefs.

31 It had been established in Vancouver in 1985, owing mainly to the efforts of Adam Eneas, chief of the Penticton band.

32 There was never any thought given to a "one Indian, one vote" system, such as might be inferred from the terms "parliament" or "congress."

33 Adam Eneas had suggested, not too seriously at first, that the differing views as to the definition of "first nation" could be accommodated by creating the utterly ambiguous term "indigenous communal entity" (ICE) and granting each ICE equal representation. In effect, Eneas's suggestion did survive, with "first nation" replacing "ICE" as the suitably ambiguous term.

34 Kathryn Teneese, interview, 28 October 1988, Vancouver.

35 Accounts in both *Kahtou* (7 November 1988) and the *Vancouver Sun* (28 October), based on misleading comments by one or two speakers at the meeting, erroneously stated that the Union's 1975 assembly at Chilliwack had been larger and more representative.

36 CBC Radio News, 27 October 1988.

37 Ibid.

38 *Kahtou*, 7 November 1988.

39 The essential point was to allow representation to either communities or tribal groups. United Native Nations locals would also be eligible.

40 No one voted against it, although Terry, several other Union officials, and the delegates of the Shuswap Nation all abstained.

41 Mathias resigned in early 1990 because of ill health. Bill Wilson was elected in his place.

CHAPTER SIXTEEN:
ABORIGINAL TITLE IN THE COURTS

1 See Ch. 1, above, for discussions of the proclamation and of aboriginal rights.

2 Douglas Sanders, "Pre-existing Rights: The Aboriginal Peoples of Canada" (unpublished paper; Faculty of Law, University of British Columbia, 23 October 1987), 1–2. This chapter relies heavily on this paper.

3 *Regina* v. *The St. Catharines Milling and Lumber Company*, *The Ontario Reports, 1885*, vol. x, 196–235.

4 *St Catharines Milling and Lumber Company* (1889), 14 App. Cas. 46 (JCPC). Sanders refers to the ruling as a "misreading of the Proclamation" ("Pre-existing Rights," 2). For further discussion of the case and those following it, see David Elliott, "Aboriginal Title," in Bradford Morse, ed., *Aboriginal Peoples and the Law: Indian, Métis and Inuit Rights in Canada*, Carleton Library Series (Ottawa: Carleton University Press 1985), 48–121, and William B. Henderson, "Canadian Legal and Judicial Philosophies on the Doctrine of Aboriginal Rights," in Menno Boldt and J. Anthony Long, eds, *The Quest for Justice: Aboriginal Peoples and Aboriginal Rights* (Toronto: University of Toronto Press 1985), 221–9.

5 See above, Chs. 6 and 7.

6 *Re Southern Rhodesia Land* (1918), 88 LJPC 1, p. 12, quoted in (1970) *13 Dominion Law Reports (3d)* [1970], 65, 66.

7 *Amodu Tijani v. Secretary, Southern Nigeria*, (1921) 2 AC 399, 402–4, 409–10, quoted in *Calder* v. *Attorney-General of B.C.* (1973), *34 Dominion Law Reports (3d)* [1973], 175, 187, 208 [Supreme Court of Canada].

8 Judges, however, must use their own discretion in deciding which previous rulings are relevant. In the end, it is the highest appeal court which has the say as to which previous rulings, if any, provide authoritative precedents.

9 In 1949 the Supreme Court of Canada became the highest appeal court. Its nine judges are appointed by the federal government. Within each province is a hierarchy of courts whose judges are also appointed by the federal government. In BC these courts, from the highest to lowest, are the BC Court of Appeal, the Supreme Court of BC, and, across the province, a number of County Courts (Supreme and County courts were being merged in 1989). Still lower are Provincial Courts, formerly called magistrates' courts, whose judges are appointed by the provincial government. Cases are tried first at one of the lower levels and then may be appealed to a higher court. Cases involving obligations of the federal government itself may be tried in the Federal Court of Canada, with appeal to the Supreme Court of Canada.

10　As was suggested above, in Ch. 9, removal of the provisions was prompted also by the possibility of international criticism that they violated human rights.

11　"Appendix No. 1: The Royal Proclamation, October 7, 1763," *Revised Statutes of Canada, 1970* (Ottawa, Queen's Printer 1970), 123–9.

12　"The Hidden Constitution," in Boldt and Long, eds., *The Quest for Justice*, 122.

13　The contention that the proclamation had not applied to BC attained its first judicial credibility in 1964 in the dissenting opinion of Mr. Justice Sheppard, of the BC Appeal Court, in *Regina* v. *White and Bob (50 Dominion Law Reports (2d)* [1965], 620–1). Whether or not it had applied became irrelevant, at least as far as pre-existing title was concerned, as a result of the Supreme Court of Canada's ruling on the Nisga'a case in 1973. Oddly enough, it was after this time that BC government officials began embracing the contention in their public statements.

14　The phrase "implicit extinguishment" is mine; it characterizes the lawyers' argument but was not used by them.

15　See above, Ch. 1, for texts and discussion of the treaties.

16　Undoubtedly, other treaty Indians had been arrested and convicted previously in exactly the same circumstances on Vancouver Island.

17　Maisie Hurley was also known by her original married name of Armitage-Moore. Tom Hurley had defended many Indians in BC courts. He and Berger had become friends through having offices in the same building.

18　*Regina* v. *White and Bob* (1964), 627ff. [BC Court of Appeal]. Sanders, "Pre-Existing Rights," 6ff.

19　*Regina* v. *White and Bob* (1964), 626–7. [BC Court of Appeal]. Their argument showed also that they could not conceive of pre-existing Indian title; for, if such title had existed, and if the Douglas agreements had no force, then the title continued in effect.

20　Ibid., 647. See also 663–4.

21　*Regina* v. *White and Bob* (1965), *52 Dominion Law Reports (2d)* [1965], 481 [Supreme Court of Canada].

22　Sanders, "Pre-Existing Rights," 6.

23　Frank Calder and Berger were at this time both NDP members of the BC legislature.

24　*Calder* v. *Attorney-General of B.C.* (1973), *Supreme Court Reports* [1973], 313. [Supreme Court of Canada]. In formal terms the suit was brought by Frank Calder and four other senior chiefs—James Gosnell, Maurice Nyce, William McKay, and Anthony Robinson.

25　*Calder et al.* v. *Attorney-General of B.C.* (1969), *8 Dominion Law Reports (3d)* [1969], 59–83 [Supreme Court of BC].

26　He had been born in Victoria in 1899 and called to the bar in 1921, at the height of the political efforts of the Allied Tribes and at the time that Viscount Haldane delivered his ruling in the Nigerian case (*Canadian Who's Who* [1969]).

27 He alluded to Haldane in passing, but quoted at length from Sumner's opinion. *Calder et al.* v. *Attorney-General of B.C.* (1970), *13 Dominion Law Reports (3d)* [1970] 66–7 [BC Court of Appeal].

28 Ibid.

29 Ibid., 67–8.

30 BC, Legislature, *Sessional Papers*, 1887, 264. For an account of Smithe's meeting with the north coast chiefs, see above, Ch. 5.

31 *Calder et al.* v. *Attorney-General of B.C.* (1970), *13 Dominion Law Reports (3d)* [1970], 70 [BC Court of Appeal]. Tysoe relied on Wilson Duff's low estimate of pre-contact Nisga'a population.

32 "It is true, as the [Nisga'a] have submitted, that nowhere can one find express words extinguishing Indian title but 'actions speak louder than words' and in my opinion the policy of the Governor [Douglas] and the Executive Council of British Columbia and the execution of that policy was such that, if Indian title existed, extinguishment was effected by it" (ibid., 95).

33 See ibid., 107 and above, Ch. 4.

34 Before the Supreme Court of Canada's decision, Berger was appointed to the BC Supreme Court by the government of Pierre Trudeau. Berger resigned from the court in 1982 in the aftermath of his criticism of the treatment of aboriginal rights in the proposed Canadian Constitution.

35 *Calder* v. *Attorney-General of B.C.* (1973), *34 Dominion Law Reports (3d)* [1973], 281 [Supreme Court of Canada]. Hall began his opinion by rejecting the notion that the Nisga'a had been primitive; he viewed the notion as a holdover from a time "when understanding of the customs and cultures of our original people was rudimentary" (169).

36 *Calder* v. *Attorney-General of B.C.* (1973), *Supreme Court Reports* [1973], 328 [Supreme Court of Canada].

37 *Calder* v. *Attorney-General of B.C.* (1973), *34 Dominion Law Reports (3d)* [1973], 208, 210, 223 [Supreme Court of Canada].

38 Ibid., 160.

39 He was in the department's Vancouver district office on an unrelated matter when an official suggested he might be interested in examining the file on the lease.

40 *Guerin* v. *Regina* (1984) *6 Western Weekly Reports* [1984], 495 [Supreme Court of Canada].

41 Haldane, said Dickson, had approved "the principle that a change in sovereignty over a particular territory does not in general affect the presumptive title of the inhabitants" (ibid., 496).

42 Ibid., 497.

43 Supreme Court of BC, "Reasons for Judgment of the Honourable Mr. Jus-

tice Gibbs in Chambers [*Martin et al.* v. *Regina in Right of B.C. et al.*]" (25 January 1985), 6. (Cited hereafter as Gibbs, "Reasons for Judgment.") The trial of the claim, part of the larger Nuu'chah'nulth claim, had not yet begun in 1989.

44 Sanders, "Pre-Existing Rights," 14.

45 Gibbs, "Reasons for Judgment," 39-41.

46 *Martin et al.* v. *Regina in Right of B.C. et al.* (1985), *3 Western Weekly Reports* [1985], 583-93 [BC Court of Appeal].

47 Ibid., 607.

48 Ibid., 595.

49 Ibid., 603. It was only a few months later that the provincial attorney-general, Brian Smith, stated: "You start negotiating land claims and you're down the Neville Chamberlain route" (see Ch. 18, following).

50 Lambert concurred completely in Seaton's opinion (ibid., 597).

51 The Supreme Court has consistently refused to hear such appeals from pre-trial orders; it was thus not indicating any position on the merits of the appeal.

52 In a related case in early 1989, a non-Indian holding title to land claimed by the Kamloops band, and which the band claimed had been improperly excluded from its reserve a century ago, was prevented from developing the land.

53 In a further case in early 1989, the courts declined a Musqueam application for an injunction to block transfer of ownership of the University Endowment Lands from the province to the Greater Vancouver Regional District, but a BC Appeal Court judge did state that it would be unjust were the fact of the transfer later taken as impairing the Musqueam claim.

54 The Appeal Court ruled that Sparrow had to be retried. *Sparrow* v. *Regina* (1986) *2 Western Weekly Reports* [1987], 577-609 [BC Court of Appeal]. Sparrow appealed to the Supreme Court of Canada, arguing that no new trial should be required. The court had not released its decision at the end of 1989.

55 Ibid., 595. Moreover, the actions and role of the province are central in the land question, while fisheries are a matter of exclusive federal jurisdiction.

56 *Delgumuukw* v. *Province of B.C and Attorney-General of Canada.*

57 In 1989 the longstanding "BC vacancy" on the Supreme Court of Canada was filled by the appointment of Madam Justice Beverly McLachlan, who had only recently become Chief Justice of the BC Supreme Court. It was she who had granted the McLeod Lake injunction.

CHAPTER SEVENTEEN: THE PROVINCE AND LAND CLAIMS NEGOTIATIONS

1 Monique Michaud, "The JBNQA: Its Origin, Content and Effects," *Rencontre* (September 1985): 5-7.

2 Anthony Hall, "Indian Treaties," *Canadian Encyclopedia*, 2nd ed. (Edmonton: Hurtig 1988), 1056. A further agreement, with the Dene-Métis, was reached in the Northwest Territories in 1988. In 1989 the eastern Arctic, the traditional territory of the Inuit, was the only area in the territories not yet the subject of an agreement, and negotiations were underway.

3 Council for Yukon Indians, "Yukon Indian Land Claim Framework Agreement" (mimeo, 30 November 1988).

4 In May 1989 John Walsh, policy adviser to the leader of Yukon's NDP territorial government during the latter stages of the Yukon negotiations, became chief policy advisory to Michael Harcourt, leader of BC's NDP.

5 Gardom was attorney-general from 1976 to 1979; Williams, 1979 to 1983; and Smith, 1983 to 1987. Gardom was minister of inter-governmental relations, and thus involved in the first ministers' conference process, from 1979 to 1983.

6 Most of the statements were made by Smith and Gardom, since Williams had left politics by this time. Williams, having a more accommodating personal style and having served in a less contentious period, was more favourably regarded by Indian political leaders than were the other two, whose attitudes and statements engendered strong hostility.

7 Garde Gardom, "Why Land Claims in B.C.?" *Province*, 8 December 1985. Perhaps Gardom's ambiguity was intended to deflect precise refutation while still giving support and comfort to those government followers whose image of Indians and view of land claims were similar to his. See below in this chapter for discussion of the image of Indians that was implicit in the comments of Gardom and Smith.

8 BC Legislature, *Debates*, 3 August 1977, 4283; see also 23 July 1979, 949 (cited hereafter as BC, *Debates*).

9 Garde Gardom, "Land Claims: Harmony Must Begin in Ottawa," *Vancouver Sun*, 9 September 1986.

10 *Vancouver Sun*, 13 June 1985.

11 See above, Ch. 5.

12 *Vancouver Sun*, 13 June 1985.

13 Tierney, pers. comm., 19 June 1985.

14 He was referring to proposals made at the 1984 first ministers' conference, and alluding to the terrorist Front for the Liberation of Quebec (*Vancouver Sun*, 13 March 1984).

15 Gardom's inability was peculiar, especially in light of his being a lawyer and of his own claim to have spent "some 25 years of working with BC Indians, both outside and inside government" (*Vancouver Sun*, 9 September 1986).

16 BC, *Debates*, 21 October 1983, 2934.

17 Ibid., 25 March 1986, 7523.

18 *Vancouver Sun*, 13 June 1985.

19 Ibid., 9 September 1986.
20 Ibid., 18 October 1986.
21 On the other hand, even Joseph Trutch reserved his more contemptuous comments for private correspondence.
22 *Vancouver Sun*, 2 August 1985.
23 Ibid.
24 Ibid., 9 September 1986.
25 Ibid., 18 Oct. 1986. Many of Gardom's statements contained provocative red herrings; in this case it was the linking of "sovereignty" with Indian title.
26 *Vancouver Sun*, 9 September 1986.
27 BC, *Debates*, 9 February 1984, p 3211.
28 *Calder et al.* v. *Attorney-General of British Columbia*. (1969), *8 Dominion Law Reports 3rd*, 61 [British Columbia Supreme Court].
29 BC, *Debates*, 18 March 1986, 7388.
30 *Vancouver Sun*, 9 September 1986.
31 BC, *Debates*, 25 March 1986, 7523.
32 Ibid.
33 "The Aboriginal Title Question in British Columbia," *Indians and the Law III* (Vancouver: Continuing Legal Education Society of British Columbia 1986), Ch. 2.2, 8.
34 Ibid., 7–8.
35 Child care agreements, allowing de facto Indian control of child welfare, were reached between the province and several communities and tribal groups. The United Native Nations received a provincial grant to study and report upon urban Indian child care needs. Ed John, chairman of the Carrier-Sekani Tribal Council, was appointed to the board of directors of British Columbia Rail Corporation.
36 The conferences were Wilson's idea. He had mentioned it first to Bruce Buchanan, president of British Columbia Packers, who had pledged to ensure industry participation if Wilson would get Indian leaders to attend. Waterland, who had been minister of forests in the Bill Bennett government, was by 1988 a firm supporter of land claim negotiations.
37 I took part in the first conference, giving an opening talk on the history of the land question.
38 As Vaughn Palmer put it, "The thinking in government circles is that the court will probably recognize aboriginal title . . . that it still exists today." He also observed that "the key figure in shaping Victoria's legal position on claims is Attorney-General Bud Smith. Long a hardliner on land claims, he has come round to the idea that some degree of recognition and negotiation is inevitable. No doubt his thinking has been helped along by similar movement in the BC business community" (*Vancouver Sun*, 26 February 1990).

Bibliography

ARCHIVAL MATERIALS

Canada. National Archives, RG10, vols. 1648, 3669, and 3696
Canada. Department of Indian and Northern Affairs. Regional Archives. Vancouver
Maracle, Len and Kitty. *The Maracle Papers* (Collection of personal papers 1969–1980, University of British Columbia Special Collections)

COURT CASES

Calder et al. v. *Attorney-General of British Columbia* (1969), *8 Dominion Law Reports (3d)*, 59–83 [Supreme Court of British Columbia]
Calder et al. v. *Attorney-General of British Columbia* (1970), *13 Dominion Law Reports (3d)*, 64–110 [British Columbia Court of Appeal]
Calder v. *Attorney-General of British Columbia* (1973), *34 Dominion Law Reports (3d)* [1973], 145–226 [Supreme Court of Canada]
Calder v. *Attorney-General of British Columbia* (1973), *Supreme Court Reports* [1973], 313–427 [Supreme Court of Canada]
Guerin v. *Regina* (1984), *6 Western Weekly Reports* [1984], 481–529 [Supreme Court of Canada]
Martin et al. v. *Regina in Right of British Columbia et al.* (1985), *3 Western Weekly Reports* [1985], 577–611 [British Columbia Court of Appeal]
Regina v. *The St Catharines Milling and Lumber Company* (1885), *The Ontario Reports, 1885*, vol. x, 196–235
Regina v. *White and Bob* (1964), *50 Dominion Law Reports (2d)* [1965], 613–66 [British Columbia Court of Appeal]
Regina v. *White and Bob* (1965), *52 Dominion Law Reports (2d)* [1965], 481 [Supreme Court of Canada]
Sparrow v. *Regina* (1986) *2 Western Weekly Reports* [1987], 577–609 [British

Columbia Court of Appeal]
Supreme Court of British Columbia, "Reasons for Judgment of the Honoura-
    ble Mr. Justice Gibbs in Chambers [*Martin el al* v. *Regina in Right of British
    Columbia et al.*]," 25 January 1985

GOVERNMENT PUBLICATIONS

British Columbia. Commission Appointed to Enquire into the Conditions of
    the Indians of the North-west Coast. *Papers relating to the Commission* . . . Vic-
    toria: Government Printer 1888
—. Legislature. *Journals* [1871–95]
—. Legislature. *Sessional Papers* [1871–95]
—. Legislature. *Debates* [1974–89]
—. *List of Proclamations for 1858* . . . *1864*. New Westminster: Government Print-
    ing Office n.d.
—. *Papers Connected with the Indian Land Question, 1850–1875*. Victoria: Govern-
    ment Printer 1875. Reprinted, Victoria: Queen's Printer for British Colum-
    bia 1987
—. Royal Commission on Indian Affairs for the Province of British Columbia.
    Evidence. Victoria: Acme Press 1916
—. *Report*. Victoria: Acme Press 1916
Canada. "The Royal Proclamation, October 7, 1763" *Revised Statutes of Canada
    1970*. Appendix No. 1. Ottawa: Queen's Printer 1970
—. Department of Indian and Northern Affairs. Task Force to Review Compre-
    hensive Claims Policy. *Living Treaties: Lasting Agreements*. Ottawa: Depart-
    ment of Indian and Northern Affairs 1985
—. Department of Indian Affairs. *Annual Reports* [1871–1989]
—. House of Commons. *Debates* [1871–95, 1916–28, 1960–89]
—. Special Committees of the Senate and House of Commons . . . to Inquire
    into the Claims of the Allied Indian Tribes of British Columbia. *Proceedings,
    Reports and the Evidence*. Ottawa: King's Printer 1927
—. Special Joint Committee [to consider] the Indian Act. *Minutes of Proceedings
    and Evidence*. Ottawa: King's Printer 1947
—. Special Joint Committee [to consider] the Indian Act. *Minutes of Proceedings
    and Evidence*. Ottawa: Queen's Printer 1960
Brown G., and R. Maguire. *Indian Treaties in Historical Perspective*. Ottawa:
    Research Branch, Deparment of Indian and Northern Affairs 1979
Cooke, Katie. "Images of Indians Held by Non-Indians: A Review of Current
    Canadian Research." Ottawa: Research Branch, Department of Indian and
    Northern Affairs 1984
—. "Splinter Groups, Factions and Group Cohesion in the Comprehensive
    Claims Context." Ottawa: Office of Native Claims, Department of Indian
    and Northern Affairs 1983

Hendrickson, James, ed. *Journals of the Council, Executive Council and Legislative Council of Vancouver Island, 1851-1871*. *Ha-Shilth-Sa* Victoria: Provincial Archives of British Columbia 1980

INDIAN NEWSPAPERS

Ha-Shilth-Sa. Port Alberni: Nuu'chah'nulth Tribal Council [1973-89]
Native Perspective. Ottawa: Native Council of Canada [1977-8]
Indian Voice. Vancouver: Indian Homemakers' Association of BC [1969-85]
Kahtou. Vancouver: Native Communications Society of BC, [1985-9]
Native Voice. Vancouver: Native Brotherhood of BC [1946-1968, 1970-89]
Nesika. Vancouver: Union of BC Indian Chiefs [1971-6]
Nicola Indian. Merritt: Nicola Valley Indian Administration [1976-83]
Non-Status News. Vancouver: BC Association of Non-Status Indians [1971-5]
UNN News. Vancouver. United Native Nations [1981-2]

GENERAL NEWSPAPERS

Bridge River-Lillooet News [1969-89]
Vancouver Sun [1965-90]
Province (also published as *Vancouver Province* and *Daily Province*) [1979-89]
Kamloops Daily Sentinel [1969-89]
Colonist (also published as *Daily Colonist* and *Daily British Colonist*) [1858-95]
Globe and Mail [1979-89]

UNPUBLISHED MATERIAL

British Columbia Association of Non-Status Indians [Minutes and records of conferences, annual assemblies, and meetings of board of directors, 1969-76]
British Columbia Chiefs Conference Planning Committee, "First Meeting of BC Chiefs Conference Planning Committee, October 18 and 19, 1969, Kamloops." Mimeographed
Braker, Hugh. "Native Brotherhood Policy Resolutions." Unpublished manuscript materials, University of British Columbia 1982
Bryant, Michael. "Canada and United States Public Policy on Aboriginal Land Claims, 1960-1988: Alaska and British Columbia Compared." MA thesis, University of British Columbia 1989
Buckle, Vincent. "Local Government in Action: The Nicola Valley Indian Administration." Unpublished manuscript, University of British Columbia 1982
Bush, Pamela. "See You In Court: Native Indians and the Law in British Columbia, 1969-1985." MA thesis, University of British Columbia 1987

Canada. Department of Indian Affairs and Northern Development. "British
    Columbia-Yukon Regional Indian Advisory Council . . . Vancouver, BC [Min-
    utes]." 1965-8
—. Federal-Provincial Relations Division. "Regional Advisory Committee on
    Indian Affairs-National Indian Advisory Board." Memorandum, 24 Sep-
    tember 1964
—. Department of Indian and Northern Affairs. "Minutes of the Regional
    Management Committee Meeting held at the Empress Hotel, Victoria, BC
    December 4, 5 & 6, 1979." Mimeographed
Council for Yukon Indians. "Yukon Indian Land Claim Framework Agree-
    ment." Mimeographed, 30 November 1988
Harrison, Isabel. "Native Courtworker and Counselling Association of British
    Columbia: Development, Structure and Activities." Unpublished manuscript,
    University of British Columbia 1981
—. "Of Ostriches, Assimilation and Self-determination: Public Policy and
    Indian Land Claims in British Columbia." Unpublished manuscript, Univer-
    sity of British Columbia 1981
Hendrickson, James. "The Aboriginal Land Policy of Governor James Douglas,
    1849-1864." Paper delivered at the BC Studies Conference, Simon Fraser
    University, 4-6 November 1988
Hudson, Stephanie. "The Role of Indian Agents in British Columbia." Unpub-
    lished manuscript, University of British Columbia 1987
Kopas, Leslie. "Political Action of the Indians of British Columbia." MA thesis,
    University of British Columbia 1972
Matthew, Robert. "Central Interior Tribal Councils: Reaction to the Rejection
    of Funds in 1975." Unpublished manuscript, University of British Columbia
    1986
May, Edwin. "The Nishga Land Claim, 1873-1973." MA thesis, Simon Fraser
    University 1979
Mitchell, Darcy. "The Allied Indian Tribes of British Columbia: A Study in
    Pressure Group Behaviour." MA thesis, University of British Columbia 1977
Morrison, Wendy. "This Decision Is Final: The 1927 Indian Act Amendments
    and the Report of the Special Committee." Unpublished manuscript, Univer-
    sity of British Columbia 1985
O'Donnell, Jacqueline. "The Native Brotherhood of British Columbia
    1931-1950: A New Phase in Native Political Organization." MA thesis, Univer-
    sity of British Columbia 1985
Patterson, E.P. "Andrew Paull and Canadian Indian Resurgence." PHD. diss.,
    University of Washington 1962
Peigan, Ron. "Injunctive Relief in Native Land Claims." Unpublished manu-
    script, University of British Columbia 1989
Rudnicki, Walter. "The Native Core Funding Program: An Interim Review pre-
    pared for the Secretary of State Department." Mimeographed, 30 April 1980

Salonas, Verne. "The McLeod Lake Indian Band: Adhesion to Treaty 8 versus Comprehensive Claims." Unpublished manuscript, University of British Columbia 1985

Sanders, Douglas. "Pre-existing Rights: The Aboriginal Peoples of Canada." Unpublished manuscript, University of British Columbia 1987

Shankel, George. "The Development of Indian Policy in British Columbia." PHD. diss., University of Washington 1945

Thomson, D. Duane. "A History of the Okanagan: Indians and Whites in the Settlement Era, 1860–1920." PHD. diss., University of British Columbia 1985

Union of British Columbia Indian Chiefs. [Minutes and proceedings of conferences, annual assemblies, and meetings of chiefs' council, 1969–83]

United Native Nations. [Minutes and proceedings of conferences, annual assemblies, and meetings of board of directors, 1976–88]

Weaver, Sally M. "Recent Directions in Canadian Indian Policy." Paper presented at the annual meeting of the Canadian Sociology and Anthropology Association, London, Ontario, May 1978

Webber, Andrew. "The Negotiation Process Concerning the Capilano Indian Reserve and Adjoining Cut-Off Lands." Unpublished manuscript, University of British Columbia 1981

Zirnhelt, David. "The Caribou Tribal Council." MA thesis, University of British Columbia 1976

ARTICLES AND BOOKS

Anon. "H.A. ("Butch") Smitheram." *Native Perspective*, 2, no. 10 (1978)

Barth, Fredrik. *Ethnic Groups and Boundaries: The Social Organization of Cultural Differences*. Boston: Little, Brown 1969

Berger, Thomas. "Native History, Native Claims and Self-Determination." *BC Studies* 57 (Spring 1983)

Cail, Robert. *Land, Man, and the Law: The Disposal of Crown Lands in British Columbia, 1871–1913*. Vancouver: University of British Columbia Press 1974

Drucker, Philip. *Indians of the Northwest Coast*. Garden City: Natural History Press 1963. First published 1955

—. *The Native Brotherhoods: Modern Intertribal Organizations on the Northwest Coast*. Smithsonian Institution. Bureau of American Ethnology Bulletin 168. Washington: Government Printing Office 1958

Duff, Wilson. "The Fort Victoria Treaties." *BC Studies* 3 (Fall 1969)

—. *Histories, Territories, and Laws of the Kitwancool*. Anthropology in British Columbia, Memoir No. 4. Victoria: Provincial Museum 1959

—. *The Indian History of British Columbia, Vol. 1, The Impact of the White Man*. Anthropology in British Columbia, Memoir No. 5. Victoria: Provincial Museum of British Columbia 1964

Elliott, David. "Aboriginal Title," in Bradford Morse, ed. *Aboriginal Peoples and the Law: Indian, Metis and Inuit Rights in Canada*. Carleton Library Series. Ottawa: Carleton University Press 1985

Fiedel, Stuart J. *Prehistory of the Americas*. Cambridge: Cambridge University Press 1987

Fisher, Robin. "Joseph Trutch and Indian Land Policy." *BC Studies* 12 (Winter 1971–2)

—. *Contact and Conflict: Indian-European Relations in British Columbia, 1774–1890*. Vancouver: University of British Columbia Press 1977

Foster, Hamar. "How Not to Draft Legislation: Indian Land Claims, Government Intransigence, and How Premier Walkem Nearly Sold the Farm in 1874." *The Advocate* 46 (1988)

Fried, Morton. *The Evolution of Political Society*. New York: Random House 1967

Gardom, Garde. "Land Claims: Harmony Must Begin in Ottawa." *Vancouver Sun*, 9 September 1986

—. "Why Land Claims in BC?" *Province*, 8 December 1985

Haig-Brown, Celia. *Resistance and Renewal: Surviving the Indian Residential School*. Vancouver: Tillacum Library 1988

Hall, Anthony. "Indian Treaties." *Canadian Encyclopedia*, 2nd ed. Edmonton: Hurtig 1988

Hawthorn, H.B. et al. *The Indians of British Columbia*. Toronto: University of Toronto Press 1960

Henderson, William B. "Canadian Legal and Judicial Philosophies on the Doctrine of Aboriginal Rights." In Menno Boldt and J. Anthony Long, eds. *The Quest for Justice: Aboriginal Peoples and Aboriginal Rights*. Toronto: University of Toronto Press 1985

Hertzberg, Hazel. *The Search for American Indian Identity: Modern Pan-Indian Movements*. Syracuse: Syracuse University Press 1971

Johnson, Basil. *Indian School Days*. Toronto: Key Porter 1988

Karr, Clarence G. "James Douglas: The Gold Governor in the Context of His Times." In E. Blanche Norcross, ed. *The Company on the Coast*. Nanaimo: Nanaimo Historical Society 1983

Kincade, M. Dale and Wayne Suttles. "New Caledonia and Columbia [Linguistic Families]." In R. Cole Harris, ed. *Historical Atlas of Canada, Vol. 1*. Toronto: University of Toronto Press 1987

Knight, Rolf. *Indians at Work: An Informal History of Native Indian Labour in British Columbia, 1858–1930*. Vancouver: New Star Books 1978

LaViolette, Forrest. *The Struggle for Survival*. Toronto: University of Toronto Press 1961

Lemert, Edwin. "The Life and Death of an Indian State." *Human Organization* 13, no. 3 (1954)

Lillard, Charles, ed. *Warriors of the North Pacific: Missionary Accounts of the Northwest Coast, the Skeena and Stikine Rivers and the Klondike, 1829–1900*. Victoria: Sono Nis 1984

M'Gonigle, Michael and Wendy Wickwire. *Stein: The Way of the River*. Van-
    couver: Talonbooks 1988
Madill, Dennis. "No Deal!" *Horizon Canada* (January 1987)
Manuel, George, and Michael Posluns. *The Fourth World*. Toronto: Collier-Mac-
    millan 1974
McCardle, Bennett. "Frank Arthur Calder." *Canadian Encyclopedia*, 2nd ed.
    Edmonton: Hurtig 1988
Michaud, Monique. "The JBNQA: Its Origin, Content and Effects." *Rencontre*
    (September 1985)
Mooney, Kathleen. "James Alexander Teit." *Canadian Encyclopedia*, 2nd ed.
    Edmonton: Hurtig 1988
Morley, Alan. *Roar of the Breakers: A Biography of Peter Kelly*. Toronto: Ryerson
    Press 1967
Ormsby, Margaret. "Sir James Douglas." *Canadian Encyclopedia*, 2nd ed.
    Edmonton: Hurtig 1988
Patterson, E. P. "Andrew Paull." *Canadian Encyclopedia*, 2nd ed. Edmonton:
    Hurtig 1988
Pethick, Derek. *James Douglas: Servant of Two Empires*. Vancouver: Mitchell Press
    1969
Ponting, J. Rick. "George Manuel." *Canadian Encyclopedia*, 2nd ed. Edmonton:
    Hurtig 1988
—, and Gibbins, Roger. *Out of Irrelevance*. Toronto: Butterworths 1980
Ralston, Keith. "William Smithe." *Canadian Encyclopedia*, 2nd ed. Edmonton:
    Hurtig 1988
Raunet, Daniel. *Without Surrender, Without Consent: A History of the Nishga Land
    Claims*. Vancouver: Douglas and McIntyre 1984
Sanders, Douglas. "The Aboriginal Title Question in British Columbia." *Indi-
    ans and the Law III*. Vancouver: Continuing Legal Education Society of Brit-
    ish Columbia 1986
—. "The Indian Lobby." In Richard Simeon and Keith Banting, eds. *And No
    One Cheered*. Toronto: Methuen 1983
Sewid-Smith, Daisy. *Prosecution or Persecution*. Campbell River: Nu-Yum-Baleess
    Society 1979
Spradley, James. *Guests Never Leave Hungry: The Autobiography of James Sewid, a
    Kwakiutl Indian*. New Haven: Yale University Press 1969
Slattery, Brian. "The Hidden Constitution," In Menno Boldt and J. Anthony
    Long, eds. *The Quest for Justice: Aboriginal Peoples and Aboriginal Rights*.
    Toronto: University of Toronto Press 1985
Smith, Allan. "The Writing of British Columbia History." *BC Studies* 45 (Spring
    1980)
Sproat, Gilbert Malcolm. *The Nootka: Scenes and Studies of Savage Life*. Edited
    and annotated by Charles Lillard. Victoria: Sono Nis 1987
Stewart, George. *Canada under the Administration of the Earl of Dufferin*. Toronto:

Rose-Belford 1878

Tennant, Paul. "Native Indian Political Activity in British Columbia, 1969–1983." *BC Studies* 57 (Spring 1983)

—. "Native Indian Political Organization in British Columbia, 1900–1969: A Response to Internal Colonialism." *BC Studies* 55 (Autumn 1982)

Thomas, R.K. "Pan-Indianism," In D.E. Walker, Jr., ed. *The Emergent Native Americans: A Reader in Culture Contact*. Boston: Little, Brown 1972

Titley, E. Brian. *A Narrow Vision: Duncan Campbell Scott and the Administration of Indian Affairs in Canada*. Vancouver: University of British Columbia Press 1986

Upton, Leslie. "Contact and Conflict on the Atlantic and Pacific Coasts of Canada." *BC Studies* 45 (Spring 1980)

Veillette, John, and White, Gary. *Early Indian Village Churches: Wooden Frontier Architecture in British Columbia*. Vancouver: University of British Columbia Press 1977

Wallace, A.F.C. "Revitalization Movements." *American Anthropologist* 58, no. 2 (1956)

Weaver, Sally M. *Making Canadian Indian Policy: The Hidden Agenda 1968-1970*. Toronto: University of Toronto Press 1981

Williamson, Barbara. "The Pizza Syndrome." *Project North B.C. Newsletter* (Fall 1989)

Index

provincial politicians, 228–35; Indians as primitive, 87, 219–20; Indians as similar to "wild beasts," 58; recency of land claims, 110, 229; role of white agitators and advisers, 87, 111, 229

White paper, 149–50

"Whites," usage of term, xi-x

Williams, Allan, 202, 228–9, 279 n. 5

Williams, Guy: in NBBC, 119, 120, 131; and Indian Non-Partisan Party, 122; in Big Five, 135; in RIAC, 143–4; in consultation process, 147; and founding of UBCIC, 265 n. 9; appointed to Senate, 165

Willie, Ernie, 187, 196

Wilson, Bill: background and education of, 139, 156, 270 n. 8; in UBCIC, 156, 157–8, 174, 179, 180, 266 n. 10; and BCANSI, 168–9, 173, 174; statement of, on "Aboriginal Title" (1972), 173–4; on tribalism and all-Indian unity, 157–8, 173, 176–7, 199; in Chilliwack assembly (1975), 178, 179; and George Watts, 185; in Coalition of Native Indians, 188–9; in Aboriginal Council, 198–9; in Tribal Forum, 196–7; as president of UNN, 186, 192, 199; as vice-president of NCC, 200, 204, 210; as tribal council official, 210; and Whistler conference with industrial leaders, 236; elected chairman of FNC and BC vice-chief of AFN, 275 n. 41

Wilson, Ethel (later Ethel Pearson), 139

Wilson, Richard, 56, 57, 62

World Council of Indigenous Peoples, 261 n. 3

Yukon land claim agreement, 228

Zirnhelt, David, 236